Moral Movements
and Foreign Policy

Why do advocacy campaigns succeed in some cases but fail in others? What conditions motivate states to accept commitments championed by principled advocacy movements? Joshua W. Busby sheds light on these core questions through an investigation of four cases – developing-country debt relief, climate change, AIDS, and the International Criminal Court – in the G-7 advanced industrialized countries (Canada, France, Germany, Italy, Japan, the United Kingdom, and the United States). Drawing on hundreds of interviews with policy practitioners, he employs qualitative, comparative case study methods, including process-tracing and typologies, and develops a framing/gatekeepers argument, emphasizing the ways in which advocacy campaigns use rhetoric to tap into the main cultural currents in the countries where they operate. Busby argues that when values and costs potentially pull in opposing directions, values will win if domestic gatekeepers who are able to block policy change believe that the values at stake are sufficiently important.

JOSHUA W. BUSBY is an assistant professor at the LBJ School of Public Affairs at the University of Texas at Austin. He is also the Crook Distinguished Scholar at the Robert S. Strauss Center for International Security and Law and a fellow with the RGK Center for Philanthropy and Community Service.

Cambridge Studies in International Relations: 116

Moral Movements and Foreign Policy

Cambridge Studies in International Relations is a joint initiative of Cambridge University Press and the British International Studies Association (BISA). The series will include a wide range of material, from undergraduate textbooks and surveys to research-based monographs and collaborative volumes. The aim of the series is to publish the best new scholarship in International Studies from Europe, North America, and the rest of the world.

Cambridge Studies in International Relations

115 Séverine Autesserre
     The trouble with the Congo
     Local violence and the failure of international peacebuilding
114 Deborah D. Avant, Martha Finnemore, and Susan K. Sell
     Who governs the globe?
113 Vincent Pouliot
     International security in practice
     The politics of NATO–Russia diplomacy
112 Columba Peoples
     Justifying ballistic missile defence
     Technology, security, and culture
111 Paul Sharp
     Diplomatic theory of international relations
110 John A. Vasquez
     The war puzzle revisited
109 Rodney Bruce Hall
     Central banking as global governance
     Constructing financial credibility
108 Milja Kurki
     Causation in international relations
     Reclaiming causal analysis
107 Richard M. Price
     Moral limit and possibility in world politics
106 Emma Haddad
     The refugee in international society
     Between sovereigns
105 Ken Booth
     Theory of world security
104 Benjamin Miller
     States, nations, and the great powers
     The sources of regional war and peace

Series list continues after index

Moral Movements and Foreign Policy

JOSHUA W. BUSBY
University of Texas at Austin
LBJ School of Public Affairs

CAMBRIDGE
UNIVERSITY PRESS

CAMBRIDGE UNIVERSITY PRESS
Cambridge, New York, Melbourne, Madrid, Cape Town, Singapore,
São Paulo, Delhi, Dubai, Tokyo, Mexico City

Cambridge University Press
The Edinburgh Building, Cambridge CB2 8RU, UK

Published in the United States of America by Cambridge University Press, New York

www.cambridge.org
Information on this title: www.cambridge.org/9780521125666

First published 2010

Printed in the United Kingdom at the University Press, Cambridge

A catalog record for this publication is available from the British Library

Library of Congress Cataloging in Publication data
Busby, Joshua W.
Moral movements and foreign policy / Joshua W. Busby.
    p.   cm. – (Cambridge studies in international relations ; 116)
Includes bibliographical references and index.
ISBN 978-0-521-76872-6 (hardback)
1. Social action – Case studies.   2. Nonprofit organizations – Case studies.
3. Pressure groups – Case studies.   4. Values – Case studies.
5. International relations – Case studies.   I. Title.   II. Series.
HN57.B88   2010
303.48′4 – dc22   2010020576

ISBN 978-0-521-76872-6 Hardback
ISBN 978-0-521-12566-6 Paperback

*To my wife Bethany whose willingness to share
in adventures is a constant joy*

Contents

List of figures   *page* x

List of tables   xi

Acknowledgments   xiii

1 States of grace   1

   Appendix 1A: Transnational principled advocacy
                    movements in the post-Cold War era (1990–)   17

2 Movement success and state acceptance of normative
   commitments   33

3 Bono made Jesse Helms cry: Jubilee 2000 and the
   campaign for developing country debt relief   70

4 Climate change: the hardest problem in the world   104

5 From God's mouth: messenger effects and donor
   responses to HIV/AIDS   151

   Appendix 5A: Evaluations of actual fair share
                    contributions to global AIDS efforts   202

   Appendix 5B: Mission and dominant frame of
                    various advocacy organizations   205

   Appendix 5C: Reasons for foreign assistance   207

   Appendix 5D: Aggregating support for foreign assistance   208

6 The search for justice and the International Criminal
   Court   210

   Appendix 6A: Additional opinion polls on support
                    for human rights   254

7 Conclusions and the future of principled advocacy   255

Bibliography   273

Index   314

Figures

2.1 Stages of issue development   *page* 38
2.2 Coercion–conversion continuum   39
2.3 Veto players in the G-7   62
3.1 G-7 disbursements to the HIPC Trust Fund   78
3.2 Mapping of bilateral debt burdens and religiosity   84
4.1 Mapping of emissions and environmental values   124
5.1 Messengers, messages, and gatekeepers   169
5.2 Mapping of fair shares and support for foreign
    assistance   175
6.1 *Financial Times* articles on the International Criminal
    Court, 1997–2007   228
6.2 Mapping of troop deployments and support for
    human rights   234

Tables

2.1 Intersection of influence and outcomes   *page* 40
2.2 Intersection of costs and values   56
2.3 Costs/values, gatekeepers, and advocacy success   60
3.1 Pledges and shares to the HIPC Trust Fund   77
3.2 G-7 debt holdings circa 1998–1999   79
3.3 G-7 measures of religiosity   84
3.4 Costs/values, veto players, and advocacy success   86
4.1 Kyoto and EU bubble commitments and emissions trends   111
4.2 Environmental values and distance from Kyoto target   121
4.3 Constitutional veto players for international treaty ratification   133
4.4 The number of treaty gatekeepers   135
5.1 G-7 Global Fund contributions and share of world income   157
5.2 G-7 bilateral aid to combat HIV/AIDS, 2000–2005   158
5.3 Average GDP growth rate, 1999–2003   161
5.4 Initial AIDS contribution fair shares and foreign assistance   162
5.5 Number of international NGO secretariats, 2003   163
5.6 Interest-based accounts of AIDS spending   164
5.7 Messenger similarity in the United States   170
5.8 Intersection of fair share costs and public support for foreign assistance   171
5.9 US funding for global HIV/AIDS   179
5.10 Public opinion and global AIDS efforts   191
5A.1 G-7 share of world GDP   202
5A.2 Assessments of fair shares and contributions   203

5C.1 Public opinion: reasons for supporting foreign
        assistance   207
5D.1 Public opinion: support for foreign assistance   209
 6.1 G-7 signature and ratification of the Rome Statute   219
 6.2 Overseas force deployments of the G-7, 1998–2000   223
 6.3 Freedom House and Polity ratings, 1998–2000   231
 6.4 Support for human rights, 2008   233
 6.5 Continuum of rhetorical entrapment   237
 7.1 Comparison of financial costs of major expenditures
        by the US government   258

Acknowledgments

I would especially like to thank my parents Mark and Linda Busby who read the entire manuscript and helped make the prose crisper and the writing more accessible. Thank you so much.

Over the course of this project, I was able to conduct hundreds of interviews in a variety of locations including Berlin, Bonn, Brussels, The Hague, London, New York, Paris, Seattle, Tokyo, Vienna, and Washington, DC. I would like to thank all of the people who agreed to be interviewed for this project. Only a fraction of them are ultimately cited in the manuscript, but I learned so much from all of you.

I would like to thank colleagues and friends at a variety of institutions where I had the opportunity to write and develop this research including Georgetown University's Department of Government, the Brookings Institution's program in foreign policy studies, Harvard University's Belfer Center for Science and International Affairs, Princeton University's Niehaus Center for Globalization and Governance, and the LBJ School of Public Affairs, including the Strauss Center and the RGK Center where I enjoy affiliations. I would especially like to thank my dissertation committee: John Ikenberry, Andrew Bennett, Jeff Anderson, and Leslie Vinjamuri.

I would like to thank the anonymous reviewers and the editors at Cambridge University Press, especially John Haslam and Carrie Parkinson for their skillful guidance of the manuscript through the publication process.

I also received support from the Berlin-based Stiftung Wissenschaft und Politik (SWP) during one of my research trips and want to thank the people at SWP, particularly Josef Braml and Alexander Ochs, for providing me with office space in winter 2003. I would also like to thank Joe Cerrell and Michelle Milford from the Gates Foundation for supporting me with office space in summer 2008 in Seattle. I would like to thank Mohamed Bouabdallah for his translation help and research support during my trip to Paris in spring 2007. Thanks to Klaus

Dingwerth, Philipp Pattberg, and Andrew and Philippa Tucker for their generosity with their flats during my research trips to Europe.

I would like to thank Jon Rosenwasser and Janine Davidson whose comments and camaraderie on this project at the dissertation stage were extremely valuable. I would especially like to thank Ron Krebs, Mike Tierney, and Kate Weaver whose advice in the publishing stage was especially helpful.

Finally, I would like to thank my friends from activism days at the University of East Anglia where this interest in global social movements really flourished. I would particularly like to thank and honor my late friend Guy Hughes who was the most serious and seriously organized advocate I ever met. We miss you every day.

1 | *States of grace*

In June 1999, 35,000 protesters descended upon Cologne, Germany, the site of that year's G-8 summit of advanced industrialized countries. Most came from across Germany, called by the country's church-linked development advocacy groups. Others came from countries farther afield, such as the UK, with a smattering of campaigners from as far away as Africa. Advocates converged downtown in the shadow of the famous cathedral that somehow survived the ravages of World War II. They formed a human chain around the city center; another 15,000 mobilized in a parallel protest in Stuttgart. The actions in Germany followed a similar protest of 70,000 the previous year in Birmingham, England. The campaign was Jubilee 2000, which drew on scripture for inspiration. The imagery of bondage was symbolic: external debts were seen as a new form of slavery, and advocates asked rich creditor governments to forgive the external debts of developing countries in time for the new millennium. In Cologne, prompted in large part by advocates, rich governments agreed to significantly expand the scope of debt reduction available to poor countries. Then US president Bill Clinton hailed the agreement as "an historic step to help the world's poorest nations achieve sustained growth and independence."[1]

More than a year later, however, the campaign's political success remained in doubt. The United States Congress had yet to honor the financial commitments President Clinton had made in Cologne. Transnational advocates supportive of debt relief sought to engage congressional gatekeepers directly, including North Carolina's Senator Jesse Helms, the conservative head of the Senate Foreign Relations Committee. In September 2000, the Irish rock star Bono met with Helms and urged him to support developing country debt relief. Helms was known for equating foreign aid with throwing money down "ratholes." However, after their meeting, Helms embraced debt relief

---

[1] Quoted in Babington 1999.

and, later, also supported funding to combat AIDS in the developing world. How can we explain this change? Bono claimed that Helms wept when they spoke: "I talked to him about the Biblical origin of the idea of Jubilee Year... He was genuinely moved by the story of the continent of Africa, and he said to me, 'America needs to do more.' I think he felt it as a burden on a spiritual level."[2] Of his meeting with Bono, Helms said, "I was deeply impressed with him. He has depth that I didn't expect. He is led by the Lord to do something about the starving people in Africa."[3] The story of Helms' tears may be apocryphal, but it speaks both to the peculiar religiosity of the United States and more generally to the power of a compelling argument to persuade key veto players or "policy gatekeepers" to support a morally motivated policy.

Jubilee 2000 was but one of a number of advocacy movements that emerged in the 1990s and early 2000s that made celebrity activists a familiar presence as champions of aspirational causes and star interlocutors to decisionmakers. The campaign's human chain was also one of many audacious actions contemporary movements have inspired among their passionate supporters in this era of low-cost travel, information technology, and ubiquitous media. The human chain became one of the iconic images of late twentieth-century advocacy, rivaled by the large papier mâché puppets of world leaders and elaborate costumes of turtles that became familiar, even notorious, in the wake of the 1999 World Trade Organization (WTO) protests in Seattle and the following year's International Monetary Fund (IMF)/World Bank protests. Together, the chains and the puppets joined the ranks of earlier protest imagery, of environmental protesters rappelling off the roofs of skyscrapers with unfurled banners, of small inflatable rafts intercepting Japanese whaling boats, and, earlier still, of stoic marchers being run down by dogs and sprayed with water hoses in the American South and suffragettes marching in front of the White House. It is easy to romanticize the protests of advocates and credit their success to the boldest actions in their repertoire or to the flexibility of their coalition structure in an era of networked communication. As superficially satisfying as these stories of pluck may be, they do not tell us why

---

[2] Quoted in Dominus 2000, 6.   [3] Quoted in Wagner 2000.

some international mass movements work and others fail, why some campaigns succeed in some places and fail in others.

In the post-Cold War era, states increasingly came under pressure to adopt policies championed by transnational advocacy groups. The cases were distinctive because the primary advocates were motivated not by their own material self-interest but by broader notions of right and wrong. These "principled advocacy movements" were different from many of the kinds of social movements of old where groups with local and parochial grievances and perceptions of injustice (workers, women, African-Americans, gays and lesbians) organized to extend their rights and the spheres of politics in which they were entitled to participate.[4] In the late twentieth- and early twenty-first-century context of deepening economic interdependence and reach of global media, the world witnessed a surge in campaign activity by groups motivated primarily if not exclusively by concerns about the effects on distant others (Darfur, AIDS in Africa, Tibet) or the world as a whole (climate change). Issues that fell under this rubric included campaigns *for* the International Criminal Court, fair trade, and religious freedom in China and the Sudan, as well as campaigns *against* global warming, AIDS, child labor, landmines, small arms, and sweatshops (see Appendix 1A for a non-exhaustive list of campaigns).

While beyond the scope of this book, the field of movement advocacy has also broadened beyond states and transnational organizations to include the private sector, with campaigns targeting mining companies, clothing manufacturers, oil companies, pharmaceuticals producers, and timber companies, among others.[5] Campaigners have even targeted consumers, seeking to cultivate a market for fair trade products and ethical investment. Even as important new actors emerged as an object of advocates' concern, states remained the principal organizing units on the international stage and the primary targets of movement

---

[4] Sell and Prakash see the distinction between principled advocacy movements and self-interest-based organizing as artificial. Given that many groups are moved by a desire for survival, contracts, or job security, principled advocacy may be less principled than appears at first blush (Sell and Prakash 2004). Cooley and Ron make a similar point with respect to operational international relief non-governmental organizations (Cooley and Ron 2002).

[5] For illustrative examples in the environmental realm, see Bartley 2007; Dingwerth 2008; Pattberg 2005.

advocacy. Of these, the advanced industrialized countries, epitomized by the annual G-7/G-8 meetings,[6] have been the main recipients of the most visible mobilized advocacy of the past decade and are the states of principal concern in this book.

Even if the contemporary era has been rich with this kind of transnational protest activity, the phenomenon is not new. Although the terminology of transnational social movements is of recent coinage, the tradition of mobilization across borders by groups that have moral attachments to events far from home has a storied history, whether it be the abolitionist movement of the eighteenth and nineteenth centuries,[7] transnational campaigns for humanitarian intervention in the nineteenth and early twentieth centuries,[8] the early twentieth-century campaign to stop Belgian depredations in the Congo,[9] the British advocates against female footbinding in early twentieth-century China, colonial expatriates railing against female circumcision in Kenya during the same time period,[10] transnational relief efforts after the Russian famines in the early 1920s,[11] or the nineteenth- and twentieth-century efforts by the UK and the United States to rein in the human rights abuses of strategic allies.[12] While less clearly altruistic (though no less interested in imposing their values across borders), émigrés often sought to generate transnational concern for the fate of their homelands or, in the case of the Jewish diaspora at the turn of the twentieth

---

[6] The Group of Seven (G-7) refers to the annual meetings of finance ministers and heads of state of seven advanced industrial democracies – Canada, France, Germany, Italy, Japan, the United Kingdom, and the United States. Formed in 1975, G-7 meetings allowed rich countries to coordinate economic policy and increasingly broader sets of issues. Russia was invited to join in 1997, making it the G-8. Here, G-7 refers to the seven advanced democracies; G-8 refers to the meetings. After the 2008 global economic crisis, the G-8 was superseded in 2009 by the G-20, a broader group of advanced and developing countries thought important for international economic coordination.

[7] Kaufmann and Pape 1999.

[8] Bass 2008. Noting a complex of imperial and humanitarian motives, Bass recounts efforts to address the decline of the Ottoman Empire in the late nineteenth and early twentieth centuries in the lead-up to World War I, including the support for Greek independence in 1825, a European drive to save the Maronite Christians of Syria and Lebanon in 1860, the British response to the Bulgarian atrocities in 1876, and American actions after the Armenian genocide of 1915.

[9] Hochschild 1998. [10] Keck and Sikkink 1998.

[11] McElroy 1992. [12] Walldorf 2008.

century, international political momentum for the creation of a new Jewish homeland.[13]

Why does the subject of transnational advocacy then deserve fresh treatment? Numerous books and articles have been written in recent years to describe and capture the processes of transnational contention, of mobilization, of actions by advocacy movements to take a stand and compel, browbeat, and persuade decisionmakers to accept what activists consider to be the right thing.[14] Perhaps the foundational work on this topic in international relations is Margaret Keck and Kathryn Sikkink's *Activists Beyond Borders* (1998).

Few books have rivaled (or even sought to rival) its impressive, ambitious breadth, wide historical sweep, and scope. The book's special appeal is that it captured the ethos of the age – the rise of non-state actors with a do-it-yourself mentality that anything was possible. The Internet was relatively new, and the mobilization of attention and people across borders through new media and communications was fresh and novel. This was also a time of, *pace* Francis Fukuyama, post-history; with the end of the Cold War, traditional security threats had largely receded, opening space for new issues and actors of a variety of stripes to push their agendas. The normative promise led scholars in this tradition to hype the potential for transformative change through social movement advocacy.[15]

A decade on – given everything that has transpired – the late 1990s seem quaint. It would be easy to assume that, with the attacks of September 11, 2001, and the subsequent wars in Afghanistan and Iraq, the landscape for advocacy would have changed entirely. On one level, one would have expected that the profoundly changed security environment would have driven these new issues off the agenda. Policymakers, consumed by terrorism and security, would have no time for offbeat causes such as climate change and global public health. But did the policy agenda really change that much? While security concerns certainly have risen to the top of the agenda, a number of

---

[13] Tarrow 2005. Tilly mentions other historical transnational antecedents, including the temperance movement, movements for women's rights, and the Irish independence movement (Tilly 2004, 113).

[14] Betsill 2000; Bob 2005; Hawkins 2004; Hertel 2006; Kolb 2007; Price 1998, 2003; Risse, Ropp, and Sikkink 1999; Risse-Kappen 1995a; Rutherford 2000; Staggenborg 2008; Tarrow 2005; Tilly 2004; Wapner 1995.

[15] Florini 2000; Mathews 1997.

non-traditional issues, including climate change and HIV/AIDS, have continued to receive attention and resources but not all of them equally so. With greenhouse gas emissions ascending nearly unabated, the continuation of killings in Darfur, the estimated two and a half million new HIV/AIDS infections each year, and persistent poverty affecting hundreds of millions particularly in Africa, the issues that animated moral outrage in the first place have not gone away.

At the same time, the literature on social movements has not quite moved on or progressed beyond the initial documentation of the relevance of social movements and the variety of mechanisms by which they exercise influence. The first cohort of research, including Keck and Sikkink's work, focused primarily on advocacy movements in developing countries and how, when faced with local state intransigence to their demands for protection of human rights or environmental enforcement, these campaigns might enlist the support of global partners to pressure their home governments. These outside–in processes were aptly titled, one being the now famous "boomerang model," and the other its illustrious counterpart, the "spiral model."[16] But what of efforts to move stronger governments and already manifestly liberal democracies? Do the same processes apply in societies with a more established democratic culture and role for internal free expression and mobilization?

The accumulated wisdom of more than a decade of scholarship on social movements has focused on a few key factors – whether or not the messages resonate with local value structures, the relative openness of the process to civil society input, and the ability of different groups to mobilize.[17] The mechanisms of influence have largely focused on mobilizing information to persuade and attention to praise and shame decisionmakers for good and bad behavior. What is missing in all these accounts is a more conditional understanding of the circumstances that facilitate successful social movement action. As Richard Price notes, the next generation of this kind of research needs to answer: "*Why* do some campaigns succeed in some places but fail in others?"[18] We can also turn this question around to ask: *When* will states take on these new normative commitments championed by principled advocacy movements?

---

[16] Keck and Sikkink 1998; Risse, Ropp, and Sikkink 1999.
[17] McAdam, McCarthy, and Zald 1996. Kolb makes a similar assessment (Kolb 2007).
[18] Price 2003, 586.

In this line of study, it is tempting to look at the material through the lens of the advocates, the structure of their networks, the nature of their messages, and other elements of what they do and what they can control. If we study what advocates can control, we can potentially provide policy advice. If only you tweak your message, raise more money, or improve your governance structure, then you will likely have more success.[19] In reality, much is outside advocates' control, once they have decided on an issue to work on. Some problems are simply harder to solve than others. More than that, most issue areas, even if unsettled, already have a cohort of professionals inside and outside governments and international institutions who are tasked to have a say over how that issue is handled.

In slightly more technical terms, advocacy involves a strategic interaction between agents and structures.[20] In other words, some things are under the control of advocates – the agents – but whether or not advocates succeed is mediated by the context, the nature of the issue, what else is going on in the world, which agencies and international organizations have a say over this problem, and so on. As the field on this topic has long recognized, the "political opportunity structure" matters greatly. If advocates cannot monitor or participate in an international conference or even get a meeting with staff at an international institution, they may be constrained from having input on the process, let alone influence. Another wrinkle in this story is that there are other agents in the narrative; you have advocates and their allies, but also you often have opponents and their coterie. More than this, on the other side of the institutional wall, both in governments and in international institutions, are people with varying degrees of authority who can, at some level, choose to act based on information and appeals. Understanding when those decisionmakers can or will listen and respond to advocates therefore is a central question in this book.

We can identify a number of reasons to explain why a given campaign succeeded, and political scientists, myself included, have written article after article about individual campaigns and single-issue areas

---

[19] Kolb critiques this line of argument (Kolb 2007). Staggenborg describes this as the "resource mobilization" school in social movement theory (Staggenborg 2008). For an illustration of this kind of perspective applied to a recent movement, see Randle on Jubilee 2000 (Randle 2004).

[20] Lake and Powell 1999.

dispensing such sage explanation and advice.[21] But how much do we really know about why some campaigns work and others fail? It is both easy and hard to offer a coherent narrative to explain many cases. Readymade, off-the-shelf answers that emphasize costs and difficulty are available from scholars in the "rationalist" tradition in political science. On one level, we can expect movement success when what is asked is easy and consistent with what states and decisionmakers wanted to do anyway.[22] However, while a good beginning, we need a more nuanced explanation that can encompass when states do what is apparently the hard thing, when the costs of action or policies are not manifestly clear, and when states seemingly act against their short-run interests or act for reasons other than for obvious material gain.

This book looks at cases of success and failure by transnational advocacy movements in different national contexts. Here, success is primarily defined in a political rather than a policy sense. What this concept means is that the focus is principally on the early stages when a country has been asked to make a domestic decision about an international commitment.[23] At this early stage, advocacy typically focuses on securing either (1) commitments of funds or (2) support for international treaties. For financial commitments, the end result involves an appropriation of money. In the case of treaties, this action entails domestic ratification. To a certain extent, this issue raises the important question of whether countries make international commitments because they engage in cheap talk, relatively painless acts of international solidarity.[24] I will come back to this discussion over the course of the coming chapters, but compliance is not the central focus of this book for a number of reasons. First, since many of these cases are live issues, the degree to which individual countries have complied with their international commitments remains an open question. Second, this project concerns states taking on international commitments championed by principled advocacy movements, not about the wisdom or the efficacy of those commitments. While I understand and have

---

[21] Cardenas 2004; Carpenter 2005; Price 1998; Rutherford 2000; Sundstrom 2005.

[22] Downs, Rocke, and Barsoom 1996, 380; Goldsmith and Posner 2003–2004, 2005; von Stein 2005a, 612; 2005b.

[23] In the life cycle of norms, Checkel refers to this early stage before internalization as "empowerment" (Checkel 1997, 479).

[24] On cheap talk, see the literature in game theory by Farrell and Rabin 1996; Morrow 1994.

analyzed the question of effectiveness (one that is intimately bound up with compliance), whether what advocates propose is wise (i.e., likely to work) is simply beyond the scope of this book. Any project has to be bounded. While subsequent chapters examine whether or not states can make commitments and later fail to abide by them, the initial commitment is a significant decision in its own right. Importantly, in countries such as the United States where the international rhetorical commitment has to be matched by domestic action (i.e., advice and consent of the Senate for treaties and congressional appropriations of funds), this book focuses on the domestic approval stage, a harder and higher bar of commitment than a leader merely announcing his or her intentions publicly.

I try to provide a generalizable explanation and approach that can explain why some countries accept commitments championed by principled advocacy groups while others reject them. The scope of the argument is both multi-issue and multi-country, with limitations on the number of issues and countries a function of using case study methods. I look at four substantive issues – debt relief, climate change, HIV/AIDS, and the International Criminal Court (ICC). For each, I examine why the campaigns for action succeeded in some country cases and failed in others. For the purposes of symmetry, the universe of potential cases is the same for all four issue areas, the seven most advanced industrialized countries (the G-7): Canada, France, Germany, Italy, Japan, the United Kingdom, and the United States. For each of the substantive empirical chapters, I provide a more extended discussion of some of the most interesting country cases within the G-7. The object for each is to subject my argument to some tougher tests, where it would not be expected to do well or where it is hard to show what I propose to show.[25] At the same time, I also seek to analyze cases that are important in terms of their global significance as well as likely to be of interest to a general audience.[26]

Invariably, a desire for relevance and significance leads me to use the United States as a country case, making this book as much about the peculiar patterns of US engagement with the world as it is about social movements. Here we have two cases – debt relief and HIV/AIDS – where the United States has been an important partner to and leader

---

[25] George and Bennett 2005.
[26] On the selection of important cases, see Van Evera 1997.

of international action and two cases – climate change and the ICC – where the United States has sought to undermine whatever counter-leadership efforts that have emerged from other countries without, as yet, putting forward much of an alternative vision. As George W. Bush left the stage and President Barack Obama assumed office, whether the United States would become a more robust supporter of multilateral cooperation remained an important and live question.[27]

Some might ask "why these cases and not others?" with respect to both the substance and the breadth of country cases. I wanted a diversity of issue areas – international economics and development (debt relief), environment (climate change), public health (HIV/AIDS), and justice/security (the International Criminal Court) – as well as a diversity of country cases. To be able to make more generalizable claims, I particularly needed cases of both successful and failed advocacy – in other words, of successful and failed state acceptance of commitments championed by social movements. While there was some overlap of coverage of the United States, I sought substantive cases where the country acted differently in some cases. At the same time, I wanted to include a variety of country cases, some cases including Japan, others Germany, some the UK, others with France or Canada. Only one country of the G-7 does not get an extended treatment, and that is Italy.

During my research for this book, I conducted several hundred interviews over eight years, many of them face to face, some by phone, and some over e-mail with a variety of people, including activists, government officials, staff of international organizations, academics, members of the business community, international lawyers, physicians, clergy, and scientists, among others. This project has taken me to Berlin, Bonn, Boston, Brussels, The Hague, London, Milan, New York, Paris, Seattle, Tokyo, Vienna, Washington D.C., and beyond. This book would not have been possible without the collaboration of the many people I interviewed.

Those interested in "external validity" or broader generalizations across larger numbers of countries and cases may find fault with a case study approach. A number of scholars have begun to apply advanced

---

[27] Brooks and Wohlforth 2008; Busby and Monten 2008b; Ikenberry 2003; Kagan 2003; Keohane 2005; Kupchan 2002; Kupchan and Trubowitz 2007; Lepgold 2001; Moravcsik 2005; Walt 2005.

statistical techniques to the study of international commitments.[28] While statistics lend themselves to broader crosscountry generalizations, this project was intended to explore the outliers and difficult cases and to understand causal processes more clearly, areas for which case study methods are simply better suited.[29] I also sought to explore in some depth country cases for which many of the dominant accounts, what I term "interest-based arguments," ultimately have some difficulty explaining.

What then is the arc of the book that you have before you? In Chapter 2, I provide an overview of the main argument. In brief, I posit that whether states accept commitments made by principled advocacy movements depends primarily on how three factors conjoin: (1) the balance of material incentives facing states, (2) the cultural resonance of the messages, and (3) the number and preferences of policy gatekeepers. I make the case that states will support moderately costly actions against their material self-interest when the issue is framed to fit with the country's values and when policy gatekeepers personally consider these attributes important.

While this argument serves as the master template that guides me throughout the book, I do something a little different in each chapter. I seek to provide a more supple approach, a family of related arguments that explain the conditions under which advocacy movements will be successful.[30] Each of the cases therefore focuses in more detail on a piece of the larger argument. So, while many things are potentially relevant, I choose to illuminate different aspects of the argument in each chapter, while retaining rigorous standards of social science inquiry. Each substantive issue and all the country cases can be explained through the lens of the core theory. Indeed, I replicate the same essential set-up in each empirical chapter, looking at the intersection of indicators of costs and values for every substantive issue to map the country cases in both dimensions. However, in the process of conducting this research, I found each substantive case raised interesting issues that deserved expanded treatment. My hope is that the additional theoretical contributions explored in successive empirical

---

[28] Hafner-Burton 2008; Hafner-Burton and Tsutsui 2005; Kelley 2007; Sandholtz 2005; von Stein 2005a, 2005b.
[29] George and Bennett 2005.
[30] For a similar approach, see Bueno de Mesquita *et al.* 2003, 37.

chapters ultimately make for a more engaging read than a formulaic application of my core argument.

In Chapter 3, I look at the Jubilee 2000 campaign in more detail, and I assess why the campaign had such difficulty in the United States, in what looks on some level to be an easy case. I also explore why the Japanese, who held much higher levels of developing country debt, resisted debt relief for so long. This chapter adheres most clearly to the theory laid out in Chapter 2, in the sense that I look at the intersection of the three factors identified above: *costs, values,* and *gatekeepers.* In the United States, the message of Jubilee 2000, with its roots in religious scripture, had deep moral appeal but, given the diversity of players who had to agree on actual appropriations of money for debt relief, President Clinton had difficulty bringing the United States on board when his administration warmed to the idea. Advocates succeeded only when they were able to convince Republican chairs of key congressional committees to support the cause; many of them, such as Senator Jesse Helms and Congressman Spencer Bachus, were moved by their faith to support the cause. However, the religious moral arguments that proved powerful in Western countries lacked cultural appeal in Japan, particularly given the importance Japan placed upon building up a "credit culture" of sound borrowing in its own rise to wealth. Japan did prove willing to write off the debts of the world's poor countries when the argument was reframed as a test of Japan's international contribution. Being a good international citizen and leader has significant cultural appeal in Japan. The contribution of this chapter to our overall understanding is that states are willing to support some forms of costly moral action, within bounds, when gatekeepers are convinced the cause is important enough.

In Chapter 4 on global climate change, I examine why some countries facing costly emissions profiles like the United States – namely Japan and Canada – ratified the Kyoto Protocol despite facing high costs.[31] Building on the analysis in the previous chapter, I expand on

---

[31] Some might argue that climate change is different from the other policy issues covered in this book because the consequences of climate change (or self-interest) may drive policy rather than morality or principle. While advocates do (increasingly) care about the consequences of climate change for their own countries and localities, advocates were initially moved by the planetary implications of climate change, with the consequences for distant others and ecosystems an important part of campaigners' motivations.

the discussion of reputation to assess why some states may make commitments that seem contrary to their material interests. In both Japan and Canada, the decision to ratify the Kyoto Protocol appeared to be deeply symbolic behavior, consistent with how the leadership at the time and the citizenry saw their role on the world stage as "good international citizens." Reputation, as used in this chapter, is not a new concept or factor to explain foreign policy outcomes. Rather, my discussion of reputation extends the argument in Chapter 3. Reputational concerns, in my view, represent a subset of the kinds of value claims that campaigners can tap into through framing. Recognizing that reputations can also be rooted in self-interest, I use this chapter to explore the extent to which reputational concerns are instrumental or are animated by ideas and beliefs that are less clearly self-serving. Interestingly, in neither Canada nor Japan has the government done much substantively with respect to actual implementation of their climate commitments, leading to a discussion of the importance of commitments versus compliance. I also raise the counterfactual, "what if?" question. If the United States had behaved differently, would Japan and Canada have been able to avoid converting their rhetorical commitments into concrete action? I discuss how neither environmental values nor reputational concerns were sufficient to offset the opposition of powerful legislative gatekeepers in the US context. While recognizing that opponents of action on climate change funded a vigorous disinformation campaign, I also emphasize how the environmental movement framed the problem as an urgent crisis and tied that frame to policies that exacerbated a number of gatekeepers' fears about precipitous action on climate change.

> A senior official in the Japanese environment ministry was asked what would have happened if the 1997 negotiations in Kyoto had been held in some country other than Japan. Would Japan have still ratified? The official said they would have tried. He said the situation would have been "very different. The Japanese public was not so greatly concerned with the international regime. Not to have the Japanese town's name, the Japanese situation would be very different."[32] If a decision as significant as ratification of a treaty is influenced by whether or not the country in question was host to the negotiations, what is going on?

---

[32] Shimizu 2004.

In Chapter 5, I look at why some advanced industrialized countries have been more generous donors than others to efforts to combat HIV/AIDS in the developing world. Here I expand on the argument developed in Chapter 2 by introducing a new but related concept, the role of messengers. Building on the concept of source effects from social psychology, I suggest that messengers who share attributes with policy gatekeepers are more likely to be successful than those who do not. In looking at the case of one relatively generous country (the United States) and two less generous countries (Germany and Japan), I find that messengers are most likely to be effective when they face a favorable material environment but also, crucially, where they possess shared attributes with decisionmakers and frame their arguments to fit the values of their target country. While the concept of messengers is a new contribution, the claims of this chapter are rooted in the core argument developed in Chapter 2.

> Franklin Graham is head of a Christian relief charity, Samaritan's Purse, and the son of longtime presidential pastor Billy Graham. In 2000, Franklin Graham offered the prayer to open George W. Bush's 2000 inaugural. In February 2002, Samaritan's Purse hosted a national conference, Prescription for Hope, to highlight the role of the evangelical community in addressing HIV/AIDS. Graham sought to recast the evangelical community's understanding of the disease, arguing that "each of the 40 million men, women, and children worldwide who are infected with the HIV virus are precious to God. And if they're precious to God, then by God, they should be precious to us."[33] Between 1997 and 2004, the amount of funding the United States dedicated to fight HIV/AIDS increased from $170 million per year to $2.2 billion per year. How did this happen?

In Chapter 6 on the International Criminal Court, I primarily examine two cases, France and the UK, though I include some discussion of the United States. All three had much higher military deployments than other G-7 countries, which made ratifying the Rome Statute, the treaty creating the ICC, potentially costly. By costly, I mean that creation of the Court could potentially subject the countries' soldiers to prosecution for individual war crimes, genocide, or crimes against humanity (though, as we will see, there were some carefully crafted protections that may have made this unlikely). Both the UK and France ratified the treaty in the early

[33] Quoted in Sheler 2002.

stages, while the United States signed the treaty in President Clinton's final weeks in office, only to have President George W. Bush repudiate that signature and then actively seek to undermine the Court. What is interesting in this case is how the UK and France had opposite reactions to the perceived costliness of the ICC. The UK always saw its risks and costs as manageable and supported the Court. The French military vigorously opposed the Court and were supported by President Jacques Chirac until an election brought the more favorably inclined Socialists into government to share power. In this chapter, through the UK case, I discuss the importance of perceived costs as an important mediating factor and how what may appear costly objectively may not be subjectively.[34] The addition of perception suggests that, like values, impressions of the costliness of what advocates want are mediated by ideas, blurring the distinction between costs and values as meaningful categories. While an important realization, this refinement adds but slight nuance to the core argument. In my discussion of France, I emphasize the importance that elections serve to bring in to government new gatekeepers potentially more sympathetic to campaigners' aims. In the process, I discuss how rhetorical commitments by the new cohabitation government made them more vulnerable to shaming efforts by weak actors and

> The British government was an early and strong supporter of the International Criminal Court. Despite having extensive numbers of troops deployed overseas, the British, unlike the French and the Americans, never regarded the Court as a risk to British soldiers. As the lead negotiator for the British said, "The prospect of an ICC Prosecutor setting out to pull the noses of powerful law-abiding states strikes me as so remote as hardly to enter into the realm of serious policy-making, and the prospect that, if he *were* foolish enough to try to do so, it would survive the scrutiny of the judges at the pre-trial level, is even more fanciful still."[35] Why did the United Kingdom not see the ICC as a threat or serious problem as France and the United States did?

their allies. Shaming is a close cousin of framing and is often implicitly referenced as a kind of framing. Where framing efforts, in my view, can rely on appeals to actors' better angels and ideas about what is good and right, shaming efforts seek to punish and rhetorically bludgeon actors for failure to live up to their values. As a consequence, shaming

---

[34] This is akin to the addition of subjective assessments to offense–defense theory. See Christensen and Snyder 1990.

[35] Berman 2002.

has a more coercive feel. Because advocates frequently rely on this strategy when positive framing efforts fail, I discuss in this chapter how shaming represents a theoretical bridge between approaches that focus on self-interest and those that emphasize the importance of ideas, morality, and norms.

The concluding Chapter 7, in addition to evaluating the contributions of this book, assesses the future of transnational principled advocacy in light of the severe economic downturn of 2008. That financial crisis may pose a more significant and lasting systemic constraint on advocacy success than anything the world has endured since the end of the Cold War, including the attacks of September 11, 2001. That said, the crisis may prove in time to be much less severe than analysts feared, making this chapter appear as a snapshot reminder of unfounded anxiety. Nonetheless, its inclusion is meant to acknowledge the extraordinary times of the post-Cold War world where, the events of September 2001 notwithstanding, existential threats to countries' security and the global economic system receded to minor preoccupations. Compared to periods such as the Great Depression, World War II, and the era of the Cuban Missile Crisis, the international system after the Cold War, with all of the promise of emergent technologies, was a favorable one for transnational principled advocacy. The threat of worldwide economic calamity reminds us that this era may not last.

One final point of departure. This book is meant to be accessible to all readers, not just those grounded in the sometimes obscure debates of international relations and political science. To that end, I have embedded some discussions of international relations theory in footnotes, where readers with an interest in arcane disciplinary issues can find more information and citations. While Chapter 2 is unavoidably more theoretical than subsequent chapters, I sought to make the chapter readable for a non-specialist audience, using everyday language wherever possible, explaining terms when necessary, and providing illustrative examples.

Appendix 1A
Transnational principled advocacy movements in the post-Cold War era (1990–)

Campaign/ movement	Primary area	Target(s)	Goal	Leading advocacy organizations	Time frame	Outcome	Political success/ failure	Scholars
CASE STUDIES IN THE BOOK								
1 Jubilee 2000	Economic	States	Write off unpayable third world debt	Jubilee 2000, church groups, CAFOD, Action Aid, World Development Movement	1996–2000	G-8 meeting agreement Cologne 1999, Gleneagles 2005	Success	Donnelly
2 Climate change	Environment	States, sub-national governments, firms	Reduce greenhouse gases	World Wide Fund for Nature, Greenpeace, Friends of the Earth, Climate Action Network	1989–	1992 Rio, 1997 Kyoto Protocol	Mixed (United States not in)	Betsill, Cass, Newell, Victor, von Stein

(cont.)

Appendix 1A (cont.)

Campaign/ movement	Primary area	Target(s)	Goal	Leading advocacy organizations	Time frame	Outcome	Political success/ failure	Scholars
3 AIDS campaign	Health	States, multinational corporations	Generic drug access for developing countries, aid for treatment	Doctors Without Borders, Consumer Project on Technology, DATA, Samaritan's Purse, Global Aids Alliance, Health GAP, ACT UP	1999–	2002 Global Fund created	Success	de Waal, Drahos, Drezner, Kapstein, Lieberman, Patterson, Prakash, Sell, Shadlen
4 International Criminal Court	Security, human rights	States, individuals	Create court to hold individuals to account for war crimes, genocide, crimes against humanity	International Coalition for the International Criminal Court, Amnesty International, Human Rights Watch	1995–1998+	Rome Statute 1998	Mixed (United States not in)	Hawkins, Kelley, Sandholtz, Struett

OTHER CAMPAIGNS

1 Anti-Iraq war protests	Security	States	Stop the United States from invading Iraq and ending the US occupation	ATTAC, ANSWER, Moveon.org, Not in Our Name, United for Peace and Justice, Canadian Peace Alliance, Stop the War Coalition	2003–	Some European countries did not join the Iraq coalition and some, like Spain, withdrew	Failure	Della Porta, Tarrow
2 Anti-GMOs	Environment	States	Banning the use/sale of genetically modified organisms	Via Campesina, Greenpeace, Consumers International	2004–	Some European bans	Mixed (United States not in)	Carlsson, Nielsen, Palme, Sindico
3 Anti-smoking/ tobacco	Health	States, individual behavior	Reducing/ eliminating tobacco use	Framework Convention Alliance	1999–	World Health Organization Framework on Tobacco Control	Mixed (United States signed but not ratified)	Hu, Pechmann, Tonneson, Warner
4 Anti-structural adjustment/ anti-IFI	Economic	States, IGOs	End of conditionality, end of the IFIs, adjustment with human face	ATTAC, 50 Years Is Enough, Oxfam	1994–	Some changes in IFI structural adjustment policies	Mixed (some change in IFI policies)	Brown, della Porta, Fox, Smith, Tarrow

(cont.)

Appendix 1A (*cont.*)

Campaign/ movement	Primary area	Target(s)	Goal	Leading advocacy organizations	Time frame	Outcome	Political success/ failure	Scholars
5 Anti-toxics	Environment	States, MNCs	Banning the release of toxics into the environment	International POPs Elimination Network	1998–	2001 Stockholm Convention (ratified in 2004)	Mixed (United States signed but not ratified)	Szasz
6 Biodiversity	Environment	States, MNCs	Preserving biodiversity	Friends of the Earth International, World Wide Fund for Nature, Greenpeace, Wildlife Conservation Network	1961–	1993 Convention on Biological Diversity, 2010 biodiversity target adopted in 2002	Mixed (United States not in)	Ferraro, Hanley, Kramer, Perrings
7 Child labor	Economic	States	Ban or reduce child labor	Global March Against Child Labour, International Labour Organization, Child Labor Coalition	1989–	UN Convention on the Rights of the Child	Success	Basu, Hertel

| 8 | Child soldiers | Human rights | Ending the use of child soldiers | Coalition to Stop the Use of Child Soldiers, Human Rights Watch, Global Action for Children | 1998– | Child Soldier Prevention Act, Optional Protocol to the Convention on the Rights of the Child on the involvement of children in armed conflict | Mixed (US bill introduced, optional UN bill) | Carpenter, Singer |
| 9 | Civilian protection | Security | Protect civilians from warfare | Genocide Intervention Network, International Crisis Group, International Committee of the Red Cross, Refugees International, R2P Coalition | 1949– | 1949 Geneva Convention, 1998 Rome Statute of the International Criminal Court | Success | Carpenter |

(*cont.*)

Appendix 1A (cont.)

Campaign/ movement	Primary area	Target(s)	Goal	Leading advocacy organizations	Time frame	Outcome	Political success/ failure	Scholars
10 Cluster bombs	Security	States	Ban cluster bombs	Cluster Munition Coalition, International Committee of the Red Cross, Human Rights Watch	2003–	2008 Cluster Munition Convention	Mixed (United States not in)	Bilukha, Brennan
11 Dams	Environment	International organizations, states	Reduce environmental damage due to dams	International Rivers, Wetlands International, Friends of River Narmada	1985–	International Commission on Large Dams, World Commission on Dams	Mixed (no binding agreements but international cooperation via UN/ICOLD)	Dingwerth, Khagram
12 Darfur intervention	Human rights	States	Humanitarian intervention in Darfur	Genocide Intervention Network, Human Rights Watch,	2003–	African Union peacekeepers, referral of	Failure	Belloni, de Waal, Mamdani, Prunier, Straus

				Amnesty International, Enough, Save Darfur				
13 Female circumcision campaign	Health	States	End practice of female genital mutilation	No Peace Without Justice, Foundation for Women's Health, Research, and Development, Tostan, RAINBO, Center for Reproductive Rights	1983–	1997 WHO Interagency Statement on Eliminating Female Genital Mutilation	Failure	Boyle, Greunbaum, Shell-Duncan, Toubia
14 Free Tibet	Human rights	States	Ending Chinese control of Tibet	Free Tibet, International Campaign for Tibet	1987–	No outcomes	Failure	Barnett, Mingxu, Sautman
15 Human trafficking	Human rights	States, private actors	Stop human trafficking	Amnesty International, Human Rights Watch, Anti-Slavery International, Somaly Mam Foundation, Polaris Project, Coalition Against Trafficking in Women	2000–	UN 2000 Convention Against Transnational Organized Crime	Success	Aradau, Jackson, Laczko, Salt

(cont.)

Appendix 1A (cont.)

Campaign/ movement	Primary area	Target(s)	Goal	Leading advocacy organizations	Time frame	Outcome	Political success/ failure	Scholars
16 Humanitarian intervention	Security	States	Encourage states to stop committing human rights abuses against their own citizens	International Crisis Group, Refugees International, Humanitarian Policy Group, Partnership for Effective Peacekeeping	1979–	Responsibility to Protect	Mixed (inconsistent actions by UN/states)	Bass, Finnemore, Holzgrefe, Kuperman, Mason, Parekh, Weiss, Wheeler
17 Internally displaced persons (IDPs)	Human rights	States	Protection of and humanitarian assistance to civilian populations internally displaced from their homes	Brookings–Bern Project, Internal Displacement Monitoring Center (IDMC), Norwegian Refugee Council, Refugees International	1992–	Guiding Principles on Internal Displacement	Mixed (no binding agreements)	Cohen, Deng, Lischer
18 Landmines	Security	States	Ban landmines	International Campaign to Ban Landmines, Vietnam	1991–	International treaty to ban landmines	Success	Price, Rutherford

#	Name	Type	Actors	Goal	Organizations	Years	Outcome	Assessment	Key figures
19	Make Poverty History	Economic	States	Ending global poverty	ONE, Make Poverty History, Christians Ending Poverty, Millennium Promise	2005–	Could take credit for G-8 Gleneagles pledges on foreign assistance and debt relief	Mixed (pledges at Gleneagles have not been fulfilled)	Hodkinson, Sachs, Satterthwaite
20	Marine conservation	Environment	States, MNCs	Preservation and protection of marine ecosystems	Oceana, Sea Watch, Consortium for Wildlife Bycatch Reduction, Project Global, Greenpeace, Marine Conservation Biology Institute, Marine Bio, Ocean Conservancy, Save the Whales, Whaleman Foundation, Sea Shepherd	1969–	Johannesburg Declaration, Ad Hoc Open-ended Informal Working Group, CITES, International Whaling Commission, Convention on Fishing and Conservation of Living Resources of the High Seas	Mixed (few binding international agreements, mixed domestic legislation)	Alverson, Barlow, Carr, Freeman, Hall, Johannes, Lewison, Lubchenco, Mooney, Norman, Northridge, Vitousek

(cont.)

Appendix 1A (*cont.*)

Campaign/ movement	Primary area	Target(s)	Goal	Leading advocacy organizations	Time frame	Outcome	Political success/ failure	Scholars
21 Maternal mortality	Health	States	Reducing maternal mortality	IMMPACT, Partnership for Maternal, Newborn, and Child Health, Center for Reproductive Rights	2000–	Millennium Development Goal 5	Mixed (one of MDGs but no real progress)	Freedman, Graham, Hounton, Shiffman
22 Millennium Development Goals (MDGs)	Health, economic, environment, human rights	States	Eliminate poverty, achieve universal primary education, gender equality, improve maternal health and	InterAction, International Committee of the Red Cross, International Medical Corps, International Rescue Committee, International Union for the	2001–	Some increases by governments in foreign assistance to meet MDGs	Mixed (some progress but unclear if goals will be reached by 2012)	Haines

#	Issue	Category	Actors	Goal	Organizations	Date	Outcome	Success	Authors
				reduce infant mortality, combat disease, promote development and environmental sustainability	Conservation of Nature, Mercy Corps, Oxfam, Millennium Promise, Save the Children, Wildlife Trust				
23	Nuclear non-proliferation	Security	States	Reducing the number of nuclear weapons and preventing the creation of new weapons	Arms Control Association, Carnegie Endowment, Center for Arms Control and Non-Proliferation	1968–	NPT, START	Mixed	Bailey, Mazarr, Paul, Quester, Reiss, Sagan, Utgoff
24	Privacy protection	Human rights	States, MNCs	Protection of citizens from privacy invasions	Privacy International, Electronic Privacy Information Center	1990	Various national privacy legislation	Mixed (success varies)	Bennett, Farrell, Tavani
25	Rainforest preservation	Environment	States, MNCs	Preservation of rain forests	Rainforest Action Network, Rainforest Conservation Fund, Sierra Club	1985–	No outcomes, groups still active	Failure	Taplin, Trapasso

(cont.)

Appendix 1A (cont.)

Campaign/ movement	Primary area	Target(s)	Goal	Leading advocacy organizations	Time frame	Outcome	Political success/ failure	Scholars
26 Refugees	Human rights	States	Protection and humanitarian assistance for refugees	Refugees International, Women's Refugee Commission, European Council on Refugees and Exiles, Norwegian Refugee Council	1979–	United Nations Convention Relating to the Status of Refugees, Protocol Relating to the Status of Refugees	Mixed (no binding agreements since UN Convention/ Protocol specifically relating to refugee protection)	Barnett, Chimni, Emizet, Feller, Finnemore, Hathaway, Weiner
27 Religious freedom	Human rights	States	Protect religious freedom in Sudan, China	International Coalition for Religious Freedom, International Association for Religious Freedom	1976–	International Convenant on Civil and Political Rights, International Religious Freedom Act of 1998 (US)	Success	Hertzke, Shadid

28	Small arms	Security	States, firms	Reduce export of small arms to developing countries	International Action Network on Small Arms, Human Rights Watch, Amnesty International, Oxfam	1998–	No outcomes	Failure	Brehm, Muggah, O'Dwyer
29	Space weapons	Security	States	Preventing the militarization of space	Global Network Against Weapons and Nuclear Power in Space	1992–	No outcomes	Failure	Baum, Mowthorpe, Stares
30	Sweatshops	Economic	States, firms	Reduce unsafe working conditions	International Labor Rights Fund, United Students Against Sweatshops, Sweatshops Watch, National Labor Committee, Worker Rights Consortium	1981–	Codes of conduct, Fair Labor Association – little has happened lately, groups still active	Success	Hapke, Louie, Moran, Varley

(cont.)

Appendix 1A (cont.)

Campaign/ movement	Primary area	Target(s)	Goal	Leading advocacy organizations	Time frame	Outcome	Political success/ failure	Scholars
31 Torture	Human rights	States	Ban torture	Human Rights Watch, Physicians for Human Rights, Amnesty International	1987–	Torture convention, targets on individuals, Rome Statute 1998, UN Istanbul Protocol (1999)	Mixed (not clearly defined)	Donnelly, Hawkins, Ignatieff
32 Transparency	Economic	States, firms	Reduce corruption through transparency	Transparency International	1993	Extractive Industry Review, EITI	Success	Alt, Grigorescu, Lassen
33 Violence against women	Human rights	States	Reduce/ eliminate violence against women	Women Thrive Worldwide, Amnesty International, Open Society Institute,	1993–	International Violence Against Women Act, Declaration on the	Success	Dobash, Heise, Joachim

				Advocates for Human Rights, End Violence Against Women International, Human Rights Watch, Women's Edge Coalition			Elimination of Violence Against Women	
34 War crimes tribunals	Security	States	Pursuing justice against the instigators of human rights abuses, ethnic cleansing, and genocide in Yugoslavia and Rwanda	Crimes of War Project, Track Impunity Always (TRIAL), Prevent Genocide International, Public International Law & Policy Group War, International Center for Transitional Justice	1998–	International Criminal Tribunal for the Former Yugoslavia, International Criminal Tribunal for Rwanda	Mixed	Bass, Snyder/Vinjamuri
35 Water conservation	Environment	States	Reducing demand for water through conservation	Circle of Blue, International Rivers, Water Environment Federation	1982–	No outcomes	Failure	Dinar, Kilgour, Meinzen-Dick, Moench, Pretty, Rosegrant, Vickers

(cont.)

Appendix 1A (cont.)

Campaign/ movement	Primary area	Target(s)	Goal	Leading advocacy organizations	Time frame	Outcome	Political success/ failure	Scholars
36 Women's reproductive rights	Human rights	States	Protecting women's reproductive rights (largely birth control)	Center for Reproductive Rights, Women's Global Network for Reproductive Rights	1984–	1994 Cairo Programme, 1995 Beijing Platform; little since then	Failure	Copelon, Correa, Hertel, Joachim, Petchesky

I thank Ben Gonzalez for his research support in compiling this list. On the margins were cases such as the anti-WTO protests of 1999 in Seattle where ideological opponents of globalization were joined by unionized workers who had a more direct material stake in the outcome of the protests.

2 | Movement success and state acceptance of normative commitments

Why do movements succeed in some places but not others? Why do some states accept commitments championed by principled advocacy movements while others do not? These questions animate this book. This chapter seeks to provide several alternative explanations for differences in movement success and state behavior that I then apply in later chapters to the four substantive cases and the seven advanced industrialized countries that make up the G-7.

I start with the most spare and obvious kinds of explanations that are typical in much of political science, those that emphasize self-interest and costs (i.e., "states will act in accord with their self-interests" and "movements will succeed when what they ask for is not costly").[1] I then demonstrate that such explanations, while a helpful beginning, cannot explain behavior in all circumstances. There are a number of instances even among these few cases where states seemingly acted against their

---

[1] This book seeks to overcome limitations of the main schools of thought in international relations theory. The dominant traditions – neo-realism and neo-liberalism – assume the state as unitary actor has interests that can be objectively read from material conditions in the international system. The major difference between them is in their assessments of how much cooperation can be fostered by institutions. Thus, both can be said to be *utilitarian*, where states respond to material calculations of cost/benefit. If states embrace a new policy commitment, the cause is reasonably straightforward: material self-interest. Neither approach looks inside the state to examine the impact of domestic politics, and neither is able to account for actors being motivated by moral concerns. While rational choice methods get at the micro-foundations of state behavior, actors are primarily, though not essentially, understood to be self-interested utility-maximizers. Other accounts that look inside the state – liberalism and pluralism – also primarily emphasize rational action defined in utilitarian terms (Milner 1997). Moravcsik's discussion of ideational and republican liberalism is an exception (Moravcsik 1997). Neo-classical realists are more eclectic and have started to bring in domestic-level variables, including ideas, to explain foreign policy outcomes.

short-run material interests – for example, Japanese and French ultimate support for debt relief, Japanese and Canadian ratification of
the Kyoto Protocol, and British and French ratification of the Rome
Statute creating the International Criminal Court. Even in cases where
self-interest seems like a plausible explanation for a state's behavior
(such as US contributions to combat the global AIDS pandemic), more
complex explanations are needed and are more persuasive.

In this chapter, I make the central case that states may accept reasonably costly international commitments when advocates have framed
their messages to fit with the values of the polities they are targeting.
Where costs and values clash, I emphasize the importance of *policy
gatekeepers* who serve as final arbiters of whether or not actions that
are costly are worthy of support. In the debt relief chapter, I employ
the basic argument, emphasizing the role of gatekeepers. In each subsequent empirical chapter, I layer this basic argument with intervening
factors. In Chapter 4 on climate change, I focus on a specific kind
of frame, where advocates go beyond basic moral argumentation to
invoke a country's national *reputation*. In the AIDS chapter, I flip the
argument around to bring in the importance of *messenger effects* and
how attributes of advocates can be as important – if not more so –
than the content of the message. Finally, in Chapter 6 on the ICC, I
explore two issues. First, in discussing Britain's accession to the Rome
Statute, I emphasize how costs can have a *subjective quality*, where
decisionmakers regard costs as manageable despite objective measures
that suggest the policy is potentially costly. Second, in examining
France's ultimate support for the Court despite initial opposition, I
look at how decisionmakers can become *rhetorically entrapped*, where
statements of support for movement ideals are contradicted by state
action.

Defining terms: movements, movement success, and state acceptance

In this section, I define key terms, beginning with a definition of movements, before turning to movement success and then state acceptance.
This discussion sets the stage for the next section on different explanations of movement success. In the process, I discuss why this book
focuses on states as the primary targets of advocacy rather than other
kinds of actors, such as firms or international organizations.

Movements

Social movements, as Charles Tilly describes them, are seen as a way for "ordinary people [to] make collective claims on public authorities."[2] They are a "distinctive form of contentious politics" and have three broad categories of attributes: (1) they involve campaigns of collective claims on target authorities; (2) they include an array of claims-making performances including special-purpose associations, public meetings, and demonstrations; and (3) they involve public representations of the causes' worthiness, unity, numbers, and commitment.[3] Unlike more established lobby groups, social movements are perceived to be more organic, less organized representations of public preferences that, at least initially, have more outsider status than traditional interest groups.

In practice, this distinction does not always hold, as already well-established groups may join or even foment movement activity, but the notion of a social movement seems to capture this sense of activity coming initially from outside the political mainstream, which lacks regularized channels of political influence and therefore engages in a variety of activities to get the attention of political insiders. Leaving aside acts of violence against property or people, these activities can range from forms of civil disobedience such as targeted transgressions of laws to large-scale demonstrations to tamer forms of political expression such as petition drives, letter-writing campaigns, and telephone calls and meetings with decisionmakers. While states are not the sole targets of movement activities, this book focuses on principled advocacy movements that primarily seek policy changes by governments. While a number of campaigns – against blood diamonds and sweatshops, for example – emerged in the 1990s to focus on firms as political targets, the dynamics of what makes profit-seeking businesses vulnerable to citizen/consumer mobilization may be quite different than what makes states and political leaders vulnerable. As a consequence, I leave explanations of why those kinds of movements succeed and fail for subsequent inquiry.

[2] Tilly 2004, 3.
[3] Tilly 2004, 7. The claims are the group's demands, the performances are demonstrations of collective action, and the representations are a way to foster group cohesion and to convince authorities why the movement has sufficient coherence, dedication, and strength to be worth listening to.

This book focuses on transnational campaigns where the primary motivation of advocates is principled rather than self-interested. How can we identify their dominant motives? We can examine whether the main groups supporting a cause had strong material incentives at stake in the outcomes they were advocating. For example, labor unions that support rules to restrict trade from sweatshops overseas have a clear material stake in the outcome, whereas campaigners seeking developing country debt relief have little to gain personally from such a situation (unless one assumes campaigners were primarily seeking to retain their jobs in the organizations where they worked). In coalition settings, where materially motivated organizations work alongside principled advocates, the main bases of funding of coalition organizations may be a good indicator of their biases. Groups primarily or significantly supported by union dues or industry backing, for example, would suggest important material motives. Groups primarily funded by individuals or foundations with no direct financial or material stake in the outcome of advocacy efforts can be thought of as principled.

Movement success/state acceptance

Movements seek changes in the world, sometimes without clarity about what specific policies they desire; sometimes their goals change over time. Because movements often comprise coalitions of different groups, they may share some goals and not others. Those differences and varying views on strategy can lead to some movement incoherence about the policy aims they seek. At the most general level, movements often seek an aspirational goal or pursuit of a norm, an assessment of what activists regard as a right and appropriate outcome such as "provide treatment to all of those infected with HIV" or "take action to halt global warming."[4] However, rather than ask, "When do states accept

---

[4] This research is also part of the now large literature on the importance of ideas and international relations (Blyth 2003; Goldstein and Keohane 1993; Hall 1989; Katzenstein 1996; Legro 2005b; Yee 1996). The third emerging theoretical competitor in international relations – constructivism – takes ideas, culture, and values more seriously than do neo-realism and neo-liberalism but has difficulty explaining under which conditions ideational factors and norms matter (Checkel 1997, 476; Kowert and Legro 1996, 486). The emphasis is on regulatory norms, the social conventions or rules, procedures, and principles that establish the standards of behavior for members of a group in a given

new norms?" it may be helpful to focus on when states accept policies that are based on those norms.[5] This distinction avoids the trouble that potentially bedevils much research where it is difficult to discern if decisionmakers are embracing the norm or acting for other reasons. While a norm is often abstract, a norms-based policy reflects a situation where activists have claimed that injustices need redress. For example, in the case of debt relief, advocates believe high levels of developing country external debt constitute a wrong that creditor nations have a moral obligation to address. In response to their activism, decisionmakers draft a policy. Thus, the norm ("the unpayable debts of the poorest countries ought to be forgiven") becomes embodied in a policy (the Highly Indebted Poor Country [HIPC] initiative). Even if the norms-based policy is accepted, advocates may continue to be unsatisfied because the norm remains unfulfilled, in part because they themselves move the goalposts of what they consider is needed to reach their normative ideal.

What then do we mean when we label a campaign such as Jubilee 2000 a success? Here, I am most interested in political successes rather than policy successes. We can judge a movement's political success based on whether or not countries important for implementation have accepted the policy that advocates are pursuing through some domestic decisionmaking process. Advocates, particularly in the early phases of transnational issue advocacy, have typically focused their activities on securing two different kinds of commitments from

context, that is, what actors "ought" to do (Finnemore and Sikkink 1999, 251). The notion of "oughtness" has been termed the logic of appropriateness. In contrast to the logic of consequences, where actors are motivated by the costs and benefits of different actions, logics of appropriateness reflect notions of right and wrong, of good and bad ethical behavior (March and Olsen 1998).

[5] Inspired by scholarship on two-level games, this book seeks to get at the question of when ideas and norms matter by focusing on the process of domestic acceptance after an international agreement has been negotiated and decisionmakers have to take a policy home for approval (Putnam 1988). I focus on what Checkel calls "empowerment," when states are first passing measures in support of a norm (Checkel 1997, 479). Thus, empowerment is distinguished from more long-lived processes of compliance. I am interested in policies that are based on norms. States may embrace policies for a range of reasons, without a desire by policymakers to embrace the norm. However, a state that is initially pushed to embrace a policy may in time find the norm internalized as an accepted part of the political discourse.

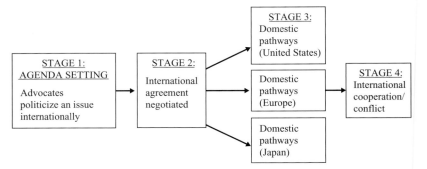

Figure 2.1 Stages of issue development

countries: (1) pledges (and appropriations) of funds and (2) ratification of international treaties. In terms of policies that involve financial support, such as contributions to a debt relief initiative or international AIDS programs, the important test is whether or not states have appropriated those funds through some domestic approval process. For international treaties, the most important test is whether or not those countries have ratified the treaties domestically (a more complicated process in some countries than others). For example, in the case of climate change, an agreement that fails to include the United States, one of the world's two largest emitters of greenhouse gases, has to be judged as less of a political success than one that includes the United States (see Figure 2.1 for a representation).[6] Since most of the issues in this book deal with long-term problems that have yet to be fully resolved, it is, in a sense, too soon to offer definitive judgments on whether or not the movements or the agreements in question have made the world better.

In this book I focus on Stage 3 of the policy process and seek to explain differences in movement success in different places.

---

[6] Of course, in policy terms, there might not be an equivalence: a non-binding agreement such as the 1992 UN Framework Convention on Climate Change is very different from the 1997 binding Kyoto Protocol. Nonetheless, in political terms, the non-participation of the United States in the Kyoto Protocol makes the agreement less of a political success (though one could argue the support of a majority of the world's countries and major greenhouse emitters still qualifies as a victory).

Coercion	Negative incentive	Positive benefit	Attention shift	Conversion

Military force | Sanctions, shaming | Reward, praise | Strategic framing (rhetorical action) | Consensual dialogue (communicative action)

Figure 2.2 Coercion–conversion continuum

Explaining movement success/state acceptance

How do movements get what they want? Scholars have identified coercion and persuasion as two primary mechanisms.[7] However, rather than conceive of movement options in dichotomous, either/or terms, we can identify a range of tools and mechanisms along a *coercion–conversion* continuum by which advocacy groups may effect change (see Figure 2.2).

On one extreme, military action forces a state to accept a policy. By definition, this option is not available to the kinds of non-violent protest movements explored in this book. That said, movements may occasionally turn violent, with factions prepared to commit acts of terrorism (such as the Weather Underground in the 1960s or the Red Army Faction in the 1970s) or, as occurs more often in developing countries, by becoming rebel groups (such as the Zapatistas in Mexico in the 1990s). Movements periodically engage in less violent protest activity, such as strikes, where advocates may end up in confrontations with the police or with private actors (as has periodically occurred between anti-whaling activists and fishermen). Sometimes, these events degenerate into rock-throwing or damage to property (as engaged in by some protesters during the WTO protests of 1999).

---

[7] For surveys of these mechanisms, see Cardenas 2004 and Cortell and Davis 2000. Early accounts of persuasion by Finnemore and Sikkink (1999) ultimately relied on more instrumental pressure from lobbying and strategic use of language. Those who study processes of norms diffusion recognize this point, suggesting that in pluralistic, liberal polities such as the United States, advocates of norms generally succeed through instrumental pressure/lobbying. Persuasive dynamics of social learning are thought to occur in more statist regimes (Checkel 1999, 89; 2001). However, this move concedes too much empirical terrain to explanations that rely on coercion, material sanctions, and political pressure.

Table 2.1 *Intersection of influence and outcomes*

Degree of influence Desired Outcomes Undesired	*Lucky (I)* Not influential, desired outcome *Unlucky (III)* Not influential, undesired outcome Not influential ←	*Skilled (II)* Influential, desired outcome *Unskilled (IV)* Influential, undesired outcome → Influential

On the other extreme, policymakers experience what some scholars describe as "true persuasion" where, once presented with "good arguments," they undergo an epiphany and change their minds.[8] Unfortunately, this portrait of political change may be rather rare in political life.[9] The middle options between the semi-coercive (civil disobedience and large-scale protests) and the semi-persuasive (strategic communication) may be the areas where groups in democratic countries with limited coercive means will concentrate their efforts; therefore, this is where I focus my attention.

Looking at the mechanisms of movement influence does not quite answer the question about what leads states to change their behavior to accept movement demands. Sometimes weak actors may get what they want ("good" outcomes for them) not because they were influential but because their demands were consistent with what governing parties wanted ("Lucky," see Cell I in Table 2.1). For example, it is unclear how much influence French human rights organizations had in influencing France's accession to the International Criminal Court.[10]

[8] Several academics influenced by the German scholar Jürgen Habermas, drawing from his theory of communicative action, differentiate "true" persuasion from rhetorical action, distinguishing a logic of argumentation distinct from logics of consequences and appropriateness (Risse 2000). "True" persuasion ideally involves situations cleaved of material and social power; such accounts of persuasion are based on a mechanism of dialogue, consensus, and actors embracing norms as a result of deeper preference change (Payne 2001).
[9] Krebs and Jackson 2007.   [10] Cohen 2005.

As former French foreign minister Hubert Védrine told me when I interviewed him in his Paris office in the spring of 2007, if the French had not signed up to support the ICC: "It wouldn't have had any political impact. It would have had a psychological impact and impact on image," but there would have been no resignations. This issue was an "important" but not a "vital" one for France.[11] In the French case, pressure from other European Union (EU) partners may have been more important than any action that French (or even international) non-governmental organizations (NGOs) took.

Other instances demonstrate more clearly where governments were pushed to act in ways they otherwise would not have, as the next chapter on debt relief concludes ("Skilled," Cell II in Table 2.1). In some instances, interest groups may not get what they want, through no fault of their own ("Unlucky," Cell III). For example, advocates of global limits on small arms have had considerable difficulty gaining traction, largely because of countermobilization by the National Rifle Association, which has globalized the second amendment to the US Constitution (which protects the rights of American citizens to bear arms) to the international arena and blocked progress. In other cases, advocates may have contributed to outcomes they did not like ("Unskilled," Cell IV). For example, having pressed the Clinton administration to embrace deep, binding emissions cuts as part of the Kyoto Protocol, climate change advocates found themselves unable to get any movement on US policy for ten years.

There is an inevitable tension in this book between ascribing the outcomes to movement influence and looking at what led states to alter their behavior, independent of whether movements were decisive in bringing about that result. I am more interested in the question that sidesteps influence to understand when it is that movements get what they want.

Despite a more varied array of mechanisms by which movements may affect outcomes, we can group explanations of state behavior into families to lay bare the underlying motivations that shape decisionmakers' attitudes and ultimately state behavior. We can roughly distinguish between arguments that are interest-based, which I alternately refer to as "utilitarian," "self-interested," and "materially rational," and those that are values-based, which I refer to as "altruistic,"

---

[11] Védrine 2007.

"normative," "ethical," "ideational," or "morality-based."[12] I do not claim, as some political scientists do, that state behavior is almost exclusively explained by one of these motivations. It would be foolish to claim, for example, that interests or costs do not matter. By the same token, it would be reckless to suggest that moral concerns are always the dominant motive. What I primarily try to do in this book is to carve out space for values to be an important motive and to specify the conditions under which values-based appeals, in combination with other factors, influence state behavior.

Some people may think this task is unnecessary, that I have created a straw-man counterargument: "Everybody knows both interests and values matter." My response is twofold: (1) the relationship between interests and values has not been fully explored, and (2) interest-based accounts still have a privileged position in much of political science. Despite overtures by academics to admit that "Values matter too!" the straw-man objection seems to be an attempt to make the argument go away. Nevertheless, the circumstances under which values and values-based appeals matter remain an important question.

Another objection might come from a different quarter, the "constructivist" camp in international relations theory. In their view, threats to or costs for the country's material interests require that leaders have a prior set of ideas about what the state's interests are. To the extent that costs and interests are constructed by or filtered through some sense of national identity or ideas about the consequences of action, the clear distinction between material factors and ideas may break down. I recognize these concerns but still believe that it makes sense to distinguish between (1) the likely or perceived consequences of action for an actor's interests and (2) whether or not the action is thought to be morally right, just, or appropriate.

A partial explanation: material interest

As suggested above, a simple but unsatisfying set of explanations to the questions explored in this book are based on material self-interest,

---

[12] The distinction between interest-based arguments and values-based arguments roughly mirrors the distinction in political science between logics of consequences and logics of appropriateness, discussed in n. 4.

what I have labeled "interest-based" approaches. This family of arguments includes a number of variants. Here, I emphasize two: one focuses on *state interests*, the other on the micro-motives of *individual* politicians.

State interest arguments

State interest arguments would explain movement success (and state acceptance of movement demands) based on the balance of material incentives facing the state. Often, this approach gets reduced to a simple metric of costs: How costly is it for the state to take action to support the policy? The baseline argument of this perspective is that states are most likely to accept new normative commitments when the material benefits are clear or when the costs are low.[13] A more sophisticated version of this argument would recognize that, even if there are high costs associated with the policy solution, the net cost–benefit ratio might be positive, either because of large potential benefits or if proponents are able to impose high costs on decisionmakers who fail to acquiesce.[14] For example, despite the high implementation costs of measures to combat the ozone hole in the 1980s, policymakers quickly recognized that phasing out chlorofluorocarbons in hairsprays and refrigerants would avoid the tremendous costs of additional skin cancers that were projected if nothing were done.[15]

While the direct costs of the policy measure are a simple indicator for whether a policy will likely find state support, other factors also typically figure into a state's assessment of the net costs of a particular policy:

(1) What else is happening in the world?
   – Countries consumed by external threats might believe that they cannot afford to be charitable or generous.

[13] The policy diffusion literature makes this argument. See Simmons and Elkins 2004.

[14] The ability of advocates to impose costs on leaders is a function of what the social movement literature calls "mobilizing resources" (McAdam, McCarthy, and Zald 1996).

[15] See chapter 10 in Sandler 2004.

(2) What is the current state of the global and/or national economy?
   – Countries with poor economic conditions would likely be less supportive of movement demands than countries doing well.

(3) If the problem is not addressed, what direct costs or threats to the country might result?
   – Despite high costs, a policy might be worth pursuing because it either will yield net benefits or avoid higher net negative costs.

(4) What costs can the movement itself impose on the state for failure to accept their demands?
   – The net cost–benefit calculation of action could be positive if movements possess sufficient organizing clout that they or their allies can impose high costs on states for inaction (through strikes, boycotts, campaign contributions, etc.).

These questions, particularly the first two, suggest that the international context can be permissive or obstruct the acceptance of a movement's aims. A high security threat or a more generalized economic malaise may crowd out social movements and focus the attention of decisionmakers on higher-order political priorities.[16] In the 1990s, this factor was mostly a constant; material threats were low and economic circumstances for most advanced industrialized countries were generally positive (with Japan a possible exception). Thus, to generalize about advocacy in the 1990s, the context – including advances in telecommunications and transport – was a permissive one for most campaigns. Before we privilege this dimension of state interest, it should be noted that campaigns for HIV/AIDS funding and debt relief were successful after September 11, 2001. This result suggests that a favorable international context may be neither necessary nor sufficient for successful advocacy.

As I argue later, aggregating the net costs and benefits of movement demands can be difficult, especially when we consider the time dimension and concepts such as discounting, which suggest that people value present costs and benefits much more than distant ones. Thus, the seemingly straightforward exercise of "assessing the costs" is more complex than appears at first blush. Nonetheless, the clearest

---

[16] Social movements refer to this concept as the international "political opportunity structure" (McAdam, McCarthy, and Zald 1996).

expression of this approach is that states will do what serves their material interests.[17]

Individual interest arguments

While state interest arguments derive their explanatory power from the mix of material incentives facing states, arguments based on *individual interest* (what I sometimes term a "pluralist" perspective in later chapters) would explain state acceptance of movement demands based on politicians' potential electoral rewards (or punishment) from acting (or failing) to support what advocates want.[18] Some explanations go back a step to identify the source of societal preferences that in turn affect decisionmakers' incentives. Collective preferences of different groups, sectors, or classes are derived from how well they fare under different policies. For example, high-skill groups that do well from globalization are thought to favor free trade, while low-skill workers, who are thought to do badly under globalization, are predicted to favor protectionist policies.[19] These accounts are materially rational all the way down, meaning that ideas about morality and justice really have minimal importance as motivations for what people or governments do.[20]

Thus, one could explain differences in states' patterns of support for movement demands based on the level of political mobilization by groups favoring and opposed to the policies advocates champion. Individual interest explanations would suggest countries that lead the way to support movement demands typically respond with greater

[17] In Chapter 4 on climate change, I distinguish between two versions of this argument, one that I call "minimalist" and another that I term "institutionalist."

[18] This approach is consistent with rational choice accounts that get at the micro-foundations of political behavior. Examples include Bueno de Mesquita *et al.* 2003; Mayhew 1974.

[19] Rogowski 1989.

[20] Proponents of individual interest arguments might accept that the mass public can be moved by religious values or other non-material motivations but deny that politicians in democratic societies can afford to allow such motives to enter their decisionmaking calculus. This distinction between public and elite motives becomes harder to sustain and likely is variable. Some politicians, perhaps incumbents in safe districts, can afford to be more value-oriented. Some are dispositionally more motivated by these non-material metrics.

support because their leaders were pressured by politically powerful constituencies. One could chart the relative strength of the advocacy community in those countries, as reflected by the resources and membership of advocacy groups in favor of the movement's policy aims.[21] From this perspective, countries with more robust pressure groups for transnational social causes (such as the UK) might be more politically successful than those from countries such as Japan where such groups are underfinanced and weak.[22]

The limits of explanations based on self-interest

Despite the plausibility of interest-based explanations, such arguments provide an incomplete account of decisionmakers' motivations. As Jon Elster noted, they are potentially "just-so" stories that impute self-interested motives when something else may also have been going on.[23] By narrowly casting the argument in terms of material self-interest, such accounts miss important elements that also affect individual motivations and shape policy outcomes, namely normative concerns about right and wrong. While material incentives matter, other mediating factors additionally shape political outcomes. The primary advantage of interest-based arguments is how lean they are, what academics call "parsimony." One can generate relatively simple, testable hypotheses; arguments based on state interest can avoid the interior messiness of domestic politics by treating the state as a single actor rather than a collection of competing interests and factions. Abstracting from the cacophony of potentially relevant variables to a few hypotheses, one can reduce state behavior to either macro- or micro-level material incentives. Unlike factors that depend on people's beliefs and ideas, material incentives (such as costs) have been thought to be easier to measure. One can assume that states seek to maximize their interests

---

[21] One should take into account countervailing political power by groups opposed to a more aggressive response such as pharmaceutical companies or opponents of foreign assistance.

[22] Elsewhere, I collected data on resources, membership, and staffing levels of British, American, German, and Japanese development NGOs. I concluded that the British development advocacy sector was the most powerful, followed by the Americans and the Germans, with the Japanese having the weakest sector. See Busby 2004a.

[23] Elster 2000, 693.

derived from a narrow set of objectives. Alternatively, one can understand individual decisionmakers' behavior based on the desire for re-election.

While scholars in this rationalist tradition acknowledge that decisionmakers can have morality-based or altruistic preferences, most accounts still identify preferences based on narrow material grounds (i.e., "What's in it for us?").[24] One reason why "ideational" arguments based on morality, values, or beliefs have not gained as much traction in political science as those based on material self-interest is because scholars fear that seemingly counterproductive behavior will be explained away as consistent with what the actor wanted, potentially contributing to underspecified theories and a proliferation of post hoc explanations made to fit the facts (i.e., "He acted against his material interests because that's what he wanted"). That said, just because one can make a plausible account that material interests explain policy outcomes, that does not make it so. As Robert Keohane writes:

Signalling theory indicates that cynically self-interested statesmen should sound as moralistic as truly moralistic statesmen in environments that reward such talk . . . The theory that leaders of some states are influenced by moral norms may under some conditions imply the same behavior as the theory that all leaders act on the basis of narrow self-interest.[25]

In other words, we may not be able to tell the difference between behavior motivated by self-interest and behavior motivated by morality, altruism, or other logics that are seemingly not rational from a purely instrumental, cost–benefit calculation.

One way to escape this conundrum is to examine what game theorists call "separating equilibria," where the costs of different courses of action force actors to reveal their "type" or true intentions. In these instances, morally committed actors are prepared to incur higher costs, such as larger donations to combat HIV/AIDS. By looking for cases where countries acted against their short-run, material interests or where their material interests were not clear-cut, we can get a better handle on what drove decision making. Where material incentives clash with an actor's values, this conflict or contrast sets the stage

---

[24] Levi 1997; O'Neill 1999.   [25] Keohane 2002, S310–S311.

for "hard cases" of "costly moral action."[26] These cases potentially pose difficult tests for arguments purporting to show that values matter because the expectation of most theories would be that concerns about costs should matter more.

Several chapters in this book, those on debt relief, climate change, and the International Criminal Court, seek precisely to examine these hard cases where states seemingly acted against their material self-interest. Unfortunately, finding hard cases like these is not always possible. For example, in the chapter on HIV/AIDS, I note that leading countries that were prepared to spend more to stem the global AIDS pandemic likely had some instrumental reasons to support funding. While the relative costs of global AIDS policies for the United States were fairly significant, the country enjoyed higher growth and lower unemployment than some of its peers. Moreover, getting out in front on AIDS could help diminish the backlash against US military activity in the "war on terror" and Iraq. However, even if the United States (and the UK) enjoyed some permissive economic conditions and self-serving reasons to bolster their global standing, those policy incentives do not explain why they chose AIDS policy over other options. As I argue in Chapter 5, we need to understand the role values played in shaping both the level and the character of the overall response.

If we want to understand both motivation and how the policy came together, "process-tracing" offers a way to understand the entire chain between cause and effect. Process-tracing is a kind of qualitative case study method that political scientists use to look in detail at how decisions were made all along the way and, to the extent we can know, how they were justified internally and externally. Process-tracing involves careful reading of press reports, government documents, advocacy publications, and memoirs, and, in my case, conducting interviews with participants. How is process-tracing different from traditional historical research? Political scientists, more so than historians, are often interested in self-conscious, systematic efforts to test alternative explanations. They ask themselves, "If my argument is right, what should I expect to see?"[27] Even if one believes states respond only

---

[26] Kaufmann and Pape 1999.
[27] For a discussion of observable implications, see King, Keohane, and Verba 1994.

to self-interested motivations, one still needs a theory of how those incentives are translated into policy. If this cause explains that effect (i.e., if moral concerns explain US willingness to support greater spending on HIV/AIDS), what are the intermediate steps that link that cause and that effect? At the same time, political scientists will go through a similar exercise with alternatives, as I have done here with interest-based arguments. Good political scientists will acknowledge when the facts fail to fit their pet theory.[28]

In many cases, scholars will offer alternative explanations and different predictions of what they expect to see along that chain between cause and effect. For example, in cases where interests and values clash (i.e., where it is costly for a country to follow the policies favored by an advocacy group), interest-based arguments and values-based arguments may make different predictions. In this book, process-tracing also reveals the importance of morality and values even in cases where indicators are potentially consistent with interest-based arguments, as we will see in the chapter on HIV/AIDS.

A more complete explanation: framing-meets-gatekeepers

State interest and individual interest are useful constructs that can help conceptualize the incentives governments and decisionmakers face as they deal with international problems such as climate change, debt relief, HIV/AIDS, and crimes against humanity. However, rarely are material incentives so clear that a "right" policy answer is obvious. Moral concerns can provide extra weight for, or against, a policy. The accompanying moral arguments can serve as tip-balancers to legitimate action, for those for whom self-interested justifications do not seem convincing. They may also influence the character of the policy. In other words, in addition to asking, "Will it work?" and "How much will it cost?" decisionmakers will ask, "What is the right thing to do?"

However, whether moral concerns figure into the equation depends in part on how the issue has been framed. Only a handful of issues rise to the attention of busy policymakers. Whether an issue gets their attention is sensitive to the episodic flow of events. Even when crises or annual meetings such as the G-8 focus attention, cases do not

---

[28] For an extended discussion of the methodology, see George and Bennett 2005.

generally speak for themselves. Agents are required to champion a problem, frame how it is interpreted, and suggest possible remedies. Different constituencies, both inside and outside government, may compete for how an issue is understood, focusing on one or more evaluative dimensions to get decisionmakers' attention.[29]

The concept of framing,[30] the strategic use of rhetoric, is drawn from the social movement literature in sociology. Framing is a particularly potent strategy by which weak actors are able to exercise influence and induce states to embrace new policy commitments inspired by norms.[31] Such "symbolic politics" are necessary given the relative weakness of proponents and because, as Martha Finnemore and Kathryn Sikkink note, new ideas about right and wrong emerge "in a highly contested normative space where they must compete with other norms and perceptions of interest."[32] Advocacy movements for these new international issues rarely have sufficient political power to alter elections. However, advocates can shape the general image and reputation of decisionmakers through praise and shame (see Figure 2.2), making them "look good" or "look bad." The less coercive side of framing appeals to mass publics and policymakers, engaging them on grounds they already agree with. If advocates' appeals to decisionmakers' existing values initially fall short, they and their allies can become more coercive, beginning with shaming other policymakers for failure to uphold societal values.[33]

Bringing in framing adds an element of agency and contingency. Frames serve as mental shortcuts by which policymakers can sort information and understand a problem's causes, its consequences, and what solutions exist.[34] While policy entrepreneurs may invent new rhetoric, they typically find a repertoire of arguments to

---

[29] Jones 1994.
[30] Zald, Snow, Tarrow, and others pioneered the concept (Zald 1996; Snow *et al.* 1986).
[31] Betsill 2000; Sell and Prakash 2004.   [32] Finnemore and Sikkink 1999, 257.
[33] Several articles have taken steps in this direction; see Acharya 2004; Carpenter 2005; Hawkins 2004; Joachim 2003; Schimmelfennig 2001; Sundstrom 2005. This book seeks to augment the contributions of this research. For example, Hawkins, like Finnemore, focuses on the importance of international normative pressures in shaping state behavior (Finnemore 1996). However, as both Acharya and Sundstrom argue, international norms are less likely to be effective without domestic bases of support.
[34] Entman 1993; Zald 1996, 262.

appropriate, what Ronald Krebs and Patrick Jackson call "rhetorical commonplaces."[35] Nonetheless, framing is a synthetic activity rather than a purely evocative one. Advocates create something new when they frame debates, their innovations a sort of recombinant rhetoric akin to sampling in popular music. Habits and societal traditions establish limits for what kinds of frames possess domestic legitimacy.[36] These elements may constrain the substance of claims as well as the form. Self-interested claims in democracies typically do not succeed, leading groups to dress up what is good for their parochial interest as good for the country as a whole.[37] In some countries, rowdy street protests may be considered legitimate, while in others the same actions would be inappropriate. What protest activity is considered legitimate can change over time. After September 11, 2001, large-scale public demonstrations in the United States and other Western countries initially appeared threatening and generated concerns about public safety and terrorism.[38]

Boosting an issue's profile requires that champions frame their arguments for successful alliance-building.[39] For a small moral interest group to succeed, what Chaim Kaufmann and Robert Pape call a "saintly logroll," they must appeal to principles backed by the "main political factions." Moral movements, they argue, are more likely to be successful when they link their arguments to domestic reformist movements seeking to root out domestic corruption.[40] While movements need to tap into the traditions and culture of the broader society, notions of morality and what kind of role the country should play internationally may also be sufficiently resonant for actors to create winning coalitions of political support.

As I explain in greater detail (pp. 55–56), these frames, for their success, therefore depend broadly upon their "cultural match" with the values of the country they are targeting. Frames thus work through two causal mechanisms, one informational/ideational and one instrumental. First, frames get the *attention* of decisionmakers and individuals on the basis of ideas and values they already think are important. Based on those frames, citizens and like-minded elites then mobilize *political pressure* to influence others.

[35] Krebs and Jackson 2007.   [36] Payne 2001, 38–39.   [37] Risse 2000, 17.
[38] ACLU 2003.   [39] Keck and Sikkink 1998, 17.
[40] Kaufmann and Pape 1999, 663–664.

Should we regard frames as coercive? Krebs and Jackson suggest successful framing denies opponents the rhetorical resources to respond. When coupled with shaming efforts, such moves are more coercive as advocates seek to impose political costs on decisionmakers.[41] In my view, a frame becomes more fully coercive when combined with material power. Weak actors try to convince decisionmakers that other dimensions of a problem are important and create the political conditions in which potentially sympathetic targets can publicly affirm their support without fear of political consequences. Whether decisionmakers heed those cues is often out of the hands of campaigners. While civil disobedience raises the costs of non-action, the capacity of social movements to alter the cost–benefit calculus of decisionmakers may be limited. Their more established allies – political parties, public officials, labor unions, lobbying groups – have the resources and political wherewithal to make a difference, though social movements in time may become sufficiently entrenched and financially powerful to exercise more coercive power. That kind of political pressure is familiar. Indeed, it is what animates individual interest-based arguments. While acknowledging the importance of interest group pressure, I focus more on the less coercive side of framing, where advocates initially appeal to decisionmakers' better angels.

Successful strategic framing is thus, in theory, distinguishable from more fundamental belief change *and* from more coercive efforts that rely mostly on shaming and political pressure.[42] From this perspective, we should view framing exercises as defining situations and activating existing preferences. Policymakers care about many things, not all of them equally. Circumstance may make a new issue salient, much the way September 11 altered the perspectives of decisionmakers. "Salience" means that an issue becomes temporally compelling to decisionmakers. If a group of decisionmakers rejects a policy one year and then affirms it the next, this change would suggest incoherent preferences. However, it may be that their attention has shifted from one

---

[41] Krebs and Jackson call this kind of successful framing "coercive constructivism" (Krebs and Jackson 2007).

[42] That said, even if deeper persuasive dynamics do occur, it may be difficult to differentiate in practice between "complex social learning," where actors are persuaded by better arguments, from more strategic calculations of actors who are moved by rhetorical efforts praising or blaming them for their behavior (Hawkins 2004, 783; Parsons 2003, 16–17).

aspect of a particular problem to another. A politician, for example, may care about both poverty in the developing world and effective use of government resources. In the midst of a recession, concerns about the costs of foreign aid might become more important. These serial shifts in attentiveness make sense of efforts to cue emotional/moral frames and boost the salience of one dimension of a problem over another.[43]

The guiding assumption here is that actors' basic preferences with regard to outcomes – what they value most – are largely stable in the short run. Preferences about means (that is, about specific policies) are less deeply rooted. While some decisionmakers identify particular policies strongly with or against their long-term preferences, new problems and policy arenas may spur uncommitted thinking. Frames thus link specific policies to a particular evaluative lens, facilitating shifts in support for the policy even as long-run values remain largely unchanged.[44]

While advocacy groups may employ a single dominant frame, they may also be strategically ambiguous in their framing in an effort to say the same thing with different meanings for different groups.[45] Advocates may also employ multiple messages to appeal to different groups. For example, HIV/AIDS has been framed as a public health issue, a human rights issue, a justice issue, a moral problem, an issue of intellectual property rights, and a security problem.

As this multiplicity of frames implies, not all frames tap into moral values. Some frames make claims about what is true, and others make claims about what is right.[46] In other words, some frames appeal to

---

[43] These situational redefinitions are similar to "heresthetics" (Riker 1986; see also Jones 1994, 83).

[44] This understanding of preference change may be problematic for some rationalists and constructivists, going too far or not far enough. For a sophisticated treatment of this issue, see Fearon and Wendt 2003. The assumption of largely stable preferences does not preclude long-run preference change, as has taken place on civil rights in the American South. Jones makes the distinction between preference change (when minds change) and attention shifts (when the focus changes) through use of two-dimensional spatial models. Where a change in the ideal point reflects preference change, changes in the shape of indifference curves reflect attention shifts, where an actor becomes increasingly willing to trade off one good for another (Jones 1994).

[45] This effort to speak simultaneously to multiple audiences has been called "multivocality" (Padgett and Ansell 1993, 1263).

[46] On cognitive heuristics and bounded rationality, see Jones 2001.

actors' causal beliefs about the likely effects of different policies, while other frames appeal to their principled beliefs about right and wrong.[47] For example, a frame that suggests "AIDS is a national security threat" seeks to make a causal connection between the disease's consequences and its implications for the target's interests. Frames that rely on causal claims as the logic to animate decisionmaking depend primarily on credible evidence. By contrast, a frame that suggests "AIDS demands Christ-like compassion for the sufferers" relies more upon community values and morality for its persuasive appeal.[48] Not all frames evoke moral considerations, though even truth-based frames will feed into prescriptive recommendations. For frames that invoke causal claims, technical experts, "epistemic communities," can validate whether or not an issue is really a problem.[49]

To the extent that debates about causes, consequences, and policy solutions are settled, evidentiary support can buttress the claims of those arguing for renewed and sustained public action. Where advocates' claims are contested, those opposing action have more scope to challenge their concerns. Nonetheless, connections between these policies and state interests may remain opaque or be inadequate justification to overcome opposition. Accompanying moral arguments, by creating additional incentives to support a policy, then may serve as "tip-balancers" to legitimate action. Because this book is focused on the role of morally motivated advocacy groups, I emphasize the role of frames that appeal to principled beliefs.

Advocacy groups often find themselves in pitched rhetorical battle with opponents seeking to counterframe the issue, either by making alternative claims about what is right or wrong, by disputing the causal claims about the nature of the problem, or by challenging the adequacy of advocates' preferred policies.[50] Winning these "frame contests" can shape whether the issue gets on the agenda and what policy instruments and resources are mustered to address the problem. What determines

---

[47] Goldstein and Keohane 1993, 8–9.
[48] For this distinction, see March and Olsen 1998. As Sell and Prakash argue, actors that promote logics of appropriateness often have intermingled concerns about consequences, whether they be organizational survival or funding. Likewise, businesses that seem to care only about consequences also believe their actions are right (Sell and Prakash 2004).
[49] Haas 1992.
[50] See Schimmelfennig 2003 for a similar characterization.

whether any particular frame or combination of frames wins?[51] A synthetic combination of three factors – low costs, high fit, and supportive policy gatekeepers – provides a relatively spare way to explain and potentially predict successful framing.[52] In shorthand, I call this argument "framing-meets-gatekeepers" or simply "framing/gatekeepers."

As I have already noted, proponents of interest-based arguments would accept that states are most likely to accept new normative commitments when the material benefits are clear or when the costs are low.[53] However, as I have already also argued, costs are not the sole drivers of policy. Perhaps the dominant theme in much of the related literature is that countries are most likely to embrace normative commitments that are framed to fit with local cultural traditions.[54] Frames that lack such a cultural match should be less successful. Movement actors that adopt anarchist, anti-capitalist rhetoric in the United States, for example, are less likely to succeed than those that tie their arguments to religious values.

How can we determine whether a frame possesses high value fit or cultural match? Since values are supposed to be relatively long-lived (as opposed to short-run attitudes subject to swings in public opinion), it makes sense to look at public attitudes over longer periods of time. For example, in the Jubilee 2000 campaign, the debt relief effort was framed primarily in religious terms. We can thus assess whether or not the main moral message invoked by campaigners matched the cultural context in different countries. As I discuss in Chapter 3, four waves of data from the World Values Survey dating back to the 1980s track

[51] Payne cautions that we may not be able to know in advance (Payne 2001, 44).
[52] As I suggested above, successful advocacy and influence are not synonymous. Just because a frame "wins" does not mean that the primary reason is a result of influential advocacy. It could be that the nature of the situation or issue favored success. I elaborate on these issues in the concluding chapter.
[53] The policy diffusion literature makes this argument. See Simmons and Elkins 2004. A useful caveat, based on the earlier discussion, is: even if there are high costs associated with the policy solutions, the net cost–benefit ratio might be positive, either because of large potential benefits or if proponents are able to impose high costs on decisionmakers who fail to acquiesce.
[54] Different terms describe this concept: grafting (Price 2003), cultural match (Cortell and Davis 2000, 73; Checkel 1999, 86), fit (Betsill 2000; Kingdon 1995), the nature of political discourse (Hall 1989, 363–365), resonance (Snow *et al.* 1986; Snow and Benford 1988), political culture (Risse-Kappen 1995b, 188), legitimacy (Jacobsen 1995, 295), concordance/intersubjective agreement (Legro 1997, 35), localization/congruence (Acharya 2004), salience (Entman 1993), and shared lifeworld (Habermas 1996, 358).

ıle 2.2 *Intersection of costs and values*

Costs / Values	Low costs ⟶	High costs
High fit	*Low costs, high fit* Cheap moral action VALUES win (1)	*High costs, high fit* Costly moral action AMBIGUOUS (2)
Low fit	*Low costs, low fit* Indifference AMBIGUOUS (3)	*High costs, low fit* Hostility COSTS win (4)

religious attitudes in different countries. By taking the average across waves, I capture a rough, and by no means definitive, measure of variation in country religiosity. The higher the country's average religiosity, the greater the prospective fit or cultural match of the Jubilee 2000 frame. For each empirical chapter in this book, I seek an indicator of cultural match based on the way advocates framed the issue or its default policy area. Where possible, I provide data from multiple years to derive measures of value fit.

High value fit and low costs together are most likely cases for successful framing. Other cases – namely ones where both value fit and costs are high – are less clear and require integration of another factor: supportive policy gatekeepers. Policy gatekeepers are influential actors with sufficient power to block or at least delay policy change. Where there are many gatekeepers (based on the concept of what political scientists call "veto players"), this number establishes a higher bar for frame success as more views make it harder to please everyone.[55]

To lay bare differences between this framing/gatekeepers argument and more streamlined interest-based accounts, I have created a basic two-by-two table (Table 2.2) to look at the intersection of costs and values. While something of an oversimplification, I assume movement demands can have either a high or a low cost. I also assume that

[55] Tsebelis 2002, 25. Veto players theory is rooted in comparative politics but has been increasingly incorporated into international political economy (Keefer and Stasavage 2003; Mansfield, Milner, and Pevehouse 2005; Tsebelis 1995; Vreeland 2004).

advocates have a dominant message, which can have either a high or a low fit with a country's cultural values. There are then four possibilities: (1) cheap moral action – low costs, high fit; (2) costly moral action – high costs, high fit; (3) indifference – low costs, low fit; and, finally, (4) hostility – high costs, low fit.

In Cell 1, it is not costly for the country to embrace a new issue, and the values are consistent with the country's values, what we can call cases of "cheap moral action." Cases that fit into Cell 1 are the most likely to achieve successful framing.

In Cell 4, there are high costs, but the way the issue has been framed does not resonate with the country's values. Therefore, we should observe that material interests dominate, and thus "hostility" best describes the probable country position. The country will oppose the policy unless countervailing power coerces them, they become convinced that the benefits of the policy are greater than the costs, or the issue is reframed to appeal to a different set of values. Cases of "hostility" are perhaps the toughest cases for successful framing since both values and costs are aligned against advocates. Because both my argument and interest-based arguments expect advocates to fail under these circumstances, these cases do not provide a clear contrast in predictions. That said, where advocates succeed despite facing high costs and low value fit, then such cases can potentially be instructive, particularly if the way that states change their behavior is consistent with a framing/gatekeepers argument. Japan's transformation on debt relief after the issue was reframed as a test of its international contribution is a good example that is explored in Chapter 3.[56]

Cells 2 and 3 are more ambiguous. In Cell 3, low value fit and low costs should make a state "indifferent" to accepting the new policy. Because the stakes are so low, interested policymakers may support a policy in the absence of compelling reasons. In Cell 2, costs and values are misaligned. While values are supportive, costs are not. In this instance, interest-based arguments would generally predict that cost concerns should trump values, unless coercion alters the cost–benefit calculus or long-run benefits clearly warrant short-run pain.[57] There may be cases – as in the British position against the slave trade – of

---

[56] US support for global AIDS intervention, discussed in Chapter 5, also shares some commonalities with Japan's debt relief case.
[57] Axelrod 1990.

states engaging in what Kaufmann and Pape call "costly moral action."[58] These are cases where states – motivated by morality at some level – absorb short-run costs even if long-run benefits are uncertain.

The distinction between costly and cheap moral action plays an important role in identifying cases for consideration here and, for several cases, allows me to differentiate my argument from a strictly material interest explanation. As a consequence, how can we distinguish between cases of costly and cheap moral action? In Kaufmann and Pape's study of the slave trade, they calculate that Britain spent on the order of 1.78 percent of their GDP per year for sixty years on the cause and lost on the order of 5,000 soldiers, mostly through disease.[59] They note that such action is exceedingly rare. However, if that magnitude of costs is the threshold for costly moral action, then it is not surprising that there have been few instances in human history of such behavior.

Kaufmann and Pape's threshold is too restrictive. While the objective measure of costs as a proportion of a country's overall GDP provides a good beginning, whether an action is costly may be domain-specific. While a policy may be relatively inexpensive as a share of national wealth, the action might require a large proportion of existing resources for particular purposes (such as for foreign assistance or environmental protection). An overall policy might not be especially costly, but if the action requires burden-sharing among several partners, one country bearing a disproportionate share might be considered costly. Thus, the distribution of costs may be as important as the overall amount. Moreover, some costs are not strictly financial, as the British loss of soldiers in the slave trade demonstrates. In these instances, costs take on a broader meaning of "difficulty," as in "How hard are these sacrifices?" As I discuss more fully in Chapter 6 on the International Criminal Court, what is considered costly has a subjective quality and is not necessarily fixed over time. The British and French, despite comparable numbers of overseas troop deployments, saw the costs (or risks) of supporting the International Criminal Court quite differently. While debt relief measures in the 1990s were considered politically costly in the United States, their financial cost was much lower. By the 2000s, the country was prepared to spend several times that sum on HIV/AIDS relief.

---

[58] Kaufmann and Pape 1999.   [59] Kaufmann and Pape 1999, 635–637.

Scholars may be mistaken if they impose their own notion of what is costly; if participants themselves believe an action is costly, such ideas may have political consequences, even if they are mistaken. While this discussion does not provide a single metric of the threshold between high and low costs, the approach I take is to look at the distribution of costs across all players and consider several domain-specific metrics of costs. These judgments provide an indicator of the spread of costs for different players, giving a measure of both relative and absolute costs. For each case, I then try to justify a threshold between high and low costs, leaving it to the reader to judge if this is appropriate.

Under what conditions might states engage in costly moral action? Here, the role of policy gatekeepers is critical. If the country's gatekeepers believe the values at stake are important enough, then resistance due to high costs may be overcome. Similarly, supportive gatekeepers can overcome indifference due to lack of cultural match. Where there are many gatekeepers, it will prove difficult to satisfy them all simultaneously. Whether gatekeepers are supportive depends on their own assessment of the relative importance of costs and fit with their values. This fine-grained distinction allows us to draw deeper contrasts between interest-based argument and a framing/gatekeepers argument. Cell 2 in Table 2.2 contains critical, tough cases for my argument. Interest-based arguments would generally predict that gatekeepers will be against a policy if the costs are high and if long-run benefits are uncertain. I argue that gatekeepers, motivated by non-material metrics, may decide to engage in costly moral action despite high costs.[60]

The intersection of costs and values provides a first approximation of the likelihood of advocates' success. However, as I have just argued, the country's gatekeepers also mediate the process, privileging some elites as they interpret the costs and values at stake.[61] To identify whether gatekeepers are supportive, we ideally need to know their number and the spread of their preferences. In this case, the number

---

[60] That said, while decisionmakers may be willing to absorb high costs to support values, such willingness is not without bounds. Bass makes a similar argument in his discussion of states' willingness to support human rights (Bass 2000).
[61] The literature on domestic structure has long recognized the importance of the institutional context (Checkel 1999; Risse-Kappen 1991). While that literature relied on ideal types of state structure, veto players theories are based on quantitative datasets and can be tested using statistical techniques.

ɔle 2.3 *Costs/values, gatekeepers, and advocacy success*

Low likelihood	⟵⟶	High likelihood
Hostility + high veto	Indifference + high veto	Cheap moral action + low veto
Hostility + low veto	Cheap moral action + high veto	
Costly moral action + high veto	Costly moral action + low veto	Indifference + low veto
Coercion		*Conversion*

of gatekeepers serves as a preliminary first cut to understand the likely outcome. With more gatekeepers, it becomes harder to alter the status quo. Where there are many independent gatekeepers, as in the United States, advocates will have a harder time convincing them all to agree, especially when costs are high. In these instances, advocates' arguments will have to be finely tuned to the specific interests and values of gatekeepers. Given such pluralism, advocates will have to develop a larger repertoire of arguments to convince them.

Table 2.3 presents predictions for the likelihood of successful framing; it incorporates measures for costs and values with a dichotomous value for the number of gatekeepers. The third row combines these features with the "coercion–conversion" continuum, suggesting, moving from left to right, the mechanisms that advocates must rely on to induce policy change can be less coercive.

Gatekeepers analysis is based on veto players theory in political science, but I use the term "gatekeeper" because it reflects the importance of actors who are able to slow down, if not formally block, policies. Indeed, the term gatekeeper is a more accurate description of their powers.[62] For example, even the US president can have his veto overridden by a supermajority of the Congress.[63]

---

[62] Although this chapter discusses some of the findings of veto players theory, I try to use the term gatekeeper when referencing my own argument rather than using the terms interchangeably.

[63] My emphasis on gatekeepers also focuses more on the individuals empowered by their institutional position to block or slow policy change, rather than the institutions that may be collectively thought of as possessing a veto.

One of the advantages of veto players analysis over other arguments that bring in the importance of domestic institutions is that it provides a numerical index by which we can rank order states. Indeed, this kind of analysis may provide a better representation of institutional configurations in advanced industrialized countries. For example, in the domestic structure literature in political science, the UK is classified as "liberal," meaning that political pressure is the most likely mechanism of policy change.[64] However, in veto players analysis, the UK possesses few gatekeepers, making it more like "statist" regimes where the influence of a few individuals is important such that it is their beliefs and learning that matter most.

Datasets of veto players often focus on *institutional* actors accorded influence under a country's constitution (this issue gets at the influence of the legislative and judicial branches) and *partisan* actors (this issue gets at the influence of political parties in coalition governments).[65] Other studies also look at dispersion of authority by taking into account federal structures and the use of referenda.[66] Figure 2.3 illustrates one measure of veto players. The average number of veto players in 1996 for twenty-three members of the Organisation for Economic Co-operation and Development (OECD) in this dataset was 1.78.[67]

[64] Checkel 1999, 88; 2001; Risse-Kappen 1991.
[65] Tsebelis 2002.
[66] Huber and Stephens 2001, 55–56.
[67] Fig. 2.3 data from Armingeon *et al.* 2005. This is an additive index of five measures of constitutional structure including federalism (none, weak, strong), presidentialism (absent, present), bicameralism (absent, weak, strong), proportional representation (none, modified, majoritarian), and use of popular referenda (absent, present). The original data from eighteen countries were from Huber, Ragin, and Stephens and were expanded to include five other countries. The Huber *et al.* data go through 2000 with the number of veto points unchanged for the original eighteen countries (Huber *et al.* 2004). These patterns are supported by other measures. Henisz has a dataset that includes presence/absence of (1) an executive, (2) a lower house, (3) an upper house, (4) federalism, and (5) a judiciary (Henisz 2000; Henisz and Zelner 2006). Henisz also takes into account partisanship to see if legislative branch(es) or the judiciary are aligned with the executive. This approach is based on Tsebelis' absorption rule, the suggestion being that, where preferences are aligned, the effective number of veto players goes down. While Henisz creates an index that heavily weighs party fractionalization, all five are summed up here with aligned legislative and judicial branches subtracted. Where the legislative branches were not aligned with the executive but were with each other, I subtracted one veto player rather than two. The average number for the twenty-three OECD countries in 1999–2000 was 2.53. On the lower end, the UK and Italy had two veto players, the French, Germans, Japanese, and Canadians had three, and the

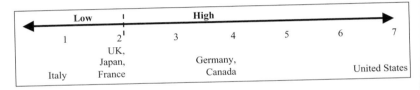

Figure 2.3 Veto players in the G-7
Source: Data from Armingeon *et al.* 2005.

Since the dataset is based on whole numbers, it makes sense to round up and make the threshold between high and low a whole number. We can thus classify countries above two veto points as high and those below as low. The United States, as befits its reputation, is an outlier with the most veto points.

However, this measure of veto players may not be sufficiently fine-grained, another reason that I prefer the term gatekeeper for the purposes of this book. Datasets for veto players miss some actors and include others that may not be relevant. For example, the datasets do not capture actors with issue-specific, effective blocking (or at least slowing) power, namely bureaucratic actors with delegated responsibility, legislative actors with committee oversight over spending programs, or societal actors with informal influence.[68] Moreover, international relations are not exactly like domestic politics. For many international issues (especially security issues), the number of veto players is often truncated so the judiciary or subnational units that are included in some datasets are not likely to be relevant. For treaties, countries have idiosyncratic rules, such as the US system where a two-thirds' Senate majority is required for advice and consent. On technical issues such as those explored in this book, we would expect these kinds of issue-specific veto players to be based on functional delegation. In the UK, for example, the chancellor of the Exchequer is the dominant player on funding decisions with the power to approve policy

United States averaged four and a half veto players. These results are a little less clean if we use Keefer and Stasavage's database, which is based mostly on executive–legislative electoral competition and intra-coalition government dynamics. Their variable for veto points, CHECKS, produces an average in 1999–2000 of four veto players for the twenty-three OECD countries with the G-7 as follows: three (Canada, Germany, Italy, Japan, UK), four (France, United States). The average for the entire dataset of 177 countries is three veto players (Keefer and Stasavage 2003).

[68] Tsebelis 2002, 81.

relatively unencumbered by parliamentary or bureaucratic obstacles. In the United States, the president can make commitments at G-8 meetings, but his ability to deliver is highly dependent upon congressional appropriations. Despite the limitations of existing data on veto players, they provide a baseline of the institutional variation in different country contexts.

The depiction thus far is of costs and values potentially being the most salient points of division. There may be situations of one set of values clashing with another set (such as those who support abortion rights in conflict with those worried about the rights of the unborn).[69] When two norms that both have domestic bases of support clash and are the primary source of contention, this disagreement is akin to instances of costly moral action (or Cell 2 in Table 2.2). Similarly, in other cases, the primary cleavage may not be between costs and values, but between a frame based on causal claims and another based on culturally appropriate values. In those instances, which idea wins may not be a product of overwhelming material incentives but may instead need to be resolved by gatekeepers. For example, in the case of debt relief, one could argue that concerns about moral hazard constituted a rival idea to the normative agenda of Jubilee 2000. The religious appeal of Jubilee 2000 gave debt relief plausible cultural match, but this issue also had to overcome concerns about moral hazard. As I argue in the next chapter, division among economists about the continued importance of moral hazard concerns slightly tilted the playing field so that supporters of debt relief could use both moral arguments and causal claims to win over policy gatekeepers.

When are advocates influential?

While structural factors constrain the influence of advocates, campaigners do have agency to affect outcomes. I account for the

---

[69] Typically, these are situations where powerful international norms face opposing domestic norms. Scholars assessing those cases find that international norms succeed when powerful states coerce or socialize weaker ones to accept them (Farrell 2001; Ikenberry and Kupchan 1990). Another view suggests that in industrialized countries international norms may gain traction after foreign pressure or crisis delegitimate domestic norms and create space for actors to claim the new ideas serve the national interest (Cortell and Davis 2005). In these explanations, material incentives – foreign pressure, self-interest, and local lobbying – resolve which norms win. Thus, the costs vs. values cleavage presented in Table 2.2 is still the best way to capture case dynamics.

differential success of campaigns by focusing on two dimensions: framing (or the content of messages) and the characteristics of the messengers who deliver them. In Chapter 6, I also discuss framing's close relation, shaming. The evocation of messages and messengers naturally raises the question: When do they matter? And, relatedly, under what circumstances are frames important and when are messengers important? In this final section, I group framing and messengers together under the broad rubric of "messaging" before discussing them separately.

The issues covered in this book are not typically central to either the domestic politics of the countries or their foreign policies, although they may be subject to intermittent, focused attention. Debt relief, climate change, AIDS, and the International Criminal Court are all novel, complex problems that sit uneasily in a single policy domain and often require significant technical expertise – economic, scientific, medical, legal, ecclesiastic – to understand and interpret.[70] As a result, by their nature, these issues may typically be more subject to the influence of framing effects of messengers than issues that already have established understandings in the public sphere. Messengers and messaging, particularly early on in an issue's emergence, can define the perceived costs of the policy, the interests of the state, and the moral match of advocates' demands with the country's values.[71]

However, despite their novelty and complexity, these issues are at least initially interpreted through existing understandings by bureaucracies that claim jurisdiction for foreign assistance, environmental problems, health issues, and human rights. And, once these issues have been in the public arena for some time, as AIDS and climate change have been, it becomes harder to change the established narratives about them, in terms of both the relative costliness of addressing the problem and the moral prism through which they are viewed.

In terms of judging the role for messaging, in addition to the stage of the issue's emergence, we also need to distinguish between movement success and influence. As I suggested, activists may be lucky and get what they want, though their influence on the outcome may be limited.

---

[70] Gormley 1986.
[71] Litfin 1995. Keck and Sikkink make similar claims about advocates being most influential in the early agenda-setting stage of the issue cycle, becoming more attenuated as the issue gets closer to an actual decision (Keck and Sikkink 1998).

They may also demonstrate skill and be decisive players (they may also fail through no fault of their own or as a result of bad strategy). This book focuses on the broader question of under what conditions states take on commitments championed by principled advocacy movements (or when do movements get what they want?), with less attention paid to tracing and determining the fingerprint of movement influence on those outcomes. As I argue later, the influence of messaging on outcomes increases as the likelihood of advocacy influence declines.

Where the default frames – of environmental protection, for example – are strongly consistent with a country's values, then the role for messaging may be relatively uncomplicated and straightforward. Where state or individual interests are also well served by supporting the policy (or the costs are minor), then we should expect movements to have the highest probability of success, provided that both the default frame and material interests are obvious and relatively uncontested. In such cases of "cheap moral action," messengers need merely to remind decisionmakers what values and interests are at stake. In such circumstances, messaging is actually less important and less decisive on policy outcomes since decisionmakers have material and moral reasons to support a policy in any case.

Where the default cultural resonance of the policies favored by advocacy groups is low, such as low support for foreign assistance in the United States, then messaging becomes somewhat more difficult but also potentially more important. The effort by advocates in the United States to move HIV/AIDS from being seen as a typical issue of foreign assistance to a moral calling is indicative of the power of compelling frames and effective messengers. In circumstances where states or decisionmakers do not have strong countervailing material incentives to oppose the policy favored by advocacy groups, we would expect messaging to be important in reframing the issue (potentially transforming an issue from one of "indifference" to one of "cheap moral action").

On par or perhaps more difficult for successful advocacy are situations where an easy fit with cultural values coincides with the apparent high costs of action. In such cases, messengers can make the case that the values at stake are worth the costs. Where perceived costs of action are high, as in the case of climate change, a more difficult gambit is to seek to recast the argument as much less costly and amenable to solutions. Former US vice president Al Gore's effort in 2008 and 2009 to suggest "We Can Solve It" is just such an effort to rebrand climate change.[72] If movements succeed despite the impediment of high costs, this is a fairly strong indication of their influence (barring some other change such as the election or appointment of more favorable gatekeepers).

Where strong material incentives against a new policy exist alongside low cultural salience of the default understanding of the issue, advocates face the least permissive conditions for success (cases of "hostility"). By reframing, advocates can succeed in transforming an issue from one of low cultural resonance to strong cultural match, a movement from "hostility" to "costly moral action." The effort to tap into Japanese concerns about national reputation in the Jubilee 2000 debt relief campaign is illustrative of such a dynamic. In such circumstances, decisionmakers will remain troubled by the high perceived cost of the policy advocates support, making them still difficult decisions. Alternatively, messengers can convince decisionmakers that the costs of the policy are actually less onerous than they appear or that the benefits are larger (moving the issue from Cell 4, "hostility," to Cell 3, "indifference"). Truly skilled advocates would simultaneously reframe the issue to be perceived as less costly and consistent with a country's values (a move from "hostility" to "cheap moral action"). In such situations, advocates face barriers in terms of costs and values so, when movements succeed under such unfavorable circumstances, their influence on outcomes is likely to be the most significant (barring some external shock).

Gatekeepers pose a further institutional impediment to advocacy success. Where gatekeepers are opposed to movement aims and where there are many of them, advocates are less likely to be successful. When a movement achieves its aims despite facing a difficult institutional environment, as advocates did in the United States on debt relief and AIDS policy, then messaging is more likely to have played an influential role in that outcome.

In this section, I have treated messaging, which encompasses framing and messengers, as a single complex, identifying the circumstances under which messaging influence is likely to be most significant if advocacy movements get what they want. In Chapter 3 on debt relief, I focus on the role of framing, while in Chapter 5, on HIV/AIDS, I focus on messengers. What determines the relative balance of importance

---

[72] See www.wecansolveit.org/.

between the messengers and the content of the messages? While a full accounting is beyond the scope of this chapter, I sketch out some provisional thoughts.

In political psychology, upon which some of this work is based, scholars often conduct experiments in a lab setting or in a survey to assess political attitudes. In these studies, scholars manipulate one variable at a time to demonstrate that the variable they are interested in has an independent effect on the audience. They often look for relatively small but statistically significant effects from which they can infer a causal relationship. Real world cases often do not afford us the luxury of changing one factor while holding others constant. I sought to develop a generalizable and spare argument to evaluate and explain state behavior across diverse issue areas. Foreign policy outcomes are likely explained, at some level, by multiple causes with many moving pieces operating at the same time. In such circumstances, teasing out relative causal weight, particularly using case study methods, becomes exceedingly tricky. In cases where advocacy movement success is unexpected, both framing and messengers are likely responsible. It is more important in these cases to show that one cannot explain the outcome without including an element of messaging, either the content of the message or the attributes of the advocates. The differential emphases in Chapters 3 and 5 on messages and messengers respectively are intended to highlight different attributes of the broader messaging complex rather than the relative importance of one or the other.

The messaging mechanism of movement influence is not the only path to movement success. As I suggested, in cases of cheap moral action, decisionmakers may realize that they have strong material and moral incentives to act. Here, the role of movements may be incidental or merely facilitate the realization by elites of their country's interests and appropriateness of the policy favored by advocates. In other circumstances, campaigners may, on occasion, mobilize enough political pressure or material backing from powerful allies to change the cost–benefit calculus of states to support a movement-backed policy. Given that the policies supported by principled advocacy movements tend primarily to benefit foreigners and/or future generations, the framing/gatekeepers mechanism is likely to be the more dominant one in which we observe states seemingly engaged in moral action that involves significant costs. If the cases of foreign policy change discussed here can ultimately be better explained through the lens of interest-based calculations, then my argument would contribute little to the discussion. However, such interest-based arguments often fail to capture what we observe in terms of outcomes and decisionmaking processes. For that reason, I believe we are better served by a framing/gatekeepers approach, but I acknowledge that it is an open empirical question as to the frequency with which we observe costly moral action actually occurring and whether framing/gatekeepers explains such instances better than interest-based arguments.

Conclusion

To summarize, as interest-based arguments suggest, the relative cost and benefits of policy solutions provide a preliminary point of departure to understand whether principled advocacy groups will get what they want. However, interests alone do not determine outcomes. Whether advocates are able to invoke culturally resonant values provides a second test for movements. That said, even if the advocates have framed an issue to be a good fit, one that enjoys cultural match, the policy still has to be approved by the relevant policy gatekeepers. Success at this stage depends on the number of gatekeepers and their preferences; where there are many gatekeepers with diverse views, movement success becomes harder.

In subsequent empirical chapters, I open with some context of the choices faced by the seven advanced industrialized countries. I outline each country's interests in supporting movement demands and whether advocates' dominant frames enjoyed cultural resonance. At the most basic level, I assess how costly it would be for the countries to implement the proposed policy. I typically relate those costs to some broader metric of the countries' overall budgets or budgets for that particular policy domain, or set them against national economic circumstances relative to global or peer-group averages. In other cases, financial costs are less clear-cut, so I assess the relative difficulty of implementing the policy on its own terms. For example, in the chapter on the International Criminal Court, I use the number of troops deployed overseas as the main metric of difficulty, on the assumption that countries with larger deployments would be more likely to be worried about their troops being subject to human rights tribunals. In Chapter 3 on debt relief, I hew most closely to the argument outlined in this chapter, looking at the specific role of gatekeepers in adjudicating the between costs and values. In the chapters that follow, I layer tl argument by looking at other mediating factors or drilling mor into the particular aspects of state motivations. In all of the empirical chapters, I pursue the framing/gatekeepers argument in more depth by exploring dynamics in selected country cases.

3 | *Bono made Jesse Helms cry: Jubilee 2000 and the campaign for developing country debt relief*

I opened the book with the story of the Jubilee 2000 campaign. To dramatize the issue of developing country debts, advocates surrounded two consecutive meetings of the world's advanced industrialized countries with human chains in the late 1990s. I retold the perhaps apocryphal story of the pop music star Bono's meeting with Senator Jesse Helms of North Carolina, the powerful, yet curmudgeonly chair of the Senate Foreign Relations Committee. Although Helms had famously derided foreign assistance as throwing money down ratholes, he was reportedly brought to tears by Bono's invocation of Christian faith as a reason for supporting debt relief. This chapter, through a case study of Jubilee 2000 and selected country responses to the debt relief campaign, seeks to explain how states may be moved to support "moral action."[1]

The Jubilee 2000 campaign – the campaign that sought to write off external debt of the world's poorest countries – provides an interesting case study. The case is a puzzle because some states acted in a manner that was contrary to their narrow material interests, apparently at the behest of a transnational advocacy group. This case is also interesting because debt negotiations are normally discussed in a rarefied world of central bankers and finance officials, multilateral bureaucrats, and private financiers, nearly all of whom are committed to minimizing moral hazard and are thus skeptical of writing off external debts. Two economists called the campaign "by far the most successful industrial-country movement aimed at combating world poverty for many years, perhaps in all recorded history."[2] It earned the endorsement of leaders of diverse ideological and professional orientations – the Pope, Bono, economist Jeffrey Sachs, and the right-wing televangelist Pat

---

[1] I follow other work on the role of morality in foreign policy by McElroy 1992 and Lumsdaine 1993.
[2] Birdsall and Williamson 2002, 1.

70

Robertson. The campaign gained the support of strong political allies in the UK and US governments, making it harder for other creditors – such as Japan, France, and Germany – to oppose debt relief.

Organized around the coming of the twenty-first century, Jubilee 2000 was an international campaign that aimed to relieve the world's poorest countries of their "unpayable" external debts. The reference to Jubilee comes from the biblical notion in the Book of Leviticus of a time to relieve the debts of the poor.[3] In the early 1990s, Martin Dent, a professor at Keele University in the UK, came up with the idea for a "Jubilee year," end of the millennium campaign, inspired by his knowledge of the Bible and ethical commitment to the third world.[4] Dent's advocacy began with his students but soon attracted Christian Aid, the World Development Movement, and other UK charities. Jubilee 2000 was launched formally in April 1996. The movement blossomed, galvanizing millions worldwide to participate in letter-writing efforts and protests before the official campaign closed at the end of 2000. In policy terms, Jubilee 2000's efforts moved donors to more than double the amount of debt relief that had previously been offered: by May 2006, nineteen states already qualified to have $23.4 bn of their debts written off through the Highly Indebted Poor Country (HIPC) initiative.[5] In 2005, rich creditors committed to write off 100 percent of the debts that the poorest countries owed to the World Bank, the IMF, and the African Development Bank. Moreover, the liberal–religious conservative coalition that came together on debt relief presaged advocacy efforts that would play an important role in the Bush administration's $15 bn financial commitment to fight AIDS, discussed in Chapter 5.

This chapter proceeds in four stages. The first section provides additional background on debt relief. The second develops a partial explanation for supporting debt relief based on material interest and describes the limitations of such an argument. In the third section, I discuss how a framing/gatekeepers explanation improves upon material interest arguments. In the final section, I explore the causal processes of debt relief in the United States and Japan.

---

[3] Leviticus 25:10 reads, "Consecrate the fiftieth year and proclaim liberty throughout the land to all its inhabitants. It shall be a jubilee for you; each one of you is to return to his family property and each to his own clan."
[4] Dent and Peters 1999.　　[5] World Bank 2006.

Background on debt relief

Debt relief for poor countries emerged as an issue in the wake of the oil price hikes of the 1970s. However, external debt problems of the poorest countries initially took a back seat to those of middle-income countries. After the Mexican government defaulted on its foreign debt in 1982, decisionmakers in Western industrialized countries feared that the large exposure by private banks such as Citicorp and Bank of America to middle-income countries' debts could potentially contribute to a meltdown in the international financial system.[6] The US government, most notably through the 1989 Brady Plan, moved to corral private creditors into an agreement that would ease middle-income country debt burdens and prevent broader financial system instability. Concurrently, the Paris Club also began to address external debts of the poorest countries.[7] However, where commercial banks had been the dominant creditors for middle-income countries, multilateral and bilateral institutions held most of poor countries' debt. Since few of these countries had much access to international financial markets, dealing with poor country debts primarily had implications for the financial integrity of the multilateral lending institutions and the budgets of creditor governments.[8] Beginning in 1988 with the "Toronto terms," the major creditor countries began to offer poor countries limited bilateral debt relief by way of new loans to continue payments on old loans.[9]

In October 1996, after years of rolling over poor country debts and providing modest debt reduction, several developed countries, the World Bank, and the IMF decided upon a joint approach for Highly

[6] Lipson 1981.
[7] The Paris Club is an informal group of creditor governments, established in 1956 with a permanent secretariat in the French Treasury to coordinate policies among bilateral creditors.
[8] In 1997, HIPC countries owed $201 bn, $174 bn of this in long-term debt and $27 bn in short-term debt. Of the long-term debt, $170 bn was public and publicly guaranteed. Within that total, $148 bn was owed to official creditors ($64 bn to the multilaterals and $84 bn in bilateral aid) and $21 bn to private creditors. Only $4 bn of the total was private, non-guaranteed debt (World Bank 1999a).
[9] Debt relief programs evolved from Toronto terms, which reduced debt repayments by 33% in 1988, to Naples terms, which reduced them by a further 50–67% in 1994, to HIPC I, which added a still further reduction of up to 80% in 1997 (Schuerch 1999; for information on HIPC I, see p. 73).

Indebted Poor Countries (hereafter HIPC I).[10] HIPC I incrementally increased bilateral debt reduction and broke new ground with respect to multilateral debt with the creation of a Trust Fund to pay for multi- lateral debt relief. HIPC I also increased the level of possible bilateral debt reduction. Countries deemed eligible for debt relief reached a "decision point," and, if they followed sound macroeconomic poli- cies for several years while enjoying reduced debt payments in the interim, they would reach a "completion point" and be eligible for actual reduction of debt stock.

HIPC I, despite some influence by Oxfam and other development charities, was primarily a top-down affair. While advocates played a background role, the real change agents in this story were Kenneth Clarke, Britain's Chancellor of the Exchequer, and the World Bank's president James Wolfensohn.[11] The main obstacle to HIPC I was the fear of "moral hazard," that definitively writing off poor country debts would reward bad behavior and encourage states to accumulate unsus- tainable debt burdens again.[12] These fears were partially undercut by the recognition that these debts were unlikely to be paid back any- way, so clearing the books of bad debt was simply good accounting.[13] Moreover, economists also suggested that developing countries could experience problems of "debt overhang," where the existing stock of debt obligations was so large that private actors had a disincentive to invest in the economy, since productive investment would likely be taxed to pay off external debt obligations.[14] At the very least, these arguments legitimized the idea that broader debt relief could poten- tially work.

---

[10] Forty-one countries were initially listed as HIPCs: thirty-three in Africa, four in Latin America, three in Asia, and one in the Middle East (World Bank Undated-b). Eligibility was based on threshold indicators beyond which a country's external debt was deemed "unsustainable": the net present value (NPV) of its debt-to-export ratio, the NPV debt-to-revenue ratio, and the export to GDP and revenue/GDP ratios. Debt relief was conditional upon good policymaking, in terms of both macroeconomic policy and poverty reduction. The original list of potential HIPCs included thirty-two countries that had a 1993 GNP per capita of US $695 or less and a 1993 NPV debt/exports ratio higher than 220 percent or an NPV debt/GNP ratio higher than 80 percent. Nine others were included because they were eligible for Paris Club concessional lending (IMF 1998, 7).

[11] Mallaby 2004.   [12] Easterly 2001.
[13] Summers 2000.   [14] Krugman 1988.

While the story of HIPC I is largely top-down, the same cannot be said for the subject of this chapter, the expansion of HIPC that took place at the 1999 Cologne G-8 summit (hereafter HIPC II). Just as creditors finally reached agreement on a program to partially write off multilateral debt, NGOs were gearing up their own campaign to pursue more wide-ranging debt forgiveness in time for the new millennium. Jubilee 2000, with its explicit connection to religious traditions and the coming of the new millennium, represented a "rebranding" of the debt campaigns that had been around for a number of years, according to Jamie Drummond, Jubilee 2000's former global strategist.[15] Prior to 1994, campaigners had tried without much success to draw attention to the debt issue along with IMF- and World Bank-administered structural adjustment programs. Jubilee 2000's primary complaint about HIPC I was that it was not fast, broad, or deep enough and was insufficiently attentive to basic human needs.[16] By mid-1998, still only one country – Uganda – had reached the completion point.

As advocates clamored for additional debt relief, HIPC's original champion, James Wolfensohn, cooled to the idea, in part (in one observer's opinion) because it was not his.[17] Campaigners hastened awareness of the limitations of HIPC I. With debt relief under HIPC proceeding slowly, a focal point for the campaign became the G-8 summit in Birmingham, England, in May 1998 when 50,000 campaigners ringed the summit in a human chain. The campaigners later met in Rome in November 1998 where they designed a loosely affiliated coalition of autonomous national campaigns.[18] In January 1999, the Pope announced his support for debt relief. Activists meanwhile conducted high-profile events with celebrities, including mass concerts, rallies, and other attention-getting actions.

Before the G-8 summit in Germany in mid-1999, the UK, the United States, and Canada led efforts to enhance HIPC. In late 1998, newly elected chancellor Gerhard Schröder signaled a softening in Germany's longstanding reluctance. Pressure mounted on Italy, France, and Japan to be more supportive. In March 1999, then US president Bill Clinton announced a plan that established the contours for what would come

---

[15] Drummond 2001.   [16] Jubilee 2000 Undated-b.   [17] Mallaby 2004, 250.
[18] Supporters minimally agreed there should be (1) a one-off debt cancellation (2) of the poorest countries' unpayable debts (3) by the end of the year 2000 through (4) a fair and transparent process.

out of Cologne, including front-loaded relief, an increase in bilateral debt relief to 90 percent, and additional multilateral financing.[19] The plan also linked debt relief to Poverty Reduction Strategy Papers to guarantee that savings would be invested in education, health, and other worthy expenditures.[20] With 30,000 protesters ringing the summit, G-7 countries in Cologne in June 1999 announced the expansion of HIPC, promising about $27 bn in new debt reduction on top of debt relief that HIPC countries were eligible for under traditional mechanisms.[21]

Cologne partly involved bargaining by creditors on how much each would contribute to the HIPC Trust Fund and how much bilateral debt relief they would support. The US contribution was $920 mn spread out over three years, of which $600 mn was to be dedicated to the Trust Fund. However, this amount was contingent upon Congress appropriating the funds and authorizing the sale or revaluation of IMF gold.[22] The $600 mn was roughly equivalent to the EU's pledged contribution and three times that of Japan. In September 1999, President Clinton announced the United States would write off 100 percent of bilateral debts, followed soon by the other main creditors. US funding, however, remained in doubt until October 2000. Congress finally appropriated $435 mn for the initial US commitments to the HIPC Trust Fund and bilateral relief.

Through 2000, campaigners complained that the pace of debt relief was too slow and that few countries were being processed.[23] Continued pressure sped things up. By December 2000, although Uganda was still the only country to have reached the completion point, twenty-two countries had reached the decision point.[24] When the Jubilee year ended, a successor campaign, Jubilee+, was created to monitor the

[19] William Jefferson Clinton 1999.
[20] Poverty Reduction Strategy Papers (PRSPs) were supposed to be country-owned development strategies to take advantage of the savings from debt relief for productive purposes. PRSPs were instituted by the World Bank and the IMF as a replacement for structural adjustment programs which were seen as externally imposed.
[21] The $27 bn figure was in net present value terms. HIPC II also lowered the threshold of what were deemed sustainable debt targets, including: a debt-to-export ratio of 150% down from 200–250%, a debt-to-revenue ratio of 250% down from 280%, and a lowering of the export/GDP and revenue/GDP thresholds to 30% and 15% (World Bank 1999b).
[22] Hart 2001.   [23] Jubilee 2000 2000a.   [24] World Bank 2001.

pace and breadth of implementation with calls for an independent arbitrator to take charge. Finance ministries, for their part, feared haste would compromise the quality of debt relief. As a result of depressed commodity prices, rich countries pledged in June 2002 an additional $1 bn to "top up" the Trust Fund. By August 2005, eighteen countries had reached the completion point and had $22.1 bn of their debts written off; another ten had reached the decision point and were eligible for nearly $11 bn of debt relief if they maintained sound policies.[25] After the Jubilee year, many campaigners thought they had pushed the debt agenda as far it could go and initially turned to new issues such as AIDS and trade. However, dissatisfaction with the pace of implementation fed renewed calls for debt relief, led by aggressive efforts from the UK and bolstered by a high-profile public campaign. In summer 2005, these efforts yielded the Multilateral Debt Relief Initiative (MDRI), a commitment by the G-8 and international financial institutions (IFIs) to write off all the remaining debts owed by HIPC countries to the World Bank, the IMF, and the African Development Bank. Partly contingent upon financing and the eligibility criteria of poor countries, MDRI meant debt relief potentially totaling $57.5 bn.[26]

While the 2005 decision to write off most multilateral debts is historic, this chapter seeks to explain (1) donors' decisions to support enhanced debt relief at Cologne and (2) the appropriations process thereafter. For most of the G-7, the first decision was the significant one. Once the countries' gatekeepers decided to support enhanced relief, compliance with 100 percent bilateral relief and their Trust Fund pledges were largely foregone conclusions. For countries with more gatekeepers, the United States in particular, the Cologne commitment and the pledge of 100 percent bilateral relief were symbolic but dependent on home appropriations. Since all members of the G-7 agreed to the Cologne deal, we can track variation in behavior by looking at (1) the timing of support for 100 percent bilateral

---

[25] Both the $22.1 bn and the $11 bn figures were in net present value terms (World Bank 2006). In April 2006, a nineteenth country, Cameroon, reached the completion point.

[26] HIPC debt holdings by the multilaterals in 2005 included $42.5 bn from the World Bank, $5 bn from the IMF, and $10 bn from the African Development Bank (World Bank Development Committee 2005). In 2006, four countries were deemed potentially HIPC-eligible including Eritrea, Haiti, the Kyrgyz Republic, and Nepal.

Table 3.1 *Pledges and shares to the HIPC Trust Fund (in millions of dollars)*

	Canada	France	Germany	Italy	Japan	UK	United States
Bilateral pledges	$102	$21	$72	$70	$200	$221	$600
All pledges (including bilateral and EU)	$102	$199	$252	$162	$200	$316	$600
GDP as % of total world economy 1999	2.15%	4.74%	6.99%	3.85%	14.55%	4.77%	30.16%
Bilateral pledges as % of total world pledges	5.97%	1.23%	4.21%	4.10%	11.70%	12.93%	35.11%
All pledges as % of total world pledges	4.18%	8.15%	10.32%	6.63%	8.19%	12.93%	25.56%

Source: World Bank Undated-a.

relief, (2) the size of the initial financial pledges donors made to the HIPC Trust Fund as of April 2000, and (3) how long it took them to come through on those pledges. What are these patterns? Support for 100 percent bilateral relief began with the United States in September 1999. The UK followed in December 1999, then Italy in February 2000, Canada in March 2000, with Germany, France, and Japan, the three most reluctant members of the G-7, not announcing their support until April 2000.[27] As for pledges to the Trust Fund, Canada, Italy, the UK, and the United States made pledges larger than their country's share of global GDP. French, German, and Japanese pledges were less generous by this measure (see Table 3.1). When we include EU pledges to the Trust Fund, French and German support for the Trust Fund looks larger, since they both contributed funds to the EU enterprise in addition to their bilateral contributions.

In terms of the time taken to comply with their pledges (Figure 3.1), Canada is an outlier, completing its pledge very early. France waited nearly three years to make any contribution, while the United States took two years to make its first contribution. Germany, Italy, Japan,

---

[27] Jubilee 2000 Undated-a.

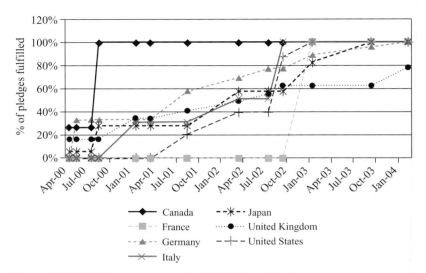

Figure 3.1 G-7 disbursements to the HIPC Trust Fund
Source: World Bank Undated-a.

and the UK made early contributions and then contributed 100 percent of their pledges even later than France and the United States.[28]

A partial explanation: material interest

I provide a partial explanation of these patterns based on material interest and suggest its merits and limitations. Arguments based on *material interest* focus on the costs and benefits of debt relief. As suggested in the previous chapter, two variants potentially explain outcomes. The first – *state interest* – presents the state as a unified actor responding to material constraints. States should support debt relief and comply with their commitments when the benefits exceed the costs. This variant would discount the influence of advocates. Policy change from this perspective would be a result of two mechanisms,

---

[28] The UK's apparent lag in Trust Fund contributions is explained by legislation that prevents funds from being disbursed without an assurance that they can be spent within three months (Jenns 2006). The figure does not include other UK contributions to the Trust Fund for Ugandan debt relief. Data on pledges and disbursements to the Trust Fund come from periodic HIPC Status of Implementation reports (World Bank Undated-a). Economic data on the G-7 come from the World Economic Outlook (IMF 2005).

Table 3.2 *G-7 debt holdings circa 1998–1999 (in millions of dollars)*

	Canada	France	Germany	Italy	Japan	UK	United States
Bilateral debt relief claims of forty countries	$711	$13,033	$6,586	$4,311	$11,200	$3,092	$6,210
as % of donor's GDP	0.1%	0.9%	0.3%	0.4%	0.3%	0.2%	0.08%
as % of total G-7 claims	1.57%	28.9%	14.6%	9.5%	24.8%	6.8%	13.8%

Source: GAO 2000; IMF 2005.

either (1) simple adaptive learning (that creditors' interests would be better served by debt relief) or (2) coercion/inducement by other states (that raises the costs of inaction). Delays in policy change could be explained as a byproduct of collective action problems of policy coordination.[29] The second variant – *individual interest* – sees state behavior through the lens of decisionmakers' incentives for political survival. In this view, politicians support policy change when it is (1) politically advantageous to do so or (2) politically costly to fail to do so. A movement's relative political strength – as measured by membership, resources, protests, and ability to leverage coercive influences domestic and foreign – determines its success or failure.[30]

In 1996, when the HIPC initiative was created, creditors recognized additional debt relief was warranted. At the same time, they wanted to retain elements of conditionality to prevent debtors from returning to bad practices. Jubilee 2000, by contrast, wanted complete and unconditional debt relief. While some individuals in creditor countries were supportive of additional debt reduction beyond HIPC I, states such as Japan and Germany and important players within other creditor countries did not think that expanding HIPC was a good idea. Indeed, HIPC I did not have much time to be implemented, so revisiting the agreement was not the highest priority from a state interest perspective. What about the costs and benefits of debt relief? As depicted in Table 3.2,

[29] Olson 1965.
[30] "Mobilizing resources" in the social movement literature (McAdam, McCarthy, and Zald 1996). This pluralist account is familiar. Research that incorporates domestic structure argues that liberal polities – such as the United States – are typically moved by bottom-up pressure.

the main creditors – the G-7 – had different levels of bilateral (country-to-country) debts. They also made different promises to underwrite debt relief for money owed to multilateral financial institutions (with the Europeans double-giving through the EU). Donors also had different accounting rules that affected their actual costs of debt relief (some already having made provisions for bad debts by setting money aside).[31]

The patterns here provide some support for material interest arguments. Some states, namely Japan, Italy, and Germany (before the Schröder era), were strongly against debt relief, and other creditors had to make repeated attempts to get them to change their policies. Given that the laggards – France and Japan – had the largest outstanding bilateral debt, their initial opposition to debt relief seems consistent with material interest arguments. Since Britain and Canada – the leaders – were the smallest holders of bilateral debts, one could also explain their enthusiasm accordingly. The timing of Italian and German support for debt relief (i.e., following the leaders) is also consistent with their debt holdings. However, the compliance patterns are less clear. While the costs of debt relief for the United States were small, it took a long time to fulfill its pledge to the HIPC Trust Fund. Japan faced high costs of debt relief, but it began to comply with its commitments faster than either France or the United States.

Like debt levels, coordination problems over burden-sharing also provide a partial answer to why getting an agreement proved difficult. If creditors want to give poor countries a fresh start, not only must multilateral debt be forgiven, but also each bilateral member has to be convinced to write off its debt. However, if the United States, for example, wrote off its bilateral debt, then other donors might be more likely to be repaid at its expense.[32] In the absence of a coordinating mechanism, no country has an incentive to forgive its debts unilaterally. While one might expect that IFIs could help resolve these collective action problems, they have their own disincentives to cooperate. They fear moral hazard, and the loans from multilaterals are spread among them. As with bilateral creditors, being the first IFI to forgive debt

---

[31] GAO 2000. Japanese and French costs were each about $8 bn, as neither did much provisioning for bad debts. US costs were about $3.7 bn due to provisioning for bad loans. Costs for HIPC have risen with the inclusion of new debtors and topping-up to account for commodity price shocks.

[32] This idea of Paul Krugman's is related to commercial debt in Crook 1991.

would mean other multilateral lending institutions would more likely be paid off. Ultimately, the IFIs depend upon member governments for support, so the institutions become forums for those distributional battles.

John Serieux and Yiagadeesen Samy argued that the insignificance of poor debtors for international financial stability, coupled with coordination problems, delayed the response to debt relief and created the need for a movement to break the impasse.[33] Debt levels suggest why some states were more enthusiastic than others, and coordination problems help us understand the delay. Neither, however, explains why a new agreement was reached in 1999.

Individual interest arguments offer another possible mechanism. In this view, campaigners made it politically costly for actors to ignore their concerns. Indeed, one cynical version of this argument suggests promises of debt relief provided politicians with cheap public relations gains. Leaders have either failed to implement debt relief or used it as a substitute for other forms of foreign assistance.[34] Lobbying by campaigners is one of the mechanisms that put this issue on the agenda. However, the G-8 protests aside, the campaign was able to bring only modest pressure to bear in different national contexts. In the United States, for example, 6,000 people attended the national rally campaigners organized in April 2000, hardly comparable to the hundreds of thousands that participate in marches against hot-button issues such as abortion. While celebrity participation enhanced the visibility of the campaign, Bono himself acknowledged, "in the US, Jubilee 2000 had been a lot slower to catch on. We were running out of time to grow the grassroots. I had to go straight to the decision-makers."[35] Former Treasury secretary Larry Summers made a similar observation when I interviewed him: "We could have not done it, and it wouldn't have been a political disaster."[36]

As for the claim that debt relief represents public relations window-dressing, twenty-two countries had reached the HIPC completion point as of August 2007 and were thus eligible for more than $21 bn in cumulative debt service savings.[37] The World Bank estimated that the ratio of debt service to government revenue for HIPC countries fell from

---

[33] Serieux and Samy 2003, 4.   [34] Arslanalp and Henry 2006.
[35] Bono and Assayas 2005, 89.   [36] Summers 2004.
[37] The figure is in net present value terms for the end of 2006 (IMF 2007).

23.5% in 1998–1999 to 11.7% in 2005, which has freed up resources for investments in health, education, and other sectors.[38] Moreover, contrary to claims of aid substitution, from 1999 to 2004, G-7 donors collectively increased their non-debt relief foreign assistance to HIPCs by 37%.[39] Thus, while both state and individual interest arguments provide a partial understanding of donors' willingness to support debt relief, an expanded agreement on debt in 1999 was not inevitable, nor was the emergence of Jubilee 2000 structurally determined. An analysis that fails to reflect advocates' efforts, including their moral claims, would tell us little about how states and key leaders came to support expanded debt relief in HIPC II.

A more complete explanation: framing-meets-gatekeepers

What value-added benefit does a strategic framing/gatekeepers argument have?

There are four observable implications. While acknowledging that advocates are (1) most likely to succeed when there are low costs, cultural match, and supportive gatekeepers, a strategic framing argument would also recognize (2) possibilities for costly moral action where gatekeepers believe the values at stake are important. Where there are many gatekeepers, (3) advocates will have to make more arguments to bring them all on board. Finally, we should (4) *not* be able to identify clearly overwhelming material pressures supporting the decision. If we observe such pressures, it would be impossible to detect if framing matters.

To lay bare differences between framing/gatekeepers and material interest arguments, we can look at the intersection of costs and values using Table 2.2 developed in the previous chapter. Country cases can be mapped in two dimensions, with costs on the X axis and the frame's value fit on the Y axis. Tracking costs and values is complex. Various potential indicators could be used, and defining thresholds between high and low is complicated. As Tables 3.1 and 3.2 show, G-7 countries varied in their bilateral debt holdings and their pledges to the HIPC

---

[38] World Bank 2006, 28.
[39] Large increases in US aid largely drove this result. The UK and Canada also increased their aid, while the other donors had flat or slight decreases in their non-debt relief foreign aid (OECD 2006).

Trust Fund. Their national economies are of different sizes, so debt write-off for one country might be considerable in aggregate terms but only a small percentage of its GDP. As a percent of GDP, even the extreme cases are modest (0.9% France, 0.3% Japan). However, setting these costs against the backdrop of GDP may be misleading. Judgments of relative costs may depend on what policy area we are discussing. Debt relief might not require a lot of money, but it might constitute a large share of a country's total foreign assistance budget, limiting discretion for other purposes. Even if total costs are modest, donors are likely to be sensitive that their own country is bearing a disproportionate share of the costs. Japan and France together, for example, accounted for more than 53 percent of the G-7 countries' debt holdings. Finally, the monetary costs of debt relief might pale in comparison to the political costs. Foreign aid, for example, is a small part of the US budget, yet it can be politically costly to support.[40]

As for values, there are a number of different ways to get at this question. The debt relief effort in 2000 was framed primarily in religious terms. Thus, one way to assess the potential cultural resonance of the frame is to examine attitudes toward religion.[41] Since values are supposed to be relatively long-lived, I look at average religiosity across the four waves of data from the World Values Survey dating back to the 1980s.[42] The higher the religiosity, the greater the likelihood the public can be mobilized on that basis. As Table 3.3 shows, the United States, Italy, and Canada are more religious than other G-7 countries. Eastern Germany, having recently emerged from Communism, is much less religious than western Germany. The Japanese are the least religious (and have a different tradition) which helps explain the country's initial reluctance to support debt relief. Like Japan, France never developed a strong debt movement, perhaps linked to its anti-clerical past.

What does the mapping of costs and values reveal? In Figure 3.2, the G-7 share of bilateral debts and religiosity scores are plotted in

---

[40] Larry Summers thought $435 mn for debt relief in 2000 was "a big amount," noting that many foreign aid expenditures start out in the $20 mn range (Summers 2004).
[41] Here, use of the religiosity indicator is meant to track the cultural resonance of the Jubilee 2000 frame, not the cultural resonance of debt relief as a policy.
[42] Except for British attitudes on religion, values were very consistent across waves.

Table 3.3 *G-7 measures of religiosity*

	Canada	France	Germany	Italy	Japan	UK	United States
% answering "Yes" to "Are you religious?"	73.37	49.97	W 63.68 E 31.27	84.63	26.02	51.5	82.5

Note: The four waves of the World Values Survey were taken in 1981, 1990–1991, 1995–1998, and 1999–2001 (Inglehart 2005).
Source: Inglehart 2005.

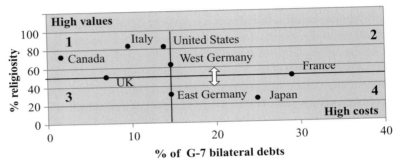

Figure 3.2 Mapping of bilateral debt burdens and religiosity
Note: The arrow between East and West Germany reflects shared debt holdings but different levels of religiosity.

two-dimensional space. Anything above 50% religiosity is coded as "high" value fit with the religious frame. The threshold for "high" costs is defined as anything above the mean share of bilateral debts (14.3%). This threshold is based on what decisionmakers thought about the problem, in terms of the domain ("As foreign aid, was this costly?") and in terms of the relative costs ("Who bears the burden?"). Looking at relative G-7 debt holdings is useful because it reveals the differences in the potential political costs of supporting debt relief. The precise threshold between high and low costs may be less important than the general patterns observed; of particular importance is the fact that Japan and France faced a disproportionate share of total costs of debt relief.

In this representation, four countries (Canada, Italy, the United States, and the UK) were cases of "cheap moral action" in Cell 1 of Table 2.2. Two countries, France and Japan, were cases of "hostility" (Cell 4), of high costs and low value fit. One country, Germany, was a case of "costly moral action" (Cell 2), with both high costs and high value fit.

When we look at the religiosity of most G-7 countries, there is a fount of religious belief that served the debt relief campaign well in even more secular countries such as the UK. At the G-8 meetings in Birmingham and Cologne, the majority of protesters were from church groups and church-linked charities. Similarly, faith groups were the main supporters in the United States, where local clergy encouraged members to contact their legislators. The religious symbolism, coupled with the timing of the new millennium, was such that the campaign was able to attract a wide swath of support from North and South, left and right. Whereas radical elements tended to bash capitalism in the 1999 WTO protests in Seattle, Jubilee 2000 brought on board influential supporters from the entire ideological spectrum as well as ordinary citizens, what Drummond called "establishment taxpayers."[43] Debts were also rhetorically linked to cuts in education and health care and, in turn, to death, malnourishment, and poverty, particularly among children. This argument helped recast the issue from fear of corruption to one of morality and justice. As a columnist for the *Financial Times* argued: "[T]he intellectual argument in favor of debt relief has largely been won – few countries argue any more that relief will by itself create large moral hazard problems."[44] As an editorial in the *Guardian* concluded: "Yes, Jubilee 2000 had successfully shifted the development agenda from one of charity – of the 'poor little things they don't have enough to eat' variety – to one of justice."[45] The *Washington Post*'s Sebastian Mallaby concurred, saying: "Late last year, during the endgame of the budget fight, the Republican line was that aid would drain money from Social Security; it was a choice of 'Ghana vs. Grandma,' they exclaimed, ridiculously. But you don't hear that so much now."[46]

While Figure 3.2 provides a representation of cost and values, the role of gatekeepers complicates the so-called easy cases in Cell 1 of Table 2.2. Table 3.4 presents predictions for the likelihood of successful framing generated by combining the measures for costs and

---

[43] Drummond 2001.   [44] Beattie 2000.
[45] Guardian 1999.   [46] Mallaby 2000.

Table 3.4 *Costs/values, veto players, and advocacy success*

Low likelihood	← →	High likelihood
Hostility + high veto	Indifference + high veto	Cheap moral action + low veto (UK, Italy)
Hostility + low veto (Japan, France)	Cheap moral action + high veto (USA, Canada)	
Costly moral action + high veto (Germany)	Costly moral action + low veto	Indifference + low veto
Coercion		*Conversion*

values with a dichotomous value for the number of gatekeepers. The table includes the "coercion–conversion" continuum from Chapter 2, suggesting that, as you move from left to right, the mechanisms that advocates use to induce policy change can be less coercive. The table also includes measures of veto players from the previous chapter and demonstrates that the United States and Canada were harder cases for successful framing because of this institutional dimension.

The depiction thus far is of costs and values being the most salient points of division. As suggested in the previous chapter, there may be situations of values *versus* values or norms clashing with other norms. One could argue that concerns about moral hazard constituted a rival idea to the normative agenda of Jubilee 2000. Jubilee 2000's effort to connect debt relief with religious values gave its policy aims plausible cultural match at the societal level in a number of countries, but debt relief also had to dislodge moral hazard and survive the scrutiny of gatekeepers. Fortunately for advocates, moral hazard had already been partially delegitimated as an overarching concern, in part by creditors' initial acceptance of broader debt relief in 1996 but also as networks of experts provided credible information that external debts were preventing countries from getting their finances in order.

Jubilee 2000 and debt relief in the United States and Japan

We can get leverage on the relationship between costs, values, and gatekeepers by looking at two creditors in more detail – the United

States and Japan.[47] What justifies studying these two country cases? By looking at a seemingly easy case (the United States) and a hard case (Japan), we can better understand the mechanism by which framing can connect to ideational currents in different national contexts with distinct institutions and decisionmaking processes. The US case is closer to Cell 1 of Table 2.2, a case of "cheap moral action." It is a critical case for strategic framing in that, if the causal mechanism does not apply in this easier case, the theory is unlikely to have explanatory power in harder cases.[48] Moreover, when we add in the institutional dimension of policy gatekeepers, the case looks more puzzling. Jamie McCormick, a former committee staff member to US Congressman Jim Leach, the lead sponsor of a House bill on debt relief, got at the political difficulties for debt relief in Congress:

> One of the reasons I was so stunned that the whole debt relief initiative took off is that the campaign seemed to fly in the face of so much the new and more conservative Republican House caucus/leadership stood for. After all, this all came about shortly after the Contract for America, pledges to cut foreign aid, eliminate the Commerce Department, downsize the State Department . . . [49]

The United States was experiencing divided government between Democrats in the executive branch and a Republican-controlled Congress. The president was weakened by scandal. At a time of heightened isolationism, debt relief was one instance when campaigners were able to induce the United States to support a new multilateral initiative. President Clinton's difficulties in getting appropriations for debt relief continued patterns of conflict over foreign policy such as the deadlock between the administration and Senator Helms over UN funding. For those interested in what it takes to move the world's most powerful nation, debt relief can shed light on other areas. The coalition of liberal Democrats and conservative Republicans that came together on debt had a lasting impact on other issues, namely HIV/AIDS.

The Japanese case is a harder case for framing. The costs of debt relief were higher for Japan, and the initial religious frame did not enjoy

---

[47] For a more extended discussion of dynamics in Germany and the UK, see chapter 4 in Busby 2004a.
[48] For a discussion of easy or most likely cases as critical cases, see George and Bennett 2005, 121–122.
[49] McCormick 2005.

local cultural resonance. However, if we can demonstrate support for the framing/gatekeepers theory in this tough case, we can be more confident that the argument is generalizable to other domains.

The United States

For most issues, the United States possesses many policy gatekeepers, and debt relief was no exception. In addition to the president and Treasury secretary, a number of congressional committees and sub-committees also had jurisdiction, including House and Senate Banking (then chaired by Jim Leach and Phil Gramm, respectively), a House Appropriations subcommittee (chaired by Sonny Callahan), a House Banking subcommittee (chaired by Spencer Bachus), Senate Foreign Relations (chaired by Jesse Helms), and House Budget (chaired by John Kasich).[50] The large numbers of players involved in foreign aid and appropriations complicated the executive branch's pledges. With more gatekeepers, we would expect that more arguments would be needed to persuade them and that political pressure would be among the mechanisms that shifted lawmakers. After Cologne, other coun-tries hesitated in fulfilling their commitments while the US contribution remained in doubt. On September 29, 1999, President Clinton agreed to cancel 100 percent of bilateral debts, but had yet to secure funding. Not until October 2000 was he able to secure a $435 mn appropri-ation, which included the country's first (and critical) contribution to the HIPC Trust Fund. How were the key policy gatekeepers – Trea-sury Secretary Summers and members of Congress including Kasich, Leach, Bachus, Callahan, Helms, and Gramm – convinced to support (or drop their opposition to) debt relief?

Although interest-based arguments help explain the outcome, they alone are not determinative. Part of the explanation lies in the actions of advocates who influenced policymakers through (1) appeals to causal beliefs, (2) appeals to religious morality, and (3) political pres-sure. Between 1997 and 2000, debt relief advocacy in the United States

---

[50] Other executive branch actors with minor influence included the Office of Management and Budget, the Council of Economic Advisors, and the State Department. In the US legislative branch, all committee and subcommittee chairs come from the party that has a majority. Between 1995 and 2001, Republicans narrowly controlled both the House and the Senate.

would grow from being inconsequential to become a small, robust movement. In the 1980s and early 1990s, advocates had pushed debt relief through the Debt Crisis Network (1985–1990) and a later Debt Action Coalition (1991–1993). Formed by development NGOs and religious groups, both dissolved in part because activists could not find a suitable "handle" by which to influence policymakers.[51] In April 1997, meetings between British activists and a religious working group on the IMF/World Bank led to the launch of Jubilee 2000/USA.[52] Other elements were the liberal arm of the Catholic Church and the mainstream Protestant denominations. Both had strong connections to developing countries through missionary activities.

Because the US development advocacy sector is smaller than that in the UK, there was no large mass movement to generate political pressure.[53] Nonetheless, the religious frame resonated with churchgoers. Members of Congress began to get mail, phone calls, and visits in their districts in small but significant numbers. Campaigners such as Bono inductively learned the importance of connecting directly with gatekeepers. Realizing that President Clinton's support would not be enough, Bono asked guiding questions for lobbying: "Who can stop this from happening?" and "Who's the Elvis here?"[54] Advocates began to cultivate ties with Republican committee chairs and build support from unlikely quarters. After the president's announcement of intent to cancel 100 percent of bilateral debt, Bono came to the United States and forged links with the administration, including Summers and members of Congress. The Shriver family introduced Bono to Arnold Schwarzenegger, who counseled him to link up with Republicans such as Representative John Kasich. Kasich in turn brokered meetings for Bono with other Republicans including Senator Orrin

[51] Elizabeth A. Donnelly Undated.
[52] The IMF/World Bank Working Group included groups such as the 50 Years Is Enough US Network for Global Economic Justice, the Maryknoll Office for Global Concerns, the Africa Faith and Justice Network, and the Columban Justice and Peace Office, among several others.
[53] While major charities such as CARE are based in the United States, there are few development advocacy organizations, Oxfam USA and Bread for the World being among the most prominent. InterAction, which serves as the coalition for more than 150 development and relief organizations in the United States, is also important. Newer groups include Bono's DATA (Debt, AIDS, Trade, Africa).
[54] Bono and Assayas 2005, 91.

Hatch of Utah, Representative Dennis Hastert of Illinois, and Representative Dick Armey of Texas.[55]

Because of the large number of gatekeepers, advocates developed multiple arguments to appeal to them. Adrian Lovett, former deputy director of Jubilee 2000 and later campaign director for Oxfam, noted that, in the case of Treasury officials and those with more of a focus on technical aspects of finance, one could argue that these were bad debts that were not going to be repaid. The spiritual appeal offered another approach. A third argument was that the United States had a chance to change its international image. One of those arguments typically worked.[56]

In March 1999, in the lead-up to Cologne President Clinton's plan for an enhanced HIPC initiative was announced. At the same time, US campaigners such as Tom Hart, director of government relations for the Episcopal Church, had formed a lobby group. Hart's group approached Congressman Jim Leach, a moderate Iowa Republican, who agreed to introduce a debt relief bill, HR 1095, on March 11, 1999, just days before President Clinton announced his plan. By approaching a Republican committee chair, campaigners made what proved to be an excellent tactical move to broaden their base of support. In the meantime, campaigners, particularly from Bread for the World, had encouraged members of Congress to co-sponsor the bill. Grassroots efforts by religious groups in the Midwest and the South made inroads, particularly with Bachus, an Alabama Republican known for being a "conservative's conservative," who became one of the bill's strongest supporters.[57] As chair of the House Banking Subcommittee on Domestic and International Monetary Policy, he could have blocked consideration of the bill. Conservatives such as Bachus attracted attention because their support was so unexpected.

Three prominent actors – Summers, Kasich, and Leach – were all persuaded that debt relief was the right thing to do based on technocratic ideas. While Summers, who had succeeded Robert Rubin as secretary of the Treasury in June 1999, had concerns about debt relief cutting off poor countries from capital markets, he ultimately

---

[55] Jonathan Peterson 2001. The Shriver family is a prominent American political family linked to the Kennedys. Eunice Shriver, younger sister of John F. Kennedy, is married to Robert Sargent Shriver. Their daughter Maria is married to bodybuilder/actor/Republican politician Arnold Schwarzenegger.
[56] Lovett 2003.   [57] Grunwald 1999.

recognized that those countries were unlikely to be getting much access. Moreover, in Summers' view, there was no good reason to maintain the pretense that these countries were creditworthy. Continuing defensive lending so countries could pay off old loans with new loans was "phony." Because these debts were not going to be paid anyway, it was sound financial practice to write them off.[58] Like Summers, Kasich found this argument appealing. According to Scott Hatch, a former Republican leadership staffer and confidant of Kasich, the Congressman responded because he thought debt relief was a viable way to free resources for poor countries to spend on education and health care.[59] Leach's support was motivated by a similar dynamic. His former staffer McCormick suggested the Congressman thought debt relief was the right thing to do, noting that Leach came at the issue more from a financial perspective than a religious one.[60] However, this argument alone was not sufficient to generate a majority coalition for debt relief.[61]

The religious case for debt relief had direct appeal to important individual lawmakers and also created some measure of political mobilization that pressured skeptics. Alongside activists and leaders such as Pat Robertson, prominent congressional Republicans – Bachus and Helms in particular – found the religious message compelling.[62] Asked about his position, Bachus said, "This bill is a gift of life. Jubilee 2000 is a celebration of the 2000th birthday of Christ . . . What more appropriate time to give to these poor in celebration of the birth of Jesus, who gave us life?"[63] Hart suggested that legislators such as Bachus were amenable to the message of Jubilee because it came from people with deep roots in local institutions.[64] Like Bachus, Helms was moved by his faith. Mark Lagon, former senior staff member to the Senate Foreign Relations Committee under Helms, suggested that Christian conservatives had reached the senator before his meeting with Bono. That meeting left Helms a "bit choked up about children in need,"

---

[58] Summers 2004.   [59] Hatch 2005.   [60] McCormick 2005.
[61] Evidence of the insufficiency of a technocratic argument is the 216 to 211 vote in July 2000 for an amendment that boosted the HIPC Trust Fund appropriation by $155 mn. It passed with only twenty-six crossover Republican votes, including a number of religious conservatives including Representatives Aderholt, Bachus, Cubin, Ehlers, English, Smith-NJ, and Wolf.
[62] On the broader mobilization of religious conservatives on international issues, see Hertzke 2004.
[63] Quoted in McManus 1999.   [64] Hart 2001.

even as he insisted that debt relief should not end up supporting corruption.[65]

Why had Helms and others not experienced this epiphany earlier? Part of the story is about agency by advocates. The appeal to them on religious grounds had not been made. Helms' support was not foreordained, but an appeal based on religious morality was more likely to succeed in the United States than in less religious countries, particularly among lawmakers such as Helms, who had a record of policy decisions guided by moral concerns.

How did these gatekeepers then exercise influence over their peers? Hatch argued that Kasich's influence was based less on his role as a committee chair and more on his informal influence, with Kasich using "political muscle" and "personal credibility" with his Republican colleagues as a fiscal hawk and solid conservative to get debt relief through the House.[66] Helms' influence on this question – like that of Kasich – was also more informal. Lagon said the "striking thing" about Senator Helms' support for debt relief was that "it left people with the idea, 'Oh well, if Helms thinks this is okay, it must be the right thing to do.'" It was certainly "hard to be outflanked on the right." In Lagon's view, Helms' support could potentially sway up to twenty-five of the most conservative and committed free marketeers in the Senate.[67] In sum, their acceptance of new causal and principled beliefs about the efficacy and legitimacy of debt relief gave their congressional allies, who knew little about the issue, the confidence that the measure was worthy of support.

Gatekeepers who remained opposed to debt relief – Sonny Callahan and Phil Gramm – appear to have been moved in the end by political pressure, lobbying, and shaming. In the weeks before the October 2000 vote, Pat Robertson asked Texas viewers of the 700 Club to "let Senator Gramm know that this is a good initiative."[68] Another pressure was a threat of a presidential veto of the budget. Summers likened the bargaining process over the omnibus appropriations bill in fall 2000 to a "game of chicken." For opponents, the specter of a veto forced them to ask if they wanted to be known for denying education spending just to prevent spending on debt relief.[69]

When I talked with Representative Callahan, he argued that given the ubiquity of veto threats that he "never paid much attention to that."

[65] Lagon 2005.   [66] Hatch 2005.   [67] Lagon 2005.
[68] Quoted in Hoover 2001.   [69] Summers 2004.

He did not object to debt relief but worried that without "contingencies" states would return to their bad behavior. He acknowledged the role of lobbying pressure: "All I did was make a little fuss over it and I incurred the wrath of the church community worldwide." Callahan suggested that he and other members of Congress were ultimately responsive because they were getting a lot of flak in their districts from the church community. "I was always swimming upstream," Callahan said, "but I had a powerful enough oar to delay" the appropriation for foreign operations "against the will of a majority of Congress." Realizing supporters had the votes to amend the appropriations bill on the floor, Callahan let the appropriation for debt relief go forward.[70] As Callahan admitted, "The debt relief issue is now a speeding train. We've got the Pope and every missionary in the world involved in this thing, and they persuaded just about everyone here that this is the noble thing to do."[71] So, while moral reasons motivated many supporters, opponents found themselves subject to the piety of their peers, evidence that a well-chosen frame can elicit the semi-coercive pressures of social shaming in the absence of a well-financed campaign.

Japan

The original religious appeal of Jubilee 2000 lacked local cultural foundations in Japan, and the costs of debt relief, while a small share of its GDP, were much larger than for other G-7 countries. Thus, Japan represented a case of "hostility" in which we would not expect advocates to be successful unless Japan were coerced or the issue were reframed to appeal to a different set of values. Reframing the issue as a test of Japan's international contribution proved compelling, moving Japan from "hostility" to being a case of "costly moral action."

While the Japanese public was generally supportive of foreign aid, the government, particularly in the Finance Ministry – the dominant gatekeeper – found debt relief inimical.[72] Where did these views come

---

[70] Callahan 2005.   [71] Quoted in Kahn 2000.

[72] Oversight and control of overseas development assistance in Japan have been traditionally fragmented among several powerful ministries. Until a major government reorganization in 2001, overseas development loans fell under the aegis of the Ministry of Foreign Affairs (MOFA), the Ministry of International Trade and Industry (MITI), the Ministry of Finance, and the Economic Planning Agency in the prime minister's Cabinet Office. Another nineteen

from? To understand the evolution of Japan's policy on debt relief, one has to retrace the roots of Japan's foreign assistance programs. Japan's overseas development assistance (ODA) has evolved from its original mercantilist origins. In the 1950s and 1960s, Japan's aim of assistance was to promote its own economic growth.[73] In that context, commercial interests "reigned supreme" as Japan sought to use foreign assistance to create export markets and to obtain natural resources. Traditionally, Japanese aid was concentrated in Asia but, beginning in the 1970s, Japan diversified beyond Asia and began to use aid for more strategic and diplomatic purposes. At the same time, Japan began to direct more of its assistance through multilateral institutions. As the US economy stagnated, it cut back on foreign assistance. Japan's economic growth brought increased expectations, particularly on the part of the United States, of greater burden-sharing by Japan.[74]

Given constitutional restrictions on playing a military role in international affairs, the Japanese chose instead to become the biggest provider of foreign assistance, building on their experience in East

ministries and agencies were in some way involved in the administration of technical assistance in the implementation and oversight of overseas development assistance (Japan Forum on International Relations 1998). The most important ministry dealing with overseas development loans and debt issues is the Ministry of Finance, with MOFA second. Historically, official overseas development assistance (ODA) loans were made by the Overseas Economic Cooperation Fund (OECF) with loans and loan guarantees also extended by the Ex-Im Bank of Japan (JEXIM). The two merged in 1999 to form the Japan Bank for International Cooperation (JBIC). Until January 2001, JBIC was jointly supervised by the Ministry of Finance and the Economic Planning Agency, the latter overseeing ODA loans (previously the OECF side) and the former focusing on others (the JEXIM side). After the government reorganization in January 2001, the Economic Planning Agency was abolished and merged into the Cabinet Office. OECF loan oversight was transferred to MOFA, and MOFA was also explicitly tasked to coordinate ODA issues within the government. Whereas technical expertise on debt issues rests largely with the Ministry of Finance, MOFA is tasked more with the diplomatic issues (including G-8 summit meetings) and overall coordination of Japan's foreign assistance. For a more extended discussion of the structure of Japanese foreign assistance, see Busby 2004a. In late 2008, the concessional loans side of JBIC merged with the Japanese International Cooperation Agency (JICA), the agency that coordinates Japanese ODA. Until 2003, JICA had been under the aegis of MOFA, but it became independent after a government reorganization.
[73] Pempel 1978.
[74] Yasutomo 1995. See also Islam 1991, 13; Kato 2002, 106; Lincoln 1993.

Asia. Japan, in an effort to demonstrate its role as a reliable ally and as a great power, decided that ODA would be its international contribution. As Dennis Yasutomo argues, "ODA is considered a key to Japan's status and survival as an accepted member of the world community."[75] At the 1977 Bonn summit, Japan announced its intentions to double its provision of ODA in five years. It was able to do so in three years, and this increase proved to be the first of several aid-doubling plans.[76] Edward Lincoln suggests that the Japanese did not have a clear idea of how the country could make an international contribution and that it sought to increase foreign aid as a way of keeping good standing in the international club of rich countries.[77] Moreover, initially there was more emphasis on quantity than quality, though this may well have been motivated by efforts to close the burden-sharing deficit with the United States.[78]

The energy crisis of the 1970s prompted Japan and other creditors to revisit the terms for loans to poor countries. In 1978, Japan created a grant aid for development program; in exchange for debt repayment, Japan would provide partial debt relief through grants.[79] The debt crisis of the 1980s devastated the economies of middle-income countries, particularly in Latin America. Japan sought to recycle its enormous trade surpluses of nearly $100 billion through increased development assistance. By 1985, Japan was the world's largest creditor. Between 1986 and 1989, Japan devised three debt relief plans totaling $65 billion. By the 1990s, Japan held the number two position in financial institutions in terms of contributions and voting shares. Japanese support for overseas development, which had long remained at 80 percent, began to waver as the Japanese economic miracle ran out of steam in the early 1990s.[80] While Japan moved to improve the quality of its lending, being the top donor for much of the 1990s was still a source of pride. A 1998 advisory committee seeking to reform ODA noted

---

[75] Yasutomo 1995, 3–6.
[76] Yasutomo 1995. In 1980, ODA totaled $3.3 bn; by 1986, it had reached $50 bn, and then $70–75 bn in 1993.
[77] Lincoln 1993, 116. These motivations for cultivating global respect and goodwill are discussed by Tamamoto 1993 and Islam 1991.
[78] Orr notes that some of the incoherence in foreign aid programs stemmed from interagency rivalry (Orr 1990), which is supported by Lancaster 1999.
[79] Japan, Ministry of Foreign Affairs 1999.   [80] Yasutomo 1995.

that development assistance was one of Japan's few diplomatic tools by which it could achieve foreign policy objectives:

> There is little point to being overly fixated on claiming the No. 1 spot, especially as quality may be more important than quantity, but at the same time the title of top ODA donor is no small coup for Japan's foreign policy.[81]

Japan experienced new demands for debt relief just as it became a major lender on the international stage and simultaneously faced an unprecedented economic slump. By the late 1990s, the international political environment had changed, with persistent poverty, particularly in sub-Saharan Africa, motivating debt forgiveness.

Japan, however, opposed these debt relief plans,[82] in part because of ingrained antipathy to moral hazard on the part of its financial technocrats.[83] Japanese views on moral hazard were summed up by Tamaki Tsukada of the Ministry of Foreign Affairs: "Just giving money like a handout isn't good for the [recipient] country in the long run."[84] Given their own experience in East Asia, the Japanese were very uneasy with debt relief. The Japanese belief in the importance of self-help, noted a former official in the Economic Cooperation Bureau of the Ministry of Foreign Affairs, derives from their experience after World War II. Japan was able to develop by using loans productively and repaying its debts.

Japan fostered high rates of growth in Asia using a similar strategy. This became its "central way of thinking" when the country gave aid. Loans used for productive purposes became a way countries could help themselves and learn "credit culture" and responsible fiscal management. Forgiving debt would invite moral hazard and might reward countries that adopted bad policies while penalizing countries that had the right policy and made efforts to repay. Another potential problem with debt relief, the official mentioned, was the reluctance by Japanese taxpayers to extend new loans to countries whose debts were canceled. Grants would have to be given for the foreseeable future, but that would likely lead to a lower flow of new resources to those countries. Faced with that dilemma, Japan let developing countries choose

---

[81] Japan Forum on International Relations 1998, 22.
[82] Katsouris 1998; Oxfam 1998. See also Chote 1999; Collins 1999; Jubilee+ 2001; Undated.
[83] Horiuchi 1999.   [84] Castellano 1999.

whether to accept debt relief and no new loans or keep trying to repay old loans in exchange for being eligible for new lending.[85]

Takehiko Nakao, then director of the coordination division in the Ministry of Finance's International Bureau, echoed these comments.[86] Debt relief, he noted, was initially seen as a very radical idea in Japan. Nakao also expressed concern that debt relief would jeopardize the "credit culture" of developing countries. From its own experience, Japan recognized the need to borrow money to develop. Japan believed there was simply not enough money for developing countries to depend on grants. Debt relief, it was feared, would cut other developing countries off from capital markets. To get the kind of higher growth rates a number of Asian countries experienced, developing countries would need private sources of finance. The Japanese believed that their ODA loans had been indispensable tools that had contributed to the long-term growth and development of their neighbors; such loans had built much of the vital infrastructure of Malaysia, Thailand, and South Korea, among others. Japanese policies in Asia were regarded as very important elements in accelerating growth in those countries, before international finance markets were well developed.[87]

Despite Japan's opposition to debt relief, once the United States had made a commitment at Cologne in summer 1999 and expanded it that fall, the Japanese were under intense pressure to yield. Fellow creditors and advocates alike used international isolation, embarrassment, and shaming efforts to tag the Japanese as out-of-step with international opinion.[88] While Japan signed on to the enhanced debt relief program at Cologne, it remained unenthusiastic about complete bilateral relief. In the lead-up to the Okinawa G-8 meetings in July 2000, Japan announced it would accept 100 percent bilateral relief.[89]

Japan's change in policy actually unfolded in stages. Continuing a practice dating back to 1978, Japan initially decided in 2000 that it would reimburse debt service in the form of grants. It was not until December 2002 when the government announced that the Japan Bank

---

[85] Japanese MOFA official-a 2004.
[86] From 2002 until July 2004, Nakao served as director of development policy and was Japan's head delegate to the Paris Club. From 1998 to 2000, he was director of international organizations, charged with oversight of G-7 summits and the IMF.
[87] Takehiko Nakao 2004a. These concerns are echoed by Rieffel 2003, 181.
[88] MacAskill 1998; MacAskill, Pallister, and Norton-Taylor 1998.
[89] Takehiko Nakao 2004b.

of International Cooperation (JBIC) would actually cancel all ODA debts of eligible HIPCs; it would do this by using the bank's surpluses, which had increased as East Asian countries repaid their loans.

Before the 2000 Okinawa summit, many members of the G-8 started discussing the idea of voluntary cancellation of 100 percent of non-ODA loans. Instead of waiting, Japan decided to go ahead, since it was preferable for it to be a Japanese initiative than one they were pushed into.[90] Japan's April 2000 announcement (along with those from Germany and France) that 100 percent of bilateral, non-ODA debt would be reduced was greeted with some skepticism. Instead of writing off the debt, Japan decided it would "reimburse debt service in the form of grants for the purchase of Japanese goods."[91] As noted previously, this practice dated back to the late 1970s when Japan, responding to a request from the United Nations Conference on Trade and Development (UNCTAD), reduced the debt burden of developing countries adversely affected by the first oil crisis.[92]

Critics of this program suggested that it was a reflection of the country's past practice of using development assistance to facilitate Japanese exports. Since the grant aid would be in yen and could only be used to buy goods from OECD countries, Japanese companies were seen as likely beneficiaries. Critics also charged that Japan was discouraging some countries from applying for the HIPC program by suggesting that they would be ineligible for receiving new loans from Japan.[93] In December 2002, this program was discontinued. The government announced that JBIC would cancel all ODA debts of eligible HIPC countries by using the bank's account surpluses.[94]

Why did Japan maintain the grant aid for debt relief program in April 2000? Here, it is clear that Japan's thinking on debt relief had not really changed. Japan was a reluctant participant because the government was not convinced it was the best policy. A former MOFA official suggested that the Japanese government maintained the grant aid program because of its concern that the credit culture among borrowers would be damaged through debt cancellation. The grant aid program was also seen as a way Japan could exercise some control

[90] Takehiko Nakao 2004a.   [91] Jubilee 2000 2000b.
[92] Japan, Ministry of Foreign Affairs 1999. For a more full discussion, see Crane 1984.
[93] Jubilee 2000 2000a.   [94] Japan, Ministry of Foreign Affairs 2002.

over how debtors used the funds, preventing their use for military goods. However, the official argued that Japanese leaders discovered the program suffered from several problems. Countries would retain high levels of debt for a very long time since those reaching a completion point would have their debts rescheduled over a forty-year period. Moreover, some countries simply lacked the foreign exchange to be able to pay back their debts in return for equivalent grants and would be subject to additional accumulation of interest while the debts remained on the books.[95]

What then led to the discontinuation of the scheme in December 2002? Finance and Foreign Ministry officials, including Nakao, initiated discussion to eliminate the grant aid for debt relief scheme in summer 2000. Despite its many reservations about debt relief, Japan found itself subject to several criticisms from NGOs about its grant aid program. In Nakao's estimation, the past practice of offering grant aid for debt relief had become embedded policy, and no one sought to make changes in 2000 because it was assumed to be too difficult.

By 2002, the situation was different. The year before, several problems had created a need for reform in the foreign aid architecture, leading to the creation of an independent advisory group.[96] That group proposed various measures, including a reexamination of the grant aid program. In December 2002, the government announced that the relevant ODA debts owed to JBIC would be canceled, and that JBIC would use its surplus revenue to pay for the major part of this measure.[97] Some portion of the cost of this measure would be subsidized by contributions from the central government budget. Between 1998 and 2000, JBIC's finances improved, in part because of continual replenishment by the Japanese government, but also because lower interest rates reduced its borrowing costs. The government realized that it could use JBIC's profits to cancel much of the debt, and

---

[95] Japanese MOFA official-a 2004.

[96] An embezzlement scandal in the Ministry of Foreign Affairs in early 2001 was a contributing factor to the formation of the advisory group (Takehiko Nakao 2004a). This account is supported by Japanese MOFA official-a 2004.

[97] All ODA debts coming under the enhanced HIPC initiative would be canceled as well as loans from some countries eligible for debt relief under the Trade and Development Board (TDB) meeting of UNCTAD in 1978. This meant that Japan wrote off the debts of a handful of non-HIPC countries, notably more than $1.2 bn (146.8 trillion yen) in Bangladeshi debts.

therefore debt cancellation under HIPC would require a much smaller budget outlay.[98]

Although the mechanics of how Japan came up with the funds to pay for debt relief are clear, we still need to understand why Japan ultimately decided to change its policies. Essentially, the argument was recast by activists and other creditor governments as something Japan could do to be a solid contributor to the international community. In the lead-up to the G-8 meeting in Okinawa, Marc Castellano of the Japanese Economic Institute saw Japan's changing policy in these terms: "The country's reputation as a global leader also is on the line."[99] Henry Northover, of the UK-based Catholic charity CAFOD, argued that the Japanese were not going to stand out against the majority within the G-7. His sense was that the Japanese saw themselves as responsible members of the international community and were loath to step out of line.[100]

This interpretation of Japanese policy is supported by my interviews with Japanese officials. Takehiko Nakao of the Ministry of Finance provided an authoritative account. Japan, Nakao said, appreciated that other G-7 countries supported debt relief. If all other G-7 countries support an initiative, Japan tends to agree. Nakao said that Japan attaches a lot of importance to G-7 summits, the UN General Assembly, and the OECD. While the United States–Japan bilateral security relationship is strong, Japan is not a member of the North Atlantic Treaty Organization (NATO). Since the country is limited in its ability to participate in military operations, Japan wanted to be recognized as a good member and contributor to the international community. To that end, Japan assumed a big responsibility by contributing to the IMF and the World Bank and through bilateral ODA.[101]

Some might ascribe this policy change to coercion. The picture of intransigence and policy movement in the face of international bullying is familiar; the Japanese word for this kind of external pressure is *gaiatsu*.[102] However, other G-7 creditors were unlikely to punish the

---

[98] Takehiko Nakao 2004a. That conclusion is supported by a Japanese MOFA official (a 2004). Interestingly, contrary to expectations, the media did not criticize cancellation of debt as a failure of Japanese ODA policies, and Nakao said that many NGOs in this area appreciated this decision.
[99] Castellano 2000.   [100] Northover 2003.
[101] Takehiko Nakao 2004b. On reputational concerns in Japanese foreign assistance, see also Lumsdaine 1993.
[102] Schoppa 1993.

Japanese for failure to support debt relief. Donor agreements are not legally binding; instead they are recommendations to sovereign governments. An IMF report on free-riding behavior and debt relief found that "moral suasion" was the primary tool donors possessed or were willing to use to persuade recalcitrant creditors.[103] Leonard Schoppa argues that *gaiatsu* is more likely to be successful when "latent support for foreign demands exists outside the privileged elite."[104] External pressure must go through domestic actors and find bases of support.

What about ascribing this change to domestic political pressure? Japanese civil society tends to be very weak. In her 1999 book, Carol Lancaster estimated there to be four hundred NGOs working on development issues, most of them small and financially weak.[105] As discussed more fully in Chapter 5 on HIV/AIDS, the historically restrictive rules for forming non-profit organizations in Japan have contributed to the financial and organizational weakness of Japanese civil society. In my 2004 study, Japanese development NGOs tended to be the weakest and least well-financed of four countries with Germany, the United States, and the United Kingdom all having better resourced and staffed organizations.[106]

Japanese campaigners support this observation. Yoko Fukawa of the Pacific Asia Resource Center (PARC) was one of the leaders of the Jubilee 2000 campaign in Japan. She noted that the number of activists involved in Jubilee 2000 was very low compared to Europe. This modest level of advocacy was reflected in minimal public awareness. Fukawa stated that the "Japanese people do not know what the debt issue is." Nonetheless, Japanese NGOs were able to collect 500,000 signatures to petitions in Japan, which Fukawa thought an unusually high number. Interestingly, more than 40 percent came from Protestant and Catholic groups alone, in a country where only 1 percent of the population is Christian. She noted that the Jubilee 2000 message, with its Christian appeal, made it difficult for campaigners in Japan, because opponents could say the campaigners were puppets of Europeans. They sought to avoid this problem by focusing on debt relief rather than the

---

[103] Nankani and Geithner 2003.   [104] Schoppa 1993, 385.
[105] Takehiko Nakao 2004a. On the rather limited role of the prime minister, the Diet and NGOs in foreign aid, see Lancaster 1999, 176–177.
[106] Busby 2004a. This conclusion is also reached by JANIC 2001–2004; Lancaster 1999, 177–179; Söderberg 2002. It is also discussed in relation to environmental NGOs by Schreurs 2002.

Jubilee 2000 campaign name, which was something of a stumbling block.[107] In the lead-up to the 2000 Okinawa summit, the broader global community of Jubilee 2000 activists sought to compensate for Japan's weak domestic organizations. However, unlike Cologne in Germany, Okinawa was a remote location and, in the wake of the WTO protests in Seattle the previous year, Japan's visa process was highly restrictive.[108] Despite the limits on NGO activity within Japan, NGO criticism of Japan fed into the reappraisal of Japan's position on debt. The Japanese government was aware and took note of the Jubilee 2000 campaign.[109] For example, before the G-8 meeting, the campaigners sent postcards and held a weekly demonstration outside the Japanese embassy in London. The embassy took these activities seriously enough to count the number of demonstrators and send back the tally to Japan.[110]

As Nakao noted, Japan wanted to do a good thing for developing countries and be appreciated by the international community. However, Japan found the demands of the debt campaign to be extreme and not a particularly good idea in terms of the potential damage to the creditworthiness of poor countries. Nonetheless, with widespread public support for debt relief around the world, Japan was willing to reconsider its previous position. The religious appeal for debt relief did not resonate in Japan. Northover noted that the Japanese often said debt relief was not part of Asian culture and that debts have to be repaid. However, as he also pointed out, Japan had written off some of its own domestic debt in the banking sector and with bullet trains.[111] In spite of this, the Japanese had long held values about thrift and about what countries at a different stage of development ought to be doing to grow. As Lincoln argued:

This intellectual position in favor of loans is a central feature of what might be considered a Japanese approach to foreign aid. Charity based on immediate humanitarian concerns has played a far less important role in Japanese society in general than it has in the United States or some other Western nations. But programs to reduce the need for charity in the long run have been important... Foreign aid loans, then, are a means of enforcing a discipline on development nations consistent with this philosophy.[112]

---

[107] Fukawa 2005.   [108] Fukawa 2005.   [109] Japanese MOFA official-a 2004.
[110] Barrett 2003; Lovett 2003.   [111] Herskovitz Undated; Northover 2003.
[112] Lincoln 1993, 123.

However, saying the millennial frame for developing country debt relief did not match Japan's values is quite different than saying there are no circumstances under which debt relief could be framed to be consistent with Japan's values. The frame – where debt relief was seen as a test of Japan's international contribution – tapped into the domestic conversation about "internationalizing" Japan, which had been nearly a national "obsession" in the 1980s.[113] By the 1990s, polls consistently showed that more than 80 percent of the Japanese public thought that "internationalizing" Japan was either "necessary to ensure Japan's future prosperity" or appropriate because "now that Japan has become a major developed country, it has to become more internationalized."[114] Reframing debt relief as a diplomatic issue also empowered the Foreign Ministry in internal bureaucratic debates with the other main gatekeeper, the Finance Ministry.

In a broader sense, Japanese national interest could have suffered from incremental "reputational" damage as an unreliable partner.[115] I explore the role of reputational motives more fully in the next chapter on climate change, where I argue that concerns about national prestige and trying to be good allies and global citizens are more deeply rooted than a materialist, cost–benefit calculation. As Robert Keohane argued, normative foundations ultimately underpin support for "diffuse reciprocity." He noted that "the actor making a short-run sacrifice does not know that future benefits will flow from comparable restraint by others, and can hardly be regarded as making precise calculations of expected utility."[116] Indeed, Japanese decisions to be reliable cooperators are based on an embedded idea of material interest that, in a sense, has become an end in itself.[117]

---

[113] Ohta 1995, 247.   [114] JPOLL Undated.
[115] Simmons 1998.   [116] Keohane 1982, 342.   [117] Legro 2005b, 7.

4 | Climate change: the hardest problem in the world

In mid-November 2000, the US elections remained in suspended animation while the world awaited the outcome of the Bush–Gore contest. Continents away, delegates gathered for the climate change negotiations in The Hague, Netherlands. Climate campaigners from the Dutch branch of the environmental group Friends of the Earth built a dike of sandbags, nearly two and a half meters high and stretching for 500 meters around the conference center, a symbolic reminder of the potential disruption posed by climate change.[1] With signs that read "You've sunk the world" and "Industry Lobbyists (and the government officials who do their bidding): How Will Your Grandchildren Forgive You?" activists pushed delegates to maintain strong environmental standards as they negotiated the implementation rules for the Kyoto Protocol.[2]

For officials of the departing Clinton administration, this was their final hurrah, their last chance to influence climate policy. While the Kyoto Protocol had dim prospects for ratification in the United States, a successful set of negotiations might have made it more politically palatable for the US Senate to eventually provide their advice and consent. Moreover, a breakthrough in The Hague could have made it harder for President Clinton's successor to back away from the international negotiations. It was not to be.

European and American diplomats had a falling-out in the final days of the negotiations, in part as a consequence of the kinds of normative and electoral pressures they were facing from advocates. The primary basis of disagreement was the question of "sinks" or how much credit countries would receive for having large forest reserves take carbon dioxide out of the air. European negotiators and environmentalists were concerned that countries would be able to meet their Kyoto

---

[1] Martens and Rafferty 2002.
[2] The Kyoto Protocol is the 1997 climate agreement negotiated in Japan's ancient capital. Kyoto bound some rich countries to significantly reduce their greenhouse gas emissions by the period 2008–2012.

commitments through existing land-use practices and thus not have to alter their environmentally destructive behavior. In the end, the two sides could not agree on a common figure for how much credit to give the United States for its forests.[3] (As an aside: the Europeans would later grant Russia, Japan, and Canada generous credits for their forests to save the Kyoto agreement.)

By mid-December, the US Supreme Court decided in George W. Bush's favor on the recount of ballots in Florida. Shortly after taking office, the new Bush administration declared the Kyoto Protocol "dead" and sought to undermine international climate policy for the remainder of its eight years.[4] Despite the US refusal to ratify the Kyoto Protocol, the agreement remained on life support, bolstered by much of the rest of the world. By October 2008, more than 180 countries had ratified it. Most interesting was the decision by countries such as Canada and Japan to ratify Kyoto. Both accepted significant emissions reductions targets under the agreement, yet they faced emissions profiles more like the United States. In this regard, their decision to ratify Kyoto most closely resembled cases of "costly moral action" (see Table 2.2).

In this chapter, I seek to explain why the United States rejected the Kyoto Protocol while Japan and Canada ratified the agreement. In so doing, my examination of climate change is part of a larger discussion of why some principled advocacy movements succeed in some places and fail in others. I conclude that countries are willing to accept costly normative or moral commitments championed by principled advocacy movements, but their willingness to accept costs has limits. With respect to Canada and Japan, I argue that prestige motivations ultimately drove their decisions to ratify. I contend that this form of reputational concern is not purely instrumentally rational. Reinforcing the argument of previous chapters, I also recognize that treaty ratification is institutionally far easier in Canada and Japan than in the United States.

Although Japan and Canada ratified the Kyoto Protocol, by 2008 they had failed to enact significant implementing legislation, in part

---

[3] The United States initially asked for 320 million tons of carbon (MtC) credits; it subsequently reduced its demand to 125 MtC in credits and then 75 during the negotiations. Frank Loy, the US delegation lead negotiator, reportedly went even lower to 40 or 50 MtC in credits (Kerr 2000; Müller 2000, 94).

[4] Kluger 2001; Pianin 2001b.

because the United States had done nothing about its own emissions. Advocates were in part to blame for this predicament. Having prodded and praised legislators for accepting deep emissions reductions in Kyoto, advocates largely defined the terms of what constituted environmentally sound behavior in the climate arena for politicians who wanted to get credit for being green. This dynamic set up Kyoto for inevitable failure, given the resistance to ratification by key gatekeepers in the United States in the face of the potentially high costs of implementation.

This chapter unfolds in four sections, beginning with an overview of the climate problem and emergent responses. In the second section, I critique a material explanation as the only rationale for state ratification of international obligations, including the Kyoto Protocol. In the third section, I focus on how the environmental crisis frame evoked by activists was tied to policy solutions that were more expensive for some countries than for others. In that context, the relative ease of treaty ratification in Canada and Japan compared to the United States enabled them to ratify, despite their facing high costs. In the final section, I complement the institutional discussion of the third section by reviewing the motivations of Japanese and Canadian leaders and by extending the discussion from Chapter 2 on values and non-material motives to include concerns about reputation and international prestige. I conclude with a short discussion of the implications for advocacy.

Background on climate change negotiations

Despite almost a century of knowledge of the possibility of global warming (also referred to as "the greenhouse effect"[5] or "climate change"), the issue emerged on the policy agenda only in the late 1980s. By the mid-1980s, environmentalists picked up warnings from the

---

[5] The "greenhouse effect" is a natural phenomenon that warms the earth to be sufficiently habitable for life. The greenhouse effect refers to the atmospheric gas conditions around the earth which are transparent to incoming ultraviolet radiation but absorb large amounts of outgoing infrared radiation (heat), thereby trapping it in the atmosphere and raising ambient temperatures. Global warming refers to an enhanced warming effect resulting from increased concentrations of greenhouse gases (GHGs) that, in turn, keep more heat in the atmosphere (Schneider 1997, 55). Global surface temperature data show a 0.5 °C increase over the last 100 years and a 30 percent increase in GHGs in the past 200 years (Shogren and Toman 2000, 5).

scientific community.[6] A number of entrepreneurial scientists working with advocacy NGOs helped politicize the issue and translate scientific concern into the basis for government action.[7] By the late 1980s and early 1990s, politicians (and the media) were sufficiently aware of "global warming" that they folded the issue into international environmental negotiations.

The US Congress held hearings in 1988 to assess National Aeronautics and Space Administration (NASA) scientist James Hansen's claims that the earth's surface temperature seemed to be rising in concert with man's emissions of carbon dioxide. The scientific community was then further mobilized to assess the validity of this finding and the implications for humans and natural ecosystems.[8] In that same year, the Canadian government hosted an important meeting on the global atmosphere that was attended by scientists, government ministers and civil servants, industrialists, and environmentalists. While not a treaty negotiating session, the participants agreed on a statement that called on developed countries to cut CO_2 emissions by 20 percent from 1987 levels by 2005. The "Toronto goal" was one of the first international efforts to set "targets and timetables" for emissions reductions of GHGs.[9] Soon after the Toronto conference, the Intergovernmental Panel on Climate Change (IPCC) was established to summarize the peer-reviewed science on the subject.[10]

The transnational advocacy network for climate change came into being in 1989 when an umbrella organization, the Climate Action Network (CAN), was created to coordinate the NGO response. By 2008, CAN had more than 365 organizations from 85 countries participating in its network, with seven regional offices across the world coordinating activity. Network partners include many new organizations

---

[6] Sarewitz and Pielke 2000.   [7] See chapter 3 in Betsill 2000.

[8] Though knowledge of the potential for human-inspired climate change was recognized in the 1950s (and even as far back as 1898), the issue did not really begin to capture the attention of the scientific community or policymakers until the late 1970s (Morrissey 1998).

[9] Haigh 1996; Pomerance 1989.

[10] This has been the most influential of the many research efforts on climate change. The IPCC is composed of more than 2,500 scientists who, rather than conduct independent research of their own, evaluate and summarize published and peer-reviewed studies. It has issued four influential assessments (1990, 1995, 2001, and 2007) that have successively sharpened their judgment of the human role in climate change; see www.ipcc.ch. For a detailed review of the history of scientific inquiry on climate change, see Morrissey 2000, 42.

as well as established environmental groups such as Greenpeace, Friends of the Earth, and the World Wide Fund for Nature (WWF), among others. CAN also includes groups representing students, labor, faith concerns, environmental justice, relief organizations, and local governments. This diffuse, transnational network organized around a common concern in preventing dangerous climate change leads me to classify it as a social movement, even if it includes established interest groups.[11]

These developments set in motion a series of international meetings geared to produce a treaty for signature at the 1992 Earth Summit. The final negotiations of the United Nations Framework Convention on Climate Change (UNFCCC) took place in Rio de Janeiro, Brazil.[12] However, prompted by lobbying by the George H. W. Bush administration, no binding targets on CO_2 emissions were negotiated.[13]

Subsequent studies produced near unanimity of scientific judgment that global warming was indeed a serious concern,[14] giving incentive for additional negotiations on specific commitments. In 1995, at the first Conference of Parties (COP)[15] meeting in Berlin, states

[11] While not inclusive of all non-governmental organizations mobilized on climate change, the group is the main transnational advocacy hub for NGO activity, as represented by the daily newsletter *ECO*, prepared during the annual Conference of Parties to the UN climate negotiations. See the CAN website and regional website for more information on members: www. climatenetwork.org/.

[12] The UNFCCC was signed by 154 nations at Rio and later ratified by 181 nations. It came into force in March 1994 (Sarewitz and Pielke 2000). On September 8, 1992, President Bush transmitted the UNFCCC to the Senate for advice and consent, and the full Senate consented to ratification on October 7, 1992, with a two-thirds' majority vote (Justus and Fletcher 2001).

[13] Though emissions reductions pledges at Rio were non-binding, 1990 emissions levels were established as the base year at which level countries should seek to stabilize emissions.

[14] The IPCC published its second report in 1995 which concluded there was a "discernible human influence on global climate" (quoted in Shogren and Toman 2000, 7). Average surface temperatures were projected to rise by between 1 and 3 °C by 2100 over 1990 levels. To stabilize emissions at twice pre-industrial levels, the report concluded, global emissions needed to be 50 percent below then-current levels.

[15] There have now been fifteen negotiating rounds or COP meetings of the UNFCCC since 1995: COP-1 Berlin (spring 1995), COP-2 Geneva (July 1996), COP-3 Kyoto (December 1997), COP-4 Buenos Aires (November 1998), COP-5 Bonn (October–November 1999), COP-6 The Hague (November 2000), COP-7 Marrakesh (October–November 2001), COP-8 New Delhi (October–November 2002), COP-9 Milan (December 2003), COP-10 Buenos Aires (December 2004), COP-11 Montreal (December 2005),

agreed that voluntary targets would not be enough and that a round of negotiations would be needed to identify what were enigmatically referred to as Quantified Emission Limitation or Reduction Objectives (QELROs).[16] Importantly, the principle of "differentiated responsibilities" was recognized in Berlin, meaning that developing countries were exempt from having to make any binding commitments through this process. In Geneva the following year, the United States went beyond the ambiguous QELRO terminology and formally embraced a "realistic, verifiable and binding medium-term emissions target."[17] Despite the tentative steps to move closer to the European position, the United States, along with the loosely aligned group of states JUSSCANNZ,[18] continued to clash with the Europeans and developing countries over the institutional climate architecture. The Americans pushed for a multi-gas regime, emissions trading, carbon sinks, and credit for action in developing countries, while the Europeans and environmental campaigners insisted that domestic action be the primary basis of emissions reductions.

Going into COP-3, the European Union's (EU) Environment Council, composed of the environment ministers from member governments, made an informal proposal in March 1997 to cut the combined emissions of three greenhouse gases (CO_2, methane, and nitrous oxide) in industrialized countries by 15 percent by 2010.[19] At the end of September 1997, Japan announced a −5 percent target for greenhouse gases, with countries with better energy efficiency or higher population growth eligible for lower reductions targets.[20] The Clinton administration, for its part, announced on October 22, 1997, a target

---

COP-12 Nairobi (November 2006), COP-13 Bali (December 2007), COP-14 Poznan (December 2008), and COP-15 Copenhagen (December 2009). Once the Kyoto Protocol entered into force, the Conference of Parties to the United Nations Framework Convention also doubled as the Meeting of Parties (MOP) to the protocol. COP-11 represented the first Meeting of Parties (MOP-1) since Kyoto entered into force.

[16] The Berlin negotiations are described in Grubb, Vrolijk, and Brack 1999 and Oberthür and Ott 1999.

[17] Wirth 1996.

[18] JUSSCANNZ consisted of Japan, the United States, Switzerland, Canada, Australia, Norway, and New Zealand. Later, this group came to be known as the Umbrella Group (Oberthür and Ott 1999, 17–18).

[19] Oberthür and Ott 1999, 55.

[20] Oberthür and Ott 1999, 117. The Japanese energy efficiency proposal meant that Japan's 5% reduction would have actually been 2.5%, Germany's 3.7%, etc.

of stabilizing emissions of all six greenhouse gases at 1990 levels by 2008–2012.[21]

In December 1997, negotiations on these targets culminated in the Kyoto Protocol through which a number of industrial countries (so-called Annex I or Appendix B countries)[22] committed themselves to reductions in CO_2 (and five other greenhouse gases).[23] For the three major greenhouse gases, CO_2, methane, and nitrous oxide, Annex I countries pledged to reduce average emissions by 6%–8% below 1990 levels by the "commitment period" between 2008 and 2012. The United States, at the time the single largest emitter, with 23% of the world's CO_2 emissions, committed to a 7% reduction after Vice President Al Gore made a last-minute intervention at Kyoto to help strike a compromise.[24] Europe collectively agreed to an 8% reduction while Japan and Canada agreed to a 6% reduction. However, the Kyoto commitment included the use of forests as sinks, reducing the US actual obligation to about a 4% reduction.[25]

In June 1998, the EU negotiated an intra-EU burden-sharing agreement or "bubble" by which to achieve its −8% Kyoto target. The bubble allowed some countries, such as Germany and the UK, to accept ambitious emissions reductions targets (−21% and −12.5% respectively), while poorer industrializing members committed to restrain the rate of emissions growth (e.g., Ireland +13%, Spain +15%) (see Table 4.1 for the distribution of G-7 Kyoto and EU bubble commitments).[26]

---

[21] William Jefferson Clinton 1997.
[22] Annex I countries, named after an annex in the Framework Convention (known as "Appendix B" countries in the Kyoto Protocol), are the thirty-eight industrialized countries, plus the European Union. For a full list, see UNFCCC Undated.
[23] The six gases included carbon dioxide (CO_2), methane (CH_4), nitrous oxide (N_2O), hydrofluorocarbons (HFCs), perfluorocarbons (PFCs), and sulfur hexafluoride (SF_6) (Fletcher 2001).
[24] The 7% reduction based on the 1990 base year was for CO_2, CH_4, and N_2O. A 1995 base year was used to calculate reductions for other greenhouse gases, HFCs, PFCs, and SF_6 (Parker and Blodget 1998).
[25] Moreover, as noted earlier, the Kyoto reduction moved the base year forward from 1990 to 1995 for emissions reductions for three greenhouse gases. Because emissions for those gases had risen, this change reduced the US obligation still further, perhaps to 3 percent (Ott 1998).
[26] Gugele, Huttunen, and Ritter 2003, 12. The Germans and British were willing to accept such steep reduction targets in part because structural changes in their economies (German reunification and fuel switching from coal to gas in the UK) radically reduced their emissions of greenhouse gases in the early 1990s.

Table 4.1 *Kyoto and EU bubble commitments and emissions trends*

Countries	Canada	France	Germany	Italy	Japan	UK	United States
Ratified? (year)	Yes (2002)	Yes (2002)	Yes (2002)	Yes (2002)	Yes (2002)	Yes (2002)	No
Commitment (A)	−6%	0%	−21%	−6.5%	−6%	−12.5%	−7%
GHG emissions 2000 (MtC)	191.3	147.8	274.7	145.7	358.3	173	1868.4
% change 1990–2000 (B)	21.2%	0.2%	−15.7%	6.1%	11.2%	−11.4%	14.6%
% distance from Kyoto target in 2000 (A+B)	27.2%	0.2%	5.3%	12.6%	17.2%	1.1%	21.6%
Per capita carbon emissions in 2000 (tons)	6.2	2.5	3.3	2.6	2.8	2.9	6.6

Note and source: Emissions trends and per capita emissions are from WRI 2006. Emissions data include all five main greenhouse gases but exclude land-use changes.

However, Kyoto left unresolved the mechanisms by which countries would attain those reductions as well as excluding a number of developing countries such as China and India from mandatory CO_2 emissions reductions.[27] Anticipating such a result, the US Senate passed a non-binding "sense of the Senate" resolution S. Res. 98 (the so-called Byrd–Hagel resolution) by a margin of 95–0. The Byrd–Hagel resolution suggested the Senate should not support any climate change treaty that did "serious harm" to the American economy or failed to include "specific scheduled commitments" by developing countries in the same compliance period.[28]

At Kyoto, the United States successfully pressed for flexible market mechanisms (including an emissions trading system) to achieve reductions at the least cost.[29] Although conceptually these ideas were agreed to, it was again left up to later negotiations to specify the precise form of these tradable permits and other flexibility mechanisms.[30] Having theoretically achieved agreement on such mechanisms, the Clinton administration signed the Kyoto Protocol on November 12, 1998,[31] but indicated that it had no intention of ratifying the treaty without it being altered to include "meaningful participation" by developing countries.[32]

[27] The US Energy Information Agency projected that China and India's emissions would increase by 136% and 103% respectively between 2000 and 2025 to reach 1,844 MtC and 506 MtC, 17.8% and 4.8% of the world's total (WRI 2004).

[28] Fletcher 2001. See the text of the S. Res. 98 at thomas.loc.gov, under the 105th Congress.

[29] The idea behind emissions trading is that it may be more expensive for different firms and different countries to comply with Kyoto reductions targets. Thus, if it is cheap for one firm (or country) to reduce emissions and expensive for another, emissions reductions should occur where it is cheapest to do so. Through trading, the firm (or country) for which emissions reductions is expensive can purchase emissions credits from the other and thereby reduce total abatement costs (Weiner 1997).

[30] The two other flexibility mechanisms elaborated at Kyoto included joint implementation (JI) and the clean development mechanism (CDM). JI, launched with the Framework Convention, is "project-based activity in which one country can receive emission reduction credit when it funds a project in another country where the emissions are actually reduced" (Fletcher 2001). Whereas JI was restricted to developed countries, CDM provisions in Article 12 of Kyoto allowed for developing country emissions reductions to apply to developed country emissions reduction targets (Toman and Cazorla 1998).

[31] At the COP-4 meeting in Buenos Aires, both Argentina and Kazakhstan announced their decision to agree to voluntary emissions reductions (Depledge 1999).

[32] United States, White House, Office of the Press Secretary 1997.

Ultimately, negotiations that would have settled questions left over from Kyoto foundered in November 2000 in The Hague.[33] As noted in the introduction to this chapter, the disagreement was over how to treat forests as sinks for CO_2. Following The Hague meeting, George W. Bush became the US president. Despite an indication during the 2000 US presidential campaign that he would promote mandatory CO_2 emissions reductions, Bush made an abrupt turnaround on March 13, 2001, overruling pleas by Christine Todd Whitman, the administrator of the US Environmental Protection Agency.[34] Moreover, the Bush administration soon announced its intent to withdraw from the Kyoto Protocol, even though Bush had not sent it to the Senate for advice and consent.[35]

In reaction, Europe spearheaded an effort to save Kyoto in Bonn, Germany, and then Marrakesh, Morocco, by making concessions on sinks to the Japanese, Canadians, and Russians.[36] In 2002, European countries took the lead in ratifying and encouraging other key signatories to ratify the Kyoto Protocol. On May 31, 2002, the fifteen member states of the EU ratified the Protocol,[37] followed by Japan on June 4.[38] In December 2002, Canada did the same.[39] To enter into force, Kyoto required that fifty-five countries and Annex I countries responsible for

---

[33] Drozdiak 2000.

[34] Pianin 2001b; Pianin and Goldstein 2001; Washington Post 2001. Whitman had publicly stated the administration's serious consideration that it would honor the Bush campaign pledge to regulate power plant emissions of CO_2. In his speech "A Comprehensive National Energy Policy" delivered on September 29, 2000, in Saginaw, Michigan, then-candidate Bush said: "[W]e will require all power plants to meet clean air standards in order to reduce emissions of sulfur dioxide, nitrogen oxide, mercury and carbon dioxide within a reasonable period of time" (Bush 2000).

[35] Pianin 2001c.

[36] Pianin 2001a. Among the changes were provisions allowing for market mechanisms (emissions trading provisions) as well as carbon sinks (forest reserves) as ways to meet CO_2 reduction commitments. In addition, penalties for failure to comply were also negotiated. The agreement salvaged the Kyoto framework for the moment. There were fears Japan would drop out since it takes many of its cues on climate change from the United States (Pianin 2001d). The Bonn agreement allowed Annex I countries to receive credits for forests, the Canadians receiving a cap of 12 million tons per year, Japan 13 million tons, and Russia 17.63 million tons. Those credits were worth about 10% of Canada's base year emissions and 4% of Japan's base year emissions (Pew Center on Global Climate Change 2001a, 2001b). At Marrakesh, the Russians successfully pushed to have their credits for forest reserves doubled (Dessai 2001).

[37] Lynch 2002.   [38] BBC 2002b.   [39] CBC 2002.

55 percent of carbon dioxide emissions in 1990 ratify the treaty.[40] With the United States and Australia (at the time) opposed to ratification, the only way the treaty could clear the hurdle of 55 percent of Annex I country emissions was to persuade the Russians to come on board.[41] They proved difficult to convince. In May 2004, after the EU announced it was willing to look positively upon Russia's application to the World Trade Organization (WTO), President Vladimir Putin strongly signaled intent to ratify. Actual ratification was not forthcoming until November 2004, which finally allowed Kyoto to enter into force in February 2005.[42]

Since Kyoto entered into force, perhaps the most significant climate policy that has been enacted is the European Emissions Trading System (EU ETS). The first phase of EU ETS came into operation on January 1, 2005, and lasted through 2007. It covered about 11,400 installations and encompassed the power sector (including all fossil fuel generators over twenty megawatts), oil refining, cement production, iron and steel manufacture, glass and ceramics, and paper and pulp production. It included only CO_2 emissions and excluded emissions from transportation, agriculture, and households and small businesses. The EU ETS therefore covered only about 45 percent of the EU's total CO_2 emissions.[43]

Despite some setbacks in implementing the emissions trading system, Europe, thanks to large emissions reductions from the UK and Germany, had begun to reduce its emissions below 1990 levels. In 2004, emissions by the fifteen EU members were 0.9 percent below 1990 levels.[44] This was about a tenth of the way toward the EU-15 Kyoto target. The EU, nonetheless, remained confident that a mix of measures – emissions trading, sinks, and additional domestic policies – would bring emissions down to 8 percent below 1990 levels by 2010.[45] In early 2007, even as some national governments sought generous caps

---

[40] Fletcher 2001.

[41] In 1990, the Russian Federation's CO_2 emissions accounted for 17.4 percent of Annex I country emissions (UNFCCC Undated).

[42] As of October 2008, 182 countries and 1 regional organization had ratified the Kyoto Protocol.

[43] The second phase of the EU ETS began in 2008 and will continue through 2012. For a more extended discussion of EU motivations, see Busby 2008a.

[44] This refers to the fifteen EU countries that initially ratified the Kyoto Protocol before the EU expansion to twenty-five countries in 2004.

[45] European Environment Agency 2006, 5.

for the second phase of the EU ETS, the European Commission proposed an ambitious energy plan with a goal of reducing greenhouse gas emissions by 20 percent by 2020.[46]

As Europe implemented its trading scheme with mixed success, other Kyoto ratifiers – Japan and Canada notably – faced the daunting prospect of initiating expensive climate policies despite facing emissions profiles much more like those of the United States. Both had a Kyoto target to reduce emissions to 6% below 1990 levels. Already having one of the most energy efficient economies in the world, Japan found it difficult to reduce emissions further. Even before the country emerged from its economic doldrums, its greenhouse gas emissions increased by 11.2 percent between 1990 and 2000.[47] Japanese plans for meeting their Kyoto targets relied mostly on carbon sinks from forests and the purchase of emissions credits from abroad.[48]

The Japanese, in a rare breach with the United States, nonetheless ratified the Kyoto Protocol. However, Japan subsequently sought different ways to engage its most important ally on climate change. In 2005, Japan joined with the United States and four other countries in the Asia Pacific Partnership on Clean Development and Climate (APP), a voluntary effort to foster technological cooperation on clean energy technologies.[49] In 2006, at COP-12 in Nairobi, the Japanese proposed emissions intensity targets rather than outright emission caps for the new commitment period 2008–2012 and suggested that non-compliance not be subject to penalties. Given that the Bush administration had embraced domestic energy intensity targets, it could only have been intended as another move to engage the United States.[50]

---

[46] BBC 2007a. [47] WRI 2006.
[48] After Kyoto was ratified, the plan Japan had in place to reduce its emissions envisioned that 4.4% of the 6% reduction in emissions would occur through domestic efforts. Nearly 90% of that total was projected to come from carbon sinks. The remaining 1.6% would come from Kyoto mechanisms, either through buying emissions credits from abroad or through accruing credits from financing JI or CDM emissions-reducing projects overseas. Japan's export–import bank was financing a number of these projects in 2006 in China as the Japanese sought to meet its Kyoto commitments (Japan Times 2002b; Masaki 2006).
[49] The other members are Australia, China, India, and South Korea. Canada joined in 2007.
[50] De Souza 2006. Emissions intensity reflects the quantity of emissions per unit of output; intensity targets reduce the emissions per unit of output, potentially

In Canada, the 2006 election brought the Conservatives to power for the first time in twelve years, in a minority government. Prime Minister Stephen Harper, while not withdrawing outright from the Kyoto Protocol, made it known that the country's Kyoto target was not attainable. With its booming oil economy in western Canada, Canadian greenhouse gases emissions increased by 24 percent between 1990 and 2006.[51] That recognition, however, was not received well by the public; the opposition Liberal Party sought unsuccessfully to make climate change a central issue in the 2008 national elections.[52] Climate change nonetheless remained a politically contentious issue in Canada.

What explains why some countries ratified the Kyoto Protocol while others did not? Or, why has the movement to address climate change gotten (at least part of) what it wanted from some countries and not others? While concern for and commitment to climate change were partially responsible, the decision to ratify the Kyoto Protocol by Japan and Canada (as well as the EU) was driven largely by prestige and reputational concerns. While costs certainly played an important role in affecting the US decision, cost concerns were filtered through the perceptions of policy gatekeepers. Given uncertainties about the actual costs of implementation, the United States might well have been able to ratify had it possessed different domestic political institutions with fewer gatekeepers, like the parliamentary systems of the UK and Canada. Nonetheless, as I noted in the introduction to this chapter, the failure to ratify is, in part, a failure of the Kyoto negotiations themselves. NGOs own a piece of that failure for having pushed for deep, short-run emissions cuts in 1997, despite the political realities.

A partial explanation: material interest

How would interest-based accounts explain these developments? As I noted in Chapter 2, interest-based approaches focus on the strategic maneuvers of states to maximize their long-run material benefit. From a rationalist perspective, states will act in support of climate policies

slowing the growth of emissions without necessarily contributing to an absolute reduction.
[51] Fekete 2006.   [52] CNN 2007.

when, given what everyone else is going to do, the likely benefits exceed the costs.

For some scholars who support a material interest account of state behavior, what I call "minimalists," treaty ratification is rational only from a specific and limited view of international legal agreements. Minimalists believe international institutions possess no ability to encourage countries to comply (so-called compliance-pull) because of weak or non-existent enforcement mechanisms. States will ratify treaties that specify policies they intend to enact anyway. Treaty negotiations and international institutions serve merely to coordinate collective expectations of what everyone is going to do.[53] These scholars might also note that deeper commitments in treaties constitute "cheap talk" that nations have no intention of abiding by and cannot be compelled to implement.[54] The extra concessions on sinks that the Japanese and Canadians were able to extract show how leaders made their Kyoto talk even cheaper. At most, states might take on climate commitments if they are not too costly. This minimalist approach could explain the behavior of leading nations (like the UK and Germany) and lagging states (like the United States) on the basis of this instrumental calculation: leaders faced low costs and potential net benefits, while lagging countries faced high costs in implementing climate policies. For the delays and inability to foster cooperation among all players, minimalists would emphasize the collective action problems of coordinating many actors with different interests in an area in which much uncertainty exists.[55] For minimalists, ratification is beside the point. To them, the lack of serious action to date by the Canadians and Japanese as well as the overly generous emissions caps of the first round of the National Allocation Plans (the plans which allocate emissions limits under the EU regional cap-and-trade scheme) in the EU ETS support their claims.

Others proponents of this approach – let us call them "institutionalists" – would focus on the painstaking agreements in which states

---

[53] Downs, Rocke, and Barsoom 1996, 380; Goldsmith and Posner 2003–2004, 2005; von Stein 2005a, 612; 2005b.
[54] Farrell and Rabin 1996; Morrow 1994.
[55] In game theoretic terms, while Kyoto supporters thought they were playing a coordination game, the different interests of the players suggest climate politics are more like a game of deadlock.

have engaged to create the UNFCCC and the Kyoto Protocol.[56] Proponents would likely highlight the benefits of information and coordination fostered by these agreements. These treaties must have some potential to lead countries to comply, institutionalists would argue, because otherwise why would states spend such time negotiating them? These scholars might underplay the difficulties experienced thus far as growing pains and stress that the climate regime has not yet had sufficient time to lock in benefits to participants. For institutionalists, the motive that ultimately drives state decisions to ratify treaties and live up to their commitments is reputational.[57] For these rationalists, reputations have material roots. States can gain most from cooperative endeavors when they enter into long-term relationships undergirded by a sense of "diffuse reciprocity," believing that cooperation now will be rewarded by cooperation in the long run. The cost of a bad reputation for a country may be a lost stream of benefits from missed opportunities; alternatively, at a minimum, potential partners will demand conditions before entering into agreements with unreliable collaborators.[58] Thus, for institutionalists, the decision by some countries to ratify Kyoto despite facing significant implementation costs may be seen as an attempt to avoid the reputational damage of breaking their rhetorical commitments to action on climate change. Reputational costs could come from their international partners or from domestic audiences who punish politicians for not keeping promises.[59]

Finally, arguments based on politicians' individual electoral incentives, let us call them "pluralists," would make many of the same predictions as minimalists and institutionalists. Pluralists would suggest that the high concentrated costs of implementation in certain countries led to the mobilization of interest groups opposed to more aggressive climate measures.[60] Where countries faced lower costs of complying with the Kyoto Protocol, interest group mobilization might be more balanced, with environmentalists able to convince legislators to

---

[56] In political science, this approach is known as "institutional liberal theory" or "neo-liberal institutionalism."

[57] Simmons 1998, 2000; Simmons and Hopkins 2005. For my own discussion of reputation, see Busby 2005, 2006b.

[58] Guzman 2005, 2002; Keohane 1986; Tomz 2007b.

[59] On audience costs, see Fearon 1997; Tomz 2007a.

[60] Olson 1965; Wilson 1980.

support ratification. A more nuanced argument of this kind would note the ability of environmental voters to influence national elections, particularly in Europe, through small Green parties that have often held the political balance in coalition governments.[61]

None of these explanations is able to fully explain outcomes in the climate regime. Interest-based accounts correctly capture why leading states have been reluctant to impose steep costs on themselves and provide a preliminary, first-cut explanation of why European countries were in a better position than the United States to ratify the Kyoto Protocol.[62] However, such arguments have trouble explaining the decision of Japan and Canada to ratify Kyoto, unless they dismiss ratification as mere cheap talk. Moreover, they cannot explain the willingness by the Europeans to impose modest, yet significant, costs on themselves as part of the EU ETS. While supporters of material interest explanations would highlight the lack of significant action by Japan (and Canada), they would have trouble explaining why Japan was prepared to spend hundreds of millions (and potentially billions) of dollars to buy excess emissions credits from countries in Eastern Europe in 2008 in order to meet its Kyoto commitments.[63]

Even a pluralist argument that emphasizes self-interested behavior by politicians responding to public pressure would have trouble explaining Canadian behavior, given the low salience of Kyoto ratification to voters. For example, while Canadians were generally supportive of ratification,[64] the percentage who identified the environment as their top concern ranged from 0.6% to 6% between 1995 and 2006, figures similar to those in the United States.[65] Further evidence of low

---

[61] I make this sort of argument in Busby and Ochs 2004. See also Harrison and Sundstrom 2007.

[62] For interest-based arguments on climate change and the Kyoto Protocol, see Cass 2002; von Stein 2005b.

[63] Even though it was difficult for Japan to implement more extensive reforms at home, the country nonetheless found itself bound to live up to the promises it had made. In 2008, Japan sought to meet its Kyoto commitments by buying excess emissions from the Czech Republic, Ukraine, Hungary, and Poland (Sato and Nakayama 2008). Japan would need to spend roughly $3.7 billion between 2008 and 2012 to buy 100 million MtC of credits to meet its Kyoto obligations (Reuters 2008a).

[64] A 2002 survey found that 67% of Canadians either strongly (28%) or somewhat (39%) supported ratification of the Kyoto Protocol (EKOS Research Associates 2002).

[65] Gallup data cited in Harrison 2007, 94.

salience is that fully half of Canadians were unaware their country had already ratified Kyoto by the spring of 2003.[66]

A more complete explanation: framing/gatekeepers with a focus on reputation

In the late 1980s and early 1990s, with some of the hottest summers on record, environmental activists used evocative language to make global warming viscerally compelling to policymakers. They framed climate change as an environmental crisis and warned of melting ice caps, cities inundated by rising water levels, huge storms, and unbearable temperatures, among other catastrophic consequences. Given the frame, targets and timetables for binding emissions reductions of greenhouse gases seemed like a natural policy extension, given how well a similar policy was working for the ozone hole. While there have been a few competing frames and policy orientations in the more than twenty years since climate change became a political issue, the crisis frame and the policy framework of targets and timetables retain their dominance. Looked at this way, one can understand the role advocates have had in defining the problem and how this frame became attached to policies that limited the options of politicians seeking credit for taking action.

Together, we have an environmental crisis frame (that has plausible cultural appeal in all G-7 countries) tied to policy solutions that are unequally costly for the countries to implement. However, even for those for whom implementation was costly, we have divergent behavior – Canada and Japan ratified Kyoto while the United States did not. To explain this divergence, I draw inspiration from gatekeepers analysis and demonstrate how easier ratification processes in Canada and Japan made it possible for them to ratify a costly treaty while the United States was unable to do so. I layer this argument in the final section of this chapter with a focus on reputational concerns.

To substantiate these claims, I lay out evidence that supports the broad moral/normative appeal of environmental values in the G-7 and set this against the imputed relative costs of implementation of Kyoto from Table 2.2. I have generated Table 4.2, a combined table with the intersection of costs and values for the G-7 on the Kyoto Protocol.

---

[66] EKOS data cited in Harrison 2007, 94.

Table 4.2 *Environmental values and distance from Kyoto target*

Countries	Canada	France	Germany	Italy	Japan	UK	United States
% of respondents valuing protection of the environment over economic growth	79.5%	63.5%	77%	84%	67.5%	78.5%	69.5%
% distance from Kyoto target in 2000	27.2%	0.2%	5.3%	12.6%	17.2%	01.1%	21.6%

Sources: Polling data are from Pew Research Center for the People & the Press 2007; emissions distance from Kyoto target calculated using WRI 2006 and data from Table 4.1.

From this table, we can see why Japan, Canada, and the United States are worthy of further discussion.

As I suggested, an environmental crisis frame is, at least on the surface, culturally appropriate in each of the G-7 countries, where environmentalism has attained domestic resonance. Polls conducted in 2002 and 2007 by the Pew Research Center found that more than 60 percent of publics in all of the G-7 countries strongly agreed or agreed with the statement: "Protecting the environment should be given priority, even if it causes slower economic growth and some loss of jobs" (see Table 4.2).[67]

---

[67] Pew Research Center for the People & the Press 2007. In fact, in 2007, a majority strongly agreed or agreed with that statement in forty-six of forty-seven countries polled across the world (Indonesia was the exception). The average for all forty-seven countries, combining the categories of strongly agree/agree, was 72%. The G-7 average for 2007 was 72.7%. Table 4.2 combines the strongly agree/agree categories and averages for 2002 and 2007 from the Pew Research polls. Since values are supposed to be relatively long-lived, I averaged for 2002/2007 to ensure that these did not represent a one-off anomalous poll result. Since the lead-up to ratification was in the period 1997–2002, it would be desirable to have more crossnational polling information from this time frame, but I have not found data that encompassed all G-7 countries from the earlier time period. The World Values Survey does provide crossnational data on environmental attitudes for earlier periods but mostly looks at differences in whether publics supported additional taxation to provide environmental protection (as in Canada and the United States) or wanted the state to protect the environment using existing governmental resources (as in France and Germany).

This question does not imply that environmental problems (and climate change in particular) are a political priority, only that a frame appealing to environmental values potentially has some basis of support. In fact, environmental concerns typically are low among the self-reported political priorities of most publics.[68] While there has been some variation in country concern for climate change and support for the Kyoto Protocol, most public opinion polls have shown general convergence of concern and support for the agreement, even in the United States.[69] However, because crossnational opinion polls that

[68] Evidence from Canada was presented on pp. 119–120. In the American National Election Studies conducted every two years to accompany national elections, Americans were asked to identify the most important national problem. Between 1960 and 2004, "natural resources" ranged as the top concern from 0.1% of the public to a high of 6.6% in 1990. In 2000, 2.5% identified natural resources as their top concern, compared to 43.5% who said social welfare and 22.9% who said public order (ANES 2005). Eurobarometer polls from 2003 to 2008 asked the two top issues facing each country. During this period, protecting the environment was near the bottom of national concerns, ranging as the top concern for between 2% and 7% of Europeans polled. Individual country results were similar. The average who said the environment was a top concern over those six years in France was 6.8%, Germany 2.8%, Italy 2.3%, and the UK 5.7%. However, there does seem to be a disconnect between local priorities and perceptions of problems facing the world. In June 2008, Europeans identified climate change as the second most important problem facing the world (62%), behind poverty (68%) (Eurobarometer 2008). In Japan, opinion polls put environmental concerns lower down on the list of priorities. In 1998, only 15% of Japanese, when given the option to choose as many as apply, said that "environmental issues such as pollution" were the most important problem facing the country. Compare that with 76% that said "recovery of the national economy" was the most important problem (JPOLL 1998). Between 2005 and 2006, when asked what the government should prioritize in the Nikkei opinion poll, environmental issues were near the middle-bottom of priorities identified by 16% (9/2006), 14% (12/2005), 17% (6/2005), and 18% (4/2005). In all four of these polls, social security was identified as a priority issue by more than 50% of those polled (Mansfield Asian Opinion Poll Database 2008). In a May 2007 Yomiuri Shimbun poll, 21.9% said to prioritize environmental issues, well behind social security reform (59.5%), economic conditions (51.1%), and six other issue areas (Mansfield Asian Opinion Poll Database 2007).

[69] A review of sixteen polls taken in 2006 and 2007, several of which contained multiyear tracking data, showed increased concern among Americans about climate change (Environmental and Energy Study Institute 2007). A December 2005 poll found that 76% of Americans regarded climate change as a serious problem compared to 90% of Canadians, 98% of Japanese, 94% of French and Italians, 93% of Germans, 92% of Poles, 91% of British people, and 89% of Finns (PIPA 2006). In 2006, 56% of Europeans and 46% of Americans

ask environmental questions are rare, I wanted to find examples that suggested an environmental crisis frame was at least superficially compelling (or not) in all of the country cases. Here, we have two polls from the 2000s where a large majority of publics expressed support for environmental goals even at the expense of their own material self-interest. When we combine this data with the distance G-7 countries were from their Kyoto commitments (from Table 4.1), we can create a figure representing the intersection of costs and values like the table developed in Chapter 2 and applied to debt relief in the last chapter (see Figure 4.1).

By the year 2000, when countries were preparing for ratification, the UK, France, and Germany had almost achieved their Kyoto commitments while the emissions of several countries, including Japan, Canada, and the United States, far exceeded them. For all three (and possibly Italy as well), it would potentially be costly to reduce their emissions to meet their Kyoto commitments.[70] At the very least, these countries would, barring some technological breakthrough, find it more difficult to meet their Kyoto commitments than the UK, France, and Germany.[71] However, in terms of values, all seven countries, by

regarded "global warming" as an "extremely important threat" in the next ten years. Another 34% and 36% respectively viewed it as an "important" threat. Thus, more than 80% of the public in both Europe and the United States see global warming as an important threat. That said, 16% of the Americans said global warming was not a threat at all, while only 7% of Europeans agreed with this view (German Marshall Fund 2006b). The European data reflected the opinions in twelve countries: Britain, Bulgaria, France, Germany, Italy, the Netherlands, Poland, Portugal, Romania, Slovakia, Spain, and Turkey. A 2006 Pew survey found a broader gap between the United States, some Europeans, and the Japanese on their personal concerns about climate change (Pew Research Center 2006). Elsewhere, I have explored the degree to which the American public holds views on climate change that are similar to those of their European allies (Busby 2003; Busby and Ochs 2004).

[70] Since Italy's commitments were made as part of Europe's bubble agreement, Italy's costs might not ultimately be purely its own responsibility.

[71] Given diversity in countries' economic structures and emissions trajectories, a snapshot of a country's distance from its Kyoto target in 2000 is not a perfect measure of likely costs. From Table 4.1, we see that Canada and the United States had much higher emissions per capita than other G-7 countries, which could imply some opportunities for low-cost energy efficiency gains. For Japan, the second most energy efficient economy of the G-7, it might suggest that additional efficiencies might be difficult. Ideally, we would have country-level estimates of the costs of implementation of Kyoto. Unfortunately, there is no authoritative crossnational comparison of Kyoto

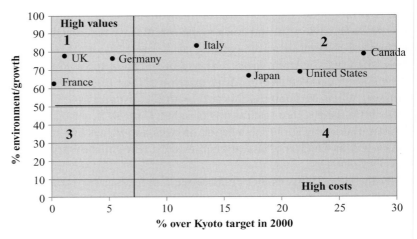

Figure 4.1 Mapping of emissions and environmental values
Note and source: This data does not include changes in land use, nor does it include extra credits the Europeans granted countries such as Japan and Canada for forest sinks. These credits effectively lowered the emissions reductions needed to meet their Kyoto commitment but do not change the broader point that implementation for Japan and Canada was still costly. In this figure, the threshold between high and low costs is somewhat arbitrary; the distribution of relative burdens is perhaps more interesting. Nonetheless, for the purpose of dividing this figure into four quadrants, the dividing line between high and low costs is for a country's emissions to be 7.15 percent above their Kyoto commitments in 2000. This is the median distance for the thirty-eight Annex 1 countries that made a commitment under the Kyoto Protocol (or the EU umbrella agreement) for which emissions data were available in the WRI CAIT database (WRI 2006).

implementation costs. The IPCC Third Assessment compared different models' estimates of the costs of implementation in Japan, Europe, the United States, and other OECD countries under a range of scenarios (with or without emissions trading). In five of nine models, it was marginally more expensive for the United States to implement Kyoto with or without global trading (in terms of the percentage of GDP lost in 2010). Most of the models also showed that it was more expensive for Europe to implement Kyoto than for Japan; for other OECD countries such as Canada, implementing Kyoto was more expensive than for either Europe or Japan, roughly comparable to the United States (IPCC 2001). Costs for the United States ranged from 0.42% of GDP to 1.96% without trading and from 0.06 to 0.66% of GDP with global trading. Cost ranges were not wildly different for the other countries. For a more extended discussion, see chapter 5 in Busby 2004a.

this measure, had environmentally conscious populations. Thus, in terms of the argument developed in Chapter 2, the United States, Canada, Japan, and possibly Italy were all cases of "costly moral action" (Cell 2 in Table 2.2), whereas France, Germany, and the UK were cases of "cheap moral action" (Cell 1).

How can we link advocacy efforts to frame the issue to successful ratification in some countries that faced high implementation costs (Japan and Canada) and failure in others (the United States)? As I suggested earlier, the environmental advocacy community had a key role in agenda-setting and shaping what kinds of commitments were rewarded politically. While their power was circumscribed by the countervailing influence of carbon-intensive industries, environmental groups defined what policies were considered "green." To understand how this later affected choices in Kyoto, we have to unpack the initial crisis frame that animated and continues to infuse climate change advocacy.

In the late 1980s when the issue first became politically visible, advocates tried to capture the public imagination by talking about coastal cities and islands inundated by rising seas, crops and lawns sunburned to a crisp, and the prospect of huge tempests and floods wreaking havoc. Michael Oppenheimer, then senior scientist for the Environmental Defense Fund, wrote in a 1984 opinion piece: "The sea level will rise as land ice melts and the ocean expands. Beaches will erode while wetlands will largely disappear . . . Imagine life in a sweltering, smoggy New York without Long Island's beaches and you have glimpsed the world left to future generations."[72] In 1988, Jeremy Rifkin warned of a dystopian world in 2035 in which Phoenix was in its third week of 130° weather, palm trees lined the Hudson River, the Netherlands was under water, and Bangladesh had "ceased to exist."[73] The director of the 1988 Toronto conference (where participants endorsed the 20 percent reduction in CO_2 by 2005) suggested that alteration of the atmosphere was akin to nuclear war: "Humanity is conducting an unintended, uncontrolled, globally pervasive experiment whose ultimate consequences could be second only to a global nuclear war."[74]

---

[72] Quoted in Sarewitz and Pielke 2000. A 1990 report by Greenpeace similarly warned of the "dire" and "dreadful" consequences, evoking past campaigns such as the abolitionist movement as parallel challenges of similar magnitude (Leggett 1999, 6–7).
[73] Rifkin 1988.   [74] Ferguson 1989.

In so doing, advocates enhanced the sense of impending doom if immediate action were not taken, making short-term emissions reductions seem to be the first line of defense against imminent disaster. While the environmental movement has experimented with alternative frames (climate change as a national security threat, an economic opportunity, or a religious moral issue), the crisis frame retains its hold on the imagination, epitomized in 2006 by former US vice president Al Gore's slide show/film *An Inconvenient Truth*: "Today, we are hearing and seeing dire warnings of the worst potential catastrophe in the history of human civilization: a global climate crisis that is deepening and rapidly becoming more dangerous than anything we have ever faced."[75]

The legacy or path dependency of framing has been highlighted explicitly by a number of authors, who emphasize that the issue was framed in urgent terms of "environmental disaster."[76] Why did activists use such a crisis lens? Activists typically succeed in getting issues on the agenda of policymakers after crisis events; this is particularly true in the United States, but is generally so of democratic polities everywhere. The electoral time horizons for most politicians are sufficiently short that they tend to respond to issues that are in the forefront of public attention, that are the most compelling at the time. Democracies are not particularly adept at long-range planning. Problems tend to be dealt with incrementally until there are colossal failures or looming crises that reorient priorities fundamentally. The response to September 11 is a case in point. As Bryan Jones and John Kingdon write, interest is not merely generated by crises. Interest can be focused through concerted advocacy.[77] Moreover, activists are aware that "necessity is the mother of invention" and therefore try to "invent necessity" by seizing upon new information or events to dramatize their perspective.

An internationally binding treaty with targets and timetables for emissions reductions of greenhouse gases appeared to be a sensible

---

[75] Gore 2006. I explore alternative possible frames in Busby and Ochs 2004. I also have been active in looking at the security consequences of climate change, part of a broader reframing effort; see Busby 2007b, 2008b.

[76] Betsill 2000; Naimon and Knopman 1999; Sarewitz and Pielke 2000; Weingart, Engels, and Pansegrau 2000. Betsill cites the Climate Action Network's newsletter *ECO* from late 1991 and early 1992.

[77] Jones 1994; Kingdon 1995.

policy solution to attach to the problem, in part because of the success of international efforts to manage the ozone hole. Because ozone had been successfully handled through a swift timetable for the phaseout of CFCs, advocates seeking models of international environmental efforts sought to emulate this approach for how to deal with global warming, beginning with the 1988 Toronto target of reducing CO_2 emissions by 20 percent by 2005.[78]

By adopting targets and timetables for binding emissions reductions of significant magnitude by a specified date, environmental groups defined for the media and broader public both what policies were considered green and what steps were adequate to address climate change. Dan Reifsnyder, then director of the Office of Global Change at the US Department of State, suggested the litmus test of being environmental in the run-up to Rio was whether a country had announced a target and a timetable for reducing its greenhouse gas emissions.[79] The United States did not have a target and a timetable, and this was seen as very bad. Having one, no matter how heavily caveated, made you green.[80] These dynamics gave rise to a sort of "green beauty contest" in which states sought to "play to the gallery" of domestic politics and outdo each other with more ambitious emissions reductions targets, none of which were based on feasibility studies.[81] The significance is that politicians who sought to be green could gain political benefit only by moving to embrace the approved policy line of the environmental community.[82] Politicians who failed to move closer to that definition

[78] Victor 2001, 14–16. Reiner (2001) dates Kyoto's problems back to the emissions reductions targets approach as does Benedick (1997). Barrett also discusses how the climate problem was modeled on the ozone issue and notes that the problems are different (Barrett 1999). See also chapter 3 of Betsill 2000; Downie 1995; Grundmann 2002; Morrisette 1991; Sandler 2004; Sebenius 1994, 283–284. Like the ozone problem, climate change started first with a framework convention before moving to more aggressive, specific targets and timetables for reducing emissions. There were only twenty-eight countries involved in the initial ozone framework convention.

[79] This view is echoed by Sebenius 1994, 293.

[80] Reifsnyder 2004. Reifsnyder noted that virtually every country that had committed to a target and a timetable had caveats; if these were parsed, one would often find less of a commitment than met the eye. But caveats were considered largely inconsequential – the point was "the commitment." See also Reifsnyder quoted in Andresen and Agrawala 2002, 44.

[81] Andresen and Agrawala 2002, 45–46.

[82] To be fair, there were and are large differences of opinion between environmental groups on the desirability of flexibility mechanisms such as

of the solution ran the risk of being branded corporate lackeys of the fossil fuel industry or "climate killers."[83]

In one sense, through their mediating role, environmental groups serve to signal to mass publics what type of leaders their politicians are. Are they pro-environment or are they not?[84] Why would decisionmakers wish to reveal their type to electorates? For pluralists, the argument is simple: to get re-elected. However, an argument based solely on the re-election motive eviscerates the insight that decisionmakers and mass publics can be moved by appeals that are not strictly utilitarian. The effectiveness of a normative appeal – to protect the planet for future generations – ultimately depends upon someone, either the politician or mass publics, believing that a course of action is the right thing to do. That said, politicians seeking to do the right thing, even if they are putting themselves on the line out of conscience, want to know they will be commended for their stance. At the very least, if politicians are taking actions that the business community finds problematic, they want to get praise from the constituency that cares passionately about the issue. In Europe, the need for politicians to pay attention to this constituency is more acute since many countries have parliamentary systems in which Green parties are represented and, as in Germany, have been important coalition partners in the ruling government.

In the context of Kyoto, non-state actors had a key role in agenda-setting and shaping what kinds of promises were rewarded politically. On one level, environmental groups pushed for a legally binding international treaty, the assumption being that other forms of agreement would be easy to disregard as well as less effective.[85] On another level, advocacy groups wanted a commitment to deep cuts in emissions in the short to medium run from governments.

---

emissions trading, with groups such as Environmental Defense being more enthusiastic and others such as Greenpeace less so. However, as noted earlier, the Climate Action Network, which includes more centrist groups such as Environmental Defense and NRDC as well as more activist organizations such as Greenpeace and Friends of the Earth, endorsed the 20 percent by 2005 reduction target.

[83] Greenpeace International 1995.

[84] While game theorists such as Morrow have ably explored the role of information in signaling types, the role of conscience is in danger of being lost in this characterization. I thank Andrew Moravcsik for pointing out the potential similarities between my argument and James Morrow's. See Morrow 1994; 1999.

[85] Raustiala 2005, 610–612.

David Sandalow, the former assistant secretary of state for oceans, environment, and science in the Clinton administration, suggested the main metric of whether a state was green was how deep the emissions cut it pledged to make. Deeper was better.[86] Nigel Purvis, former deputy assistant secretary of state for oceans, environment, and science in the George W. Bush administration, echoed those comments.[87] Purvis suggested the public saw environmental groups as the arbiters of whether or not Kyoto was considered "environmental"; they were the "deal-breakers."[88]

While governments could shape the agreement in ways that green groups may not have been enthusiastic about, the environmental lobby's focus on short-term, binding limits on emissions shaped policymakers' views about what kinds of action they could take and still get public affirmation. We can see this play out with respect to proposals to incorporate a "safety valve" in climate policy. In the weeks before President Clinton's October 1997 speech announcing the US negotiating position before Kyoto, the administration floated the idea of a safety valve, an upper bound beyond which costs to the American economy would not be permitted to rise. In a world with emissions trading, the safety valve would allow the government to offer more emissions permits in the event that prices per ton of carbon reached a certain level, thereby providing businesses with some certainty about what their expected costs would be. While the safety valve could insulate the economy from costs becoming unacceptably high, it does not guarantee a set amount of emissions reductions.[89]

When this idea was mooted, environmental group reaction was overwhelmingly negative. Seventeen environmental groups promptly sent a letter to the administration lambasting the safety valve as a "treaty-busting escape clause." Even groups in favor of trading emissions, such as the Environmental Defense Fund (EDF), denounced the idea. Fred

---

[86] Sandalow 2003. Sandalow also served jointly as senior director for environmental affairs on the National Security Council and associate director for the global environment on the White House Council on Environmental Quality.
[87] Purvis also served as senior advisor to the undersecretary of state for global affairs in the Clinton administration.
[88] Purvis 2003.
[89] The safety valve idea was developed by economists associated with the think tank Resources for the Future (Passell 1997). For a more extended discussion of the safety valve, see chapter 6 in Busby 2004a.

Krupp of EDF said of the safety valve: "This would spoil the market mechanism and remove the incentives to produce innovations."[90] Economists believed that environmental groups simply did not understand the idea. As one supporter of the safety valve argued at the time: "If they [environmental groups] want to insist that it can be done cheap and easy, why would they worry?"[91] From this perspective, the safety valve weakens a binding emissions target only if the trigger price is set too low.

Because environmental groups were unified in opposition to the safety valve, an administration that flirted with that mechanism risked incurring their wrath and damaging its green credentials. While the Clinton administration could not hope to support a plan that would be universally popular, the last thing that it wanted was a plan that was uniformly reviled. Indeed, one of the main benefits of getting out in front on climate would be recognition from the environmental community for having done so. The safety valve, when it was floated, had the support of the Clinton economic team and some parts of the State Department, and was even regarded somewhat positively by Gore.[92] However, once the environmental community vociferously attacked the idea, it was shelved.

As of 2010, binding emissions reductions may be the best strategy to send a credible signal to industry that governments are serious about the problem. On the other hand, they are not the only conceivable policy tool (one could imagine carbon taxes, technology standards, and sectoral agreements as alternatives). Even a cap could have unfolded more slowly and still have been environmentally defensible. As Dan Bodansky wrote, "Fundamentally, Kyoto treats a long-term problem as though it were a short-term crisis."[93] And, after a decade of US delay, what was a long-term problem is becoming more and more like a crisis in both the short and the long term.

The discussion here is not meant to deride environmental groups for their efforts. It could be that, given the high stakes of climate policy, any policy solution would engender intense political opposition. However, as Daniel Sarewitz and Roger Pielke note: "The point is simply that the climate-change problem has been framed in a way that catalyzes a determined and powerful opposition."[94] Importantly, some domestic

[90] Cushman 1997.   [91] Hebert 1997.   [92] Hebert 1997.
[93] Bodansky 2001, 45.   [94] Sarewitz and Pielke 2000.

systems were more poised than others to translate that opposition into political influence.

My assessment is that, as measured by broad public opinion, the environmental crisis frame did fit with broader societal attitudes in a number of national contexts, including those of the United States, Germany, the UK, and Japan. However, given the potentially high costs in at least three G-7 countries (the United States, Japan, and Canada), the position of their domestic gatekeepers crucially determined the balance between cost concerns and values. What is more, gatekeepers poised to decide on ratification were faced with an additional set of appeals that went beyond environmental values. For leaders in Japan and Canada who decided to ratify, their country's reputation – as a good international citizen – was invoked as an extra motivation. In both cases, these concerns found fertile ground, both because these values are quite important in Japan and Canada but also, crucially, because the treaty ratification process in those countries is much easier than in the United States. I first discuss those institutional differences before looking at the reputational motives of Canadian and Japanese gatekeepers in more detail in the final section of this chapter.

The United States faces the most onerous institutional barriers to ratification in the G-7. While the US president can enter into executive agreements, two-thirds of the Senate has to vote in favor of providing "advice and consent" for contentious international agreements on issues such as climate change. This requirement is an especially high bar. Andrew Moravcsik explains the paradox that the United States is home to one of the most vigorous human rights NGO communities yet has difficulty ratifying international human rights treaties:

The most immediate veto group involved with human rights treaties, a one-third minority of recalcitrant senators, is created by the unique US constitutional requirement of a two-thirds' "supermajority" vote to advise and consent to an international treaty. This is a threshold higher than that in nearly all industrial democracies, which generally ratify international treaties by legislative majority.[95]

The same could be said for the strong US environmental advocacy community and failure to ratify Kyoto. Moreover, even cutting off debate to vote on legislation in the Senate procedurally requires sixty

[95] Moravcsik 2005, 187.

votes of a possible one hundred to reach "cloture," which then ends discussion and allows for a vote on the substance of the legislation. Without such levels of support, a determined minority can filibuster debate, extending discussion of legislation indefinitely. If, for example, a US political party possesses only a 52-vote majority in the Senate, it would still need eight senators from the other party to vote with them to attain the sixty-vote margin needed for cloture, assuming strong party discipline.[96] Given the greater reliance of US politicians on private sources of finance, party discipline is weaker in the United States than in Europe.[97] Even with cloture, for treaty ratification, a dozen or more senators, assuming a few defections, could effectively veto ratification, as each one would be needed to get over the two-thirds' threshold. While on issues of war, power in the US system has become increasingly concentrated in the executive branch, it remains extremely fragmented for treaty obligations and appropriations, precisely the issue areas in this book. For example, such a high bar for treaty approval has prevented the Law of the Sea Treaty from being ratified by the United States, despite strong support by the military, business, and environmental communities.[98]

Bernard Boockmann provides a schematic of the number of constitutional veto players required for treaty ratification in different national contexts, to which I have added Canada. For legislatures, a simple majority is required, unless otherwise noted (see Table 4.3).

In the UK, treaty ratification does not have to go through Parliament.[99] Similarly, in Canada, treaty ratification is a decision of the Cabinet.[100] In parliamentary systems where the legislative and

---

[96] For a discussion of these dynamics on domestic cap-and-trade legislation in the United States, see Busby 2008e.

[97] For a more extended discussion, see Busby and Ochs 2004.

[98] Gorelick 2008.   [99] Hennessey 2001, 89–90.

[100] In the two constitutional monarchies, the UK and Canada, the head of state is the queen, but her role is largely ceremonial, leaving the prime minister as the driving force behind treaty ratification. In the UK, the Foreign Office consults with other departments that would have to implement treaties before moving forward on ratification. In Canada, Cabinet approval is required for treaty ratification. Even here, a prime minister with a strong parliamentary majority can push through ratification in the Cabinet. In both countries, Parliament generally has only a peripheral role in treaty ratification (though EU treaties in the UK require implementing legislation and therefore allow for parliamentary oversight; United Kingdom, Parliament undated). In the UK, it is also standard practice to leave a treaty for twenty-one days before Parliament.

Table 4.3 *Constitutional veto players for international treaty ratification*

	Lower house	Upper house	President/ head of state	Provincial governments
Canada	No	No	No	No
France	Yes	No	Yes	No
Germany	Yes	Yes	No	No (only through a vote in the upper house)
Italy	Yes	Yes	No	No
Japan	Yes	No	No	No
UK	No	No	No	No
United States	No	Yes (two-thirds' majority)	Yes	No

Note and source: Boockmann 2006, 176. Thurner and Stoiber provide an amplified discussion of European treaty ratification requirements and a more nuanced, contingent view of effective veto power based on whether the executive enjoyed a parliamentary majority. See Thurner and Stoiber 2001.

executive functions are fused, the fate of the government rests on support in the lower house, which reinforces party discipline. As a consequence, as Kathryn Harrison noted, authority is concentrated, and the Canadian prime minister (true also for the UK prime minister) has the ability to act on his personal beliefs in a way that US presidents do not: "With a disciplined majority in the Canadian House of Commons, Prime Minister Chrétien had the institutional capacity to deliver on his personal commitment to the Kyoto Protocol."[101] In multiparty parliamentary governments in continental Europe, treaty ratification does have to go through parliament, but ratification is something of a formality when leaders have large parliamentary majorities. In Germany, for example, the vote for Kyoto ratification was unanimous in both the lower and upper chambers.[102]

For example, the UK procedure for Kyoto ratification was described in a press release as follows: "The Protocol will be laid before Parliament for 21 sitting days. This will mean that the Foreign Secretary will be in a position to sign the UK's instrument of ratification on or after 19 April" (DEFRA 2003).

[101] Harrison 2007, 97.

[102] The sequence in Germany for ratification was prompted by actions at the EU level. The European Commission in October 2001 proposed to the Council of

In Japan, treaty ratification also has to go through the Japanese parliament (the Diet), but ratification for most issues is typically not too controversial, with the Diet exercising a less active role than, for example, the United States Senate. Commenting on the 1992 UN Framework Convention on Climate Change, Hiroshi Ohta wrote: "The process of ratification of international agreements is not so politically complicated in Japan as it is in the United States, where ratification of any major international convention is politically contested."[103] Given the potential implementation costs of the Kyoto Protocol, however, ratification (as discussed later in this chapter) appeared to be somewhere between a formality and the highly contested political process in the United States.

While Canada's federal system has given regional interests significant veto power over implementation of the country's Kyoto commitments, Canada's streamlined treaty ratification process enabled the prime minister to push through ratification despite significant opposition. As a consequence of this process, which concentrates power, the number of veto players for treaty ratification in the G-7 is slightly different than the number depicted in Chapter 2. Roughly, there are three groups of countries, ranging from countries with a high number of treaty gatekeepers to those with a medium or low number. The United States is the outlier with the requirement for a Senate majority of two-thirds. I classify countries in which parliaments have to ratify treaties as having a medium number of treaty gatekeepers and those where the government can decide without going through parliament as having few gatekeepers. This yields Table 4.4.

Given that Canada, Japan, and the United States all faced high costs, we would expect that Canada's ratification process would be the easiest of the three and the American process the most difficult. I briefly discuss their ratification experience before discussing the motivations of the two successful ratifiers, Japan and Canada.

Ministers that the EU ratify Kyoto in 2002, signaling to member states to begin the process at home. The German Cabinet, composed of all the ministers of the German government, then signed off on ratification on December 5, 2001, indicating to the German parliament to do the same. On March 22, 2002, the lower house of the German parliament ratified, followed by the upper house on April 26. For a more detailed discussion, see Busby 2004a.

103 Ohta 1995, 271.

Table 4.4 *The number of treaty gatekeepers*

Low	Medium	High
UK	France	United States
Canada	Germany	
	Italy	
	Japan	
Easy	Ratification	*Difficult*

In Canada, Prime Minister Jean Chrétien did not have to take the Kyoto Protocol to the parliament for approval, but made a symbolic vote in the House of Commons over ratification a vote of confidence in his government.[104] This gesture came about in part because Chrétien was engaged in an intra-party leadership battle with Paul Martin in summer 2002. With a majority of the Liberal Party supporting Martin, Chrétien agreed to a more progressive policy agenda and a pledge to step down by early 2004. Pressure on the government both for and against ratification built in the months before the full Johannesburg environmental conference, a ten-year follow-on meeting to the 1992 Earth Summit. Prior to Johannesburg, Chrétien announced that a vote on ratification would be scheduled for the parliament before the end of the year, even though ratification is formally a decision of the Canadian Cabinet. With much of the business community opposed and Chrétien's Cabinet apparently evenly divided for and against ratification, Chrétien made a December non-binding vote in the House of Commons a question of confidence in the government (despite having failed to secure further concessions at the New Delhi climate negotiations, where Chrétien attempted to have Canada's clean energy exports of natural gas and hydroelectricity to the United States count toward its Kyoto commitment). With defeat of the motion setting the stage for new national elections, the Liberal Party rallied to support the resolution, all Liberal Party members present voting in favor. The Senate voted two days later in favor of the same motion, and the following day the Cabinet supported the measure without debate.[105]

[104] Bueckert 2002.
[105] These dynamics are explained in more detail by Harrison 2007, 106–107.

While the Japanese Cabinet concludes treaties, it must "obtain the prior or subsequent approval of the Diet."[106] Kazuyoshi Okazawa, former director general of the Global Environment Bureau in the Environment Agency, described tough negotiations in the lead-up to ratification.[107] Just after COP-7 Marrakesh, Japanese prime minister Junichiro Koizumi held a Cabinet meeting at his residence where his government decided Japan would move forward on ratification. He justified his decision as a way to revitalize the country's economy through the export of energy efficient and clean technology.[108] The prime minister's decision thus made it difficult for any bureaucratic organization to officially oppose that direction.[109] While the Ministry for Economy, Trade, and Industry (METI) did not formally oppose ratification of Kyoto, it was reluctant to support the protocol, given the agency's long-running concerns about the country's ability to further improve its energy efficiency and the potential effect of compliance on Japanese industry. While METI was constrained and had to support the government position after the prime minister's decision was announced, the main business association, Keidanren, was not. Keidanren's opposition to the Kyoto Protocol thus threatened to derail the government's effort to establish unified public support for the protocol both inside and outside government, and, more importantly, it undercut domestic implementation after ratification.[110]

The government made some informal promises to industry not to implement the Kyoto Protocol through mandatory programs and the imposition of taxes.[111] However, prior to the ratification vote, Keidanren experienced a change in leadership. Its president until April 2002 was Takashi Imai, chairman of Japan Steel, a very energy intensive company with strong concerns about the negative impact of Kyoto on the business sector and the country's competitiveness. His successor was Hiroshi Okuda, chairman of Toyota, who oversaw the union of Keidanren with Nikkeiren (the Japan Federation of Employers' Associations) in May 2002. This shift was quite symbolic, as Toyota has

---

[106] Japan, House of Representatives Undated.
[107] Okazawa 2004b. For another detailed account of Japan's ratification, see Tiberghien and Schreurs 2007.
[108] Associated Press 2001. This meeting was already mooted in October 2001 before the final negotiations in Marrakesh (Masaki 2001).
[109] Yutaka Nakao 2004.   [110] Morgan 2003; Okazawa 2004b.
[111] Japanese industry official 2004; Okazawa 2004b.

been a leader on climate policy, as exemplified by its development of fuel-efficient hybrid electric cars.[112]

The Japanese House of Representatives has 480 seats. At the time of ratification of Kyoto, the ruling parties had 286 representatives (246 Liberal Democratic Party [LDP], 31 Komeito, 9 New Conservative Party).[113] Of those, about one hundred were initially not in favor of ratification, with factions in the LDP and the Conservative Party being those most antagonistic to the Kyoto Protocol. Leading up to the vote, intense negotiations were conducted to secure the approval of all three coalition partners in the ruling government. Those parties could not openly oppose the prime minister but nonetheless could register their objections through the Environment Ministry. This process normally takes two to three weeks, but in the case of the Kyoto Protocol those negotiations took nearly two months.[114] Meanwhile, though weaker than their counterparts in other countries, Japanese environmental NGOs – Greenpeace Japan, Kiko (Environment) Forum, WWF, Friends of the Earth, ASEED Japan, and the Citizens' Alliance for Saving the Atmosphere (CASA) – lobbied the government to support ratification.[115]

While the Cabinet decision to ratify Kyoto was taken in February 2002, the Diet did not state its intention to do so until March.[116] On May 21, 2002, Japan's House of Representatives unanimously approved legislation that made ratification possible. The bill then went to the upper House of Councilors, where it passed unanimously on June 4. Following approval by the Diet, the Cabinet ratified the protocol on June 4. On May 22, the lower house also passed a second bill

---

[112] An industry official disputed the notion that there was much difference between the two men (Japanese industry official 2004). An Environment Ministry official suggested that the difference was a reflection of the companies these men led. Where the car industry (Okuda) may see economic opportunity in climate mitigation (e.g., the Toyota hybrid Prius), energy intensive industries such as steel (Imai) have a lot to lose. However, while Okuda's early statements were more positive about the Kyoto Protocol, Shimizu suggests his later statement fell into line with that of his predecessor (Shimizu 2004).

[113] Yoshida and Takahashi 2003.

[114] The behind-the-scenes debate in the Diet is suggested in Sugiyama 2003 and Okazawa 2004b.

[115] Tiberghien and Schreurs 2007, 75. For a review of the relative strength of Japanese environmental groups, see chapter 6 in Busby 2004a.

[116] Kawashima and Akino 2001.

with the provisions necessary to implement the Kyoto Protocol, and on May 31 the upper house did the same when it passed legislation approving ratification.[117]

Reputational ratification of Kyoto in Japan and Canada

As I noted in the previous section, Canada and Japan were institutionally better placed to ratify the Kyoto Protocol than the United States. However, our understanding of Japan and Canada's ability to ratify does not explain their motivations to do so.

I have suggested that reputational concerns loomed large for both but there are limits to rationalist accounts of reputation. In institutional rationalist accounts, a bad reputation is accompanied by material punishment. These reputational costs drive states to make good on their international treaty commitments. However, as Todd Sandler notes, material sanctions are costly. Where multiple countries have been cheated on by an unreliable treaty partner, the would-be punishers will tend to free ride in the hopes that others will bear the cost of punishing the rule breakers.[118] Consequently, states are willing to impose only modest reputational costs on defectors.[119] Furthermore, as Roger Downs and Michael Jones argue, states have multiple reputations, which are domain-specific. A reputation for compliance with international agreements may be less important than a reputation for toughness.[120] So, even if a state faces some costs from breaking a particular treaty commitment, these may pale in comparison with its other material incentives.

Other actors, however, may seize on these broken promises for political advantage and act as enforcers.[121] Even if a treaty partner decides it is not worthwhile to punish unreliable allies, opposition politicians or international rivals have an incentive to punish actors for making but not keeping treaty promises. When other states, non-state actors, and domestic publics can monitor compliance, rhetorical promises made by leaders can become binding. Trapped by their earlier words (or those of their predecessors), leaders risk being shamed publicly for their hypocrisy. Public shaming can result in a decline in

---

[117] Japan Times 2002a; BBC 2002b.   [118] Sandler 2004.
[119] Guzman 2002.   [120] Downs and Jones 2002.
[121] These symbolic "audience" costs can be thought of as an extension of reputation costs (Fearon 1994; 1997; Schultz 1998; Tomz 2007a).

political standing that limit leaders' freedom to maneuver. In other words, domestic or international publics can impose costs on leaders for failure to keep their commitments.[122] Those enforcers might not particularly care about the issue in question but might simply want to censure the treaty breaker in order to enhance their own standing.[123]

While actors may find it somewhat politically costly to repudiate their Kyoto commitments, the costs of actually implementing the protocol may be so great that countries such as Japan and Canada ultimately feel they have no choice but to renege. If a state can ratify a treaty without later having to implement it, such a strategy may offer a way to reward environmentally minded publics (and avoid their sanction or punishment by political opportunists) without having to pay the long-run costs of actually implementing the agreement. As Yves Tiberghien and Miranda Schreurs contend, states may be able to get away with this shell game (at least for a while) because ratification is a "highly visible decision, one with tangible reputation stakes and multiple audiences. Implementation, on the other hand, is the outcome of countless lower-level battles, many of which are quite technical and hidden from the public eye."[124]

Individual leaders also may desire prestige, which in turn may encourage them to overpromise.[125] Some scholars believe leaders have an innate desire for prestige. The motivations are ultimately psychological, that humans are hard-wired to seek status.[126] However, the prestige mechanism can also work through the domestic benefits leaders receive from good international press. Such positive media attention can enhance leaders' stature and enable them to achieve more both internationally and domestically, even enhancing their re-election prospects or their legacy in history. The prestige motive can help

---

[122] On shaming and rhetorical entrapment, see Greenhill 2007; Keck and Sikkink 1998; and Schimmelfennig 2001; 2003. Rhetorical entrapment is similar to the mechanisms of imperial overstretch and blowback described by Snyder 1991.

[123] Greenhill describes how in 1993–1994 Jean-Bertrand Aristide used the threat of Haitian boat people to get President Clinton to reinstall him in power after Clinton-as-candidate had promised more lenient treatment of Haitian refugees (Greenhill 2007).

[124] Tiberghien and Schreurs 2007, 71–72.

[125] Prestige can be thought of as consistent with its dictionary definition: "The level of respect at which one is regarded by others; standing." See the *American Heritage Dictionary*, www.thefreedictionary.com.

[126] Larson and Shevchenko 2005; Lebow 2005; Markey 2000.

us understand what Marc Levy calls "tote-board diplomacy" where politicians engage in competitive promise-making.[127] These dynamics become especially salient if a leader hosts a meeting such as the G-8 summit or one of the Conferences of Parties, as Japan did in 1997 in Kyoto.[128]

Thus far, this reputational account is consistent with both institutionalist and pluralist arguments. However, the reputational motive may not be strictly utilitarian.[129] Punishment from broken promises will likely have only a modest influence on state behavior, particularly when the costs of adhering to an agreement are potentially quite high. Cooperative attitudes also rest on beliefs about right and appropriate behavior that may represent, as Jeff Legro argues, an embedded view of instrumental rationality that, over time, become ends in and of themselves.[130] Initially, instrumental behavior habitually repeated can alter a country's "national role conception" or the self-image leaders have of their country's role on the world stage.

As Martha Finnemore writes: "Localized social understandings among domestic groups may also influence state policy, giving states certain identities and predictable characteristics in international interactions."[131] As a consequence, decisionmakers sometimes act in accord with these established patterns of behavior, their decisions guided by whether or not a policy is consistent with the conception of their country's role on the international stage – such as being a good international citizen, a leader, a trustworthy ally, an independent agent, and so forth.[132] While states may play multiple roles, many will have dominant patterns – central tendencies if you will – of foreign policy behavior. Some states in certain circumstances may seek to develop reputations for what Oded Lowenheim calls "moral credibility."[133]

---

[127] Levy 1993.
[128] The hosts rotate. In 2008, Japan played host, preceded by Germany in 2007, Russia in 2006, the UK in 2005, the United States in 2004, France in 2003, Canada in 2002, Italy in 2001, Japan in 2000, and Germany in 1999 and so on.
[129] For a more extended discussion of reputation, see Busby 2005, 2006b.
[130] Legro 2005b, 7.   [131] Finnemore 1996, 145.
[132] On national role conceptions, see Holsti 1987; Keohane and Milner 1996; Krotz 2001; Nau 2002; Sampson and Walker 1987; Walker 1987; Wang 2004, 2001.
[133] Lowenheim 2003, 28.

While these national role conceptions may have material roots, they take on a normative status if they continue to serve a country well over time. These normative pressures can reinforce the modest reputational costs states face for non-compliance. Coupled with broader uncertainty about the consequences of action, the non-material aspects of reputation can serve in the same way moral values do and tip the balance to lead decisionmakers to support costly moral action.

Why might "moral credibility" feature prominently in a state's reputation? Cohesive, functioning states are animated by foundational myths and national self-understandings. The United States, for example, has a civic creed, based on the rights to life, liberty, and the pursuit of happiness, which were ostensibly available to all people. While they may change over time, such tenets may nonetheless be essential to bind a people together without resulting in endless fighting. Thus, a state's external orientation on the world stage is a partial reflection of domestic preoccupations. At the same time, states are part of a system that influences and is influenced by national self-understandings. The distribution of national role conceptions, or identities, can contribute to outcomes in the system as a whole. For example, a security community, what Henry Nau terms an "anarchy of friends," reflects a constellation of compatible national identities.[134] However, the potential compatibility of roles on the world stage does not lead to functionally determined benign outcomes. Local variation in cultures and governance, burden-sharing issues, and substantive differences over how to achieve shared goals all contribute to more complexity, even among similar regime types.

How can we know that leaders care about "moral credibility"? In some cases, leaders may be able to claim the moral high ground for supporting a particular policy without incurring great cost. However, the whole point of "moral credibility" is for some actors to do things that are not expedient or self-serving. When those states demand costly action from others without the willingness or ability to incur great cost themselves – or a high risk of having to do so – then their position, however sincere, can be easily dismissed as "moral grandstanding." The difficulty is that states that do not incur significant costs are, aside from what they say, potentially indistinguishable from states that do not care. As observers, whether we are academics or fellow travelers

---

[134] Nau 2002, 4–6.

in policy, we cannot tell how important the issue is to the country in question if costs are low. For example, the Canadians played a leadership role in establishing the International Criminal Court. However, they do not have many deployable troops for overseas missions. So, in a sense, it was easy for them to support because the risks for them were lower than for other states.[135] As Michael Tomz explains, a state or leader has the best chance of building a reputation when they do something they should not have done, based on their material interests.[136]

In a unipolar world, the United States, though sometimes controversially, provides security assets for the entire world (such as protecting the sea lanes to facilitate global commerce). Other states can distinguish themselves on the world stage in various ways, sometimes through pursuit of economic power like both Germany and Japan in the aftermath of World War II and like the European Union later.[137] In other cases, national role conceptions might lead states to try to serve as moral arbiters of the international system. The impetus behind investing in "soft-power" institutions and activities under unipolarity may be a desire to compensate for military inferiority and serve as the guardians of either Western or more universal values, such as climate protection.[138]

Under what circumstances will these reputations for moral credibility become important? When decisionmakers have publicly committed to a particular policy, non-governmental advocates and their powerful allies can evoke these self-images to great effect, reminding countries of right and appropriate behavior for that particular country, given how it sees itself. In that sense, advocates can reframe the issue in a way that is culturally compelling, perhaps even more so than environmental values are; additionally, these national self-understandings may also be particularly salient for gatekeepers. In institutional settings where power is concentrated (as in Canada) or where there is considerable cultural homogeneity among elites (as in Japan), elite gatekeepers are in a position and motivated to respond to these powerful cultural symbols in ways that are less possible in different institutional settings.

---

[135] This discussion of costs mirrors the game theoretic literature but also is substantiated by Larson's discussion of how states need to incur consistent costs that cut against material interests to induce another untrusting state to revisit their former evaluation of them (Larson 1997, 13–14).
[136] Tomz 1998, 2007b.   [137] Berger 1996, 1998.   [138] Nye 1990, 2004.

Japan

Since the end of World War II, the Japanese have sought to be good international citizens. In part, this was a rational strategy meant to reassure nervous states in the region about their intentions.[139] It has since taken on more normative significance.[140] When pressed in the 1970s and 1980s to play a more constructive role internationally, the Japanese sought to do so within the constraints of the pacific role mandated by their constitution. In addition to foreign aid, the Japanese have found the environmental field an important arena in which to play this role of good international citizens.[141] As Nobutoshi Akao, Japan's former ambassador for global environmental affairs, said, "The global environmental issue was 'tailor-made' for Japan."[142]

What explains the Japanese decision to ratify Kyoto? Perhaps the most basic reason, more important than international pressure, for Japanese ratification was national honor; "the Kyoto Protocol was the *Kyoto* Protocol." As Yasuko Kameyama notes, ratification became a priority for the same reasons that the Kyoto negotiations had to succeed. If the treaty did not enter into force, this would make Japan look like an unskilled diplomatic player.[143] Moreover, reputational concerns are important because "the Kyoto Protocol is the only international treaty that bears the name of a Japanese city."[144] Similarly, Yutaka Nakao, former first secretary of the environment at the Embassy of Japan to the United States, noted that public support was a main factor driving ratification, "partly because the COP-3 was held in Japan."[145]

As Yasuhiro Shimizu, head of the Climate Change Policy Division in the Ministry of the Environment, explained to me in an interview:

We hosted COP-3 in 1997. The Japanese media covered [that event] very intensively... The Japanese people regard COP-3 as a national event, an

---

[139] Midford 2002.
[140] One scholar described the search for an appropriate international role as something of a "national obsession" in the 1980s (Ohta 1995, 247). Similar dynamics are discussed by Tamamoto 1999.
[141] Lincoln 1993; Ohta 1995. This section builds on Busby 2004a, 2005.
[142] Ohta 1995, 42.   [143] Kameyama 2003, 148.
[144] Kameyama 2001; Kawashima 2001, 178.
[145] Yutaka Nakao 2004. The importance of domestic public pressure was highlighted also by Sugiyama 2003.

occasion in which Japan exercised leadership in the international field. Most people think the conclusion of the Kyoto Protocol at COP-3 was something they were very proud of.[146]

When asked what would have happened if the Kyoto Protocol had not been negotiated in Japan, Shimizu said that although his ministry would have still pushed for ratification, the situation would have been "very different. The Japanese public was not so greatly concerned with the international regime. Not to have the Japanese town's name, the Japanese situation would be very different."[147]

Tiberghien and Schreurs provide a complementary interpretation. They describe the decision to ratify as a product of "embedded symbolism" and the significance the treaty took on given its name:

The decision of earlier LDP [Liberal Democratic Party] leaders to pursue global environmental leadership, reinforced by media discourse, public opinion, and bureaucratic actions, helped to build the Kyoto Protocol into a symbol of Japan's new policy identity.[148]

The European Union and environmental campaigners sought to tap into that sentiment in the run-up to the subsequent round of climate negotiations in mid-July 2002 in Bonn. Both the EU and advocates launched a major effort to persuade the Japanese to ratify Kyoto even without the United States on board, sending a high-level delegation to Japan to meet with Koizumi and his Cabinet in early July 2001.[149] In so doing, they suggested that Japan's failure to ratify would doom the Kyoto Protocol and, as Jan Pronk, the Dutch head of the negotiations, put it, "put climate policy in jeopardy."[150] Environmental advocates buttressed the EU's pressure. As Jennifer Morgan, the head of the WWF climate campaign, noted, there was a deliberate effort to remind the Japanese government that its national honor, prestige, and reputation were at stake if the Kyoto Protocol failed. In her view, "if there hadn't

---

[146] Shimizu 2004.
[147] Shimizu 2004. Tiberghien and Schreurs make exactly this point (Tiberghien and Schreurs 2007, 71).
[148] Tiberghien and Schreurs 2007, 71.
[149] The EU delegation reacted negatively to a Japanese proposal to delay the implementation period of the Kyoto Protocol by two years (Kyodo News International 2001b).
[150] Daily 2001.

been a NGO campaign to save the Kyoto protocol, it wouldn't have happened."[151]

This outside reminder of what was at stake was bolstered by domestic public opinion, which showed strong support for Kyoto. In the same week that the EU sent representatives to Japan, WWF released a poll that showed the Japanese public strongly supported the country taking the lead on the Kyoto Protocol entering into force.[152] The poll was actually more qualified, showing that only 67% had heard of the Kyoto Protocol, and, underscoring the symbolic nature of Kyoto for the Japanese public, only 17.6% said they knew the name of the pact and its contents while 48.3% said they knew the Kyoto Protocol by name only. These efforts intensified in October 2001 during COP-7 at Marrakesh, shortly after which, having secured an even better deal for Japan, the prime minister announced the government would move forward on ratification. Kyoto thus became a symbol of the country's efforts to be seen as a global leader. As Tiberghien and Schreurs conclude: "It became a symbol of the pressing problem of global climate change and Japan's bid to be a larger foreign policy player and a leader in global environmental protection."[153]

Canada

Canada's decision to ratify the Kyoto Protocol appears to be driven largely by the decision of the Liberal Democrat leader, Prime Minister Chrétien, who was personally concerned about climate change. In the Canadian parliamentary system, much as in Britain, treaty ratification requires little legislative oversight.[154] Thus, if the prime minister is supportive and if there is not overwhelming public opposition, then he or she can usually prevail. Even though the Liberal Democrats had done little to restrain the pace of greenhouse gas emissions during their tenure in government, the measure was politically popular with much of the public (though industry and a number of provinces, including oil-rich Alberta, mounted spirited opposition). However, as suggested

---

[151] Morgan 2003. These comments are echoed by Schreurs 2002 and Okazawa 2004a.

[152] Kyodo News International 2001a.   [153] Tiberghien and Schreurs 2007, 78.

[154] While the Canadian Parliament voted in December 2002 by a margin of 195–77 to support ratification of the Kyoto Protocol, the decision was ultimately Chrétien's (BBC 2002a).

already, climate change was not so politically salient that the government felt compelled to ratify.

Rather, Canada's role on the world stage and the country's self-image relative to the United States loom large both in terms of Canada's initial Kyoto commitment and during the lead-up to ratification. As Kathryn Harrison notes, Canada's Kyoto target was intended to shadow the US position. As a member of the Canadian delegation told her: "Being good Canadians, can you imagine us letting the Americans get too far ahead of us?"[155] Perhaps more importantly, as noted earlier, the Kyoto Protocol was personally meaningful to the prime minister, important enough to him that he made the symbolic vote in the House of Commons on ratification a vote of confidence in his government.[156] Ratification was seen as part of the prime minister's legacy as he prepared to retire from politics.[157]

Prior to ratification, business groups, particularly from Alberta, claimed the costs of ratification would bankrupt the economy and cause massive job losses; Canadian NGOs dismissed these claims as alarmist. In addition, groups such as the David Suzuki Foundation critiqued the government's efforts to seek additional credit for clean energy exports with the reprimand: "Don't cheat!" The foundation also evoked the country's aspirations to be a global leader in a June 2002 report:

For many years, Canada has stated and re-stated its intention to act on climate change in a leadership role and in harmony with the international community... Further delay will betray Canada's international commitments, damage our reputation around the world, and allow global warming to continue unchecked.[158]

Harrison's account of Canadian dynamics reinforces this interpretation. Based on interviews with senior Canadian officials, she concludes:

When asked what motivated Mr. Chrétien to support ratification despite significant opposition from business and the provinces, to a one Cabinet colleagues and senior officials interviewed pointed to principled beliefs, offering

---

[155] Harrison 2007, 102.   [156] Bueckert 2002.
[157] BBC 2002a. The announcement to ratify was twinned with an expansion of the country's national parks.
[158] David Suzuki Foundation 2002, 9.

remarkably close variations on the words of one of Mr. Chrétien's Cabinet colleagues that "he believed it was the right thing to do."[159]

In his statement announcing his decision to ratify the Kyoto Protocol, Chrétien spoke in terms consistent with the country's self-image and its perception of its appropriate role on the world stage: "You say to them, Canada is a good citizen of the world." The prime minister elaborated the basis of Canada's support: "Because we believe in international institutions, we believed that we could play a positive role."[160] Chrétien defended his action, explicitly evoking his country's international reputation:

[A potential successor] has no choice because it's an international obligation we have. Canada is a country with a great reputation, that when we are involved internationally, we respect our word. It's not a political gesture. It's extremely important for future generations.[161]

A Canadian polling firm echoed these sentiments in its report on Canadian public opinion of the Kyoto Protocol in advance of ratification: "A majority of Canadians say that Canada should live up to our international commitments even if there are associated economic costs." The firm concluded that, "our research clearly shows that multilateralism and the environment are core values of Canadians."[162] US efforts functioned, as they did in Europe, to steel independent-minded Canadians to support the Kyoto Protocol, even though Canada's emissions had grown sharply, much like the United States.

Conclusion

On climate policy, non-state actors framed the issue as an environmental crisis, which shaped the kind of policies that were politically rewarded (or punished). For politicians who wanted to appear green, either because of political expedience or out of conscience, a binding international treaty with deep targets and timetables for emissions reductions was highly desirable. The agreed-upon targets of the Kyoto

---

[159] Harrison 2007, 112.   [160] Sault Star 2002.   [161] Toulin 2002.
[162] Globescan 2002. The poll found the percentage of Canadians who would disapprove of a US-like withdrawal from Kyoto fell from 70% to 59% between May and November 2002. Anti-ratification forces, particularly in western rural provinces, had succeeded in shifting some segments of Canadian public opinion, but not enough to have a majority.

Protocol were unequally costly to different countries. In the G-7, Japan, the United States, and Canada faced costly action to ratify the treaty, given their high levels of emissions in 2000. While Japan and Canada were able to ratify, the United States was not. I emphasize the institutional barriers to ratification in the United States compared to Japan and Canada and the role reputational motivations played in both ratifying countries. Reputation here is conceived as a concern for the country's prestige and role on the international stage, not just a preoccupation with the potential costs, domestic and international, of not keeping promises.

For advocates, the Kyoto Protocol provides a salutary lesson about the policy instruments that are linked to particular policy frames and the importance of the institutional environments for approving international agreements. A different policy instrument (a series of sectoral efficiency agreements for different industries, for example) might not require a two-thirds' majority of US senators to secure passage in the United States. The lessons of Kyoto are also instructive – that international agreements need domestic political support, beyond broad cultural appeal to values, environmental, reputation, or otherwise. In the case of climate policy, a number of American commentators have concluded that it must begin at home, with domestic legislation on a carbon cap by necessity preceding an international agreement and not the other way around, as was envisaged in the Kyoto Protocol.[163]

In December 2009, the Copenhagen climate negotiations, where the successor to the Kyoto Protocol was meant to be negotiated, took place. As expected, the incoming Obama administration was not able to pass domestic climate legislation in time and simultaneously fully prepare its negotiators for Copenhagen. The outcome was a non-binding political agreement. While advocates have already experimented with alternative frames to capture the attention of decisionmakers, they would be advised to consider more flexible forums and policy instruments to avoid the fate of the Kyoto Protocol, at least in the United States; these would more likely ensure meaningful action by others, including Canada, Japan, and emerging economies in the developing world, such as China and India.[164]

---

[163] Bodansky 2001. See also Lee, Cochran, and Roy 2001; Purvis 2004.
[164] See Busby 2006a.

For observers of Canadian and Japanese politics (and treaty obligations writ large), the evidence seems to support the minimalist notion that treaties have little compliance-pull, that countries are able to ratify treaties without having to implement them or pay any costs for not keeping their commitments, an attractive but inaccurate conclusion. As noted, Japan's symbolic incentives to support Kyoto have affected its behavior. To protect its image, the country (and its firms) have been prepared to pay billions of dollars to East European countries for emissions offsets.[165] In Canada, climate change remains a live issue. Although Canada's emissions are wildly off-track in terms of its Kyoto commitments, the resonance of environmental values, coupled with the country's self-image as a good international citizen and constructive multilateralist, could allow climate change to become an important wedge issue in national elections. While the economic crisis may have blunted the political support for an environmental/internationalist appeal, Australia's experience is instructive. In November 2007, Australia's right-leaning government, long opposed to Kyoto and climate legislation, was defeated by Kevin Rudd's Labor Party, with a change in climate policy part of its appeal. The Rudd-led government promptly ratified Kyoto, leaving the country with some difficult choices as it seeks to meet its Kyoto commitment (a target of an 8% increase above 1990 emissions and actual emissions 36% higher than 1990 levels in 2005).[166] Victory by the Liberal Party in Canada would bring to power a government rhetorically committed to Kyoto and climate policy, making it more likely the government would finally have to back up its words with action. With the United States poised to take action on climate policy, Canada's ability to avoid implementation will likely erode.

Whether or not treaty commitments are, in fact, meaningful depends on the balance of domestic forces and what other countries are doing and, importantly, what the United States is prepared to do. US withdrawal from Kyoto was a sufficient challenge to European credibility and leadership that the EU was prepared to assume some modest costs

---

[165] To meet its Kyoto target, Japan's power generation sector, its steel sector, and the Japanese government had plans to buy 350 million tons of emissions credits by 2012, at an estimated cost of $6.4 billion (Carr and Tomek 2009).
[166] WRI 2006.

by way of its regional emissions trading scheme.[167] Although the Kyoto Protocol was ratified by more than 180 countries, the absence of the United States, the world's second largest emitter of greenhouse gases, has undermined the broader regime. The US refusal to ratify has particularly affected the willingness by China and India to take actions to restrain the growth in their emissions. In Japan and Canada, pro-Kyoto forces were able to secure ratification, but US non-participation sapped their governments' domestic support for more costly implementation. This observation suggests that advocates have to pay much more attention to long-term policy success, rather than simply short-term political success.

[167] For a more extended discussion of the effects of US withdrawal on the EU, see Busby 2008a.

5 | *From God's mouth: messenger effects and donor responses to HIV/AIDS*

In his 2003 State of the Union address, President George W. Bush called on the US Congress to fund PEPFAR, a five-year $15 billion emergency plan to combat HIV/AIDS in the developing world. In justifying PEPFAR, the president declared:

> As our nation moves troops and builds alliances to make our world safer, we must also remember our calling as a blessed country is to make this world better... A doctor in rural South Africa describes his frustration. He says, "We have no medicines. Many hospitals tell people, you've got AIDS, we can't help you. Go home and die." In an age of miraculous medicines, no people should hear those words.[1]

The size and scope of the program left many in the advocacy community stunned. So why had the Bush administration done it? Was this announcement a calculated effort to deflect attention from the United States' imminent military action in Iraq? Was it driven by pharmaceutical companies? Could the decision have been motivated by moral concerns? This anecdote underscores a broader question: Why do some states give more than others to support international HIV/AIDS efforts? From the perspective of advocacy groups promoting efforts to address AIDS and other concerns, another question emerges: Why do some campaigns succeed in some places and fail in others?

In the twenty-five years since AIDS was first identified, more than 25 million people have died from the disease, mostly in developing countries. Tens of millions more will likely die. Since 2001, rich countries have become increasingly generous donors to global efforts to combat AIDS, prompted in part by advocacy groups such as the Global AIDS Alliance and Debt, AIDS, Trade, Africa (DATA). Many advocates for more expansive programs of donor support for HIV/AIDS were veterans of Jubilee 2000, the campaign for developing country debt relief.

---

[1] Woolley and Peters 2006. PEPFAR stands for the President's Emergency Plan for AIDS Relief.

151

In June 2001, UN secretary general Kofi Annan bolstered their cause by calling for a global fund to combat HIV/AIDS that would require $7–10 billion annually. In 2002, advanced industrialized countries pledged their support for the Global Fund to Fight AIDS, Tuberculosis, and Malaria as the centerpiece of the multilateral response. PEPFAR became the Global Fund's main bilateral companion/competitor.

This chapter addresses the politics of donor response to HIV/AIDS by the G-7 advanced industrialized countries.[2] While advanced industrialized countries are not doing enough to meet the financing needs Annan identified, some countries are doing more than others. In the period 2002–2006, the United States, Canada, and the United Kingdom did more while Japan and Germany clearly lagged behind. What explains these differences in donors' willingness to provide funding to combat HIV/AIDS in developing countries?

Material factors created a permissive context for higher spending on global HIV/AIDS programs by several leading countries and contributed to lower spending by lagging nations. However, such factors do not fully explain the divergence in spending patterns. Some leading states, such as the United States, were asked to spend a significant share of their foreign assistance on AIDS and, contrary to some expectations, they have done so (albeit the sum was less than what campaigners asked for). Moral considerations are needed to understand both the scale and the character of leading countries' responses. AIDS advocates framed their arguments to tap into moral and religious attitudes and found receptive audiences among key policy gatekeepers in leading countries. Lagging countries lacked receptive high-level leadership and had low levels of civil society mobilization. While earlier chapters focused on the content of advocacy messages, this chapter augments the earlier discussion by emphasizing the role of *messenger effects*. Drawing on findings from social psychology, I suggest that interlocutors such as Franklin Graham, the son of the Reverend Billy Graham, were successful messengers in the United States and enjoyed influence because they possessed a number of shared attributes with policy gatekeepers. Who they were was perhaps as important as what they had to say.

The chapter is divided into four sections. The first provides an overview of the epidemic and of donor responses. In the second section,

---

[2] I only tangentially discuss the politics of access to generic AIDS drugs.

I evaluate material interest-based explanations and discuss their limitations. In the third section, I augment the framing argument of earlier chapters, emphasizing the importance of messenger effects and moral motivations. In the final section, I explore three country cases: a leading country, the United States, and mini-cases of two lagging countries, Germany and Japan.

Background on HIV/AIDS and donor responses to the pandemic

The AIDS crisis is a tragedy of epic proportions. By 2007, more than 25 million people had already died from AIDS, 2 million of them in that year alone.[3] Another 33 million were living with the virus. There were an estimated 2.7 million new infections in 2007, 1.9 million in sub-Saharan Africa, the epicenter of the pandemic.[4] In 2004, it was the leading cause of death worldwide for people aged 15–59.[5] As many as 100 million may die from AIDS by the middle of the twenty-first century.[6]

In the late 1990s and early 2000s, a confluence of events created the impetus for broader international action to address the pandemic.[7] Sociologists such as Tony Barnett documented the effects of HIV/AIDS on communities in Africa.[8] Sustained media attention in 1999 and 2000, by the likes of Laurie Garrett at *Newsday* and Barton Gellman at the *Washington Post*, brought the human tragedy into stark relief. Together, these efforts pushed the issue higher on the agenda, with the number of articles in major newspapers that connected HIV and Africa spiking from 500 in 1997 to about 900 in 1999 and 1,000 in 2000.[9] The success of countries such as Brazil in putting HIV-positive individuals on treatment and Uganda's reportedly effective prevention program helped create a constituency for something to

---

[3] By way of comparison, the Black Death killed about 25 million in the fourteenth century, possibly as much as one-third of Europe's population (Susan Peterson and Shellman 2006).
[4] UNAIDS 2008.   [5] Kaiser Family Foundation 2005b.
[6] Even the best scenario, in which sub-Saharan Africa slows the tide of new infections, cumulative deaths from 1980 to 2025 are projected to reach 67 million (UNAIDS 2005a, 22).
[7] For a more detailed history of the lack of international attention, see Behrman 2004; Gellman 2000.
[8] Barnett and Whiteside 2002.   [9] Sell and Prakash 2004, 162.

be done and delegitimated arguments that new programs could not be effective. In January 2000, the United Nations Security Council hosted an unprecedented meeting focusing on AIDS as a threat to peace and security in Africa, with US vice president Al Gore presiding. Soon after, in July 2000, South Africa hosted the international conference on AIDS in Durban, widely regarded in the AIDS community as the turning point in global acceptance that extending treatment to the developing world was possible.

While organizations such as Doctors Without Borders, Health GAP, and James Love's Consumer Project on Technology battled over intellectual property rights and access to essential medicines, groups such as the Global AIDS Alliance and ACT UP demanded the extension of treatment to the developing world. South Africa's Treatment Action Campaign, founded in 1998, complemented those efforts. As the Jubilee 2000 campaign wound down, activists from the development advocacy community also turned their attention to AIDS. The Irish pop star Bono formed DATA in 2002, which included Jubilee 2000's global strategist Jamie Drummond and the Episcopal Church's Tom Hart. DATA quickly became one of the leading organizations engaged on the issue.

Until the Global Fund's creation in 2002, few resources were directed at the HIV/AIDS crisis in the developing world. In a 2001 paper in the *Lancet*, Amir Attaran and Jeffrey Sachs estimated that between 1996 and 1998 rich donors averaged about $170 million a year for HIV/AIDS activities in the developing world.[10] With the creation of the Global Fund and other bilateral and multilateral programs, donors rapidly scaled up funding for HIV/AIDS treatment and prevention programs, making available about $8 billion in 2005.[11] Treatment received the largest proportion of funds, remarkable given that the extension of anti-retroviral therapy (ARV) to the developing world had been dismissed as inappropriate for developing countries just a few years earlier.[12] In June 2001, USAID administrator Andrew

---

[10] Attaran and Sachs 2001, 57. Of this total, only $69 mn per year was dedicated to HIV/AIDS projects in sub-Saharan Africa.

[11] Estimates for 2005 include bilateral, multilateral, private, and domestic resources. Domestic resources accounted for about one-quarter of the total (UNAIDS 2005b).

[12] The original legislation for PEPFAR, for example, required by law that at least 55 percent of the funds be spent on treatment. A May 2007 US Government

Natsios had famously derided the efficacy of treatment, saying Africans could not tell time, and thus would not take the drugs at the required time intervals.[13]

While a far cry from the 8–10 million people who likely need treatment, funds from the global community put about 4 million HIV-positive individuals in middle- and low-income countries on ARV therapy by the end of 2008, up from 400,000 at the end of December 2003.[14] On the prevention side, financing supported abstinence and fidelity, programs that provided condoms, and efforts to secure the blood supply, among other measures.[15] The prevention agenda has been more politically contested, particularly in the United States, where religious conservatives have promoted abstinence while liberals have been in favor of condom use. With an estimated 2.7 million new infections in 2007, prevention has arguably been less successful, with new approaches, such as male circumcision, not getting sufficient emphasis.[16]

Annan's estimates of the need for $7–10 billion annually for AIDS have been scaled up. The Joint United Nations Programme on HIV and AIDS (UNAIDS) has come to include other needs, such as support for orphans, development of the health infrastructure, and education of health professionals. In 2005, UNAIDS estimated that $12.3 bn would be needed that year to combat the epidemic but that only $8.3 bn was going to be provided. Based on estimates of need and financing commitments, the shortfall was estimated to climb from

Accountability Office (GAO) report estimated that 32% of the Global Fund's resources for AIDS were being dedicated to treatment, compared to 30% for prevention, 14% for care and support, and 24% for other (including health systems capacity strengthening) (GAO 2007).

[13] John Donnelly 2001.

[14] UNAIDS 2009; WHO 2008. As of September 30, 2008, the United States estimated that the US government had supported more than an estimated 2.1 mn people on anti-retroviral drug therapy, up from 155,000 in September 2004 (United States, Department of State, Office of the US Global Aids Coordinator 2009). For a discussion of how the treatment regime was politically constructed, see Kapstein and Busby 2009.

[15] United States, Department of State 2006, 38–39. It is hard to gauge progress since infections averted are non-events that we cannot observe. Disentangling the effects of prevention programs is complex, and we may not know how successful these programs are until better data become available.

[16] On new infections, see UNAIDS 2008. On male circumcision, see Busby 2008d.

$4 bn in 2005 to $8.1 bn in 2007 (when more than $18 bn was needed).[17]

AIDS activists have suggested that donor countries should contribute based on an assessment of their "fair share."[18] One oft-used metric is each donor's share of world income.[19] While no country can claim to be doing enough, some countries are doing more than others. Table 5.1 shows contributions to the Global Fund between 2001 and 2006. Based on share of world income, the United States, the UK, Canada, France, and Italy were leading in their contributions to the Global Fund, while Germany and Japan lagged behind.[20] The United States contributed 28.69% of world GDP in 2004; its pledges to the Global Fund constituted 30.84% of funds actually paid between 2001 and 2006.[21]

However, many countries concentrate their HIV/AIDS spending on bilateral contributions to governments or to NGOs. Of the $5.563 bn the G-8/EC and Development Assistance Committee (DAC) members pledged to AIDS in 2006, about 83 percent was channeled bilaterally.[22] While some of the US response has been directed to the Global Fund, more than 80 percent was distributed bilaterally through US government partners in 2004–2006, mostly in fifteen target countries.[23] Consistent with the patterns of multilateral giving, the British, Americans, and Canadians all generally pledged more than their share of income (see Table 5.2). However, in contrast to their performance in the multilateral arena, the French and Italians gave less than their

---

[17] UNAIDS 2005b.   [18] Kates 2005; Oxfam 2002.   [19] Oxfam 2002.

[20] Global Fund 2005; IMF 2005. Contributions to the Global Fund also reflect support for tuberculosis and malaria prevention. Only 61 percent of Global Fund resources are dedicated to HIV/AIDS.

[21] Congress limited US contributions to the Global Fund to one-third of the Fund's total resources.

[22] Kates, Izazola, and Lief 2007. One could also impute HIV/AIDS contributions by governments to the World Bank and/or the European Union. This would boost Italian, Japanese, German, and French contributions, but their contributions would remain below their share of global GDP. The DAC is the body coordinating foreign assistance for major donors, composed of twenty-three OECD countries and the European Commission; its members are advanced industrialized countries. Since data on bilateral giving are available for DAC countries, I compare giving percentages to their share of DAC income, excluding the EU as a separate entry.

[23] Kates 2006, 2005. Countries include: Botswana, Côte d'Ivoire, Ethiopia, Guyana, Haiti, Kenya, Mozambique, Namibia, Nigeria, Rwanda, South Africa, Tanzania, Uganda, Vietnam, and Zambia.

Table 5.1 *G-7 Global Fund contributions and share of world income*

	Pledges 2001–2007	Contributions 2001–2006	% of total pledges 2001–2007	% of total contributions 2001–2006	% of world GDP 2004	2004 GDP (current prices $US bn)
Canada	$431,462,054	$320,867,690	4.71%	4.93%	2.43%	$993.442
European Commission (EC)	$775,346,567	$638,547,661			31.46%	$12,865.602
France	$778,487,913	$778,487,913	8.50%	11.96%	5.0%	$2,046.292
Germany	$409,956,988	$286,436,783	4.48%	4.40%	6.74%	$2,754.727
Italy	$801,137,155	$460,620,273	8.75%	7.07%	4.11%	$1,680.112
Japan	$662,274,702	$476,668,241	7.23%	7.32%	11.42%	$4,871.198
UK	$668,386,001	$467,147,678	7.30%	7.17%	5.22%	$2,133.019
United States	$2,731,943,055	$2,007,943,055	29.83%	30.84%	28.69%	$11,734.300
Total by government actors	$9,159,719,071	$6,510,945,700				$40,894.78

Note and source: Figures do not include contributions from private actors such as the Gates Fund, which constitute a small share of the organization's total resources (Global Fund 2007). Shares of world income are from IMF 2005.

Table 5.2 *G-7 bilateral aid to combat HIV/AIDS, 2000–2005*

	2000–2005 bilateral aid activities (nominal $ millions)	% of OECD/ DAC total bilateral aid 2000–2005	% of OECD/ DAC GDP 2004	2004 GDP (current prices $US bn)
Canada	$343.15	4.05%	3.2%	$993.442
France	$87.70	1.03%	6.6%	$2,046.292
EC	$216.80	2.56%		
Germany	$303.05	3.58%	8.89%	$2,754.727
Italy	$17.74	0.21%	5.42%	$1,680.112
Japan	$63.75	0.75%	15.07%	$4,871.198
UK	$1,146.68	13.53%	6.88%	$2,133.019
United States	$4,907.25	57.89%	37.84%	$11,734.300
Other DAC	$1,390.25			
Total by DAC	$8,476.37			$31,012.387

Sources: DAC data are from OECD 2007. For other data sources, see Kates 2005, 2006; Kates, Izazola, and Lief 2007.

share of income. The US bilateral share amounted to more than 55 percent of DAC contributions in the period 2000–2005.[24]

Based on both multilateral and bilateral measures, three countries – the United States, Canada, and the UK – contributed more than their share of GDP while two countries – Japan and Germany – lagged behind on both measures.[25]

[24] Interestingly, the United States (like the Global Fund) has had trouble in recent years disbursing all that it has committed. In 2006, it pledged far more bilateral aid than it disbursed, with only 60 percent of its pledge disbursed by year's end (Kates, Izazola, and Lief 2007).

[25] Contact the author for the data. Kates presents alternative metrics to judge "fair share" contributions by donors, including the relative share of advanced economy GNP, the share of total resources provided to HIV/AIDS (including resources mobilized by developing countries themselves), and funding provided per $1 million of gross national income. While the United States exchanges the leadership position with the UK on the latter measure, the United States, Canada, and the UK lead in all three (Kates 2005, 15). However, when she looked at the share of global resources for HIV/AIDS (including recipient country contributions), she found only the UK and Canada exceeding their share of global GDP, with the United States providing just 15.6% of global resources (Kates 2006).

However, when judged against the total need estimated by UNAIDS, donor giving patterns look less generous. By this measure, only the UK exceeded its putative fair share in 2006 and 2007 (see Appendix 5A). Moreover, if we focus solely on HIV/AIDS, there is a risk of losing sight of the larger portrait of donor countries' foreign assistance programs. US giving, for example, appears much less generous when one looks at broader patterns of foreign assistance as a share of GDP.[26] However, the fact that the United States dedicated increasing amounts of foreign assistance to HIV/AIDS when it is a stingy donor for broader development assistance suggests an even more interesting puzzle. How did AIDS advocates break through typical resistance by the US government to increase funds for foreign assistance? It remains important to understand the patterns and the reasons why some countries have been more generous donors to support global AIDS efforts while others have lagged behind.

A partial explanation: material interest

A set of partial explanations for these patterns is based on material self-interest. I review arguments based on *state interests* as well as a pluralist account based on the micro-motives of *individual* politicians before discussing the limits of interest-based explanations.

Arguments based on *state interests* would explain levels of donor giving to combat HIV/AIDS based on the balance of material incentives facing the state, including: (1) the perception of a direct threat to its domestic populations from the disease, and/or (2) the perception that its interests abroad are threatened in former colonies, areas of responsibility, or areas of financial interest (e.g., trading partners or natural resource providers). State interest arguments would also suggest (3) that donor giving is contingent upon available resources and other economic factors. Thus, countries with poor economic conditions would likely be less generous than countries doing well. A background condition affecting all countries is (4) the cost of treatment

---

[26] In 2005, the Center for Global Development ranked the United States nineteenth of twenty-one countries in terms of the quantity and quality of foreign assistance. The United States spent only 0.14% of its GDP on foreign assistance, far from the 0.7% target industrialized countries pledged in 1970 before the UN and reiterated in Monterey, Mexico, in 2002 (Center for Global Development 2005).

and prevention programs. Very high costs of anti-retroviral drugs, for example, might make treatment appear unfeasible to all of them. In addition to the overall price tag for the policy, decisionmakers would also likely judge the costliness of the policy for their country and compare their expected costs for global AIDS support relative to what they were already spending on foreign assistance. Where this proportion was high, states would be expected to be less supportive of the policy.

For the state interest argument to be valid, leading countries such as the United States and the UK would have to face greater threats from AIDS than the laggards. In reality, all advanced industrialized countries largely had the disease under control by the early 2000s.[27] Not all states had interests based on former colonial ties: The UK and France had the most at stake as the dominant former colonial powers in Africa. Proponents of state interest might also emphasize the broader strategic environment. Given the campaign against global terrorism and the potential for negative reaction to the United States' then-impending conflict with Iraq in 2003, donor action on the AIDS pandemic, according to this line of thought, served the country's interests by shoring up states vulnerable to state failure, blunting criticism, and providing cover for the administration's military agenda.

Advocates of this argument would also likely emphasize the long-running recession and unemployment problems in Japan and continental Europe at the time, in contrast to more robust economic conditions in the UK and the United States (see Table 5.3). The average GDP growth rate for advanced economies for the five-year period 1999–2003 was 2.98%, while for the G-7 it was 2.12%. Among the G-7 countries, only Canada (3.47%) had higher growth than the rich world average followed by the UK (2.95%) and the United States (2.59%). Lagging donors Germany and Japan had slower growth rates, 1.22% and 0.92% respectively. Follower countries France and Italy also had lower than average growth rates, 2.24% and 1.48% respectively.

In addition to patterns of economic growth, proponents of state interest arguments might explain why this initiative did not occur earlier – say in the late 1990s – by noting the sharp decline in ARV drug prices in 2000 and 2001.[28] While the drop in per unit ARV

---

[27] Prevalence levels for all G-7 countries was less than 1 percent; see UNDP 2004.
[28] In 2000, competition from generic producers in India and Brazil drove down the average price of a branded AIDS triple-combination therapy from $10,439 per year per patient to less than $1,000. In February 2001, the Indian generics

Table 5.3 *Average GDP growth rate, % 1999–2003*

Canada	France	Germany	Italy	Japan	UK	United States	G-7 average	Average of advanced economies
3.47	2.24	1.22	1.48	0.92	2.95	2.59	2.12	2.98

Note and source: IMF 2008. These growth rates are calculated by taking the five-year average annual percentage change in GDP in constant prices.

prices might explain the broader acceptance of treatment as an option among all donors, state interest accounts might emphasize other cost considerations, namely the size of the total obligation for each state, to explain the differential willingness of some donors to accept these costs. Advocates encouraged states to contribute to the global total (as noted earlier, the need was initially estimated to be $7–10 billion per year) based on their share of global GDP. If states agreed to advocates' demands, this would imply a commitment of new resources to foreign assistance or a reprioritization of existing resources within the overseas development assistance budget. All else being equal, it would be more costly (and more politically difficult) to approve the policy the higher the proportion of the existing foreign assistance budget that this commitment implied.[29] The midpoint in the initial $7–10 billion annual cost estimate for global AIDS policies is $8.5 billion. Taking each country's share of world GDP and this middle estimate of $8.5 billion as the size of the funding request, we can calculate the implied per country cost based on the fair share metric and compare this to country spending commitments on foreign aid.[30] Based on this indicator, it would have been more difficult in 2002 (the year after Annan's plea for resources and the year the Global Fund was created) for the

manufacturer Cipla stepped up the competition on other ARV manufacturers when it announced a triple-combination treatment for $350 per patient per year (Hellerstein 2004).

[29] Some might question this interpretation, since countries already spending a significant amount on foreign assistance would find the additional fair share to be a smaller percentage of their existing total.

[30] For both GDP and foreign aid commitments, I used the nominal $US average in the three years 1999–2001 before the Global Fund was created. Data on global GDP are from IMF 2008. Data on foreign assistance commitments come from OECD 2007.

Table 5.4 *Initial AIDS contribution fair shares and foreign assistance*

	% of world GDP 1999–2001	Average ODA commitments 1999–2001 (millions $US)	Implied fair share (millions $US)	AIDS fair share as % of ODA commitments
Canada	2.22%	$1,824.49	$188.55	10.33%
France	4.36%	$5,349.25	$371.02	6.94%
Germany	6.28%	$6,393.96	$533.81	8.35%
Italy	3.61%	$1,906.47	$307.15	16.11%
Japan	13.88%	$15,871.60	$1,179.94	7.43%
UK	4.70%	$4,237.34	$399.80	9.44%
United States	30.83%	$12,647.94	$2,620.62	20.72%

Note: Figures in column 3 reflect non-rounded percentages. For both GDP and foreign aid commitments, I used the nominal $US average in the three years 1999–2001 before the Global Fund was created.
Sources: IMF 2008 (global GDP); OECD 2007 (foreign assistance commitments).

United States and Italy to meet their fair share commitments than it would have been for countries such as France and Japan, for which the additional AIDS contribution constituted a smaller percentage of their existing foreign aid budgets (see Table 5.4).

While state interest arguments derive their explanatory power from the mix of material incentives facing states, arguments based on *individual interest* would explain donor giving based on politicians' potential electoral rewards (or punishment) from acting (or failing) to provide donor support for HIV/AIDS prevention and treatment.[31] Thus, one could explain differences in states' patterns of giving based on the level of political mobilization by groups favoring and opposed to more generous AIDS intervention policies. Individual interest explanations would suggest that politicians in leading countries responded with greater contributions because of pressure from politically powerful constituencies. From this pluralist perspective, countries with more robust internationally oriented lobby groups (such as the UK) were able to pressure their politicians to give more to AIDS efforts than

---

[31] This approach is consistent with rational choice accounts that get at the micro-foundations of political behavior. Examples include Bueno de Mesquita *et al.* 2003 and Mayhew 1974.

Table 5.5 *Number of international NGO secretariats, 2003*

	Canada	France	Germany	Italy	Japan	UK	United States	High-income countries
Number	462	1,405	987	544	264	1,923	3,305	14,939
Number per 1 million population	14.5	23.4	12.0	9.4	2.1	23.1	11.5	11.5

Source: Anheier, Glasius, and Kaldor 2004.

countries such as Japan, where such groups are underfinanced and weak.[32]

The strength of the advocacy sector is hard to assess, but two comparative measures are the number of international NGO secretariats and their organizational density in a country (the number per 1 million population). By this measure, France and the UK should have the strongest international advocacy sectors (at least in terms of density) with the United States leading the G-7 in terms of numbers of international NGOs. Japan trailed all of the countries, being weak in numbers and density (see Table 5.5).[33] These figures are likely to be only a partial reflection of advocacy for global AIDS funding, as other groups (a number of religious organizations, the gay and lesbian community, and the African diaspora) all mobilized in varying degrees to support addressing the pandemic.

One could also gauge the strength of potential opponents. While providers of health services stood to benefit from more generous AIDS programs,[34] the pharmaceutical industry might have reasons to oppose

[32] One could also chart the relative strength of the AIDS advocacy community in those countries, as reflected by the resources and membership of groups in favor of more ambitious AIDS efforts. Elsewhere, I have collected data on resources, membership, and staffing levels of British, American, German, and Japanese development NGOs. I concluded that the British development advocacy sector was the most powerful, followed by the Americans and the Germans, with the Japanese having the weakest sector. See appendix A in Busby 2004a.

[33] One should take into account countervailing political power by groups opposed to a more aggressive response, such as pharmaceutical companies or opponents of foreign assistance.

[34] On the self-interested motives of NGOs, see Cooley and Ron 2002.

Table 5.6 *Interest-based accounts of AIDS spending*

Leaders (United States, UK, Canada)	Good economy (United States, UK, Canada)
	Supporter of the Iraq war (United States, UK)
	Strong colonial ties (UK)
	Strong civil society (UK, United States, Canada)
	AIDS fair share low in relation to ODA (UK, Canada)
	AIDS fair share high in relation to ODA (United States)
Followers Italy, France	Bad economy (Italy, France)
	Supporter of the Iraq war (Italy)
	Strong colonial ties (France)
	AIDS fair share low in relation to ODA (France)
	AIDS fair share high in relation to ODA (Italy)
Laggards Japan, Germany	Bad economy (Germany, Japan)
	Weak colonial ties (Germany, Japan)
	Weak civil society (Japan)
	AIDS fair share low in relation to ODA (Germany, Japan)
All	Declining prices of anti-retroviral therapy

(or at least co-opt) policies that sanction the purchase of generic anti-AIDS drugs. However, because pharmaceutical companies might still get large orders for their products as part of the response to the pandemic, their preferences regarding enhanced global AIDS programs are not obvious. Table 5.6 summarizes interest-based accounts of the observed behavior of the G-7.

Despite the plausibility of interest-based explanations, such arguments provide an incomplete account of decisionmakers' motivations. As I noted in Chapter 2, imputing material motives to decisionmakers as a default is tempting. With state interest explanations, for example, we do not have to know much about the case or dynamics inside the country. With only a few indicators, we can explain what was going on ("Japan had low economic growth while the US economy was much more healthy, so therefore the United States could afford to support global HIV/AIDS efforts while Japan could not"). Activists themselves periodically engage in such diagnoses. As Bono said of Italian prime minister Romano Prodi in the lead-up to the 2007 G-8 summit: "He's a beautiful man, but he's broke. I don't know what to do about Italy."[35]

[35] Quoted in Dugger 2008.

Knowing something about the relative economic health in different countries is important, but such arguments should serve as a preliminary point of departure rather than a complete explanation. As I noted in the previous two chapters, states on occasion act against their short-run material interests. Material interest-based explanations on their own have difficulty explaining such cases. Moreover, as this chapter demonstrates, even when states have apparent material motivations for their behavior, something else may be going on. Concerns about morality and other motives such as prestige may shape the nature of a country's responses as much as or more than material factors. Moreover, in a number of cases, such as the United States, Germany, and Japan, material indicators gave states contradictory signals about the ease of supporting global AIDS intervention policies.

In previous chapters, I looked at cases of costly moral action, where a state seemingly acted against its material interests. In cases where it is not costly for a state to pursue its values (or where a state also has overwhelming material incentives to support a policy even if it is not expensive), it may be difficult to distinguish morally motivated behavior from self-interested behavior. For that reason, it is instructive to examine cases where states have to choose between their interests and their values. Such cases provide teachable moments about state motivations (and about the adequacy of potentially rival arguments). In the case of HIV/AIDS, leading countries such as the UK that were prepared to spend more on fighting the disease likely had modest if not overwhelming instrumental reasons to support funding, while lagging countries had plausible economic difficulties that curtailed their enthusiasm and ability to provide larger sums to combat the pandemic. The US case provides an interesting puzzle. On one level, its healthy economic growth provided a permissive context for greater spending on AIDS. However, the total request for the United States constituted a significant share of its entire foreign assistance budget. Moreover, foreign assistance is comparatively less popular in the United States than in other G-7 countries. Even if the United States had some self-interested motivations to do something, those policy incentives do not explain the choice of AIDS policy over other options.

If we want to understand both motivations and how the policy came together, process-tracing, described in Chapter 2, offers a way to understand how a policy evolved from conception to execution.

Looking in detail at how policies were made and justified can reveal that moral and other non-material motivations had a clear impact on decisionmaking, even in cases where indicators are at least partially consistent with state and individual material self-interest. For example, while the increase in overall US spending to address the global HIV/AIDS pandemic is potentially explained by permissive material conditions, the character of the US bilateral funding program can be explained only by acknowledging moral motives. As I discuss more fully later in this chapter, the US Congress required that a proportion of US funding for global AIDS programs be dedicated to abstinence-only measures, a policy motivated by the concerns of religious conservatives. While an individual interest or pluralist argument might suggest the policy was a response to political pressure, the explanation still presumes that a segment of the general public was motivated by moral concerns. Admitting that voters can have moral motivations leaves the door open to allowing politicians themselves to be so moved.

A more complete explanation: framing/gatekeepers with a focus on messengers

State interest and individual interest are useful ways to conceptualize the incentives governments and decisionmakers face as they deal with international problems such as HIV/AIDS. However, rarely are material incentives so clear that a "right" policy answer is obvious, and while issues of global altruism are periodically politically salient, provision of AIDS funds to poor foreigners is unlikely to be so important to voters that a politician could fear electoral punishment at the ballot box.[36] As I have already suggested, moral concerns and other motives such as prestige can provide extra weight for (or against) a policy. They may also influence the character of the policy. However, whether moral concerns become part of the equation depends on how the issue has been framed and on the preferences and number of gatekeepers. In this chapter, I introduce another mediating factor – the *messengers*.

Earlier in the book, I wrote about the cultural match of advocates' messages and the importance of gatekeepers; here I focus on

---

[36] For a more extended discussion, see Busby 2008c.

the messengers that bring ideas and issues to gatekeepers' attention. In addition to the content of the message being important, so too are the attributes of the source. Research in experimental social psychology has found that messengers or "sources" are quite important under certain conditions. Multiple studies have found that a variety of source attributes enhance persuasiveness including: expertise,[37] celebrity,[38] attractiveness,[39] similarity,[40] unexpected behavior,[41] and race.[42] So-called dual process models suggest there are two main pathways by which source effects matter. First, people may use these sources as *information shortcuts* and cues to decide what to do. These decisions may be either conscious or unconscious but the importance is that this mode of thinking is more reflexive than deliberative: "If s/he is for it, I am for it." Alternatively, in other cases, source attributes can be central to deliberation as *persuasive arguments*: "Coming from her, that argument makes sense." The mode of messenger influence varies with the ability and motivation of the receiver. Where issues are of low personal significance or relevance to the receiver, source effects function at best as cues to accept or reject a policy. As personal relevance increases, source effects can become

---

[37] One study by Petty, Cacioppo, and Goldman found that respondents were much more favorable to expert sources than non-experts (in this case university professors and high school students), and that they retained more of the information from the experts than the non-experts (Petty and Cacioppo 1986).

[38] In other cases, the messages of well-liked sports figures and celebrities were better received and better remembered than those of anonymous citizens (Petty and Cacioppo 1986, 143).

[39] Studies by Petty and Cacioppo, Efran and Patterson, and Chaiken found that more attractive speakers were better received: Efran and Patterson cited in Cialdini 1984, 167; Chaiken cited in Petty and Cacioppo 1981.

[40] Studies by Byrne, Rokeach, Berscheid and Walster, and Suedfeld *et al.* suggested that people found others like themselves (in terms of dress and demeanor) to be more persuasive than people who were very different: Byrne, Rokeach, and Berscheid and Walster cited in Petty and Cacioppo 1981, 63; Suedfeld *et al.* cited in Cialdini 1984, 169.

[41] Another experimental finding from Jones and Davis suggested that, when behavior from a particular person is unexpected, the inference that these are the messengers' true beliefs and that this view was credible is stronger: cited in Eagly and Chaiken 1993, 360–361.

[42] Domke found race an important influence on the perceived credibility of the messenger with a white messenger being better received than a black messenger (Domke 2000).

more central to deliberation.[43] Messengers may also play a third role; the messenger may move actors from one mode of thinking to another. Here, a trusted source may get the attention of decisionmakers, prompt them out of simple heuristic thinking to *elicit deliberation*: "I trust this source so I will give this issue more thought."

How might messenger effects function in international politics? Most studies in social psychology examine source effects on average citizens rather than elite messenger effects on other elites. Here, I focus on elite messengers, or what in policy circles are known as the "grasstops." In the field of international relations, messengers are akin to "policy entrepreneurs," but the focus in much of the literature has been on what they do (naming, framing, shaming) rather than who they are. Elite messengers or policy entrepreneurs convey their ideas both to get the attention of decisionmakers and to mobilize supporters and the general public.

For policymakers, even if they have the motivation and expertise to seek more information and judge content, they are busy and do not necessarily have much knowledge about every topic, particularly international issues that affect poor foreigners. Thus, like the general public, they likely rely on trusted sources of information, perhaps more so given the demands on their time and the multiplicity of issues. We would expect that those accepted interlocutors, whether they are policy experts or advisors, have special access and credibility. Policymakers who become champions of a cause likely are moved to deliberate by messengers. In other cases, policymakers may defer to people of their own political persuasion deemed to have expertise or seniority on issues. In these cases of more passive followers, we would expect messengers to merely cue behavior rather than inspire deliberation. In some cases, a gatekeeper who has received a message then goes on to become a messenger to other gatekeepers. For example, Senator Jesse Helms was inspired to support more robust global AIDS policies by Franklin Graham, head of the Christian relief charity Samaritan's Purse and son of Billy Graham; Helms in turn took that message to his colleagues in Congress and the executive branch. The relationship between messengers, messages, and gatekeepers is diagrammed in

---

[43] See Petty and Cacioppo 1981, 63; Eagly and Chaiken 1993, 318–320. In Eagly and Chaiken, the distinction is between "heuristic" and "systematic" information processing, whereas in Petty and Cacioppo the difference is between "peripheral" and "central" routes to persuasion.

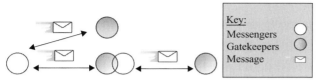

Figure 5.1 Messengers, messages, and gatekeepers

Figure 5.1. In the top pathway, messengers appeal to policy gatekeepers. In the lower pathway, messengers reach out to gatekeepers who, in turn, pass the message on to other gatekeepers.

Under what circumstances will an actor likely be an effective messenger? Here I focus on the similarity of the messengers to the gatekeepers. To understand similarity, we have to evaluate whether or not the prominent advocates, at any moment in time, on balance share characteristics with the gatekeepers. Among the attributes that affect the degree of similarity are partisanship, ideology, gender, religion, age, race, nationality, sexual orientation, profession, and special historical ties. While an oversimplification, messengers can either be *similar* or *dissimilar* to gatekeepers, with the expectation that messengers will have more success when they are similar to gatekeepers.

For example, as I argue below, Franklin Graham served as one of the main messengers to US president George W. Bush and Jesse Helms on HIV/AIDS. Graham shared with the president a number of characteristics: gender, faith, race, nationality, ideology, age, sexual orientation, and, probably, partisanship (see Table 5.7). Graham's father had ministered to US presidents dating back to Harry Truman. Interestingly, Bono was also an important messenger. He was less similar than Graham (a musician and Irish national, with a left-wing ideology), but he shared some important attributes as well (faith, race, gender, and sexual orientation). Graham was more likely on similarity grounds to be a successful messenger, but Bono had already, by virtue of previous campaign efforts on debt relief (described in Chapter 3), overcome some of the barriers to influence.

A third set of messengers who were even less similar than Bono to US gatekeepers were representatives of the group ACT UP. The largely gay and lesbian advocates from ACT UP tend to be more left-leaning and are likely supporters of the Democratic Party or are independents. While individual members may be religious, the organization is not

Table 5.7 *Messenger similarity in the United States*

Similar ⟵		⟶ Dissimilar
Franklin Graham	*Bono*	ACT UP
(1, 2, 3, 4, 5, 6, 7, 8, 10)	(3, 4, 6, 8)	(6, 7, possibly 3)

Note: Possible messenger similarity attributes are: (1) partisanship; (2) ideology; (3) gender; (4) religion; (5) age; (6) race; (7) nationality; (8) sexual orientation; (9) profession; and (10) historical ties.

known for its religious perspective in the same way that Graham (and his organization) or Bono are. Some of its leaders were likely white men, which brought them some similarity with prominent gatekeepers like Bush and Helms, but their sexual orientation created additional distance. Thus, while this group may have been effective with other strategies, their role as messenger to white heterosexual religious conservatives was likely rather limited.

We can combine the discussion of messengers with the mapping exercise in Chapter 2 of costs/values employed in both the debt relief and climate chapters. While I identified a number of measures that affected the balance of material incentives facing states, the two most salient issues in the case of HIV/AIDS appeared to be the fair share cost of global AIDS policies relative to the country's total foreign assistance budget and the relative economic health of the various countries.[44] For the purposes of mapping the intersection of costs and values, I report in Table 5.8 the relative fair shares for AIDS contributions as a proportion of each country's foreign assistance.

As for values and the cultural match of advocates' frames, determining the dominant frame of AIDS advocacy is somewhat tricky. HIV/AIDS has been framed in multiple ways: as a public health issue, a human rights issue, a justice issue, a moral concern for people of faith, an issue of intellectual property rights, and a security problem. As I suggested in Chapter 2, some frames make empirical or causal

---

[44] AIDS funding constituted a small share of GDP and national budgets, though it was a significant and rising share of foreign assistance. The fair share contribution would have been about 0.03% of GDP for G-7 countries between 2004 and 2007. In 2007, the fair share assessment would have been 0.05% of government expenditures at its most expensive. However, as a share of foreign assistance, the fair share contribution loomed much larger.

Table 5.8 *Intersection of fair share costs and public support for foreign assistance*

	Canada	France	Germany	Italy	Japan	UK	United States	G-7 average
Fair shares as a percentage of overseas development assistance	10.33%	6.94%	8.35%	16.11%	7.43%	9.44%	20.72%	11.33%
Average "strong" support for foreign assistance	51%	38.2%	24.2%	45.4%	22.1%	40.3%	20.4%	34.5%

Note and source: This table reflects strong support for foreign assistance. See Appendix 5D for a fuller description and sources.

claims about how the world works rather than claims about right and wrong. For, example scholars and advocates continue to debate whether AIDS is a security threat.[45] A security frame primarily makes empirical claims about the likely social and political consequences of AIDS, rather than explicit moral claims. By contrast, a frame that suggests "it is unjust that the developing world does not have access to AIDS treatment" makes direct moral claims about right and appropriate behavior. Given that the Global Fund came into being shortly after the UN Security Council convened a meeting on AIDS and security in Africa, one might conclude that AIDS as a security threat constituted the dominant frame for advocacy groups. Certainly, after September 11, 2001, advocacy groups such as DATA used the security frame to enhance their agenda, but variations on a broader justice theme served as the dominant frame of the advocacy community (see Appendix 5B for examples of how a variety of groups described their mission).

Most groups emphasized the need to extend treatment and to confront the AIDS crisis as a matter of conscience, while several explicitly linked that approach to an anti-corporate, anti-pharmaceutical patents agenda (Health GAP, ACT UP). Others made an appeal to human rights (the German AIDS campaign), while the "friends of" groups from the United States and Japan made more technocratic public health appeals based on extending care and saving lives. However, the moral mission, the concern about justice and fairness, provided the energy and impetus for most campaigns. In fact, President Bush's own justification for PEPFAR was based on moral concerns rather than the security logic that had led the Clinton administration to label AIDS a security threat shortly after the January 2000 UN Security Council session.[46]

If justice concerns animated AIDS advocacy campaigns, how can we evaluate the degree of cultural match of their claims? AIDS advocates were asking for higher levels of foreign assistance, so attitudes toward foreign aid provide one possible metric. However, general attitudes about foreign assistance do not tell us about the relative importance of those concerns compared to more parochial concerns. In the previous chapter, the public opinion questions about the environment explicitly

---

[45] Elbe 2006; Garrett 2005; Kassalow 2001; Susan Peterson 2002/2003; Susan Peterson and Shellman 2006; Singer 2002.
[46] PBS 2000.

addressed potential tradeoffs with economic growth and still showed that strong majorities supported environmental concerns. We do not yet have a similar metric for foreign assistance. Many survey questions, such as those in the Chicago Council on Foreign Relations polls, ask about attitudes toward current levels of spending, which do not tell us about whether, in principle, people are supportive of foreign aid. It would be preferable to have a question that gets at people's underlying values rather than a question that taps the public's perhaps ephemeral sense of current spending levels (which, in the case of foreign aid, are notoriously imprecise).

Moreover, motivations for giving foreign aid may vary. The public may support foreign aid for self-interested reasons (to shore up their nation's security, to gain allies, to secure trade partners). Fortunately, a number of surveys suggest that people's attitudes toward foreign assistance are a decent proxy for underlying moral motivations. In 2006 and 2007, when asked by the German Marshall Fund about the main reasons to provide foreign assistance, Europeans and Americans identified moral motivations as more important than strategic concerns or economic self-interest. Alleviating poverty and fighting health problems such as AIDS for five countries (France, Germany, Italy, the UK, and the United States) outranked concerns such as preventing breeding grounds for terrorism, helping poor countries trade, and gaining political allies (see Appendix 5C). Polls for Canada and Japan also show that moral motivations were the main reasons publics supported foreign assistance.[47]

It is easy to assemble poll results that show that publics across the G-7 are generally supportive of foreign aid by aggregating results where people are "strongly favorable" to providing foreign assistance (or think it is "very important") with those who merely say they are "somewhat favorable" to foreign assistance (or think it is "important").[48] By lumping these categories together, it is possible to miss out on

---

[47] In 2004, Canadians cited helping people in need and fighting poverty as the most important reasons for providing development assistance. These results mirrored earlier findings from 2002 (Environics Research Group 2004). Japanese motivations are similar. In 2004, 2005, and 2006 polls, the two motivations cited by clear majorities of supporters of foreign assistance were Japan's "humanitarian obligation" to provide assistance and its ability to contribute to the stability of developing countries and world peace (Japan, Cabinet Office 2004, 2005, 2006).

[48] For examples, see McDonnell, Lecomte, and Wegimont 2003a, 2003b.

variations in relative concern in different countries. Neither do those results fit well with poll results that consistently show that publics overestimate how much their countries provide in foreign assistance and/or want the level to be lower.[49]

For each country, there are at least four polls between 1996 and 2007 in which a comparable question about relative support for foreign assistance was asked. Except for Canada, each question had a similar structure: People had four main categories to rate their favorability to foreign aid (highly favorable, somewhat favorable, somewhat unfavorable, and highly unfavorable).[50] If we look only at the most favorable category, we observe some sharp differences on the relative importance of foreign assistance to G-7 countries. The French, Italians, and British were far more supportive of foreign aid than Germans, Japanese, or Americans, with Canadians slightly more concerned than any of the others (see Table 5.8). We should be wary of reading too much into these averages, as slight differences in question wording and variations over time make these comparisons somewhat problematic (see Appendix 5D). Nonetheless, looking at the general patterns can be a helpful way to think about different dynamics in the various countries.

I repeat the mapping exercise from previous chapters by intersecting one measure of costs (the relative fair share to ODA ratio) with the country's support for foreign assistance (see Figure 5.2). Based on the assumption that G-7 countries compare themselves to each other, I took the G-7 mean to be the threshold for high and low fair share costs and support for foreign assistance.

Thus, Cell 2 in this mapping exercise, occupied by Italy, represents a case of costly moral action, where the country had high levels of support for foreign assistance but also faced high costs relative to its foreign assistance budget. In Cell 1, Canada and the two former colonial powers, France and the UK, faced lower fair share costs and strong support for foreign assistance, cases of cheap moral action. Cell 3

---

[49] For example, in the quadrennial Chicago Council surveys of Americans between 1982 and 2004, less than 50 percent of the American public were in favor of expanding or even keeping foreign assistance spending at the same level. There was a gap of more than thirty points between public and elites on that question. See Busby and Monten 2008a.

[50] Canada had a six-point scale for which I consolidated "very strong support" and "strongly support."

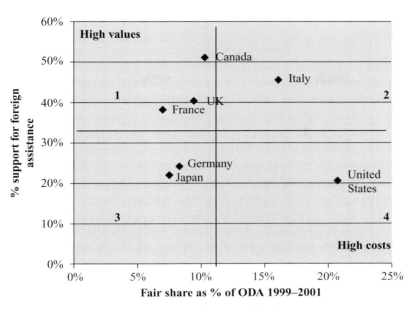

Figure 5.2 Mapping of fair shares and support for foreign assistance

includes cases of expected indifference, represented by Germany and Japan, with low fair share costs matched by below average support for foreign assistance. Finally, in Cell 4, the United States was a case of expected hostility. The United States had both high fair share costs and softer support for foreign assistance than other G-7 countries.

These maps are useful ways to think about the cases but should not be considered the only possible representation of country realities. Much depends on the chosen indicators for costs and values and on where the threshold between quadrants is drawn. For example, from Table 5.3, if we thought economic growth to be a better indicator of the perceived costliness of AIDS contributions, our results would be somewhat different. From this perspective, higher economic growth would be associated with a country having an easier time providing foreign assistance. From this perspective, the top quadrants of countries with strong support for foreign assistance would remain unchanged. Italy faced slower economic growth than its peers in the period 1999–2003, but the UK, France, and Canada all experienced economic growth that was higher than the G-7 average. However, while the US economy was strong, both Japan and Germany were growing more slowly than their G-7 peers.

From either perspective, US behavior is something of a puzzle. From Table 2.2, the United States should have been hostile to AIDS spending, facing both high costs and weak support for foreign assistance. A generic justice frame likely had limited support, given the general public's weak support for foreign assistance compared to other G-7 countries. At best, the country's solid economic performance made the country indifferent to AIDS appeals. As described in the book's opening anecdote about Senator Helms and Bono, Republican gatekeepers had long had an aversion to foreign assistance. As I discuss later in this chapter, reframing AIDS funding as consistent with Christian moral precepts overcame the ambivalence of US gatekeepers to greater foreign assistance, shifting the US case from hostility to costly moral action, from Cell 4 to Cell 2.[51] This reframing harkens back to the kind of success debt campaigners had with the Jubilee 2000 campaign in Japan. In the case study that follows, I extend the argument by looking at the role specific messengers such as Franklin Graham had in that process.

From a fair share standpoint, Germany and Japan were indifferent. In Cell 3, gatekeepers' preferences and their relative number loom large. If gatekeepers are all favorably inclined to support foreign assistance, we would expect higher levels of AIDS funding. Changes in government can bring to power new gatekeepers, who are more favorably inclined to a policy, and in the next section, I suggest that this dynamic is at least partially responsible for the change in Germany.

From an economic growth perspective, German and Japanese behavior on AIDS funding is not especially surprising. Given low economic growth and weaker domestic support for foreign assistance, we should expect the two countries to lag behind their peers in contributions. The finding here suggests that a generic justice frame, one that taps into sentiments in support of foreign assistance, is unlikely to work in Germany and Japan, meaning that more country-specific, tailored frames might be required to shift Germany and Japan out of Cell 3. Indeed, as I show in the later case studies, advocates seized on previous

---

[51] Taking economic growth as our cost indicator, this reframing would have moved the United States from indifference (Cell 3) to cheap moral action (Cell 1).

promises of AIDS funding to recast the issue as a test of German and Japanese prestige and credibility.

Alternatively, taking economic growth as the limiting material factor, we might expect a change in German and Japanese behavior if their economic fortunes improve. Barring a frame shift, rising growth would move Germany and Japan from hostility to indifference. As I discuss next, more successful advocacy in 2007 and 2008 in Germany and Japan may be a consequence of movement in both directions. Both countries started to experience higher economic growth, and the issue was reframed to fit more with each country's preoccupations with status and prestige.

Global AIDS policy in the United States, Japan, and Germany

In this section, I first focus on dynamics in the United States before providing a more cursory look at two laggards, Japan and Germany. Why choose these cases? As I just suggested, the US case is more of a puzzle than it would appear at first glance. Though the country's strong economic growth created a permissive condition for supporting AIDS programs, the advocacy community's target fair share for the United States would have consumed more than 20 percent of the country's total foreign assistance budget. However, the weakness of public support for foreign assistance made this an unlikely priority for US legislators. Given the evangelical community's existing hostility to AIDS sufferers in the homosexual community, the mobilization of Christian conservatives and President Bush on AIDS was quite unexpected and, thus, the PEPFAR announcement in 2003 caught many people by surprise. AIDS policy ultimately became the primary area where President Bush claimed a successful legacy as he left office in 2009.[52] This puzzle aside, the United States has been the largest contributor to HIV/AIDS financing, and understanding US dynamics is therefore also substantively important.

As for including Germany and Japan, both experienced slow economic growth throughout the 1990s and early 2000s, which affected their government's contributions to both debt relief and HIV/AIDS. Moreover, compared to their G-7 peers, both also had weaker levels of support for foreign aid. Furthermore, if we add in gatekeeper

[52] Alberts 2009.

politics, both have strong, tightfisted finance ministries that have been big bureaucratic players able to dominate government advocates for foreign assistance. So, what's left to explain?

In 2007 and 2008, Germany and Japan increased their commitments to global AIDS efforts, particularly to the Global Fund. While neither country has yet contributed at the levels fair share advocates wished, the shifts are important and help us understand how initially unlikely cases for successful advocacy can change, possibly because of more propitious material circumstances or efforts to reframe the issue to appeal to more culturally resonant values. Looking at these cases in more detail allows us to disentangle what led to these changes.

In Germany, elections in late 2005 brought a new chancellor, Angela Merkel, to power. In 2007, her country hosted the G-8 summit during which the feminization of HIV/AIDS was an important agenda item, championed by Heidemarie Wieczorek-Zeul, the development minister and a holdover from the previous Social Democratic-led government. How can we explain Germany's change? Was it Merkel's election? Was it Germany's hosting of the G-8 summit? Was it improved economic conditions? Was it Wieczorek-Zeul's gender bond with Merkel?

As for Japan, the country played host to the G-8 summit in 2008 (do we observe a pattern?) and, like the Germans, the Japanese upped their pledged contributions to fight global diseases. What explains the change? Japan's economy began to improve in the early 2000s. This upturn may have diminished the finance minister's control on the public purse. There was no shortage of messengers in Japan. A former prime minister and a former health minister of the ruling Liberal Democratic Party were among the lead advocates. How do improved economic fortunes, prominent messengers, and the role of G-8 summit host fit together? I try to provide a partial answer in the case material.

The United States

During the Clinton administration, funds dedicated to fighting international AIDS increased incrementally but remained below $200 mn through 1997. Not until FY2000 and 2001 was the Clinton administration able to increase spending significantly. The first George W. Bush budget in 2002 added nearly $500 mn. Spending on global AIDS

Table 5.9 *US funding for global HIV/AIDS (nominal and GDP in constant 2004 $US millions)*

	1992	1993	1994	1995	1996	1997	1998	1999	2000	2001	2002	2003	2004	2005
Nominal $	$128	$153	$161	$170	$163	$170	$179	$215	$360	$712	$1,196	$1,490	$2,253	$2,701
2004 $	$161.7	$188.9	$194.6	$201.4	$189.5	$194.4	$202.4	$239.7	$392.8	$758.6	$1,252.4	$1,529.3	$2,253.0	

Source: Kates and Summers 2004, 5.

programs continued to increase after the president announced the creation of PEPFAR (see Table 5.9).

Through the mid-1990s, US AIDS activists faced stigma and marginalization because the disease was perceived as largely affecting gay men and poor immigrants, particularly Haitians. At the time, the attitude among some Americans, particularly Christian conservatives, was that AIDS was caused by deviant behavior. This view found expression in Congress through legislators such as Jesse Helms. Helms vigorously opposed reauthorization of the Ryan White Act in 1995,[53] suggesting AIDS sufferers brought the disease on themselves for "deliberately engaging in unnatural acts" and "disgusting, revolting conduct."[54] The landscape for global HIV/AIDS programs changed dramatically in the United States in the late 1990s. The suffering of AIDS patients, coupled with advances in medical treatment, humanized those infected with the virus. By the late 1990s, a diverse movement for a more aggressive treatment and prevention response for AIDS *globally* coalesced in the United States and other rich nations. A January 2000 United Nations meeting on AIDS and the Durban AIDS conference of July 2000 signaled the issue's arrival on the world stage. In the United States, the issue gained more political visibility through the actions of gay and lesbian activists from ACT UP, who harassed both Democratic and Republican candidates about treatment access in the 2000 elections.

How can moral arguments and messenger effects help explain US generosity under President George W. Bush? Even if the case were likely on material grounds (which my previous discussion challenged), advocates still faced problems from a message and messengers perspective. In terms of messages, several understandings of HIV/AIDS competed for attention in the lead-up to President Bush's 2003 State of the Union address. While the medical and public health communities made a strong case that not enough was being done and that additional resources could be effective, advocates also made other arguments justifying why rich countries and the United States in particular should care: (1) HIV/AIDS as a security threat, (2) HIV/AIDS as a justice issue, and (3) HIV/AIDS as a matter of Christian morality. While the

---

[53] The Ryan White Act, named for a hemophiliac boy who contracted HIV, was intended to improve the quality of care for US AIDS sufferers.
[54] Dunlap 1995.

outgoing Clinton administration declared AIDS a security threat in 2000, variants of the justice frame remained the dominant one employed by campaign groups as the Bush administration took office. In May 2001, the Health GAP Project, a coalition associated with ACT UP and other groups seeking expanded access for treatment, framed the then-low US contribution in terms of not only justice but also class: "Tax cuts for millionaires, nothing left for AIDS."[55] Paul Zeitz, head of the Global AIDS Alliance, made a broader normative argument for treatment: "It is outrageous from both a practical and a moral standpoint that more than 99% of Africans are not able to obtain practical lifesaving medications."[56] This argument was perhaps not the best in terms of cultural match. A precise evaluation is beyond the scope of this chapter, but class-based justice arguments have a weak cultural fit in the United States.[57] The generic justice frame was marginally better but not especially strong, as I have suggested.

When Christian conservatives joined the cause, beginning largely in 2002, their involvement accomplished two things: (1) a Christian morality frame, which had greater cultural match, became more prominent, and (2) the advocates who championed the cause had more attributes in common with key policy gatekeepers. Religious morality has broad cultural match in the United States, as I noted in Chapter 3. The new frame moved the United States, in terms of Table 2.2, from hostility (Cell 4) to costly moral action (Cell 2). Once US gatekeepers such as President Bush and Senator Helms had given their strong support, significant new resources for HIV/AIDS were committed. This shift was reinforced by the emergence of new messengers. Until those messengers emerged, one would still have expected a disconnect between the Republican White House and prominent advocates on this issue from the gay and lesbian community, the liberal left development community, and African-Americans.

In talking about HIV/AIDS, the George W. Bush administration echoed the concerns of the evangelical community. President Bush in his State of the Union address, for example, framed the argument in

---

[55] Health GAP Coalition 2001.   [56] Global AIDS Alliance 2001.
[57] Across three waves (1990, 1995, and 1999) of the World Values Survey (WVS), Americans were asked whether or not incomes needed to be more equal based on a ten-point scale, with 1 preferring incomes the most equal and 10 believing that large income differentials were needed as an incentive. The mean was 6.07 (Inglehart 2005).

moral terms rather than using security language. He described the AIDS plan as "a work of mercy" that could help in "sparing innocent people" from unnecessary suffering.[58] How did this result come about? Christian conservatives had become a more internationally minded constituency in the 1990s, beginning with concerns for religious freedom in China and Sudan and extending to issues such as overseas abortions.[59] They were among the supporters of the Jubilee 2000 campaign. In the narrative of HIV/AIDS and the Bush administration, Franklin Graham's emergence as a new messenger looms large. The son of former presidential minister Billy Graham and head of the relief organization Samaritan's Purse, Franklin Graham was newer to the role of presidential pastor. He had offered the prayer at President George W. Bush's 2000 inauguration and, like his father, he had special access to the president.

Under Franklin Graham's leadership, evangelicals began mobilizing on AIDS in the late 1990s. Many Christians had experienced the devastating effects of HIV through their missionary work. In February 2002, Samaritan's Purse hosted a national conference, "Prescription for Hope," which featured Senator Helms as a keynote speaker before an audience of 800. The conference was an important moment in the evolution of Christian conservative attitudes about HIV/AIDS. Tom Hart, director of governmental relations for DATA, suggested this meeting represented a "recasting" of the issue.[60] Until this conference, the conservative Christian community had maintained the view that AIDS was a "sinner's disease."[61] As Franklin Graham argued, the effort was to get Christians past old views to recognize that "each of the 40 million men, women, and children worldwide who are infected with the HIV virus are precious to God. And if they're precious to God, then by God, they should be precious to us."[62]

In his conference address, Graham emphasized his view that all of humankind were sinners and that "you think of the person that you despise the most, the group of people you cannot stand the most and remember, for God so loved them, because they're part of this world too."[63] In his 2002 book *The Name*, Graham appealed to Christ's

---

[58] Woolley and Peters 2006.   [59] Hertzke 2004.   [60] Hart 2006.
[61] Sheler reported a survey that found evangelical Christians much less likely to donate to international AIDS education and prevention than non-Christians, 3% compared to 8% (Sheler 2002).
[62] Quoted in Sheler 2002.   [63] Graham 2002a.

compassion for all, writing, "When Jesus encountered people who wanted His healing touch, He never questioned them about how they became sick."[64] The "Prescription for Hope" conference took on larger significance than the organizers had imagined. Ken Isaacs, the organizer of the conference and vice president of programs for Samaritan's Purse, stated that there was no intent to create a groundswell for a new government initiative like PEPFAR. With the planning for the conference beginning in 1999, "Prescription for Hope" was organized mainly to recognize and energize Christians who were at the forefront of AIDS control efforts around the world. The conference also aimed to bring some greater acknowledgment by both the media and policy-makers that Christians were leaders in the fight against AIDS and that values-based programming on AIDS was desirable and effective.[65]

How did this moral concern then become policy? In Graham, we have much greater messenger similarity with gatekeepers compared to other potential messengers from the ideological left. Graham, along with Bono, reached out to key policy gatekeepers such as Senator Helms, who would again become Foreign Relations Committee chair in December 2002. In conversations with Helms, Graham said:

People with HIV/AIDS – many of them have made mistakes that they regret . . . But are we to throw these people out and abandon them and say, "You got what you deserved – shame, shame on you"? Or do we try to reach out and love them and to save a life and then try to prevent others from making the same mistakes? I believe this is what Jesus would have us to do.[66]

Graham's persuasive appeal was partly substantive, but, as a trusted interlocutor, his words were particularly important to Helms. Given that this was one area in which the senator already had strong and contrary views, Helms' reaction to Graham's message was likely deliberative rather than purely reflexive. The senator's speech at the conference was the apotheosis of the changed view among many Christian conservatives. While perhaps indicative of deep persuasion that constructivists write about, the basis of the appeal – Christian morality – was consistent with Helms' long-held beliefs. In his speech, Helms apologized for his prior stance and expressed shame that he had not done more before to address the pandemic.

[64] Graham 2002b, 169.   [65] Isaacs 2007.   [66] PBS 2006.

Isaacs said Helms' remarks caught the organizers by surprise: "We were all shocked by it. None of us had any idea that tide change had happened in him."[67] Les Munson, who served Senator Helms on the Foreign Relations Committee, described Helms' speech before Samaritan's Purse as "an emotional, religious, spiritual thing for him," during which time both the senator and audience broke down in tears. Munson traced Helms' 2002 speech to the president's State of the Union announcement, suggesting it was part of the "same arc of activity." Munson discussed how Helms' support helped dissolve remaining congressional opposition, asking, "Honestly, with Jesse Helms supporting international AIDS programs, who could be opposed to them?" Helms had credibility on this issue with constituencies that other advocates did not. Munson suggested that what Helms did was to "change the way the issue was presented."[68] While Helms was a recipient of the message about global AIDS, Helms himself played the role of messenger with his colleagues. However, here, the messenger effect appears to be more of a reflex cue: "If Helms is for it, I am for it." Again, like Graham, Helms shared a number of characteristics with his congressional colleagues, particularly on the Republican side: profession, age, gender, race, partisanship, ideology, and faith.

Given that conservatives had been the most likely legislators to reject greater funding for AIDS on both fiscal and moral grounds, Helms' reinterpretation of the Christian obligation on AIDS was especially significant. Not only did Helms make his views known, he and Senator Bill Frist of Tennessee, who became Senate majority leader in December 2002, championed a $500 mn amendment in June 2002 to prevent the transmission of HIV/AIDS between mothers and their children. Although Helms and Frist ultimately withdrew the amendment at the White House's request, their actions pushed the Bush administration to do more. They also set the stage for a broader change in social conservative sentiment within the Republican Party, as Senator Rick Santorum of Pennsylvania and Senator Mike DeWine of Ohio became champions for greater attention to AIDS.

Advocates for a more generous response to the AIDS epidemic also sought influence through the executive branch. Journalists' accounts emphasized the importance of moral concerns as HIV/AIDS was teed

---

[67] Isaacs 2007.   [68] Munson 2005.

up for President Bush.[69] Franklin Graham met with the president shortly after he took office and then several times over the course of his presidency. He described the president's willingness to address AIDS: "Because I think he believes in his heart that this is the right thing to do. The president is motivated by – and I cannot speak for him, but from just my observance, my opinion – what's right and wrong."[70]

Like Graham, Bono emphasized the religious and moral dimension of AIDS in his conversations with the president on the Millennium Challenge Account (MCA)[71] and AIDS. Bono may have been an unlikely messenger on some attributes (nationality, profession) but his faith, as I argued in Chapter 3, was an important bridging attribute with decisionmakers. In 2002, in the lead-up to the announcement of the MCA, Bono presented the president with a psalmbook and appealed to a passage in the Gospel of Matthew to justify why great leaders ought to help the poor: "For I was an hungred, and ye gave me meat: I was thirsty, and ye gave me drink: I was a stranger, and ye took me in."[72] Bono's reported success and rapport with policymakers suggest that his intellectual ability surpassed that of the average pop star and that he was able to overcome certain negative connotations of celebrities as messengers. President Bush set in motion a wider consultative process to respond to their concerns, suggesting that the mode of messenger influence was, as with Helms, a prompt to more deliberative behavior.

Michael Gerson, former speechwriter for President Bush, told me that much of the impetus for the president's concern about AIDS came from "his religiously informed moralism." Gerson said that President Bush is "deeply and thoroughly American," and that the AIDS plan was part of the president's "foreign policy idealism" and reflected his view that "this is what America should be known for."[73] Aside from the president, the three other main champions for an enhanced effort on AIDS in the executive branch included Gerson; Condoleezza Rice, then national security advisor; and Joshua Bolten, then deputy

---

[69] Allen and Blustein 2003; Behrman 2004; Burkhalter 2004; Stolberg 2003; Traub 2005.
[70] PBS 2006.
[71] The MCA was a new bilateral foreign assistance approach announced in 2002 in which the United States would provide larger-scale grants rather than project assistance to countries that pre-cleared certain good governance criteria.
[72] Traub 2005.   [73] Gerson 2006.

chief of staff for policy at the White House (and later head of the Office of Management and Budget).[74] Like President Bush, all are very religious.[75]

In a key White House meeting in November 2002 that preceded the president's decision to back PEPFAR in his 2003 State of the Union address, moral concerns were heavily emphasized. During the meeting, Rice told a personal story in support of the plan. She said her mother had been diagnosed with breast cancer while Rice was a teenager and that treatment forestalled her death until Rice was thirty. Rice said that "you bet those years meant a lot to me" and suggested that ARV therapy similarly would mean that many children would be able to grow to adulthood with their parents alive.[76] At the end of the meeting, the president asked Gerson what he thought. According to Dan Bartlett, counselor to President Bush, Gerson replied, "The bottom line is that we're the richest nation in history, and history will judge us severely if we don't do this."[77]

Alluding to the decline in ARV drug prices, Gerson also said he told the president that opportunity created responsibility. As for Bolten, Gerson described him as, like the president, "essentially a moralist too."[78] Like Helms, these counselors to the president were both receivers and deliverers of the messages from the advocacy community.

A state interest argument would challenge these statements professing moral motivations as self-serving cover for what Stephen Morrison, director of the Center for Strategic and International Studies' task force on AIDS, described as the real reason for the size and timing of the program: "Iraq, Iraq, Iraq, Iraq."[79] An individual interest argument might assert that the AIDS program provided a convenient way to reward the pharmaceuticals sector. While some evidence supports the former contention, there is little evidence to support the latter. The point is not that interest-based arguments had no influence but that we cannot understand US actions without understanding the importance of morality and the role played by messengers.

Asked whether the HIV/AIDS plan was announced as a way to turn attention away from the impending conflict with Iraq, DATA's Tom

---

[74] Barnes 2005; Behrman 2004.
[75] Goldberg 2006; Kralev 2000; Tyrangiel 2005.   [76] Goldberg 2006.
[77] Goldberg 2006. For a similar account, see Lefkowitz 2009.
[78] Gerson 2006.   [79] Quoted in Behrman 2004, 302.

Hart said, "I never heard that association," and "if that [was] the intent, it didn't work."[80] He added, "I don't think it was a redirect to show good, but I wouldn't be surprised if part of the rationale of the Millennium Challenge Account and PEPFAR was a demonstration of what the United States stands for abroad."[81] Asked whether the AIDS plan was seen as necessary in light of the impending conflict with Iraq, Gerson said that was not the impetus, but "PEPFAR sends an important message to the world." Further, "clearly, a lot of these efforts have been intended to show America's role is broader. I don't think anything is wrong with that." He noted that "our enemies have a vicious vision; we need our own vision." In sum, he explained that "these efforts are part of a new approach, more than pre-emption of threats, but also creation of hope."[82]

While these comments suggest that strategic concerns played some role, when we compare President Bush's spending on HIV/AIDS programs to President Clinton's, we see a dramatic shift in the amount of resources dedicated to the problem even before the Iraq war.[83] Moreover, as Dietrich argues, while the Clinton administration had embraced AIDS as a security concern, the Bush administration did not justify PEPFAR in those terms, opting for a moral case instead.[84]

Individual interest-based arguments might claim pharmaceutical companies were the main drivers that sought to channel government money for treatment to benefit their own firms. However, according to Laurie Garrett of the Council on Foreign Relations, pharmaceutical companies were not especially active in the lead-up to PEPFAR's announcement.[85] Gerson said during his time in the White House, "I never had any dealings with the pharmaceuticals industry."[86] Similarly, David Gartner, policy director of the Global AIDS Alliance,

---

[80] A 2006 survey found only 25% of Americans regarded President Bush as a leader on global AIDS, trailing Bill Clinton (50%), Nelson Mandela (50%), and Bono (47%) (Kaiser Family Foundation 2006a).
[81] Hart 2006.   [82] Gerson 2006.
[83] Clinton's FY2001 budget, passed in December 2000, was his last and contained $612 mn dedicated to fighting AIDS internationally. Bush's FY2001 budget increased this by $100 mn, making a total of $712 mn; his FY2002 budget for global AIDS added another $500 mn, to $1.196 bn (Kates and Summers 2004, 5). The FY2001 budget included $100 mn for the Global Fund, initially announced by President Bush as a contribution of $200 mn in May 2001. The actual appropriation of $100 mn was part of the July 2001 Supplemental Appropriations Act.
[84] Dietrich 2007.   [85] Garrett 2006.   [86] Gerson 2006.

said pharmaceutical companies were not especially active in the legislative appropriations process even after PEPFAR was announced: "I don't think they played much of a role. They just never engaged in a serious way."[87]

Another interest-based account might explain the change in the Bush administration's policy as a result of public pressure. What are we to make of this claim? Advocates sought to influence the White House, but the Bush administration was not particularly responsive to public opinion. The plan for PEPFAR was drafted by a small group; many senior officials in the administration were unaware that it would happen, and the announcement also took advocates by surprise. Gerson suggested that there was "very little outside pressure at least as far as I could determine."[88] While Samaritan's Purse organized the "Prescription for Hope" conference, the organization did not have a lobbying staff, and the organization did not lobby in the lead-up to PEPFAR or in the appropriations process.[89] While Bono once likened the ideal influence of groups like DATA to an "NRA for the poor," global AIDS is not an issue over which many voters are willing to throw politicians out of office.

Advocacy groups are able to exercise influence more through their access and their ability to praise behavior they like (which DATA especially is known for) and shame politicians for failure to keep promises. As Hart said, "Our design is not to elect and defeat" politicians. Rather, DATA is about having political weight and being "taken seriously."[90] Advocates had a limited role influencing the executive branch through pressure; their efforts to collect votes in the US Congress in the appropriations process were more influential. They relied as much on an inside strategy of good information, contacts, and credibility as they did on a mass strategy of brute political power. This is not to say that politics were far from the president's mind when

---

[87] Gartner 2006. Pharmaceutical companies still had an interest in protecting their patent rights for anti-retroviral medications. Initially, their concerns were bolstered by the appointment of former Eli Lilly executive Randall Tobias as Bush's first Global AIDS coordinator with the rank of ambassador. However, while they vigorously defended their patent rights in the context of the WTO, they played a limited role in PEPFAR's formation and approval. Ultimately, after considerable work by advocacy groups, their position was undermined by the adoption of a Food and Drug Administration fast-track approval system for generic ARVs in 2004.

[88] Gerson 2006.   [89] Isaacs 2007.   [90] Hart 2006.

he committed to the plan in 2003. Support for AIDS initiatives in a sense could be viewed as a low-cost way to fulfill, even outsource, the vision of compassionate conservativism by going international.

Although it may be impossible to disentangle the geostrategic and political concerns that played a role in Bush's decision, one can see the influence of moral considerations in the character of the US response. The original US legislation authorizing PEPFAR specified that 55% of the funds be allocated to treatment, with 20% for prevention, 15% for palliative care, and 10% for orphans and vulnerable children.[91] The emphases on treatment and mother-to-child transmission are less controversial than prevention, where policies get into contentious issues such as sex education, homosexuality, and prostitution.[92] The US House of Representatives also made a number of key and controversial amendments to the bill authorizing PEPFAR. One amendment offered by Representative Chris Smith of New Jersey mandated that no groups receiving funding from the US government endorse or promote prostitution. A second amendment by Representative Joseph Pitts of Pennsylvania mandated that one-third of the US money dedicated to prevention by law must go for abstinence and faithfulness programs.[93] A GAO study suggests this amendment had some counterproductive results on program effectiveness.[94] Thus, the administration supported a policy that might be ineffective but is consistent with the Christian community's moral views.[95] Even if the Bush administration were purely responding to political pressure (which seems unlikely), advocates themselves were moved by morality in articulating their concerns.[96]

[91] These were recommendations for the first two years of PEPFAR; beginning in FY2006, they were mandated by law (Kaiser Family Foundation 2006b, 7).
[92] Patterson 2006, 157.
[93] To meet that target, the Office of the US Global AIDS Coordinator (OGAC) mandated that 50 percent of prevention monies be dedicated to preventing sexual transmission of the virus and that two-thirds of that, in turn, be dedicated to abstinence and faithfulness programs. This would leave at most one-third of prevention monies for sexual transmission for condoms (Kaiser Family Foundation 2006b).
[94] GAO 2006.   [95] Patterson 2006, 149–158.
[96] Epstein argues that organizations such as Samaritan's Purse stand to gain contracts from the US government for their overseas AIDS programs (Epstein 2005). Isaacs noted that Samaritan's Purse got only 2.5 percent of its budget (which was nearly $270 mn in 2005) from the US government. He said, "We don't chase government money," and that suggestions to the contrary were "convenient and uninformed" (Isaacs 2007).

The impending Iraq war may have influenced the timing of the Bush administration's announcement of PEPFAR, but it is unclear whether the plan's size was influenced by strategic concerns. However, Gerson and others noted two material factors that made a treatment regime both feasible and morally compelling: falling ARV drug prices and the success doctors such as Paul Farmer were having providing ARV therapy in poor countries. Even if we ascribe some weight to the permissive material environment, the Bush administration did not have to respond with an ambitious $15 billion AIDS plan. The fact that it did reflects the influence of moral concerns and messengers as much as if not more than material drivers.

Germany and Japan

While the United States has been among the leading contributors to global AIDS programs bilaterally and multilaterally, Germany and Japan are two countries that have lagged behind other contributors. What explains their behavior? German and Japanese leaders had several incentives for inaction, including weak economic performance, shallow ties to Africa, and weak civil society movements. However, other countries such as Italy provided comparatively more support for the Global Fund despite facing similar economic troubles.

To understand Japanese and German behavior, we have to go beyond economic statistics to examine the consequences of comparatively lower public support for foreign assistance on awareness of the global AIDS pandemic and willingness to address the disease. In both countries, public opinion about the threat of AIDS was soft, and German and Japanese leaders have, until recent years, not felt the issue to be of sufficient political or personal concern to make the issue their own. For example, in 2002, the Pew Research Center polled publics in different countries and asked them their perception of the world's greatest threats. Japanese and German citizens were far less concerned about AIDS than were citizens of other G-7 countries. A 2005 poll by the Kaiser Family Foundation found that 68% of the Japanese did not know if their country was spending enough, the right amount, or too little to combat global AIDS. Only 32% of Germans, the next lowest in the survey behind Japan, thought their government was doing too little (see Table 5.10).

Table 5.10 *Public opinion and global AIDS efforts*

	% of public agreeing that HIV/AIDS is the "greatest danger to the world,"* 2002	% of G-7 public response when asked about their country's spending to combat global AIDS,** 2005	
		Too little	Don't know
Canada	30%	40%	16%
France	37%	52%	19%
Germany	17%	32%	16%
Great Britain	29%	42%	10%
Italy	32%	53%	21%
Japan	19%	7%	68%
United States	32%	35%	11%
G-7 average	28%	37%	23%

Notes and sources: * The survey listed five dangers: HIV/AIDS, terrorism, nuclear weapons, rich/poor gap, and pollution/environment, and asked people to identify the "greatest danger to the world." The percentage is based on the proportion of people who listed HIV/AIDS as the greatest or second-greatest threat (Pew Research Center for the People & the Press 2002).
** They asked, "Do you think [YOUR COUNTRY] is giving too much, too little, or about the right amount of money to assist the developing countries most affected by the HIV/AIDS epidemic?" (Kaiser Family Foundation 2005a).

Unlike France, the UK, or the United States where Chirac, Blair, and Bush were personally committed to the issue, there was not top-level support for global AIDS spending in Germany under Chancellor Schröder, according to Christoph Benn, formerly of the German AIDS campaign and later director of external relations for the Global Fund. The issue did not receive that kind of attention: Chancellor Schröder was very focused on domestic concerns. An exception was the 1999 G-8 summit held in Cologne, Germany, which presented Schröder with an opportunity to get international acclaim for supporting debt relief. In the United States and France, Benn noted, people living with AIDS had a strong advocacy movement (in ACT UP) that championed universal "access for all" to anti-retroviral therapy. That support was "completely absent" in Germany, though there were some efforts such as Deutsche AIDS-Hilfe, mostly geared to helping Germans with HIV.

In addition, Benn noted German journalists displayed little interest in the problem compared to Anglophone newspapers.[97]

The German AIDS campaign, Aktionsbündnis gegen AIDS (Action Against AIDS), thus faced an uphill battle.[98] In 2003, the nationwide campaign had fifty-four affiliated organizations from the development service delivery sector with the support of another 200 grassroots organizations. This total subsequently grew to 100 AIDS service delivery organizations and 270 grassroots groups. In late 2003, the nationwide AIDS campaign presented a petition with 95,000 names to Heidemarie Wieczorek-Zeul, the minister of the country's development agency (Bundusministerium für wirtschaftliche Zusammenarbeit und Entwicklung, BMZ), seeking additional multilateral and bilateral funding for global AIDS efforts and low-cost access to AIDS drugs. While campaigners had access to the development ministry, their country's G-8 coordinator (or sherpa, as it is known), and operational people in various agencies, they were not able to get meetings with the Foreign Office or Chancellory. Echoing Benn's view, Katja Roll of Aktionsbündnis gegen AIDS and later the Global Fund suggested Germany was missing commitment at the highest level under the Schröder government. Combating AIDS in the developing world was not seen as a key foreign policy goal. Her group's letters to the Chancellory and the Finance Ministry were forwarded to BMZ. As Roll noted, "BMZ has done what they can do," but it lacked the authority to allocate more money for AIDS spending without approval at the highest levels. When the campaign reminded Germany of commitments made at the special UN session on AIDS, government officials said they were doing the best they could in a difficult economic situation.[99] Claiming budget problems was a good reason to do nothing, but, as Benn noted, France faced similar problems and Chirac still made it a priority.[100]

[97] Benn 2003.

[98] In April–May 2000, the Eurobarometer poll found, compared to other EU countries, a lower proportion of Germans (16%) ranked "promoting human rights throughout the world" and the "fight against cancer and AIDS" (13%) as a high-priority action item for the European Parliament. The EU-15 averages were 22% and 20%, respectively. The priority for Germany was employment (39%). German concern about AIDS was low again in November–December 2000 (Eurobarometer 2000, 2001). In addition to the lack of popular or media interest, the campaign's frame, "Life is a human right," perhaps had weaker cultural appeal than in other EU countries.

[99] Roll 2003.   [100] Benn 2003.

Development issues finally started to get a much more favorable hearing under Angela Merkel's government, which hosted the G-8 summit in Heiligendamm in 2007. As noted in the previous chapter, hosts of G-8 meetings usually feel compelled to engage in competitive promise-making. During the summit, Merkel pledged $4 bn over five years for infectious diseases, including AIDS, and Germany then hosted the Global Fund's replenishment meeting in fall 2007. Roll suggested that the change in Germany's position on HIV/AIDS occurred as the new Merkel government was seeking themes and topics on which it could develop a profile. Since HIV/AIDS was high on the international agenda, the government was in a position to get international credit for focusing on Africa and health at the 2007 G-8 summit.[101] Joerg Maas, former executive director of Germany's Foundation for World Population (Deutsche Stiftung Weltbevölkerung, DSW), echoed this view, emphasizing that Chancellor Merkel used the summit and the EU's rotating presidency to burnish Germany's international reputation.[102]

Merkel's initial intention was to focus the agenda on traditional macroeconomic coordination among the major economies, but the mobilization of advocates at previous G-8 summits and in the lead-up to Heiligendamm helped convince Merkel of the political opportunity in including Africa and health on the G-8 agenda. Prior to the summit, global civil society organizations dispatched their messengers to Germany and put unprecedented pressure on Merkel by enlisting the support of local development organizations, celebrities, and businesses.

Bono, for example, met with Merkel in April 2007 and had tumultuous meetings with her again during the summit, in which they clashed over the extent to which Germany (and other donors) were increasing their overall aid budget. Advocates also commissioned several large advertising campaigns, particularly in and around Berlin. One such campaign, supported by DSW, emphasized reproductive health as a human right; another, supported by Oxfam Germany, DATA, and Agro-Action Germany, focused on the importance of keeping the promises made at the 2005 G-8 meeting at Gleneagles to double aid to Africa and provide 10 million people with ARV therapy by 2010. A third, "Your Voice Against Poverty," organized under the aegis of the German chapter of the Global Call to Action to End Poverty (GCAP) and supported by the Gates Foundation, enlisted the help of celebrities

---

[101] Roll 2007.   [102] Maas 2008.

such as the German pop star Herbert Grohemeyer. In advertisements, celebrities clicked their fingers, noting that "every three seconds a child dies."[103]

Of these, perhaps most successful in Maas' view was the campaign to remind Germany of previous promises. An Oxfam Germany poll released before the summit found that 71 percent said it was important or very important for Germany to keep the Gleneagles promise of doubling aid.[104] Since World War II, multilateral cooperation for Germans had become what Joachim Krause describes as "an organizing principle" of foreign policy, perceived as "good in its own right and as a foundation for a rule-based order."[105] Reminding Germans of the need to keep international promises and be good international citizens thus remained a potent cultural frame with more importance than its instrumental value. Thus, per Table 5.2, framing the German contribution in terms of its international credibility benefited from improved cultural match, moving the case from indifference (Cell 3) to cheap moral action (Cell 1).[106]

Manfred Konukiewitz, the BMZ deputy director general for global and sectoral policies, provided a different perspective. He suggested that the chancellor generally plays a limited role in specific budget items of individual ministries and that Chancellor Merkel "was not specifically involved" with Germany's enhanced contribution to global AIDS efforts in 2007. In his view, the difference on HIV/AIDS contributions between the Schröder and Merkel eras was not about personalities or political background but Germany's improved fiscal situation. Under Schröder, the austerity provisions in the budget were much stronger. In the 2006 budget, ministries received unexpected good news to plan on a growth mode rather than contraction.[107] Once the Development Ministry received authorization from the Finance Ministry for a larger budget, he argued, then it was Minister Wieczorek-Zeul, who stayed on as development minister after the 2005 elections, who ensured that more money was directed toward HIV/AIDS spending.[108] Taking economic growth as the material

---

[103] Maas 2008.   [104] Oxfam 2007.   [105] Krause 2004.

[106] If economic growth was seen as a more salient cost concern, the movement was from hostility (Cell 4) to costly moral action (Cell 2).

[107] Germany's economic growth would improve from 1.934% in 2005 to 2.424% in 2006 (IMF 2008).

[108] Konukiewitz 2008.

constraint, the movement in Table 5.2 would have been leftward, reflecting Germany's improved economic circumstances, potentially from hostility (Cell 4) to indifference (Cell 3).

While an improved fiscal environment may have facilitated Germany's enhanced contributions, it cannot explain why HIV/AIDS rather than other needs received additional resources and why Merkel allowed aid to Africa and HIV/AIDS to become high priorities of the G-8 summit. Indifference does not explain Germany's decision to increase its pledged contributions. Like Schröder's position on debt relief in 1999, the Merkel government's embrace of African issues in the year Germany held the EU presidency and hosted the G-8 summit was partially opportunistic, responding to the success advocates had in making AIDS and Africa popular causes. However, it was more than pressure that led to a changed dynamic in Germany. Internal advocates such as Wieczorek-Zeul found the new chancellor more receptive to their message. As Roll noted, advocates from the German Council on Foreign Relations (DGAP) and people such as Christoph Benn were influential because their longstanding expertise gave them credibility on the issue and high-level access. According to Maas, Merkel's three female ministers – the development minister Wieczorek-Zeul, the health minister Ulla Schmidt, and the education and research minister Annette Schavan – were instrumental in preparing the chancellor. In March 2007, for example, Merkel gave the keynote address at a conference on HIV/AIDS in Bremen that was supported by those three ministries. Throughout her remarks, she emphasized the special vulnerability of women to the AIDS virus, a theme that would become central at the G-8 meeting. While only suggestive, the transition from a male chancellor – who, according to Maas, almost "never mentioned HIV/AIDS in eight years" – to a female chancellor may have facilitated a much higher degree of similarity between messengers (such as Wieczorek-Zeul, Schmidt, and Schavan) inside the German government and the leadership.

Like Germany, Japan's major promises on foreign assistance and global public health came with its host role of the G-8 summit in 2000 and again in 2008. At the 2000 Okinawa meeting, the Japanese, despite their financial situation, pledged $5 bn over five years for the Okinawa Infectious Disease Initiative. The idea for the Global Fund came out of the 2000 Okinawa G-8 summit. The Japanese are proud to credit the idea to then prime minister Yoshiro Mori who hosted a session on infectious diseases in December 2000 and delivered the Japanese address in June 2001 at the UN special session on AIDS, even though he was no longer prime minister.[109] Despite Japan's imprimatur in the creation of the Global Fund, Japan subsequently lagged behind other donors.

According to Yoichiro Yamada, former director of the Specialized Agencies Division in the Japanese Ministry of Foreign Affairs (MOFA), the main barrier to expansion of the Japanese commitment to the Global Fund and bilateral support for global AIDS programs was the country's tough economic situation. The fiscal deficit imposed discipline on all ministries. In 2004, MOFA had a 3 percent budget cut imposed which included both voluntary and mandatory contributions to multilateral institutions. Given this fiscal climate, Yamada saw the country's contributions to the Global Fund as "exceptional." While Japan was subject to criticism about its level of contributions, Yamada commented that this critique was applicable to many countries. He noted that everybody says "Country X" should contribute more, but suggested that the Japanese were doing their best.[110] Another official from the Foreign Ministry supported this view and described Japan's contributions to the Global Fund, given Japan's declining budget for overseas development assistance over the previous decade, as a "miracle."[111] However, Japan's entire ODA budget averaged 0.23 percent of gross national income between 2000 and 2007, and HIV/AIDS funding was but a small fraction of that total.[112] The claim by Japanese officials that the country's fiscal situation prevented additional spending suggests far more structural constraint than is warranted. HIV/AIDS was just not a priority expense.

We can get a more complete explanation by looking at the interaction between Japan's advocacy community and its leadership. As I noted earlier, while the Japanese public is generally in favor of foreign assistance, polls show the people are not as strongly supportive of foreign aid as their G-7 peers. This weakened support for foreign assistance is attributed to the long-running financial problems the country experienced throughout the 1990s and beyond.[113] Together, Japan's weak fiscal position and comparatively weaker public support for

---

[109] Mori 2001. Mori's tenure lasted but a year, April 2000 to April 2001, and his successor Junichiro Koizumi, at least initially, lacked the same enthusiasm as Mori for the issue.
[110] Yamada 2005.   [111] Japanese MOFA official 2008b.
[112] OECD 2007.   [113] McDonnell, Lecomte, and Wegimont 2003a, 2003b.

foreign assistance made the country hostile to expanded AIDS funding. Taking the fair share measure of foreign assistance from Table 2.2 as the core cost constraint, Japan should have been indifferent to AIDS advocates, making gatekeepers' preferences particularly important (Cell 3 in Table 2.2). If, however, economic growth was a more significant material concern for the Japanese, then Japan's position would have been more hostile (Cell 4 in Table 2.2).

When we pull in attributes of Japanese gatekeeper politics, the situation for AIDS funding by Japan looks even more bleak. Japan's Finance Ministry is a strong player able to restrain spending on global international causes against demands from others in the Japanese government.[114] For example, in 2002, the Japanese government allocated $200 million to the Global Fund over three years. After some discussion, the Japanese government decided that one-quarter of the resources would come from the Ministry of Finance and three-quarters from the Ministry of Foreign Affairs. In 2005, however, the Ministry of Finance did not support an extension of this arrangement of continued cost-sharing between the ministries.

In this context, the arc of mobilization in Japan is frequently slower compared to other countries. However, with pressure from other governments, global civil society, and domestic mobilization, Japan often comes around to supporting popular international causes. This is particularly true when the issue is framed as a test of Japan's international leadership, a highly resonant value in Japan as we saw in Chapters 3 and 4.[115] Japan's contributions to global AIDS efforts show a similar pattern, moving Japan potentially from indifference (Cell 3 in Table 2.2) to cheap moral action (Cell 1) or from hostility (Cell 4) to costly moral action (Cell 2).

---

[114] The main ministries involved in AIDS efforts are the Ministry of Health, Labour, and Welfare (which mostly deals with AIDS internally in Japan); the Ministry of Foreign Affairs; and the Ministry of Finance. The Prime Minister's Office is also consulted when major decisions are made (such as contributions to the Global Fund), although they are not always engaged. Because the Ministry of Finance allocates budgets to each ministry, it has huge influence over how much money is provided and how much Japan ultimately contributes to multilateral institutions such as the Global Fund. The International Bureau in the Ministry of Finance is a powerful department that exercises control over budget allocation. Based on guidance from the Ministry of Finance, MOFA proposes the distribution to different international organizations, including the Global Fund (Yamada 2005, 2007).

[115] Busby 2007a; Ohta 1995.

Japan's civil society organizations working on global AIDS have been few, partly because the entire non-profit sector is weak.[116] Because of complex tax laws, fewer than 1,000 of Japan's 25,000 public interest corporations have been able to achieve special tax status. This means that Japanese NGOs are cash-poor, despite the country's wealth.[117] Among the active organizations on AIDS are Friends of the Global Fund Japan (FGFJ), founded in 2004 and chaired by former prime minister Mori, as well as a task force of parliamentarians affiliated with FGFJ that included Mori and Tadashi Yamamoto, an influential former member of the Trilateral Commission, a private organization created in the 1970s to foster cooperation between the United States, Europe, and Japan. In addition to FGFJ, a few NGOs that operate in Africa have also taken up AIDS as a community development issue, and broader efforts to address the issue in Asia are under way. Until 2005–2006, the profile of AIDS was simply too low for either public engagement and high-level attention. Despite trips to Japan by Bono and Bill Gates, the coverage on AIDS hovered around 200 media articles per year across Japan's three major newspapers between 1998 and 2004.[118] One difficulty in Japan is that HIV/AIDS, to the extent that there is awareness of it, is perhaps perceived as a problem plaguing Africa, a continent where Japan has few historic interests.

Some signs of change emerged, particularly in the lead-up to Japan's role as host of the 2008 G-8 meeting. In 2005, on the fifth anniversary of the Okinawa meeting, Friends of the Global Fund Japan hosted a conference on AIDS in Asia that secured a multiyear commitment from Prime Minister Koizumi to contribute $500 mn to the Global Fund. This amount represented a doubling of the country's annual commitment, though it is still low by comparison with other countries. With former prime minister Mori in attendance, Koizumi also pledged $5 bn over the following five years for health and development, as part of a broader effort to restore the country's foreign assistance programs.[119] At the 2005 London replenishment meeting for the Global Fund, MOFA increased its pledge to the Global Fund for

---

[116] One study suggested that there were fewer than twenty NGOs in Japan that were involved, even tangentially, in AIDS-related issues in developing countries (Japan Center for International Exchange 2005).
[117] Japan Center for International Exchange 2007a.
[118] Japan Center for International Exchange 2005.   [119] Koizumi 2005.

2006 to $130 mn (up from about $100 mn in 2005). In 2006, the pledge for 2007 increased again, to $186 mn. Yamada suggested that high-level politicians, notably former prime minister Mori and former senior vice minister for foreign affairs Ichiro Aisawa, lent their support to increased Japanese contributions.[120] Keizo Takemi, a former health minister who narrowly lost his parliamentary seat in July 2007, joined Mori as a prominent advocate for AIDS funding. As a politician with the ruling Liberal Democratic Party and son of the former head of the Japan Medical Association, he, like Mori, had a number of attributes that enhanced his credibility and congruence with decisionmakers. In fall 2007, in the lead-up to the G-8 summit, the Japan Center for International Exchange launched the Takemi Project, a series of meetings and conferences on Japan's role in global health. Acknowledging that Japan's commitments to fighting infectious diseases have been scaled up since 2005, Takemi emphasized continuity with Japan's earlier leadership role in 2000.[121] In his appeals, Takemi expanded that "leadership frame," focusing on Japan's historic success in dealing with disease in the aftermath of World War II.[122] These efforts to engage the government by framing the argument as a test of Japanese global leadership have been more successful than focusing on the issue of public health alone.

Prior to the G-8 summit, Japan also hosted the Fourth Tokyo International Conference on African Development (TICAD IV) in May 2008.[123] Just before TICAD, Prime Minister Takeo Fukuda pledged an additional $560 mn to the Global Fund to be delivered over an unspecified period of years.[124] Japan saw the summit as an opportunity to lead on health systems capacity, in addition to supporting specific diseases such as HIV/AIDS.[125] After a difficult decade, Japan sought to use the G-8 summit to reclaim the mantle of leadership on global development. As in Germany in this case as well as with climate change in Japan itself, being the host of an international meeting focused attention, created pressure for promise-making, and provided civil society with organizing hooks.

---

[120] Interestingly, Japan used a supplementary budget for this contribution, which was not subject to the strict mandatory cap mentioned above (Yamada 2007).
[121] Takemi 2008b.   [122] Takemi 2008a.
[123] Japan Center for International Exchange 2007b.   [124] Fukuda 2008.
[125] Reich *et al.* 2008.

Like Germany, Japan's improved fiscal climate may have also facilitated its ability to increase its commitments. After a decade of stagnation, Japan had one year of solid economic growth in 2000 (more than 3%) before experiencing five years of anemic economic performance. After growing by less than 1% in 2005, Japan's economy expanded by nearly 3% in 2005 and then by 2.5% in 2007. By 2008, the mobilization of influential messengers and a more focused narrative on Japan's leadership role, along with the modest recovery of the Japanese economy, provided a more propitious climate for AIDS spending. In terms of Table 2.2, Japan had moved from being hostile or indifferent to AIDS efforts to seeing the issue as costly moral action, moving leftward toward cheap moral action as its economy improved.

Conclusion

This chapter again demonstrates the importance of moral arguments, prestige motivations, and framing. Added to the mix is a discussion of messengers. Interlocutors serve both to mobilize public support and to get the attention of policy gatekeepers. In the United States, the greater similarity between emergent messengers such as Franklin Graham and key policy gatekeepers enabled them to have success employing moral arguments. The character of the US response, with its emphasis on abstinence and the proscriptions against sex workers, also reflected the values of religious advocates. While the relative health of the US economy and strategic concerns created permissive conditions and incentives for action, the fair share asked of the United States constituted a significant part of its foreign assistance budget. These mixed material indicators aside, one cannot explain US support for expanded AIDS funding without bringing in moral concerns.

In lagging countries such as Germany and Japan, while the fair share for AIDS funding asked of them was a smaller portion of their foreign assistance budgets than other G-7 countries, poor economic conditions provided them with a rationale for low contributions. Comparatively low donations for global AIDS efforts by Germany and Japan are what political scientists call "overdetermined." In addition to bad economic conditions, both countries had publics that were less supportive of foreign aid than their G-7 peers and, as a consequence, were less motivated and concerned about HIV/AIDS. When transnational advocates reframed their arguments in Germany and Japan through local intermediaries as a test of their government's prestige and credibility, they achieved modest results. These findings suggest efforts to find local support, in terms of both appropriate messengers and messages, are important determinants of whether or not advocacy movements succeed or fail.

In 2007 and 2008, Germany and Japan successively hosted G-8 summits, which created incentives for leaders to seek international acclaim by making grandiose promises. Effective summits can provide leaders with boosts in their political fortunes at home, so making pledges is rational from an individual interest perspective. G-8 summits are among the few moments when development issues receive sustained media coverage, allowing advocacy groups to get wider attention for their concerns. For causes that may be generally supported but only weakly salient to domestic publics, these high-profile venues provide tempting opportunities to grandstand and make lavish promises, since domestic publics may not care that much about punishing politicians who fail to make good on their pledges. However, as I argue in the next chapter on the International Criminal Court, unkept promises can come back to haunt politicians, as groups mobilize to remind them of or shame them for their broken pledges. So, unless leaders are confident they can keep their promises or evade punishment for breaking them, the short-run reputational gains have to be weighed against the costs of implementing the proposals or getting caught overpromising and underdelivering. When we factor in shared aspirations for global leadership and conceptions of a country's role on the global stage, the prestige motive for themselves and for their country is a powerful force, even if politicians know the risks.

Appendix 5A
Evaluations of actual fair share contributions to global AIDS efforts

The UK was the only country of the G-7 to spend more than what advocates deemed their fair share contribution to global AIDS efforts. The United States and Canada were a distant second and third, more than 50% and 60% below their fair share.[1] Japan was an outlier, falling more than 90% below what activists believed its fair share should have been. Germany and Italy were only slightly better, falling 80% below their fair share.

Table 5A.1 *G-7 share of world GDP*

	2004	2005	2006	2007
Canada	2.38%	2.52%	2.63%	2.63%
France	4.95%	4.77%	4.67%	4.75%
Germany	6.60%	6.21%	5.99%	6.08%
Italy	4.15%	3.95%	3.82%	3.86%
Japan	11.06%	10.13%	8.99%	8.03%
United Kingdom	5.28%	5.06%	5.01%	5.14%
United States	28.04%	27.59%	27.08%	25.30%

[1] It is unclear if the United States could have spent additional funds wisely. Between 2004 and 2007, the country was unable to disburse nearly $3.5 bn of its bilateral commitments, a rate of 57.9 percent. It is unclear if this was a problem of the appropriations process or if it reflected difficulty in finding suitable programs on which to spend the money. Data are from Kates 2005, 2006; Kates, Izazola, and Lief 2007, 2008.

US HIV/AIDS commitment and disbursement gap 2004–2007

$ millions	2004	2005	2006	2007	2004–2007
Commitment	$1,354.80	$1,918.70	$2,631.70	$2,362.80	$8,268.00
Disbursement	$781.20	$1,095.00	$1,589.80	$1,320.90	$4,786.90
% disbursement gap	57.66%	57.07%	60.41%	55.90%	57.90%

Table 5A.2 *Assessments of fair shares and contributions*

	2004 fair share	2005 fair share	2006 fair share	2007 fair share	2004–2007 fair share
Canada	$197,953,066.83	$309,651,208.60	$391,588,456.52	$476,196,677.62	$1,375,389,409.57
France	$410,463,480.13	$586,689,579.53	$695,402,773.74	$860,080,066.44	$2,552,635,899.84
Germany	$547,423,181.04	$763,448,132.67	$892,495,335.46	$1,101,192,921.09	$3,304,559,570.26
Italy	$344,545,573.69	$486,131,645.32	$568,975,313.70	$697,893,410.78	$2,097,545,943.48
Japan	$917,702,705.19	$1,245,970,001.79	$1,340,142,221.19	$1,452,901,799.72	$4,956,716,727.90
United Kingdom	$437,977,020.30	$622,910,007.82	$745,749,209.29	$929,932,874.50	$2,736,569,111.90
United States	$2,327,232,743.39	$3,393,641,772.45	$4,034,876,268.47	$4,578,492,817.37	$14,334,243,601.68
TOTAL NEED	$8,300,000,000.00	$12,300,000,000.00	$14,900,000,000.00	$18,100,000,000.00	$53,600,000,000.00
	2004 Actual	2005 Actual	2006 Actual	2007 Actual	2004–2007 Actual
Canada	$164,773,373.00	$93,229,982.67	$130,565,935.23	$146,565,935.23	$535,135,226.14
France	$122,180,534.50	$115,672,005.00	$218,925,779.63	$313,313,800.96	$770,092,120.08
Germany	$112,486,358.50	$109,032,384.08	$176,149,954.80	$225,374,958.60	$623,043,655.98
Italy	$76,242,200.00	$75,908,400.00	$117,528,750.00	$110,028,750.00	$379,708,100.00
Japan	$55,647,002.36	$63,880,000.00	$110,490,419.08	$133,664,146.78	$363,681,568.22
United Kingdom	$157,623,258.10	$465,153,750.39	$746,704,898.00	$990,439,440.00	$2,359,921,346.49
United States	$1,387,277,580.19	$1,254,936,862.24	$1,633,823,354.08	$2,100,461,811.12	$6,376,499,607.63

(*cont.*)

Table 5A.2 (*cont.*)

	% of fair share 2004	% of fair share 2005	% of fair share 2006	% of fair share 2007	% of fair share 2004–2007
Canada	83.24%	30.11%	33.34%	30.78%	38.91%
France	29.77%	19.72%	31.48%	36.43%	30.17%
Germany	20.55%	14.28%	19.74%	20.47%	18.85%
Italy	22.13%	15.61%	20.66%	15.77%	18.10%
Japan	6.06%	5.13%	8.24%	9.20%	7.34%
United Kingdom	35.99%	74.67%	100.13%	106.51%	86.24%
United States	59.61%	36.98%	40.49%	45.88%	44.48%

Fair share is based on UNAIDS estimates for needed resources for low- and middle-income countries for that year. Actual contributions reflect disbursements to the Global Fund and bilateral expenditures on HIV/AIDS. Since the Global Fund also addresses tuberculosis and malaria, I calculate AIDS Global Fund donations to be 61% of their total, reflecting the distribution of Global Fund resources as of December 2008. Kates uses a 58% figure in her work. Data for bilateral HIV expenditures in 2004 and 2005 come from the OECD DAC database. Data for 2006 and 2007 bilateral expenditures come from Kates, Izazola, and Lief 2007, 2008. The Global Fund data are from the Global Fund.

Appendix 5B
Mission and dominant frame of various advocacy organizations

Group name	Mission	Dominant frame
ACT UP New York	"There are 35 million people in the world living with HIV/AIDS. 95% of them lack access to the medicine that could save their lives. The US and other rich nations must rise to the occasion and address the crisis at hand." "We need a new plan for 'Equitable Access.'" "PUT CARE BEFORE PROFIT: RESPECT THE DOHA DECLARATION."[1]	*Justice, anti-corporate*
Action Against AIDS Germany (Aktionsbündnis gegen AIDS)	"Together [campaigners] are engaging in advocacy work to improve the living conditions of people living with HIV and AIDS. The campaign 'Life is a Human Right' started in 2002."[2]	*Human rights*
DATA	"DATA argues that supporting Africa is essential to our economic and national security interests. However, at the core of DATA's beliefs is a view that these issues are not about charity, but about equality and justice."[3]	*Justice*
Friends of the Global Fight (US)	"Friends of the Global Fight Against AIDS, Tuberculosis and Malaria (Friends) is an advocacy organization that works to sustain and expand US support for the Global Fund's life-saving work."[4]	*Public health*

Group name	Mission	Dominant frame
Friends of the Global Fund Japan	"The Friends of the Global Fund, Japan (FGFJ), is a private support group that works to promote a greater understanding of the Global Fund to Fight AIDS, Tuberculosis and Malaria; encourage Japan to expand its role in the battle against communicable diseases; and build cooperation between Japan and other East Asian countries in this shared struggle."[5]	*Public health, prestige*
Global AIDS Alliance	"The Global AIDS Alliance seeks to mobilize a comprehensive and compassionate response to the global AIDS crisis, while addressing the epidemic's fundamental links to social justice issues such as poverty and gender inequality."[6]	*Justice*
Health GAP	"We are an organization of US-based AIDS and human rights activists, people living with HIV/AIDS, public health experts, fair trade advocates and concerned individuals who campaign against policies of neglect and avarice that deny treatment to millions and fuel the spread of HIV . . . We believe that the human right to life and to health must prevail over the pharmaceutical industry's excessive profits and expanding patent rights."[7]	*Justice, anti-corporate*

[1] See www.actupny.org/reports/bcn/BCNbushAUpr.html.
[2] See www.aids-kampagne.de/en/home/.
[3] See web.archive.org/web/20070702154221/www.data.org/about/mission.html.
[4] See mission statement at www.theglobalfight.org/.
[5] See www.jcie.or.jp/fgfj/e/.
[6] See www.globalaidsalliance.org/.
[7] See www.healthgap.org/about.htm.

Appendix 5C
Reasons for foreign assistance

The German Marshall Fund asked people in 2006 and 2007 to state the most important reason for providing foreign assistance. Here, I have selected two more altruistic motivations and three self-interested reasons from a broader list. Alleviating poverty was the top choice for most countries both years.[1]

Table 5C.1 *Public opinion: reasons for supporting foreign assistance*

%	Alleviating poverty	Fighting health problems like AIDS	Helping poor countries trade	Gaining political allies	Preventing breeding grounds for terrorism
France	2007: 26	2007: 14	2007: 11	2007: 1	2007: 9
	2006: 36	2006: 23	2006: 9	2006: 0	2006: 7
Germany	2007: 35	2007: 10	2007: 7	2007: 1	2007: 4
	2006: 26	2006: 13	2006: 8	2006: 1	2006: 6
Italy	2007: 16	2007: 12	2007: 15	2007: 1	2007: 9
	2006: 25	2006: 20	2006: 13	2006: 1	2006: 9
UK	2007: 35	2007: 11	2007: 14	2007: 0	2007: 8
	2006: 27	2006: 16	2006: 12	2006: 2	2006: 8
United States	2007: 22	2007: 9	2007: 5	2007: 2	2007: 10
	2006: 23	2006: 15	2006: 4	2006: 4	2006: 11

[1] German Marshall Fund 2006a, 2007.

Appendix 5D
Aggregating support for foreign assistance

In 1996, 1998, and 2004, the Eurobarometer polls asked Europeans: "In your opinion, is it very important, important, not very important, or not at all important to help people in poor countries in Africa, South America, Asia, etc. to develop?" In the first two polls, Germans consistently lagged behind the British, Italians, and French. In 2004, the percentage of Europeans who thought foreign aid was "very important" spiked sharply, most likely as a response to the events of September 11, 2001.[1]

In 2005, 2006, and 2007, the German Marshall Fund asked Europeans and Americans a comparable question: "Please tell me if you have a very favorable, somewhat favorable, somewhat unfavorable or very unfavorable opinion of providing development assistance to poor countries."[2] In 1998 and 2000, Belden, Russonello, and Stewart polled the US public and asked them, "Are you generally in favor or opposed to the US (United States) giving economic assistance to help other countries?" Category responses included very much favor, somewhat favor, somewhat opposed, and very much opposed.[3]

In Japan, polling questions conflate principles in support of foreign assistance with current funding levels. In 2001, 2004, 2005, and 2006, the Cabinet Office asked, "Developed countries provide economic cooperation, including financial aid and technical assistance, for developing countries. What do you think about Japan's economic cooperation in the future?" The categories are a blend between principled support for aid and comments on current funding levels: should advance cooperation actively, current level of cooperation is sufficient, should cut cooperation as much as possible, and should stop

---

[1] Eurobarometer 1997, 1999, 2005.
[2] German Marshall Fund 2007.
[3] PIPA 2001.

Table 5D.1 *Public opinion %: support for foreign assistance*

	1996	1998	2000	2001	2002	2003 Sep.	2003 Dec.	2004	2005	2006	2007	Average
France	31.6	23.6						49	41	40	44	38.2
Germany	19.2	20.1						50	21	17	18	24.2
Italy	40.2	32.1						55	43	49	53	45.4
UK	33.1	23.7						63	41	42	39	40.3
US		18	14						21	21	28	20.4
Canada		52			58	38	56					51
Japan				24.7				18.7	22.0	23.1		22.1

completely. While not ideal, this is the best question from Japan to make a comparison with other G-7 countries.[4]

Similarly, the Canadians were asked a question that simultaneously gauged the Canadian public's sense of support for foreign aid as well as a more contemporaneous assessment of whether or not they supported the government's current aid program. Canadians were asked, "On a scale of one to six, where one means 'very strongly oppose' and six means 'very strongly support', what is your level of support for Canada's aid program for poor countries?" I consolidated the categories for very strongly support and strongly support.[5]

Combining these poll results in a single table and aggregating yields Table 5D.1.

4 Japan, Cabinet Office 2004, 2005, 2006. For 2001 data, see McDonnell, Lecomte, and Wegimont 2003a, 144.

5 Environics Research Group 2004.

6 | The search for justice and the International Criminal Court

In February 2006, Luis Moreno-Ocampo, the prosecutor of the International Criminal Court (ICC), issued a letter acknowledging that he had received more than 240 communications alleging among other things that war crimes had been committed in and after the March 2003 invasion of Iraq. The ICC was a young institution, having been created in July 2002, when its founding treaty entered into force.[1] The Court was charged to address "the most serious crimes of international concern," focusing on the crimes of individuals rather than states, looking specifically at genocide, crimes against humanity, and war crimes.[2] In his reply to the complainants, Moreno-Ocampo declined to begin a formal investigation of the charges. He noted that his office had no authority to comment on the legality of the conflict, as the rules for crimes of aggression had yet to be codified: "As the Prosecutor of the International Criminal Court, I do not have the mandate to address the arguments on the legality of the use of force or the crime of aggression." As for war crimes, Moreno-Ocampo noted that the Court's jurisdiction did not extend to non-parties (like the United States); he did evaluate whether parties to the statute (such as the United Kingdom) had been complicit in committing war crimes. The prosecutor demurred,

---

[1] The ICC headquarters is located in The Hague, Netherlands, but it can conduct its proceedings anywhere. It is technically an independent organization but has administrative and technical support from the United Nations. It consists of a prosecutor, two deputy prosecutors, and eighteen judges elected to nine-year terms by an assembly of state parties that meets once a year. As of June 2008, 561 people from 80 countries worked for the Court (ICC 2008a).

[2] Article 1, ICC 2002. The treaty creating the Court is called the Rome Statute. According to Article 5, the Court will also one day have jurisdiction for the crime of aggression, should an amendment to the treaty be agreed to by seven-eighths of the states that are ICC parties prior to it coming into effect. An amendment to the treaty could not have been considered until July 2009 (Articles 121 and 123).

suggesting any crimes committed were not of sufficient gravity to warrant the Court's jurisdiction: "The resulting information did not allow for the conclusion that there was a reasonable basis to believe that a clearly excessive attack within the jurisdiction of the Court had been committed."[3] There may never have been any doubt about Moreno-Ocampo's conclusions about these allegations. It would probably have been political suicide for the prosecutor of a newly established court to take on the great powers. Frank Berman, former legal counsel to the British government on the ICC, dismissed the concerns of critics worried about politically inspired cases being brought against soldiers and leaders of major powers: "The prospect of an ICC Prosecutor setting out to pull the noses of powerful law-abiding states strikes me as so remote as hardly to enter into the realm of serious policy-making, and the prospect that, if he *were* foolish enough to try to do so, it would survive the scrutiny of the judges at the pre-trial level, is even more fanciful still."[4]

This episode and the UK legal counsel's remarks are instructive. Countries such as the UK, which are party to the ICC, may one day find themselves subject to these kinds of legal complaints. While the prosecutor may find it prudent and even reasonable to dismiss such claims, particularly in the Court's early years of operation, an entrenched Court and emboldened prosecutor, notwithstanding a number of safeguards, may one day seek to investigate purported crimes even by soldiers and leaders of some of the great powers.[5] In 2007, Moreno-Ocampo told the *Daily Telegraph*, no friend of the Court, that he could envisage a scenario in which the British prime minister could face charges at the ICC: "Of course, that could be a possibility,

---

[3] In February 2006, the ICC prosecutor declined to begin an official investigation of human rights abuses in Iraq by an ICC party, the UK. The prosecutor concluded that there was no willful effort by the British to target civilians and that, while there was a small number of deaths (four to twelve) where individual British troops had done so, these were of a different order of magnitude than the situations in other cases the ICC was investigating where hundreds of thousands of individuals had been victimized (ICC, Office of the Prosecutor 2006).

[4] Berman 2002.

[5] In 1986, the International Court of Justice ruled that the United States had illegally mined Nicaragua's harbors in its support of the Contras (the anti-Communist guerrillas that fought against the Sandinistas). In the lead-up to the ruling, the United States withdrew its support for the compulsory jurisdiction of the Court.

whatever country joins the court can know that whoever commits a crime in their country could be prosecuted by me."[6]

Even if these prospects remain distant, at the very least, parties to the Court may believe it necessary to conduct more vigorous domestic investigations of their own to ward off attempts to take such cases to the ICC. In 2006, three British soldiers were, for the first time under the jurisdiction of the ICC, tried domestically for war crimes against Iraqi detainees. One of them was subsequently found guilty in 2007.[7] These potential implications of the Court were raised during the negotiations, and a number of safeguards (described pp. 216–218) were created to insulate the great powers from potential prosecution. Despite these risks, two G-7 countries with large troop commitments – France and Britain – nevertheless ratified the Rome Statute, the treaty creating the Court.

What is interesting about this episode is the divergence in the perceived costs of the Court in three G-7 countries – the UK, France, and the United States. All three had large overseas troop deployments, potentially making their citizens subject to complaints under the Court's jurisdiction. However, the UK believed these concerns were manageable and vocally supported the Court throughout the negotiations. France and the United States, while rhetorically committed to the Court, waged more vigorous objections to its jurisdiction. Both countries' governments were much more fearful of what might be, in their view, politically inspired tribunals. Nonetheless, like the UK, France in the end ratified the treaty, while the United States failed to do so and ultimately became a vigorous opponent of the Court for much of President George W. Bush's tenure. These results lead to the question animating this chapter: What explains why some countries ratified the treaty creating the International Criminal Court while others did not?

In this chapter, I explore a related question about why countries similarly situated in terms of overseas troop concentrations (such as the UK and France) would have such different views about how risky or how costly it would be for their countries to ratify the treaty and become a party to the ICC. In emphasizing the subjective nature of costs, I also focus on the role of gatekeepers and how the dynamics of ratification and representation in the UK and France facilitated their

---

[6] Chamberlain 2007.   [7] BBC 2007b; Blackstock and Norton-Taylor 2005.

support for the Court, while these same dynamics made US accession much more difficult. In the process, I discuss the degree to which a government that has rhetorically supported a policy favored by advocacy groups becomes vulnerable to shaming and reputational damage for perceived hypocrisy.

This chapter represents an important extension of the arguments in previous chapters that have largely examined second-tier issues of development, the environment, and health policy. While the ICC is ostensibly a case in the human rights arena, the potential prosecution of individuals for war crimes touches directly upon the security sphere, elevating the ICC from low politics to high politics, making this issue possibly more sensitive than any of the others explored in the book.

The chapter is divided into four sections. The first provides an overview of the creation of the International Criminal Court. The second section evaluates material interest-based explanations and discusses their limitations. In the third section, I expand the framing/gatekeepers argument of earlier chapters, emphasizing the importance of subjective assessments of costs and the degree of rhetorical entrapment. In the final section, I explore the cases of the UK and France, two countries that ratified the Rome Statute despite having large overseas troop deployments. In the process, I contrast their actions with those of the other country that had large troop deployments but failed to ratify the Rome Statute, the United States.

Background on the International Criminal Court

In 2002, the Rome Statute for the International Criminal Court entered into force, establishing the legal rules for genocide, crimes against humanity, and war crimes. The idea of an International Criminal Court has a long pedigree. Gustave Moynier of Switzerland, one of the founders of the International Committee of the Red Cross, proposed such a court in 1872 as a way to punish violators of the 1864 Geneva Convention for the Amelioration of the Condition of the Wounded in Armies in the Field.[8] No court came to fruition then, but the idea was revived in the aftermath of World War II. The Nuremberg and Tokyo trials were an ad hoc response to Nazi atrocities during the Holocaust

---

[8] Glasius 2003.

and Japanese crimes against humanity. The horrors of World War II also generated interest in a permanent tribunal. In 1948, the United Nations General Assembly adopted the Convention on the Prevention and Punishment of the Crime of Genocide, which called for possible "penal tribunals" for criminals. The General Assembly asked the International Law Commission (ILC) to study creation of a judicial organ to try persons charged with genocide.[9]

However, despite a draft statute from the ILC by the early 1950s, proposals for a court went nowhere for four decades, a casualty of the Cold War. By the late 1980s, with the Cold War thawing, the court would receive some renewed impetus from unlikely quarters. In June 1989, Trinidad and Tobago revived a proposal to establish an ICC as a way of combating drug trafficking in the Caribbean. The UN General Assembly asked the ILC to resume work on drafting a statute.[10]

After the failure of the world to confront ethnic cleansing in Yugoslavia and the genocide in Rwanda in the 1990s, human rights activists sought to create a more durable legal regime, which they thought would bring future killers to justice and also deter other would-be gross violators of human rights. Ad hoc courts for Yugoslavia and Rwanda were created, but advocates believed a permanent court would avoid the start-up costs of creating country-specific tribunals after violations and provide stronger deterrent and investigatory capacity.

In 1994, the ILC presented its final draft statute for an ICC to the UN General Assembly and recommended that a conference be convened to negotiate a treaty.[11] The General Assembly established an Ad Hoc Committee on the Establishment of an International Criminal Court, which met twice in 1995, to review some of the major issues. In the lead-up to actual negotiations of a treaty, the General Assembly created a Preparatory Committee on the Establishment of an ICC to prepare a draft text. The Preparatory Committee held six sessions between 1996 and 1998 in New York at UN headquarters.[12]

The ICC received broad support from activists in the human rights community. In February 1995, advocates from a number of NGOs

---

[9] Coalition for the ICC Undated.   [10] Stephen 2003.
[11] That draft envisioned a very weak court that generally protected state sovereignty. See Deitelhoff 2008, 149–150, for more details.
[12] Coalition for the ICC Undated.

met in New York to coordinate efforts of human rights organizations in support of the Court's creation. William Pace, executive director of the World Federalist Movement–Institute for Global Policy, was appointed convenor of the NGO Coalition for the International Criminal Court (CICC), which initially consisted of twenty-five organizations. The coalition was guided by a steering committee that included Amnesty International, the Spanish organization Asociación pro Derechos Humanos, the European Law Students Association, the French human rights organization Fédération Internationale des Ligues des Droits de l'Homme (FIDH), Human Rights Watch, the International Commission of Jurists, Lawyers Committee for Human Rights, the Italian NGO No Peace Without Justice, Parliamentarians for Global Action, Rights & Democracy, and the World Federalist Movement.[13] The coalition in subsequent years grew to include 2,000 organizations across the world. A number of coalition members contributed to the preparatory meetings of the draft statute of the ICC.

In June and July 1998, efforts to create an ICC culminated in negotiations in Italy with the Rome Statute of the International Criminal Court.[14] During the Rome negotiations, as many as 200 NGOs were present. They provided position papers and private commentary to delegates and lobbied them throughout the proceedings. They were even able to produce a report in the midst of the negotiations with an informal vote count of different country positions on major items of contention.[15]

The coalition provided information to supporters around the world through the *ICC Monitor*.[16] Other groups also covered the proceedings; the Inter Press Service, a quasi-advocacy media organization, produced a daily newspaper, *TerraViva*, one of three papers covering the proceedings.[17] A number of delegations included representatives of the NGO community; in fact, groups such as No Peace Without Justice provided staff for developing country delegations that lacked resources for sufficient legal expertise. Thirty-five, mostly young European lawyers joined delegations from the developing world to flesh out those countries' positions on the ICC over the course of the negotiations.[18]

---

[13] Coalition for the ICC Undated.   [14] Lee 1999.   [15] Kaul 1999, 119.
[16] See www.iccnow.org/?mod=monitor.   [17] IPS 1998.
[18] No Peace Without Justice Undated.

Leading up to the Rome negotiations, a group of like-minded states – Canada along with member states of the European Union, including Germany, Italy, and ultimately Britain – emerged as the primary supporters of the Court.[19] The Clinton administration, despite expressions of support for the Court, faced strong opposition at home from members of Congress and from the military. Throughout the course of the Rome negotiations, the Americans sought to shape the Court in ways that would shield American soldiers from ever being subject to it. At the same time, these efforts were designed to blunt congressional and Pentagon objections to the Court. Once again, as on debt relief and HIV/AIDS, Senator Jesse Helms was a major player. As head of the Senate Foreign Relations Committee, he signaled his implacable opposition to any court that might lead to the prosecution of the US armed forces. In the lead-up to and over the course of the Rome negotiations, France initially sided with the United States.

In addition to the definition of crimes, one of the principal issues of contention during the Rome negotiations was the jurisdiction of the Court. Its advocates pushed for "universal jurisdiction." They wanted the prosecutor to be independent, to be able to initiate investigations independent of member states and, in particular, of the United Nations Security Council, where veto power by any of the permanent five members would likely undercut the Court's relevance. Countries such as the United States and France, while potentially supportive of the Court, sought to limit its jurisdiction to ensure that their own soldiers would unlikely be tried before it. In addition to Security Council authorization, the United States initially sought consent of the state in which the crime was allegedly committed and the state of the nationality of the alleged perpetrator. At the very least, the United States wanted consent of the home state of the alleged perpetrator for the Court to be able to claim jurisdiction.[20] Likewise, during the August 1996 preparatory meetings, France sought to limit the Court's jurisdiction to require the "triple consent" of up to three states – that of the

---

[19] By early 1997, this group had grown to include most European countries (except France and Britain), Argentina, Australia, Canada, Chile, the Caribbean states, Lesotho, New Zealand, Senegal, Singapore, South Africa, and South Korea (Deitelhoff 2008, 167). Over the course of negotiations, the group expanded to include sixty countries.

[20] Brown 2000, 63; Elsea 2002, 5. For a critical assessment of US conduct during the negotiations, see Nolte 2003.

nationality of the accused, of the nationality of the victim, and of the location of the alleged crime – all to agree before the Court would have jurisdiction.[21] Britain, which generally holds its special relationship to the United States dear, broke ranks when it joined the like-minded group in December 2007. In doing so, the UK accepted the "Singapore compromise," which allowed the Security Council to block ICC jurisdiction but not be required to authorize every case.[22]

The Singapore compromise was one of the ways in which great power concerns were accommodated as part of the Court's mandate. A second compromise was a restriction on the prosecutor's ability to investigate or prosecute cases independently. The prosecutor could initiate a case if the Security Council referred it or if a state party requested an investigation. However, before the prosecutor could initiate proceedings independently based on petitions from individuals or organizations, s/he must first obtain the permission of the so-called Pre-Trial Chamber (Article 15). Another safeguard incorporated was that the Court could not act retroactively for crimes committed before it was created (Article 24).

A fourth safeguard for great powers in the statute was the principle of "complementarity" enshrined in Article 17. The ICC was designed to complement national legal systems and to be used only when states were unable or unwilling to prosecute crimes covered under the statute. Thus, in most cases, with functioning domestic legal systems of advanced industrial democracies, the issue of capability would be moot. However, if a country failed to conduct adequate investigations or initiate legal action against citizens who had committed crimes, the Court could potentially claim jurisdiction in the absence of a good faith effort to pursue the charges domestically. In a nod to advocates of universality, the Court has potential jurisdiction in any one of three instances: where the accused is a national of a state party, where the alleged crime took place on the territory of a state party, or where a situation is referred to the Court by the United Nations Security Council.[23]

In the waning days of the negotiations, the French negotiating team still exercised its objections and suggested that France would not be able to sign or ratify without additional freedom to maneuver. To that

[21] Eftekhari 2001.   [22] Brown 2000, 63.
[23] For a discussion, see Brown 2002, 326–328; Struett 2008, 8.

end, the French secured, after considerable negotiation, the addition of Article 124, which allowed countries to take advantage of a seven-year opt-out for war crimes.[24] The French were ultimately the only country to take advantage of this option. The American delegation unsuccessfully pursued a ten-year opt-out and could not secure permission from Washington to support the seven-year compromise.

The negotiating rules for Rome proceedings required a majority vote by the delegates before the statute could be sent forward for state signature and subsequent ratification. Of the 148 states that voted on the text of the treaty, 120 approved it; the United States was one of seven to vote against, with twenty-one abstentions.[25]

Actual treaty accession to the Rome Statute was a two-step process up until December 31, 2000. Until then, countries could sign the treaty and ratify later. By signing, countries could signal their intent to remain part of the negotiations; most European governments signed the treaty in 1998. Ratification was subject to the kinds of domestic measures described for the Kyoto Protocol (see pp. 131–136). As host to the negotiations, Italy was among the first countries to ratify the Rome Statute, depositing its instrument of ratification in July 1999. Other European G-7 countries followed in 2000 and 2001 (see Table 6.1).

On December 31, 2000, the last day countries could become parties to the Rome Statute without ratifying it, President Clinton instructed his negotiators to sign the treaty, just ahead of the midnight deadline. With three weeks to go in his administration, the decision was largely a dead letter, as the Bush administration withdrew US officials from negotiations on the Court in April 2001 and repudiated the Clinton signature in May 2002, having delayed the decision to do so in September 2001 because of the terrorist attacks of 9/11.[26] Finally, the Rome Statute reached the required threshold to enter into force on July 1, 2002, after sixty countries had ratified the treaty. Among

---

[24] This meant that the country taking advantage of the opt-out could not have its citizens prosecuted for war crimes for seven years after the treaty entered into force for that country. France ratified in 2000 but the Rome Statute did not enter into force until July 2002, meaning French nationals were exempt from war crimes under the statute until July 2009. The negotiations of the war crimes opt-out, which began with a request for a ten-year opt-out, are described in Kaul 1998.

[25] Brown 2002, 325. The others were China, Iran, Iraq, Israel, Libya, and Sudan (Elsea 2002).

[26] Lewis 2002; United Nations Association of the United States of America 2003.

Table 6.1 *G-7 signature and ratification of the Rome Statute*

Country	Signed	Ratified
Canada	December 1998	July 2000
France	July 1998	June 2000, seven-year opt-out on war crimes
Germany	December 1998	December 2000
Italy	June 1998	July 1999
Japan	-	July 2007
UK	November 1998	October 2001
United States	December 2000, repudiated May 2002	No

Source: ICC 2009.

the G-7, Japan initially stayed outside the Court for its first five years, until changing course in July 2007. By July 2008, there were 110 states that were parties to the Rome Statute, including thirty African states, fourteen Asian states, seventeen from Eastern Europe, twenty-four from Latin America and the Caribbean, and twenty-five from Western Europe and elsewhere including Canada, Iceland, Australia, and New Zealand.[27] Nearly forty had signed the statute but not ratified it.[28] As of March 2010, a number of major powers, including the United States, India, Russia, and China, have not ratified the treaty.

Like climate change, the ICC became highly contentious between the United States and Europe. After the Court was created, the Bush administration pursued special agreements to limit the jurisdiction of the Court over American soldiers. The US Congress passed the American Servicemembers' Protection Act (ASPA), threatening to cut off foreign assistance to a number of governments that did not sign bilateral immunity deals with the United States.[29] The United States concluded more than 100 such agreements, but a number of governments refused to sign them.[30] During the George W. Bush administration, the United States largely retained this antagonistic stance against the Court

---

[27] ICC 2009.   [28] United Nations Treaty Collection 2009.
[29] NATO members, non-NATO allies (Argentina, Australia, Egypt, Israel, Japan, Jordan, New Zealand, and the Republic of Korea), and Taiwan were exempt from this legislation.
[30] Kelley 2007.

and cut off military, anti-narcotics, and/or foreign assistance to almost twenty countries that refused to sign bilateral immunity agreements, Mexico among them. The United States sought to divide the loyalties of EU candidate countries such as Romania by dangling NATO membership in front of them in exchange for immunity agreements for American soldiers. In July 2002, when the United States threatened to veto the extension of the peacekeeping mandate in Bosnia, the UK brokered a compromise that secured a unanimous vote for Security Council Resolution 1422, which granted a yearlong exemption to UN peacekeepers from non-signatory countries from being referred to the ICC.[31] In October 2002, the European Council agreed to a UK compromise that allowed EU members to enter into limited immunity agreements with Americans for military or "official" personnel sent overseas by the United States.[32] The peacekeepers' exemption was renewed again in 2003 but rejected in 2004 after US detainee abuse at the Abu Ghraib prison in Iraq became public.[33]

Despite its antagonism to the Court, the United States did permit the Security Council to refer the ongoing genocide in Darfur, Sudan, to the ICC in March 2005 by abstaining on a vote to refer the case to the Court.[34] In addition, after several years in which a number of African and Latin American governments refused to sign Article 98 agreements and had their military and/or foreign aid reduced, US policymakers recognized that these restrictions were counterproductive and harmed other US interests such as counterterrorism.[35] The restrictions on military assistance were repealed in October 2006 and those on foreign assistance in January 2008.[36]

Between its creation in 2002 and 2009, the Court opened investigations in four situations – northern Uganda, the Democratic Republic of the Congo, the Central African Republic, and Darfur – issuing arrest warrants for twelve people, four of whom were in custody.[37] The Court's first trial, of Congolese militia leader Thomas Lubanga, began in January 2009.[38] In 2008, as a prelude to full investigations, the

---

[31] Lederer 2002.   [32] Dempsey 2002b.   [33] Associated Press 2004.
[34] Bravin 2006.   [35] Mazetti 2006.
[36] Arieff, Margesson, and Browne 2008.   [37] ICC Undated.
[38] ICC judges in June 2008 ordered his release due to questions about proper procedure in the collection of evidence. These concerns were addressed, and ICC judges rescinded the release order and the suspension of the proceedings in November 2008 (ICC 2008b).

prosecutor was analyzing situations in Afghanistan, Chad, Colombia, Côte d'Ivoire, Georgia, and Kenya.[39] Some scholars have questioned whether or not an International Criminal Court will actually have any deterrent qualities or help contribute to peace in post-conflict reconstruction. Without an option for exile or amnesty, leaders at risk of prosecution for crimes against their own citizens might continue to hold on to power.[40] In July 2008, the ICC prosecutor asked judges for an arrest warrant for Sudanese president Omar Hassan al-Bashir, accusing him of orchestrating genocide in Darfur. A decision on an arrest warrant was issued for him in March 2009. The arrest warrant was the first for a sitting president. The Sudanese government warned an indictment could disrupt efforts to put an end to fighting in Darfur and upset the delicate peace accords of 2005 that had ended the long-running civil war in Sudan between the north and south.[41]

A partial explanation: material interest

Why did some countries ratify the Rome Statute while others did not? Material interest-based arguments provide a partial explanation based on the costs and risks of supporting the Court compared to its benefits. Where state interest arguments would emphasize the different costs of treaty accession, individual interest arguments would stress the balance of domestic political forces organized for and against ratification. I review both before discussing their limitations.

In terms of state interest arguments, all states potentially possessed an interest in a permanent court, which would avoid the start-up costs of having to create ad hoc courts anew each time a crisis occurred. From a justice and deterrent perspective, a permanent court was thought to be more efficient and effective. However, this observation fails to explain why some countries ratified while others did not. Moreover, given doubts about the Court's effectiveness, it is unclear how strong such efficiency concerns were as a motivation for creating the Court.[42]

---

[39] Arieff, Margesson, and Browne 2008.
[40] Snyder and Vinjamuri 2003.   [41] Heavens 2009.
[42] Fehl provides a critical review of rationalist arguments for the International Criminal Court in Fehl 2004. Similar doubts are expressed by Deitelhoff 2008, 154; Kelley 2007, 576.

One potential contributor to different state interests in ratifying the Rome Statute was the unequal financial costs of underwriting the Court, which vary by a government's ability to pay. This factor placed a larger burden on richer countries. However, this detail was an unlikely impediment to ratification. The Court's budget is tiny by international standards, having grown from about €20 million (about $25 mn) in 2002–2003 to €90 million (about $115 mn) in 2008. The individual costs for any single donor were modest.[43]

Of deeper concern to states was the risk that their own soldiers would be investigated or brought to trial before the ICC for purported crimes. Some states feared unpopular military interventions might inspire politically motivated trials being brought against their soldiers for human rights abuses, though some (perhaps even all) of those risks were mitigated by the Court's safeguards. That said, critics feared the Court might ultimately contest the seriousness of domestic efforts to try cases. As I suggested in the introduction to this chapter, even in countries with a tradition of trying soldiers for crimes in war, parties may be put under pressure to pursue individuals in domestic courts for actions committed in wartime.

Perhaps the best measure of relative country risk was the number of soldiers countries had deployed overseas.[44] State leaders in countries with large deployments perceived their troops to be at greater risk of having their soldiers charged with grave human rights abuses than countries with smaller deployments.[45] Comparable data on overseas force deployments between 1998 and 2000 when states were

---

[43] Unlike the International Court of Justice, which is financed from the UN budget, parties to the ICC bear the costs of supporting it. Contributions to the Court for its 2002 and 2003 budget totaled €31,044,722, of which nearly 64 percent was paid by five members of the G-7 (Canada, France, Germany, Italy, and the UK). Canada paid €1,728,654 (5.6%), France €4,377,706 (14.1%), Germany €6,614,895 (21.3%), Italy €3,328,092 (10.7%), and the UK €3,747,689 (12.1%) (ICC 2004). When Japan joined the Court in 2007, it assumed the maximum share any single country could contribute to the organization's budget (22%) based on ability to pay. The Court's budget for 2008 was €90,382,100.

[44] Fehl calls the costs of giving up some state control over criminal justice of its nationals "sovereignty costs" (Fehl 2004, 364).

[45] See, for example, Senator Hillary Clinton's prepared remarks to the Senate Foreign Relations Committee for her confirmation as secretary of state in 2009 (question 118): "But, at the same time, we must also keep in mind that the US has more troops deployed overseas than any nation" (Hillary Clinton 2009).

Table 6.2 *Overseas force deployments of the G-7, 1998–2000*

	1998	1999	2000	Average	Average as % of country's total active duty forces 2000
Canada	1,221	2,641	2,400	2,087	4.06%
France	40,939	28,397	35,460	34,932	12.04%
Germany	3,505	7,966	8,505	6,659	2.65%
Italy	2,814	6,382	8,352	5,849	3.33%
Japan	45	45	45	45	0.02%
UK	41,179	42,156	36,273	39,869	17.07%
United States	259,871	252,763	257,817	256,817	18.88%

Note and source: International Institute for Strategic Studies 1998, 1999, 2000. US figures include both onshore and floating overseas deployments. Floating deployments averaged about 50,000 soldiers during this period (Kane 2004).

contemplating ratifying the Rome treaty are available in *The Military Balance*, a regular report issued by the International Institute for Strategic Studies (see Table 6.2).

The differences in relative force deployments are revealing. The United States was in a class by itself with deployments, more than six times its nearest competitors. Leaving aside the United States as an extreme value, the average deployment of the remaining six was 14,907. By this measure, France and the UK, like the United States, have high force deployments compared to the other G-7 members. Japan, with only a handful of troops deployed, had by far the lowest risk followed by Canada, Italy, and Germany. Alternatively, we could look at each country's overseas deployments as a proportion of its total forces. Even as a proportion of total forces, the United States, France, and the UK had outsized deployments compared to the other G-7 countries.

From a state interest perspective, enthusiasm for the Court from countries such as Canada – given their low number of troop deployments – is understandable. Some might object to the characterization of deployments from such countries as not costly. The deployment of a small number of troops from countries that formerly shunned much overseas deployment (such as Germany and Japan in the second half of the twentieth century) or from countries such as Canada that have small militaries can be quite politically sensitive.[46] Others have expressed the opposite view. As Michael Struett and Steve Weldon argued, compared to developing countries with a history of military conflict, the ICC was not especially risky for *any* of the G-7 since democratic countries with military codes of justice have effective domestic mechanisms for trying soldiers for criminal behavior.[47] However, for great powers, their peer group of comparison was other great powers and advanced industrialized countries. As already noted, great powers with larger force deployments tended to perceive greater risks from the ICC compared to those with fewer deployments. France, the UK, and the United States had the largest military deployments and have a history of sending troops to the toughest military assignments, which are more likely settings for human rights abuses. For example, in the NATO operation in Afghanistan, the Americans frequently complained that German troops had severely restricted rules of engagement, which made them less likely to get into situations where soldiers could be accused of human rights abuses.[48]

The issue of troop deployments is, in a sense, an indicator for deeper-seated concerns about the effect of the ICC on state sovereignty. For some critics, such as John Bolton, who served in the US State Department under George W. Bush and later became the country's representative to the UN, the opposition was driven by a deeply rooted, ideological aversion to international institutions as a threat to the supremacy of the US Constitution.[49] For less ideologically driven critics in the United States, the threat of prosecution would constrain

---

[46] As Lana Wylie notes, countries that supported the ICC also faced other costs besides deployment. The United States threatened to cut off military aid and economic assistance to a number of countries. While NATO allies and countries such as Japan were exempt from such restrictions, the 2002 dust-up between the United States and its NATO allies over peacekeeping suggests ICC supporters faced other costs from US coercive pressure. Wylie also argues that Canada had more than 2,000 troops deployed to Afghanistan in 2006, where there was some real risk that their soldiers might be involved in war crimes because of association with detainee policies. While true, the comparative risks for Canada were lower than for countries with greater deployments (Wylie 2006). As for the diplomatic pressure from the United States, all G-7 countries faced this pressure. Among G-7 countries, one could argue that such pressure was only unequally meaningful for Japan, a country in a dangerous neighborhood reliant on its alliance with the United States for its security.

[47] Struett and Weldon 2006.   [48] Koelbl and Szandar 2008.   [49] Bolton 1998.

great powers' freedom of maneuver to use force.[50] Given their out-sized military expenditures and commitments, the United States and other countries with a greater military footprint had more to fear in terms of the Court's effect on their ability to project military power.

Even if we accept a greater cost sensitivity for G-7 countries with larger troop deployments, Japanese, French, and British behavior on the ICC is puzzling. If troop deployments were the only cost to consider, Japan's initial opposition to the Court is curious, given the country's extremely modest troop commitments. State interest proponents could explain Japan's behavior from a broader geostrategic perspective. In this view, Japan's dependence on the United States for security meant that a break with the United States over the ICC could have had rather severe implications for the country's security alliance. However, if this view was true in the early 2000s, it was also valid in 2007 when Japan changed course and ratified. Several observers have explained that Japanese leaders were initially wary of the Court because of fears on the Japanese right that the ICC would be used to retroactively punish Japan for crimes committed during World War II.[51] Given that the Court explicitly precluded retroactive punishment of crimes, Japan's reported fear suggests that the costs of treaty ratification for countries have a subjective quality beyond any objective measure such as troop deployments, a theme to which I will return when I examine the British case.

A state interest perspective would also have difficulty explaining French and British ratification of the Rome Statute, given their sizable overseas troop deployments.[52] Proponents might downplay the significance of those forces and suggest that the United States is a special case, given how many more US soldiers are stationed around the world. Moreover, in this view, the seven-year opt-out for war crimes

---

[50] Wedgwood 1998; Wippman 2004.

[51] Goold 2002; Higashizawa 2007. Noguchi notes that Asia is underrepresented in the ICC, in part as a product of a strong attachment to sovereignty on crime and punishment; until Japan's accession, only twelve countries in the region had ratified the Rome Statute. A number of countries, each with more than 100 million population, had not ratified including Bangladesh, China, India, Indonesia, and Pakistan (Noguchi 2006).

[52] Sandholtz and Kelley find no statistically significant relationship between military expenditures and ratifying the Rome Statute, while Struett and Weldon do find a positive relationship (Sandholtz 2005; Kelley 2007; Struett and Weldon 2006).

insulated France from absorbing many actual costs in support of the Court. In the same vein, the decision in 2002 and 2003 by US allies to exempt non-parties involved in UN peacekeeping missions from being subject to the ICC suggests only a modest willingness by the G-7 to absorb costs. However, such an argument still has trouble explaining differences in French and British reactions to the Court. If French and British troop deployments were not meaningful compared to the United States, then what explains why some French elites shared US fears of politically inspired cases? Why did the French feel compelled to pursue a war crimes opt-out while the British did not? Taking into account the potential diplomatic costs of refusing to follow the United States would make British behavior even more puzzling, given its closeness to the United States on foreign policy as part of its much-vaunted "special relationship." Furthermore, even if France reduced its potential vulnerability to the ICC through the opt-out on war crimes, this fact fails to explain why the United States did not avail itself of this option as well.

A pluralist argument based on the individual interest of politicians in securing re-election provides little additional traction on the ratification of the Rome Statute by some countries and not others. From this perspective, the strength of the human rights community in parties to the Rome Statute compared to non-parties resulted in ratification by some countries and not others. However, an assessment based on the strength of the human rights community alone is unsatisfying, given that the world's largest and best-financed human rights organizations, such as Amnesty International and Human Rights Watch, are centered in the United States.[53] A pluralist might refine the argument by looking at the relative political power of human rights organizations compared to opponents. In the US context, the primary opponents were members of the military. However, the military, as part of government, is not just another interest group. As I argue below, treaty ratification requirements and gatekeeper politics better explain why the United States, arguably possessing the strongest human rights advocacy community, failed to ratify the Rome Statute.

---

[53] Human Rights Watch had a $35 million budget in fiscal year 2006–2007 (Human Rights Watch 2007). Amnesty International USA had a $47 million budget during the same time period (Amnesty International USA 2007). FIDH, the French human rights organization, had a 2006 budget of €3.91 million ($4.92 million), small by comparison (FIDH 2007).

A more damning critique of a pluralist argument is the lack of public salience of the International Criminal Court even in countries that strongly supported it. In June 2003, nearly a year after the Rome Statute had entered into force, only one in ten Canadians could name the International Criminal Court as the new international body for investigating genocide, crimes against humanity, and war crimes.[54] As former French foreign minister Hubert Védrine told me in 2007, if the French had not signed on, "It wouldn't have had any political impact. It would have had a psychological impact and impact on image," but there would have been no resignations. This issue was an "important" but not a "vital" one for France.[55] Jeanne Sulzer, an attorney with the French human rights organization, FIDH, supported this view. At the time of the Rome negotiations, Sulzer was one of the attorneys seconded by No Peace Without Justice to an African delegation, in her case Burundi. She suggested that French NGOs had low public visibility in the lead-up to Rome negotiations; their campaign did not hold street demonstrations, and it was extremely difficult to get media attention for their work. Moreover, relations between the French government and NGOs were "extremely hard," especially during the negotiations when it was "impossible to have a dialogue with the French delegation" which perceived NGO participation as "illegitimate."[56] In general, the Rome Statute on the International Criminal Court was not especially visible or politically salient, even in European countries, at the time when most countries ratified, in 1999 and 2000. Only later, once the Bush administration had repudiated President Clinton's signature and vigorously pursued non-surrender agreements, did the ICC begin to have broader public visibility (see Figure 6.1).

A more complete explanation: framing/gatekeepers with a focus on subjective cost assessments

While the risks to their soldiers of politically inspired tribunals provide some leverage on objections to the ICC from the United States, Russia, China, and other great powers, this metric fails to explain British support for the Court; it only partially accounts for French objections and does not explain France's eventual ratification of the Rome Statute. A framing/gatekeepers perspective can help us understand

---

[54] Dominion Institute 2003. [55] Védrine 2007. [56] Sulzer 2007.

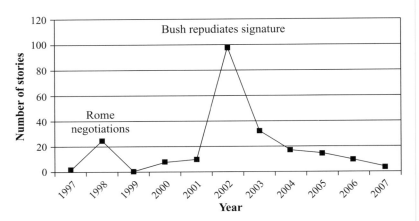

Figure 6.1 *Financial Times* articles on the International Criminal Court, 1997–2007
Source: Data are from a LexisNexis search in the headlines and lead paragraphs of the *Financial Times*.

ratification outcomes in these critical cases coupled with some observations about the subjective perception of costs and the degree to which leaders became rhetorically trapped in their support of the Court. I begin this section by evaluating some more sweeping claims about what advocates for the ICC achieved before providing a more narrow argument consistent with the analysis in previous chapters.

As Caroline Fehl notes, the ICC was largely a state-led project until the mid-1990s; the decision to create a court had been made before the NGO coalition mobilized.[57] However, once the NGO coalition supporting the Court got started, it had an important role in shaping the nature of the body that would ultimately come out of Rome. The Court was more independent from great powers than might have been expected based on the 1994 ILC draft, and its jurisdiction, even with safeguards, was closer to what NGOs and the like-minded group wanted when they advocated a fair, independent, impartial prosecutor with universal jurisdiction. The like-minded group and the NGO community often worked in tandem as collaborators in the creation of the Court. Nicole Deitelhoff credits the like-minded group and NGO community with mitigating developing country fears of great power

[57] Fehl 2004, 374.

dominance over the ICC by staging a number of regional conferences concerning the Court.[58] Struett similarly suggests this persuasive process led to an emerging normative consensus in support of a robust Court, one that would end impunity for gross human rights abuses, even by the leadership of individual countries.[59] Cherif Bassiouni, the Egyptian lawyer who chaired the statute's drafting committee, describes the emotional catharsis at the end of the Rome negotiations as delegates reacted to a failed US effort to add amendments to the final statute:

After the second vote, which was final, the delegates burst into a spontaneous standing ovation which turned into rhythmic applause that lasted close to 10 minutes, while some delegates embraced one another, others had tears in their eyes. It was one of the most extraordinary emotional scenes ever to take place at a diplomatic conference.[60]

This depiction may overstate how deeply both publics and elites around the world had bought into the idea of the Court. For example, polls in conflict regions of Congo and Uganda, two countries that ratified the statute and have had among the most intense dealings with the Court, showed low initial awareness of the ICC several years after it was created.[61] As I suggested in Chapter 2, moments of near universal normative convergence are exceedingly rare in political life. Interpretations that see the Rome Statute as exemplifying a deep normative convergence fail to accurately reflect the diversity of motivations among countries that ultimately ratified the Rome Statute. Yoweri Museveni, the Ugandan president, used the Court instrumentally in 2003 to refer the abuses by the rebel movement, the Lord's Resistance Army, to the ICC. Would-be members of the European Union may have felt the incentive to ratify based on more prosaic motives of wanting to enhance their chances of attaining EU membership. Deitelhoff hints of other state motivations in ratifying the Rome Statute: reactions to the US position. As one of her interviewees from the like-minded community noted:

[58] Deitelhoff 2008, 162.   [59] Struett 2008.   [60] Bassiouni 1998, 31–32.
[61] In a 2007 survey, only 28% of people polled in Kinshasa, Congo, knew about the Court, and only 27% in Eastern Congo were aware of it (ICTJ 2008). In 2007, a survey of northern Uganda found that 60% had heard of the International Criminal Court, up from 27% from a 2005 survey carried out before the ICC issued arrest warrants for the Lord's Resistance Army leadership (ICTJ 2007).

After we figured out [that the American delegation and its followers were explicitly interested only in a standing Ad Hoc Court that could never convict their own citizens] the 'Like-minded' have emphasized over and over again . . . that we stood for a court for all states and with equal rights and duties for all. That had a surmounting appeal, especially to developing countries because this was essentially the contrary position to the American view.[62]

As Oona Hathaway and Emily Hafner-Burton and Kiyoteru Tsutsui note, a number of countries, particularly in the developing world, have historically supported human rights treaties as a low-cost means of improving their international reputation, with little intent of following through on implementation.[63] As Judith Kelley argues, the refusal by some states to sign anti-surrender agreements with the United States (and thereby risk loss of military assistance, foreign aid, and anti-narcotics assistance) was a natural experiment that allows us to test the degree of a country's commitment to the ICC.[64] Less committed countries would likely yield to pressure and sign immunity agreements. As of August 2006, forty-three parties to the ICC had signed surrender agreements while fifty-seven had not, many of them NATO allies exempt from the punishment of the ASPA.[65] This observation suggests that for less committed countries motives other than normative consensus may have been at play in initial ratification decisions.

This point does not negate the importance of moral motivations, but we should be careful about ascribing and extending a normative consensus to parts of the world where those values have yet to be fully inculcated. I do not doubt that individual participants in the Rome negotiations may have been persuaded, but they represented a narrow subset of the elite, whose views may not have been fully indicative of their home populations. It is not entirely surprising that a meeting comprised primarily of international lawyers might find they have shared views on many aspects of criminal justice. At the same time, while the presence of numerous European advisors as part of developing country delegations provided them an opportunity to persuade those they were

---

[62] Deitelhoff 2008, 163.
[63] Hathaway 2002; Hafner-Burton and Tsutsui 2005.
[64] The willingness to sign non-surrender agreements thus was a costly signaling device that separated those with strong affinity for the Court from those who might have joined for purely expressive purposes.
[65] Kelley 2007, 574.

Table 6.3 *Freedom House and Polity ratings, 1998–2000*
PR (political rights). CL (civil liberties).

	Canada		France		Germany		Italy		Japan		UK		USA	
	PR	CL	PR	CL	PR	CL	PR	CL	PR	CL	PR	CL	PR	CL
*Freedom House**	1	1	1	2	1	2	1	2	1	2	1	2	1	1
*Polity***	10		9		10		10		10		10		10	

Notes and sources: * Data from www.freedomhouse.org/template.cfm?page=5.
** Democracy scores, measured on a ten-point scale, include some regularized procedures for citizens to express preferences, checks and balances, and guarantees of civil liberties. Autocracy reflects the restrictions on political participation and is measured on a negative ten-point scale. Adding the two yields a combined polity score. Data are available from www.systemicpeace.org/inscr/inscr.htm.

representing, delegations comprised partially of Western legal advisors were imperfect mirrors of the cultural dynamics of the countries they purported to represent.

Tracing the motivations of the developing world is beyond the scope of this chapter, as are larger questions about the degree to which the half-century turn toward human rights law is in fact a universal project or a Western phenomenon of advanced, industrialized democracies. What we do know is that the human rights agenda has largely been consolidated within the West, a world that has expanded as countries have become richer, more liberal democracies, and as the European Union has extended its reach. Looking at the G-7 countries, we observe Freedom House rankings for political rights (PR) and civil liberties (CL) on a ten-point scale, with 1 being most free. All seven achieved the highest category as "free" countries with scores of 1 for political rights and at least a 2 for civil liberties. Similarly, all seven countries scored high on the Polity IV ratings for their combined polity score, reflecting the degree of democracy and autocracy on a ten-point scale (with 10 being fully institutionalized democracies) (see Table 6.3).

We also know that G-7 countries were the most likely to ratify the Rome Statute. Parties to the statute were generally richer and more democratic, had better domestic human rights records, and belonged to the like-minded group more frequently than non-state parties.[66] Given that the United States meets three of these criteria, what then explains its non-participation in the Court? Wayne Sandholtz claims

[66] Kelley 2007. Struett and Weldon also find democracies were much more likely to ratify the ICC (Struett and Weldon 2006).

that a cultural fault line between the United States and Europe explains the divergence:

Whereas Americans are inclined to preserve sovereign prerogatives as against international norms, Europeans are more likely to place human rights – and international reinforcement of them – above sovereignty. The relative priority accorded to human rights in Europe has its roots in a legal and human rights culture that is more receptive than its American counterpart to international law and courts and more protective of human rights, in both domestic constitutions and international commitments.[67]

As support for his argument, Sandholtz found that countries that joined regional human rights organizations, and those that joined European human rights organizations in particular, were more likely to ratify the Rome Statute than states that did not join regional human rights organizations. Given the high score of the United States on Freedom House indices of rights, claiming a deeper appreciation for human rights in Europe is curious. Moreover, using treaty accession as an indicator of culture is problematic, as the extremely high bar for Senate advice and consent offers a cleaner explanation of US refusal to ratify the ICC. The same institutional barriers also explain why the United States failed to ratify other human rights treaties (the UN Convention on the Rights of the Child and the Convention to Eliminate Discrimination Against Women) and why the United States took nearly forty years to ratify the Genocide Convention.

While a strong, vocal minority vigorously opposes US treaty accession based on a concern for protecting US sovereignty, that view is hardly a widely shared cultural norm.[68] Rather, the institutional rules of US treaty accession empower gatekeepers with such idiosyncratic views to stymie ratification of human rights treaties. Despite a greater willingness to support the Court on the part of the State and Justice Departments as well as the White House, most within the Pentagon preferred not to deal with the Court, according to Ambassador David Scheffer, the lead negotiator for the US delegation in the Clinton administration. Moreover, Senator Jesse Helms was, according to Sheffer, "virulently opposed."[69] As chair of the Senate Foreign Relations Committee, Helms wielded great power over both spending priorities and treaties. Although he permitted US support for debt relief and AIDS, Helms earned his nickname as "Senator No" on the ICC,

---

[67] Sandholtz 2005, 30.   [68] Moravcsik 2005.   [69] Scheffer 2007.

Table 6.4 *Support for human rights, 2008*

	Canada	France	Germany	Italy	Japan	UK	United States
"Should human rights be a central feature of [your country's] foreign policy?" (2008)	73%*	85%	84%	80%	56%	63%	72%

Note and sources: * Canada was not included in this survey, but a 2007 survey asked Canadians whether "Canada should not seek free trade agreements with developing countries that have dubious human rights records." This question is framed in a parallel manner to the other survey with two main options (agree/disagree) and not sure (Angus Reid Global Monitor 2007).

declaring over the course of the Rome negotiations that any treaty that afforded any chance of trying an American before the Court would be "dead on arrival" in the US Senate.[70] As I argued in Chapter 4 on climate change, nowhere else in the advanced industrialized world are these institutional barriers so onerous.

If gatekeeper dynamics in the United States precluded ratification of the Rome Statute, then what explains French and British behavior on the ICC? Why were gatekeepers in the UK and France, where power was more concentrated, not similarly inclined to reject the Court on the basis of costs? Here, the way advocates framed the issue becomes an important part of the narrative. In the lead-up to the Rome negotiations, NGO advocates and governmental supporters of a robust court framed the ICC project in terms of holding individuals accountable for gross human rights abuses and preventing future abuses, what Deitelhoff called a "public interest" frame.[71]

Such an appeal had cultural resonance in every country in the G-7. In Table 6.4, we observe the appeal of supporting human rights at the level of principle across the G-7. When asked in a 2008 poll, a strong

---

[70] Pisik 1998.
[71] Deitelhoff documents a frame shift from early discussions in the 1996 preparatory meetings that focused on "political realities" and the need to protect state sovereignty and the later 1998 Rome negotiations that focused on the "public interest" and the need for a court with an independent prosecutor, wide jurisdiction, and a limited role for the Security Council (Deitelhoff 2008, 160).

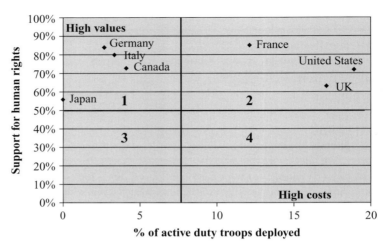

Figure 6.2 Mapping of troop deployments and support for human rights

majority of publics across the G-7 agreed that human rights should be a central feature of their country's foreign policy.[72] As Appendix 6A shows, publics in G-7 countries have consistently expressed their support for promoting human rights abroad. Even though these concerns might not always have been politically salient, advocates could tap into a reservoir of cultural support for the ICC based on a tradition of respect for human rights domestically and general support for extending human rights in principle internationally.

We can combine this information with the data on deployments to map the country cases as in previous chapters. Advocates' central message had cultural appeal, but the costs of supporting the ICC were unequally distributed, leading to the patterns observed in Figure 6.2. The average percentage of troops deployed overseas in 2000 among the G-7 was 8.29 percent.[73]

Based on this mapping, France, the UK, and the United States were all cases of costly moral action, the others, by contrast, cases of cheap

---

[72] Harris Interactive 2008.
[73] As I note in the discussion of the UK case, gatekeepers subjectively filter hypothetical costs of novel institutions. As a result, I use the average deployment as the threshold between high and low risks for illustrative purposes only to classify cases. It is more important to note the distribution of costs.

moral action. As I suggested, French, British, and potentially Japanese behavior is therefore puzzling for state interest explanations.

A framing/gatekeepers perspective provides some leverage on these cases. Support for human rights in G-7 countries was the source of political mobilization for the ICC; it was modest and mostly confined to human rights groups and lawyers when the issue was largely absent from the media. Connecting ongoing, high-profile human rights outrages such as the situation in Darfur provides a wider potential source of public support for the ICC. In the context of rights-affirming cultures, politicians of advanced liberal democracies are comfortable expressing broad support for human rights and are constrained from making explicit statements negating their importance. Officials might talk about balancing human rights with pragmatism or political realities, but they would be loath to reject human rights sentiments outright. In the context of ICC negotiations, advocates could use the broad cultural orientation to human rights, past support for the ad hoc tribunals, and explicit support for the ICC to box in leaders of democratic polities. Amnesty International's Christopher Hall explained the way groups such as his strategically sought to shame recalcitrant governments from stepping out of line:

Governments were trapped by their own rhetoric not only with regard to what they had said with regard to 1993 and 1994 on the ad hoc tribunals but also because no one wanted to go on record saying it was okay to commit genocide or war crimes. There was a framework of discussion that made it very difficult for them to be hypocritical.[74]

In the months preceding the Rome negotiations, leaders of democratic polities, including the United States, France, and the UK, were on record for stating their support for a court in principle.[75] The NGO community and like-minded groups linked the successful pursuit of justice with a court that had a strong independent prosecutor, universal jurisdiction, and a limited role for the UN Security Council. If a delegation came out against those attributes of such a court, it risked being portrayed by the advocacy community as being against justice and peace. For example, Amnesty International, in its final statement

[74] A 2002 interview quoted in Deitelhoff 2008, 161.
[75] Labour Party 1997; Rubin 1998; Védrine 1997.

reacting to the statute that came out of Rome, castigated countries that did not support the NGO/like-minded perspective:

Amnesty International is disappointed that a few powerful countries appeared willing to hold justice hostage by threatening and bullying other states and were all along more concerned to shield possible criminals from trials rather than producing a charter for victims.[76]

Efforts to portray governments that opposed the ICC as enemies of justice and human rights ultimately depended on leaders who cared or who were sensitive to the constituency that cared about those issues and who wished to avoid the reputational stain of being on the wrong side of an issue. Governments that had rhetorically supported a court were more vulnerable to these pressures than those that had not. The degree of rhetorical entrapment provides political opponents and advocates an opening to charge leaders with hypocrisy and failure to keep their word. In some contexts, domestic actors are too weak to take advantage of such disjunctures between word and deed. The famous boomerang and spiral models of the human rights literature hinge on outside allies and governments seizing on such moments to pressure governments, mostly in the developing world. However, for advanced industrialized countries, external pressure on powerful states may be less influential, although the European Union provides some extraordinary collective pressure on its members given the scope and reach of its activities.

Where domestic advocacy groups are weak, as in French human rights groups, they typically require more powerful allies within the government. Thus, the election of favorable gatekeepers may serve both to up the rhetorical ante in support of an advocate's cause and to bring into power actors capable of and responsive to pressure to conform to both internal and external demands. Since shaming constitutes an effort to damage a country's reputation, it can have material consequences, in terms of damage to a country's leverage and its leaders' political stature and influence at home and abroad. On another level, shaming challenges actors' self-conceptions as members in good standing within a community. Those that value good standing, which is somewhat independent of the utility that such standing offers, will be more responsive to shaming attempts. At the same time, shaming

[76] Amnesty International 1998.

Table 6.5 *Continuum of rhetorical entrapment*

Most	← ——————————→		Least
UK (under Tony Blair) *May 1997* ◄ — — –●	(under John Major) *November 1990*		
United States	(under Bill Clinton) *January 1993* ●— — –►	(under George W. Bush) *January 2001*	
France	(under cohabitation) *June 1997* ◄ — — –●	(under Jacques Chirac) *May 1995*	
Strong support for ICC	Modest support for ICC	Support for ad hoc tribunals	Strong opposition to ICC

efforts can operate on the individual psyche, where people feel ashamed for having acted in ways considered improper. Because these diverse effects of shaming are difficult to disentangle, like reputation itself, shaming operates on the margins between materialist and ideational influences on foreign policy outcomes.[77]

In the context of great power support and opposition to the Court, the degree to which governments rhetorically committed to it showed considerable variation, ranging from strong support under the UK's Tony Blair (whose government joined the like-minded group) to the United States under George W. Bush (whose government repudiated Clinton's signature of the Rome Statute). Several elections throughout this period brought into power governments that were either more favorable to the Court (Blair in the UK and the cohabitation government with Lionel Jospin as prime minister in France) or less so (George W. Bush in the United States). The more explicit a state's support for the Court, the more vulnerable it was to shaming efforts by advocacy groups and government supporters of the ICC (see Table 6.5).

French and British decisionmakers reacted differently to the Court, despite similar troop deployment levels. The British thought the risks

---

[77] The logic of rhetorical entrapment and shaming is explored by Greenhill and Busby 2009. Other accounts of shaming and entrapment are discussed by Hafner-Burton 2008; Risse, Ropp, and Sikkink 1999; Schimmelfennig 2001.

were manageable, but the French, at least initially, shared the Americans' fears of the Court. The differences may have been a product of the leading gatekeepers in each country. The UK's prime minister at the time, Tony Blair, was a lawyer by training and the husband of an accomplished barrister of human rights law. France's president Jacques Chirac trained at France's top school for civil servants, the École Nationale d'Administration (ENA), but also, importantly, served in the French army in Algeria. Lionel Jospin, who became the French prime minister in 1997, was also a graduate of ENA but cut his political teeth protesting against the Algerian war. Variations among different decisionmakers' reactions to the Court indicate costs have a subjective quality; objective data on deployments are mediated by the preferences and experiences of the key gatekeepers.

A rich literature in the social sciences suggests that busy decisionmakers have limited time, attention, and information to make a fully rational calculation of the costs and benefits of different courses of action, particularly for complex problems such as those explored in this book.[78] The exigencies of decisionmaking and cognitive constraints may mean that policymakers conduct "good enough" searches for alternatives and then employ simplifying metrics and heuristics to reach decisions, rather than conduct exhaustive calculations of utility.[79] In such circumstances of uncertainty and limited attention and ability of the human mind to process information, policymakers may rely on social cues from the way the issues have been framed, historical analogies, or, importantly, their own personal experiences (or those of their generation) to decide on different courses of action.[80]

In the next section, I expand on how the dynamics of framing, shaming, and gatekeepers played out in the UK and France, the two cases where states facing costly action nevertheless ratified the Rome Statute, with a short discussion on the United States by way of introduction.

Ratification of the Rome Statute in the UK and France

In the United States President Clinton's rhetorical vulnerability was not enough on its own to overcome the institutional constraints posed

---

[78] Jones 2001; Kahneman 2003; Simon 1956, 1959, 1979, 1982.
[79] Jones 1994; 2001, 25, 70, 102.
[80] Khong 1992, 2005; Lebow 1985; Mannheim 1952; Murray 1996; Roskin 1974; Schuman and Reiger 1992.

by domestic gatekeepers during his administration. In a system with many gatekeepers and the onerous treaty ratification requirements of obtaining the advice and consent of two-thirds of the US Senate, military opponents of the ICC were able to exercise their objections both through the Department of Defense and through their contacts in the legislative branch. The number of policy gatekeepers affected not only ratification but also the negotiation process. While the French negotiator was able to secure agreement between Chirac and Jospin on the seven-year opt-out in a constrained time period, the demands of intra-Cabinet coordination in the United States, where gatekeepers were divided, prevented the US delegation from being able to support the compromise opt-out provision. The Clinton administration was put in an awkward position because of its rhetoric in support of the Court. These reputational pressures, coupled with practical reasons to stay part of the negotiations to protect US interests, were perhaps sufficient to push the president to decide to sign the treaty. However, they were not enough to generate the votes needed in the Senate for ratification. With President Clinton's departure, the incoming Bush administration was even less rhetorically constrained, since a number of its leaders, Secretary of Defense Donald Rumsfeld and Undersecretary of State John Bolton, were on record as being opposed to the Court. The UK and France, by contrast, were ultimately able to support the ICC. Both the preferences and the configuration of gatekeepers were critically important, although rhetorical entrapment played a part in the French story.

In the UK, the rhetorical vulnerability of the government proved insignificant since gatekeepers and institutional dynamics favored support for the Court (though the government potentially would have had a problem had it taken a different position). The Labour Party came into power in 1997 already determined to take a supportive stance on the Court. Further, ratification of the Rome Statute was facilitated by the concentration of treaty ratification power within the UK's parliamentary system (discussed in Chapter 4). This concentration of power also permitted the government to discount the military's potential objections.

In the case of France, the degree of rhetorical entrapment under the Chirac-led government was initially modest but increased with the June 1997 election of a cohabitation government with the Socialists. Where Chirac was strongly opposed to the Court, the election brought into the government a party that was more committed to it, which led to competing gatekeepers in the government with Chirac. At the same time, the new cohabitation government became more rhetorically entrapped, having issued statements in support of the Court. This backing gave supporters of the Court, particularly from governments in the European Union and to a lesser extent advocacy groups, a means of reminding the government of its commitments and shaming it for possible bad behavior. At the same time, this position gave supporters within the French government leverage over opponents by suggesting there would be broader reputational repercussions for France if it did not join the EU consensus on the Court.

In the remainder of this chapter, I trace the dynamics of British and French policy on the ICC. For both, I highlight the role of gatekeepers and the importance each government attached to its role on the world stage. For France, I focus on the intersection between the government's supportive rhetoric of the Court and its hardline stance in the negotiations, the disconnect giving supporters of the ICC some leverage to pressure France.

The United Kingdom's accession to the International Criminal Court

In 1962, not long after the disastrous effort by the British and French governments to seize the Suez Canal in 1956, former US Secretary of State Dean Acheson remarked that "Great Britain has lost an empire and has not yet found a role."[81] If so, decisionmakers in Britain still prized having outsized influence on global affairs. Since Suez, almost all British leaders, both Conservative and Labour, have tried to punch above their weight in international affairs by cultivating an Anglo-American partnership. Sometimes, these twin goals of wanting a leadership role and a strong alliance with the United States conflict. Desires for leadership appear in the manifestos of both political parties. In 1992, the Tories proclaimed: "Under the Conservatives, Britain has regained her rightful influence in the world. We have stood up for the values our country has always represented." In 1997 and 2001, Labour for its part asserted: "We will give Britain leadership in Europe" and "turn our inner confidence to strength abroad, in Europe and beyond, to tackle global problems."[82] In the Labour era, these

---

[81] Guardian 1962.   [82] Keele University Undated.

aspirations found particular expression in the moral dimension of Blair's foreign policy, what Walter Russell Mead called the "ghost of Gladstone," the nineteenth-century reformist prime minister.[83] The British position on the ICC took on particular significance, given the tension between its aspirations for moral leadership on the world stage and its relationship with the United States. What explains the British decision to ratify the International Criminal Court despite the opposition of their closest ally?

In the lead-up to negotiations in 1998, the British elections of May 1997 brought the Labour Party to power for the first time since 1979. The Tories had been cautiously supportive of the ICC.[84] The Labour government made support for the ICC part of its manifesto:

Labour wants Britain to be respected in the world for the integrity with which it conducts its foreign relations. We will make the protection and promotion of human rights a central part of our foreign policy. We will work for the creation of a permanent international criminal court to investigate genocide, war crimes and crimes against humanity.[85]

One could interpret this policy as purely belief-driven. Upon taking office in 1997, Robin Cook, the Labour government's first foreign secretary (who died suddenly in 2005), announced an intention to implement an "ethical foreign policy." While mainly seen as an effort to rein in unscrupulous arms trading, the International Criminal Court was a core part of that vision.[86] Cook announced this new dimension to British foreign policy with much fanfare in a May 1997 speech at the Foreign and Commonwealth Office called "Human Rights into a New Century":

Britain also has a national interest in the promotion of our values and confidence in our identity . . . The Labour Government does not accept that political values can be left behind when we check in our passports to travel on diplomatic business. Our foreign policy must have an ethical dimension and must support the demands of other peoples for the democratic rights

---

[83] Mead 2001.
[84] For the rhetorical shift from cautious support under the Conservatives to more full-throated embrace of the ICC by Labour, see UK statements to the UN in 1995 before and after the election in 1997 (United Kingdom, Mission to the United Nations 1995; 1997).
[85] Labour Party 1997.   [86] BBC 2000.

on which we insist for ourselves. The Labour Government will put human rights at the heart of our foreign policy.[87]

Although Cook quickly found that some of the objectives of pursuing an "ethical" foreign policy were problematic, given the complexity of the world (indeed, he would later resign from Blair's Cabinet over the Iraq war), it would be disingenuous to dismiss Cook's mission as the personal quirks of an unreconstructed lefty on the margins of the party. The moral sentiments Cook espoused were also echoed by the most senior leaders of the British government, including Prime Minister Blair and Chancellor Gordon Brown. For example, Brown's commitment to anti-poverty measures in the developing world is attributed in part to the religious tradition of his family, his father being a minister in the Church of Scotland.[88] The ethical and religious dimensions of Blair's own worldview feature prominently in discussions of his support for the use of force in Kosovo and Iraq. Indeed, the ICC had particular salience to one member of Blair's family – his wife. Cherie Booth, a prominent human rights lawyer, was a champion of the International Criminal Court in print as a legal scholar as well as in a number of public speeches, arguing that "the international criminal court with independent prosecutors putting tyrants and torturers in the dock before independent judges reflects the postwar human rights aspiration come true. It is a shining example of how human rights might be realized under international law."[89] Thus, the Labour Party's support for the ICC can be seen as an extension of the way the government saw the country's role on the world stage.

While the Labour Party's choice may have been purely values-driven, it may also have had a strategic, symbolic component to it. At the time of Blair's ascension, the Labour Party was undergoing a historic shift in its identity from being a socialist party of old to becoming a modern center-left party. As a consequence, it was jettisoning a number of its "old-time left" commitments to unions and hostility to markets. This move made much of the traditional left uncomfortable. Although

---

[87] Cook 1997.

[88] This view is supported by Wheeler and Dunne who write that, while there is no doubt that there were important differences between Cook and Blair, they both were committed to a highly interventionist foreign policy being pursued in accordance with multilateral rules and institutions. They also maintained an unstinting belief that Britain could make a difference (Wheeler and Dunne 2004, 14).

[89] Booth 2004; Kessler 2003.

foreigners are often the main target audience in international meetings, domestic audiences are the primary focus of political manifestos. The meaning of a phrase may have particular significance in the domestic context. For Labour, strong stances on human rights and international poverty could have enabled the party leadership to signal its support for issues with which the left could identify. It was a way for the party leadership to say, "We are with you." Certainly, this is a weak signal to most voters concerned about domestic issues, but such statements also could serve to rally organized sectors of the policy community whose support or opposition could be important in mobilizing voters at election time. At the same time, an "ethical foreign policy" also served to differentiate the Labour Party from the Conservative Party, which, while in power, had blessed a number of controversial arms sales including some to Saddam Hussein and Iraq.

The British joined the like-minded group in December 1997, shortly after the Labour Party took office, and played an important role in the Rome negotiations. The Labour Party shepherded a bill through parliament in 2001 to make good on their pledge to be among the leaders in ratification of the treaty. While treaty ratification did not require a parliamentary vote, the government opted to pass domestic implementing legislation prior to ratification.[90] The House of Lords voted down a Tory amendment in March 2001 to take advantage of the war crimes opt-out clause in the Rome treaty.[91] In October 2001, the British ambassador to the UN, Jeremy Greenstock, deposited the UK ratification with the UN.

---

[90] The customary practice, dating back to 1924, is for the government to deposit a treaty with the UK Parliament for twenty-one days after it has been signed, after which time it is considered ratified. This is known as the Ponsonby Rule, after Arthur Ponsonby, Under-Secretary of State for Foreign Affairs in Ramsay MacDonald's first Labour government. Although the government may allow discussion in the House of Commons for important treaties, there is no formal requirement for consultation, and parliamentary assent is not required (United Kingdom, Foreign and Commonwealth Office 2001).

[91] When the bill was introduced in 2000 to incorporate some of the provisions of the Court into domestic law, Robin Cook stated: "The International Criminal Court Bill will enable us to achieve our target of becoming a founding member of the Court and send a clear message to the world's tyrants that Britain wants them to face international justice. We took the lead in the negotiations to agree the Treaty on the International Criminal Court. We are now taking the lead in ratifying it" (United Kingdom, Foreign and Commonwealth Office 2000). The Tory amendment on the opt-out was defeated in the House of Lords by a vote of 122 votes to 69 (Kallenbach 2001b).

The ICC became a contentious issue between Europe and the United States, and this dissension complicated the British government's higher order strategy of engagement with the Americans, described by one observer as "hug them close."[92] The British government addressed this quandary in different ways. On non-security issues such as climate change and African poverty, Blair was willing to distance the British position from that of the United States. This approach was bounded by an appreciation of the need to engage the Americans. The ICC was a different matter. As a security issue, this subject cut closer to the heart of the British–American special relationship. Because the ICC was negotiated during the Clinton administration, which was fitfully supportive of the ICC, Blair could hope the United States would ultimately embrace the Court and ratify the Rome Statute. As a consequence, Britain could support the Court and remain true to its role as interlocutor to the Americans, attempting to coax them into supporting the ICC. However, with the Bush administration aggressively attacking the ICC, the British adopted a lower profile.

Despite their continued affirmations of support for the Court, the British refrained from publicly criticizing the United States on the issue.[93] In July 2002, when the United States threatened to veto the extension of the peacekeeping mandate in Bosnia, the UK brokered a compromise at the Security Council. That same year, the British proposed a compromise to allow EU members to enter into limited immunity agreements with the Americans for military or "official" personnel sent overseas.[94] The British ultimately reached a new extradition agreement with the Americans in March 2003, promising in a side letter not to extradite any Americans to the ICC without US permission.[95] Britain's subdued support for the ICC allowed them in

---

[92] Riddell 2003, 14.
[93] When asked about potential American efforts to veto the extension of the Bosnian peacekeeping mission over the ICC, Blair's spokesman said, "the Prime Minister had no intention of acting as a commentator on the way other countries ran their affairs" (United Kingdom, Prime Minister's Official Spokesman 2002). One exception to this was a speech Cherie Booth gave at Georgetown University on the eve of George W. Bush's November 2003 visit to the UK in which she criticized the US position, saying, "With time we can but hope the US will come to share that perspective with regard to its own people, and recognize that the concerns it has expressed – legitimate as they may now seem – are not well founded" (Kessler 2003).
[94] Dempsey 2002a.   [95] Coalition for the ICC 2005.

2005 to help broker an agreement to allow the UN Security Council to refer the case of Darfur to the Court. The British worked with the original French proposal and were able to secure the Americans' willingness not to oppose the motion.[96] Given the British government's reluctance to cross the United States, it is debatable how willing the UK government was to assume costs in backing the Court. Moreover, as Chaim Kaufmann and Robert Pape argue, for a country to engage in costly moral action, decisionmakers have to acknowledge that there are costs involved.[97] The British themselves generally downplayed the risks that the ICC posed to British soldiers, as demonstrated by the quote from the British legal advisor in the opening section of this chapter (p. 211). When press reports circulated in 2001 suggesting that British field commanders as well as Admiral Sir Michael Boyce, Chief of the Defence Staff, were worried that the Court might expose British troops to the vagaries of some foreign tribunal, the government was quick to respond with two arguments.[98] First, they noted the complementarity principle meant that any legitimate grievances against British soldiers for human rights abuses would be investigated by domestic courts.[99] Second, the government argued that British soldiers would be tried under longstanding military disciplinary procedures that have historically been applied for suspected human rights violations. Neither the procedure nor the crimes for human rights violations were anything particularly new.[100] The ability of the British government to bypass these concerns from the military is a product of a parliamentary system with few veto powers.

Interestingly, even if the British government did not publicly acknowledge some real risks of becoming a party to the ICC, its experience in support of the Iraq war generated interest on the part of war opponents in using the Court against the UK. The Court's reluctance to take on the United States and other great powers undercuts the notion that the British faced real risks at the ICC. That said, pressure for domestic action to head off independent prosecutorial action on the part of the ICC may still have led the British government to conduct especially thorough or punitive cases against soldiers accused of war crimes. Given the contested legitimacy if not legality of the war

---

[96] Hoge 2005. [97] Kaufmann and Pape 1999, 633.
[98] Kallenbach 2001a. [99] Parker 2001.
[100] United Kingdom, Prime Minister's Official Spokesman 2005.

in Iraq, the British government may yet find it has the potential for problems associated with the ICC.

Military commanders in the field may still believe the government has not offered them sufficient protection from punitive trials and may think hard about ordering and conducting difficult missions on which civilian casualties are likely. Of course, this moderating influence of the laws of war is not necessarily new but may have taken on a new significance. The real problem may be a political one, where the military is reluctant to have its own personnel charged for crimes that are a product of political decisions to use force under legally ambiguous circumstances.[101]

In any case, it is clear that the British government justified its support for the ICC in terms of British values and of how the new Labour government saw itself on the world stage. At the same time, when faced with potential conflict with another key element of the UK government's longstanding foreign policy orientation to maintain close ties with the United States, the British sought a series of compromises to keep both the Court and their relationship alive. This assessment supports the framing/gatekeepers argument, although it also demonstrates that a state's willingness to absorb costs for moral purposes has limits. This issue is particularly salient as we move closer to the security arena where the consequences of morality-based policies potentially involve the survival of the state; even if a state's survival is not at stake, questions about troop deployments typically have a higher order of political significance than the other issues in this book.

France's accession to the International Criminal Court

Where the UK government believed the costs of supporting the ICC were manageable, dynamics in France were much more like those in the United States, where the military was very skeptical and worried about politically inspired tribunals pursuing French soldiers for transgressions on the battlefield. Advocates of the Court used France's traditions as a defender of human rights, the government's backing of the ad hoc tribunals, and ultimately rhetorical support for the ICC itself as a way to persuade and shame the French government into ratifying the Rome Statute on their terms. These efforts bore little fruit until the

---

[101] Observer 2005.

1997 election brought into power the Socialists, who were much more partial to the Court.

From 1996 through mid-1997, France and the United States had similar reactions to the Court. Members of the French military establishment were as worried about being called before the Court as were the Americans. Hervé de Charette, foreign minister from 1995 to 1997, described the Ministry of Defence as completely opposed to the Court and French president Jacques Chirac as "hostile."[102] Though the French had helped lead the effort to create the International Criminal Tribunal for the former Yugoslavia (ICTY), it had left a bitter aftertaste. French enthusiasm for global justice cooled after its troops were implicated in having possibly trained the Hutu militias involved in the Rwandan genocide. The French military, having also observed Dutch peacekeepers crossexamined about their role in the Srebrenica massacre, were determined not to have to testify at the ICTY.

In preparatory meetings for the ICC in August 1996, France proposed a very narrow basis of jurisdiction for the Court, requiring the "triple consent" of the state of nationality of the accused, that of the nationality of the victim, and that of the location of the alleged crime all agree before the Court would have jurisdiction.[103] ICC opponents clearly had the upper hand in this phase of the negotiations. President Chirac was deeply concerned about the proposed court. As Marc Perrin de Brichambaut, the lead French negotiator during the Rome negotiations, noted, President Chirac's views about the Court were shaped by his own military experience in Algeria. He understood that soldiers could be sent on difficult, even unsavory missions. Like the Americans, Chirac "didn't want soldiers to be hampered by legal constraints."[104]

Nonetheless, France had been one of the strongest defenders in the creation of the ad hoc tribunal for the former Yugoslavia. Chirac himself had made some statements about human rights around which supporters of the Court could mobilize. For example, in 1995, apologizing for French collaboration with the Nazis on deportations during World War II, Chirac said, "France, the nation of light and human rights, land of welcome and asylum, accomplished the irreparable . . . Betraying its word, it delivered its dependents to their executioners."[105] While this language did not create a high degree of rhetorical

---

[102] De Charette 2007. [103] Eftekhari 2001.
[104] De Brichambaut 2007. [105] Quoted in Ganley 1995.

entrapment for Chirac, these statements and the country's historic attachment to human rights put it close to the threshold between high and low entrapment.

In June 1997, the French national elections brought the Socialists into power, with Lionel Jospin as the new prime minister. This election led to a period of cohabitation, with Chirac still controlling the presidency. The Socialists were more favorably inclined toward the Court. In September 1997, Hubert Védrine, the new Socialist foreign minister, gave Court supporters plenty of reason to think the new government would be on their side, or that they could at least shame it into being so:

> To ensure the lasting settlement of conflicts, consciences have to be assuaged and justice needs to be done to put an end to the endless cycle of revenge. The perpetrators of the most serious crimes must be tried impartially . . . This is why France supports the action of the international criminal tribunals for the former Yugoslavia and Rwanda, and hopes that the forthcoming conference on an international criminal court will be a success.[106]

Védrine also had some reservations. He worried about potential trade-offs between peace and justice and that prosecuting malefactors might be counterproductive to conflict resolution. He also worried that proponents were overselling the deterrent value of the Court.[107] As he later explained, the Socialists were favorable to the Court but uncomfortable with huge expectations that existed about it, and they wanted to disabuse people of "illusions" that it would solve all conflicts.[108]

Here, the incorporation of the Socialists served to balance Chirac. Instead of having a strong military establishment demanding that France reject the Court backed by the president, France now had another gatekeeper willing to support the Court. The president of France typically has wide discretion over foreign policy and serves as the sole gatekeeper but, with cohabitation, he also had to respect Jospin's position or risk a political crisis. A crisis could be politically damaging; cohabitation had been associated with such crises and was deeply unpopular with the French public. As former foreign minister de Charette told me, Chirac changed his mind on the Court. Chirac could not do anything else, de Charette suggested, as it would not have been popular with the public to have a political conflict with the new

---

[106] Védrine 1997. [107] Védrine and Moïsi 2001. [108] Védrine 2007.

government. That said, he argued that the ICC on its own was not a big issue. Had the Socialists not made the ICC an issue, there would not have been important political consequences, as the ICC was neither a low nor a high priority for France.[109] As Ambassador de Brichambaut noted, "the NGOs were making a fuss" and "the press were against us," but even though there was a vocal constituency, the ICC did not rise to a high level politically.[110]

Going into the negotiations, Ambassador de Brichambaut suggested that the delegation's "biggest problem was infighting in Paris." While the Justice Ministry was very supportive of the Court and the Foreign Ministry was looking for an accommodation that would take French interests into account, "our Department of Defense didn't want to hear about the Court." Having been "burned" with the ICTY, the Ministry of Defence got the upper hand in initially attaining an "extremely restrictive" posture on the part of the French government vis-à-vis the ICC. Getting the opt-out for war crimes made it possible for France to support the Court. As de Brichambaut noted, that victory was hard won: "It was close, I could have missed."[111]

Given Védrine's personal skepticism, the precise source of French favorability to the Court is unclear. French human rights organizations, such as FIDH, were supportive, of course, but, despite being vocal, the French human rights community on its own did not have significant leverage. Nonetheless, international and French human rights groups, including Amnesty International-France and FIDH, appealed to the country's human rights tradition to soften its approach to the ICC. *Le Monde* and other newspapers were also quite supportive, which created an additional source of pressure. The public was perceived to be in favor, although not especially active or informed. Perhaps more important were the mobilization and support among France's European partners.

Prominent Europeans, including Louise Arbour, chief prosecutor for the two ad hoc tribunals, and Emma Bonino, the EU human rights commissioner, appealed directly to French decisionmakers and the public to change the country's stance on the ICC. In December 1997, mobilization seemed to have swung back in the direction of the military; the French defense minister, Alain Richard, described the ad hoc tribunal

---

[109] De Charette 2007.   [110] De Brichambaut 2007.
[111] De Brichambaut 2007.

for Yugoslavia as a "show trial" and suggested that French soldiers would not testify. Within days, Arbour went directly to the French press to criticize Richard; she suggested that Bosnian war criminals felt protected in the French-controlled sector of the country.[112]

In March 1998, in the face of this criticism, Védrine announced that French soldiers would be allowed to testify at the ICTY after all. By the opening of the Rome negotiations in June, the French had abandoned their demand for triple consent for ICC jurisdiction. Just as the Rome negotiations were getting started, Prime Minister Jospin further raised the rhetorical stakes in a June 1998 interview in New York:

On this issue, in agreement with President Chirac, we have shifted France's stance from the one I found when I took office. I believe people would have had difficulty understanding why France, fifty years after the adoption of the Universal Declaration of Human Rights... wasn't taking a leading position.[113]

France's isolation within Europe was quite important and arguably more influential than domestic lobbying from human rights groups.

As Ambassador de Brichambaut acknowledged, "NGOs were a major lobbying force to be reckoned with" at the Rome meetings. He added, "We were completely isolated in the European Union. The British were putting a lot of pressure." While Jospin and Védrine were not keen on the negotiations, they "understood they couldn't look bad." At the same time, the constraints from France's European Union partners made the French delegation's efforts difficult. As de Brichambaut noted, "The consultations among EU members were not an effective framework for compromise. The French position had no support among EU member states."[114] A Foreign Ministry official explained the consequences of bucking the views of France's European partners. Because France was working together with other EU countries on so many issues, he argued, if one country went against the European consensus, it could lose standing, influence, and credit on other important issues such as the Balkans and human rights.[115] Shiva Eftekhari makes a strong case for European disapproval as decisive, highlighting criticism of the French position in the press from Bonino,

[112] Trueheart 1997.   [113] Jospin 1998.
[114] De Brichambaut 2007.   [115] French Foreign Ministry official 2007.

from German foreign minister Klaus Kinkel, and from Gijs de Vries, president of the liberal group in the European parliament. In her view, the idea of the world's moral condemnation was unacceptable for "the fatherland of human rights."[116]

French negotiators upped the stakes for the country over the course of negotiations by playing a vigorous role in shaping the nature of the Court. As David Scheffer told me, French negotiators saw the ICC as an "opportunity to exert leadership on the world stage." In his view, the French saw themselves as "taking a unique lead on something which was very popular [in France] and elsewhere." He noted that the French delegation lobbied to give the Court a "French character" in a number of areas, on victims' rights for example. They also sought to shape the Court so that it would operate on lines similar to French civil law, with an inquisitorial model of courtroom justice, as opposed to the common law and adversarial traditions of the United States and the UK. Even after 1998, the French were the driving force on formulating the rules of procedure and evidence.[117]

Thus, having taken the lead on a number of aspects of the Court, it would have been quite an indignity for the French delegation to be the only member of the European Union to oppose it. Faced with strong opposition by the French military and defense establishment and countervailing pressure from its European partners and international NGOs, the French government sought a way out through concessions that would allow it to join the Court but insulate French soldiers from some areas of potential jurisdiction. By the end of the Rome negotiations, the French secured a provision that allowed them to opt out for seven years from the war crimes provisions of the Court. This move was enough to give the pro-Court forces in the government in the Foreign Ministry (and Justice Ministry) sufficient leverage to obtain permission to sign the treaty on July 18, 1998.

Thereafter, ratification, including a modification of the country's constitution, was a relatively painless process. As Scheffer remarked, the French do not have the same potential as the Americans for being blocked by their legislative branch. Although ratification requires the approval of the National Assembly, decisions there are more subject to party control than are US senators with their higher degree of

---

[116] Eftekhari 2001, 1045–1046.   [117] Scheffer 2007.

independence.[118] As de Brichambaut noted, ratification "was not a big deal." Once French negotiators were authorized to sign a deal, it was "not at all a political problem" to modify the constitution and have it approved domestically later. At that point, it became a technocratic rather than a political issue.[119]

Conclusion

Advocates of an International Criminal Court framed the issue as a way to pursue justice for gross human rights abuses and to deter future crimes. That human rights frame enjoyed broad cultural resonance across the G-7. However, the risks of the ICC were unequally shared; states with larger troop deployments perceived their risks to be greater than other states. Their main concern was the risk of politically inspired tribunals being waged against their soldiers for difficult military missions that might go awry or be seen as illegitimate by other states. Three states – France, the UK, and the United States – faced costly moral action of supporting the ICC. Of these, France and the UK supported the Court while the United States opposed it.

In this chapter, I noted that French and British ratification of the Rome Statute cannot be explained by material interest arguments. I suggest that a framing/gatekeepers argument provides better traction on this case. I conclude that the concentration of gatekeeper authority in the UK meant that a Labour Party favorably disposed to the Court could easily push through ratification, although the government later took pains to try to engage and mollify the United States as a way of retaining their special relationship. Interestingly, the British government never shared French and American fears of the ICC. While some in the military held these views, senior Labour leadership did not share their concerns, suggesting that concerns about costs are mediated by individuals' subjective assessments. In France, Jacques Chirac's initial assessment was to side with the military. However, when the Socialists were elected in 1997 to form a cohabitation government, this result added a set of gatekeepers more favorably inclined to support the Court. With the Socialists on record in favor of the Court,

---

[118] Scheffer 2007.   [119] De Brichambaut 2007.

and Europeans and international NGOs threatening to vilify France for turning its back on human rights, Chirac avoided a political crisis with his new governing partners by supporting the ICC albeit with the seven-year opt-out for war crimes. Such an explanation, based on gatekeeper dynamics and framing, provides a convincing account of why the British and French supported the ICC despite high troop deployments.

Appendix 6A
Additional opinion polls on support for human rights

	Canada	France	Germany	Italy	Japan	UK	United States
Promoting the defense of human rights – key priority (Jan. 1996)[1]		86%	79%	82%		74%	
Some people say the United Nations should actively promote such human rights principles in member states. Others say this is improper interference in a country's internal affairs and human rights should be left to each country. Do you think the UN SHOULD or SHOULD NOT actively promote human rights in member states? (2008)[2]		76%	91%	81%		68%	70%
Should have clear rules against torture (2006)[3]	74%	75%	71%	81%		72%	58%

[1] Eurobarometer 1996.
[2] Worldpublicopinion.org 2008.
[3] Worldpublicopinion.org 2006.

7 | Conclusions and the future of principled advocacy

In the wake of the 2008 financial crisis, Tom Chandy, head of Save the Children in India, articulated the fears of the advocacy community: "The impact of the American economic meltdown will be experienced everywhere." His views were echoed by Steve Radelet of the Center for Global Development who noted that US foreign assistance for strategically unimportant countries would likely be vulnerable. "The government won't take a dime out of funding Iraq or Afghanistan or Pakistan," Radelet said. "But they will be unlikely to spend money in, say, Tanzania or Senegal."[1]

In this book, I have argued that material conditions and constraints do not explain cases where states supported social movement demands despite facing high costs. I have emphasized the importance of morality and other motivations that were not strictly instrumentally rational or self-interested and how those concerns could lead to costly acts of altruism when policy gatekeepers believed those values to be important. In examining Japan's eventual support for debt relief, Japanese and Canadian ratification of the Kyoto Protocol, and French and British ratification of the Rome Statute establishing the International Criminal Court, I focused on how advocates successfully framed the issues as tests of international citizenship, tapping into desires for prestige and conceptions of national roles on the world stage. In discussing US actions on debt relief and HIV/AIDS, I went further and suggested that moral motivations were important in cases where countries faced permissive economic conditions or had other self-interested motives for supporting causes championed by principled advocates.

I noted, however, that even gatekeepers of generous states were willing to invest only limited (albeit significant) resources in acts of global altruism. Importantly, their willingness to embrace costs extended to

[1] Both quoted in Wax 2008.

255

periods of heightened security risk after the attacks of September 11. However, that generosity was predicated on a functioning global economic order. Events of 2008 and 2009 raised the specter of total economic collapse, where social movement concerns might be swept aside by bigger challenges, both domestic and transnational. In the midst of this economic turmoil, Barack Obama was elected as the first African-American president of the United States, a first for any country without a black majority. Given his politics and his Kenyan heritage, among other attributes, Obama generated intense optimism about what his election might mean for the US role on the world stage and engendered hope among many social movement activists. These twin developments – a deep and prolonged global recession and the emergence of a charismatic, biracial American president – were likely to shape the landscape for social movement activity in the decades after 2010.

In this concluding chapter, I look to the future of activism by principled advocacy movements. I consider the potential impact of the unfolding financial crisis that was placing unprecedented constraints on donor countries and that might precipitate a more durable attention shift away from global altruism than that brought on by the events of September 11. I also consider the role of the United States and leadership opportunities for other countries in light of US ambivalence and hostility to some issues (the International Criminal Court and climate change). I then discuss what lessons past failures and successes of advocacy efforts provide for future campaigns, particularly the ways in which advocates can successfully engage the United States. Although most of this book looks at campaign failures and successes, I consider failures to campaign, where movements did not emerge when they could or should have. I close with a discussion of the contributions of this book.

The financial crisis

In 2008, the world faced a deep financial crisis that emanated from the US housing market but soon spread across the globe as the fabric of crossnational financial ties roiled country after country. For principled advocacy movements like those examined in this book, the economic turmoil posed a more serious challenge to their goals than September 11, 2001. While the terrorist attacks of

2001 disrupted economic activity, the decline, though significant, was transitory and did not challenge the fundamental structure of the global economy.[2] Even as the United States reoriented its foreign policy priorities to focus on terrorism and challenges posed by radical Islam, the country's leadership still found time to address the threats of pandemic diseases such as HIV/AIDS. While the United States led the way on global public health, other states sought to lead on issues such as climate change and the International Criminal Court, despite US obstructionism.

The financial crisis that started in 2008 threatened to undermine the political will supporting global charity by governments. While structural conditions had not, even after 9/11, posed an insurmountable barrier to state support for the goals of transnational advocates, the financial crisis that began in 2008 appeared to be different. As the significance of the economic crisis became clear, advocates expressed worries that even powerful countries would turn inward to face their own problems rather than remain as engaged internationally. While declines in export demand perhaps would have the biggest effect on developing country economies, particularly in Asia, cutbacks in foreign assistance looked like another important consequence, if history is a guide. After previous financial crises, foreign assistance dipped significantly. For example, a 1991 Nordic financial crisis led to a 10% decline in Norway's foreign assistance budget, a 17% decline in Sweden, and a 62% decline in Finland. In the midst of Japan's economic malaise of the 1990s, Japan's foreign aid fell 44% between 1990 and 1996.[3] Indeed, one of the first potential casualties of the financial crisis appeared to be one of Barack Obama's campaign promises to double foreign assistance. In the vice presidential debate of October 2, 2008, Senator Joe Biden said, "We'll probably have to slow that down," suggesting the *expansion* of foreign aid would unfold more slowly than desired.[4]

---

[2] While the attacks had a direct impact on infrastructure as well as larger implications for budgetary allocations for defense, one measure of the effect was the consequence for global economic growth. A Congressional Research Service study suggested that world economic growth was one percentage point below expectations the year after the attacks of September 11, equivalent to a loss of approximately $300 billion (Nanto 2004, 4).

[3] Roodman 2008; data from peak to trough, adjusted for inflation.

[4] Reuters 2008b.

Table 7.1 *Comparison of financial costs of major expenditures by the US government*

Expense	Estimated cost	Inflation-adjusted cost
2008 bailout	$7.76 trillion (as of November 2008)	
World War II	$288 billion	$3.6 trillion
NASA	$461.7 billion	$851.2 billion
Vietnam War	$111 billion	$698 billion
Invasion of Iraq	$551 billion	$597 billion
The New Deal	$32 billion	$500 billion
Korean War	$54 billion	$454 billion
Savings and loan crisis	$153 billion	$256 billion
Race to the Moon	$36.4 billion	$237 billion
Louisiana Purchase	$15 million	$217 billion
Marshall Plan	$12.7 billion	$115.3 billion

Sources: Bloomberg 2008; Pittman and Ivry 2008; Ritholtz 2008.

In the late 1990s, it was politically difficult to dedicate hundreds of millions of dollars to development purposes such as debt relief. By the early 2000s, it was politically possible to find billions of dollars for HIV/AIDS. Even as the financial crisis deprived governments of financial means to address domestic and global challenges, the restrictions of deficit spending that had capped expenditures in previous years were set aside, at least for domestic purposes. By the late 2000s, governments were prepared to spend trillions to rescue the global financial system. For example, the US government was prepared to spend as much as $7.76 trillion for the financial bailout of 2008, exceeding all previous acts of significant government expenditure combined, including World War II (see Table 7.1).

In the midst of such tremendous increases in government spending, sustaining or even expanding levels of foreign assistance would constitute a small fraction of government budgets. It was unclear if in the toughest economic times in a half-century whether largesse for poor foreigners would be seen as a luxury or a pittance in a sea of red ink. Even as the financial crisis undermined the ability of the United States and other rich countries to support social movement aims, political developments in the United States changed global hopes and ambitions.

The United States and the world

Although the financial fallout threatened to upend commitments by rich countries to broader transnational causes, the election of Barack Obama as president potentially ushered in a new period of global engagement by the United States. Thus, even as financial chaos constrained the economic wherewithal of G-7 advanced industrialized countries, the transformation in US domestic politics brought new possibilities for breakthroughs on issues advocates care about, such as climate change and international criminal justice, and sustained and even deepened commitment in areas such as global public health where the United States had remained engaged.

Despite these portents of change, the United States still possesses the same institutional barriers to treaty ratification that allow, for example, US senators skeptical of international commitments to exercise substantial veto power. Although these constraints may have eased with a broader Democratic majority, advocates could not wave away those political barriers or the broader financial crisis. As discussed in previous chapters, in the Clinton era the United States was constrained by gatekeepers in the US Senate. The country became more obstructionist when both the executive branch and the US Congress were controlled by Republicans after the 2000 election. The tenor of US leadership between 2000 and 2008, characterized by aggressive unilateralism in a number of arenas, prompted a vigorous debate in scholarly circles about whether the relationship between the United States and its European allies was irrevocably damaged and whether the historical trajectory of US internationalism was in inexorable decline.[5] In areas where there are international treaties, ratification can be a misleading indicator of whether or not states are sufficiently internationalist or contribute to the provision of global public goods. As I noted in Chapters 4 and 6, ratification of human rights treaties in a number of developing countries may be a costless signal that allows states to curry favor internationally. In the case of the United States, it may fail to ratify a treaty, as a result of its peculiarly onerous treaty ratification

---

[5] On US relations with the rest of the world, particularly transatlantic relations, see Busby 2003, 2004b; Busby and Ochs 2004; Gordon and Shapiro 2004; Ikenberry 2002; Kagan 2002, 2003. On the potential decline in American internationalism, see Busby and Monten 2008b; Ikenberry 2003, 2005; Kupchan and Trubowitz 2007; Legro 2005a; Skidmore 2005.

requirements. However, in practice, the United States may act in keeping with the intent of the treaty, though remaining formally outside it. Such was the initial policy of the Clinton administration on the landmines ban.[6] Extensions of research on costly moral action ultimately have to go beyond treaty ratification to identify when such ratification entails high costs and instances where states may incur costs in keeping with the spirit of the treaty, even if they are constrained from formally ratifying the agreement.

While the United States has complied with yet failed to ratify some treaties, on other issues, the country has played a more obstructionist role. In the George W. Bush era, the US refusal to play a constructive role on issues such as climate change also sparked discussion about whether leadership in the global arena required the participation of the world's dominant power.[7] While there may be issues where the absence of US engagement is not an insurmountable barrier to effective problem-solving, other global problems, including but not limited to climate change, necessitate its participation since the country is a major contributor to the problem.[8] Moreover, for issues that require collective action, whether the United States is supportive can affect the behavior of other states. On climate change, for example, Japan and Canada have done little to meet their commitments under the Kyoto Protocol because the lack of US action could be used to justify inaction. Under such circumstances, advocates who seek policy instruments such as international treaties that are inherently hard to pass because of US domestic institutional constraints may doom their campaigns to failure.[9] That choice is not always a policy mistake, if the problem is amenable to collective action by a subset of international actors. However, where a particular country's participation is required for a problem to be addressed (such as China and the United States on climate change), then advocates would be wise to pay as much attention to the political viability of their preferred policies as they do to the cultural match of their messages.

[6] The United States has acted similarly on the Convention on Elimination of All Forms of Discrimination Against Women and the Convention on the Rights of the Child. I thank an anonymous reviewer for this point.

[7] Brem and Stiles 2008; Brooks and Wohlforth 2008.

[8] See, for example, my discussion of global public goods and climate change in Busby 2006a, 2008a.

[9] On the apparent preference for hard law and international treaties over soft law and informal agreements, see Raustiala 2005; Victor and Coben 2005.

Campaign failure and failure to campaign

In 2004, the controversial Danish political scientist Bjorn Lomborg convened a group of economists to rank the top problems in the world that would provide the largest benefits for the least amount of money. In a world of limited resources, this seemingly rational exercise might contribute to helpful prioritization, a triage of very important problems to distinguish among policy prescriptions that were amenable to solutions and those that might yield very little gain at very high cost. The 2004 report of the so-called Copenhagen Consensus revealed that issues such as climate change would provide few gains at high cost while other issues such as removing trade barriers, prevention of new AIDS infections, and providing micronutrients to people in the developing world could provide great benefits in incomes raised and lives saved at low cost. If the Copenhagen Consensus were adopted, foreign assistance budgets and attention would be redirected from climate change to health and, within the AIDS agenda, from treatment to prevention. Yet, as Lomborg and his colleagues lamented, the nature of the global agenda is not set through such a careful, rational process but instead is driven by swings in public opinion and media attention.[10] As the political science literature on agenda-setting has long recognized, successful political advocacy leads to episodic lurching from issue to issue without a deliberate strategy to marshal public funds for their most productive purposes.[11]

In this context, it is interesting to note how some issues get more attention than others, which is distinct from but related to the animating question of this book: Why do some campaigns fail in some places and succeed in others? While this book focuses on campaign failures (and successes), there are also instances of failures to campaign, of campaigns that advocates have not yet run. (These are the proverbial "dogs that don't bark" in Sherlock Holmes' parlance.) As for why some campaigns get started in the first place, part of the answer lies in the agency of individuals. Some campaigns may not have formed for idiosyncratic reasons: A charismatic leader with good ideas has yet to emerge. However, more systematic reasons may privilege which campaigns emerge.

[10] Lomborg 2004.
[11] Baumgartner and Jones 1993; Downs 1972; Finnemore and Sikkink 1999; Kingdon 1995.

As Clifford Bob notes in his book on rebel movements, secessionist movements in the developing world often compete for resources and support from rich Western donors. Some groups do better than others. The world knows about the Zapatistas in Chiapas, Mexico, but most would be hard-pressed to remember much, if anything, about the Popular Revolutionary Army in the same country. Bob demonstrated the inside–out version of successful framing; groups got more external support when their appeals fit the priorities and values of Western donors.[12] Those same pressures for marketing apply to advocacy campaigns.

What then determines donor priorities? Margaret Keck and Kathryn Sikkink suggest that campaigns that can appeal to protecting vulnerable and innocent individuals from bodily harm have a history of success, as do issues of legal equality of opportunity. Based on this logic, one would expect donor priorities to converge on issues of bodily harm such as torture, where one can make direct connections between actions and consequences that most people find objectionable.[13] However, rich Western donors have supported a variety of causes from environmental protection to global public health to human rights to religious freedom and more. Many different issues could potentially resonate with the donor community. That said, donor attention (and that of advocacy campaigns) may be episodic and respond to what is happening in the world. For example, in the midst of rising fuel and food prices in 2008, advocates turned their attention to those issues. That attention may be ephemeral, and difficult problems that are not easily subject to human interventions may ultimately lose appeal. From this perspective, donors go where the media go.

The work of the Gates Foundation is, in part, an example of media-driven priorities. Founded in 1994, the foundation, as one of the most richly endowed private foundations in the world, has exercised considerable control over the advocacy community agenda by creating demand for global public health campaigns. The foundation has supported many of the leading public health and development advocacy groups and think tanks around the world including DATA, Bread for the World, Oxfam, the Brookings Institution, InterAction, the United

---

[12] Bob 2000, 2002, 2005. For similar survival-seeking actions among humanitarian relief organizations, see Cooley and Ron 2002.
[13] Keck and Sikkink 1998, 27.

Nations Foundation, Results, CARE, ActionAid, and the Center for Global Development, among others.[14] Bill Gates' interest in global health reportedly came about after he saw a graphic in a 1997 *New York Times* article by Nicholas Kristof that showed the number of people who died each year of easily treatable illnesses such as diarrhea.[15] Kristof's columns, however, were meant to draw attention to neglected diseases, issues that got little attention in the policy world and were scarcely covered by the media. Thus, while Gates may have been responding to media coverage, it was not because of the frequency of articles on schistosomiasis and intestinal helminth infections. Perhaps Gates was drawn to these areas for the reasons Keck and Sikkink identified: Here were areas where innocents were clearly experiencing bodily harm and the solution appeared to be simple. The priorities of super-empowered individuals – Gates, Warren Buffett, George Soros, and others – may be idiosyncratic and difficult to explain, let alone predict, using social scientific methods, though the difficulty should not stop us from trying.

Even within the field of global public health, some issues have received more attention and resources while others have languished. AIDS, for example, has received a significant and growing share of overseas development assistance. Between 2004 and 2007, the British, for example, spent nearly 10% of their entire foreign assistance budget on HIV/AIDS while the Americans spent almost 7.5%.[16] AIDS has received disproportionate attention as a share of foreign assistance while funding for other health priorities such as family planning, water resources protection, and basic nutrition has remained flat.[17] As Jeremy Shiffman notes, deaths from HIV/AIDS accounted for about 5% of total mortality in low- and middle-income countries in 2001, but HIV/AIDS funding grew from 9% of the US foreign assistance

---

[14] For a full list, see www.gatesfoundation.org/grants/Pages/search.aspx.
[15] Cooley and Ron 2002.
[16] Data from the OECD Development Assistance Committee website. This calculation excludes aid to Afghanistan and Iraq. See www.oecd.org/dataoecd/50/17/5037721.htm.
[17] Between 2001 and 2006, OECD overseas development assistance for the health sector increased by $12.9 billion. The category for sexually transmitted diseases and HIV/AIDS increased more than any other category, by 29%. Meanwhile, ODA for family planning declined by 2.3%, water resources protection declined by 0.3%, and funds for basic nutrition increased by 0.5% (Kaiser Family Foundation 2008).

for health in 1998 to 43% in 2003.[18] In this context, understanding the dynamics of G-7 contributions to the global AIDS pandemic raises additional questions about why no comparable campaigns for maternal mortality or diarrhea emerged.

Charli Carpenter suggests that dynamics within a campaign network may affect which issues get attention. For example, in the broader network of groups concerned about the effects of war on children, she finds that few campaign groups have worked on the issue of children born of wartime rape. She concludes that, because the issue potentially touches upon concerns of several different issue networks, groups avoid the issue for fear of treading on the turf of other organizations. In a sense, the issue has no natural home or fit with organizational mandates.[19] Similarly, in the health arena, Shiffman and Stephanie Smith note that campaigns for maternal mortality never coalesced because groups lacked a defined and coherent strategy; they disagreed over the nature of the problem, and no single organizational hub emerged to tamp down on interorganizational rivalry.[20] These lines of investigation are provocative, focusing on internal dynamics of networks themselves. That kind of research demands much information and may be less amenable to crossissue, crossnational generalizations like those developed in this book. While the discussion here by necessity is partial, the underlying question about the campaigns that never were is an important one.[21]

The contributions of this book

In 2003, political scientist Bruce Bueno de Mesquita and several coauthors published *The Logic of Political Survival*, a sweeping argument explaining foreign policy outcomes.[22] For those readers unfamiliar with Bueno de Mesquita's work, his approach is an exemplar of a strictly materialist, individual interest explanation of political outcomes.[23] In their book, Bueno de Mesquita *et al.* simplify the motives of politicians to two things: to stay in office and to enrich

---

[18] Shiffman 2006.   [19] Carpenter 2007a, 2007b.
[20] Shiffman and Smith 2007.
[21] For a provisional answer, see Kapstein and Busby 2009.
[22] Bueno de Mesquita *et al.* 2003.
[23] A glowing portrait of Bueno de Mesquita was published in the *New York Times* (Thompson 2009).

themselves personally. The balance between these two choices is determined by the political incentives leaders face. In the process, leaders will provide a mix of public goods to benefit their society as a whole and private goods to enrich themselves and their political supporters. The strength of this argument is that, with but a few factors, Bueno de Mesquita and his colleagues purport to explain a variety of political outcomes across varied regime types, from authoritarian systems to liberal democracies. Outcomes include everything from the degree of corruption to whether or not states go to war.[24]

Bueno de Mesquita and his colleagues present a vignette about King Leopold II, who, in the late nineteenth century, presided over the progressive consolidation of government services in Belgium while he plundered Congo of its resources and treated its people with shocking brutality. Focusing on institutional constraints, they explain how Leopold expanded the services available within Belgium while simultaneously mistreating the people of Congo. In Belgium, Bueno de Mesquita *et al.* argue, Leopold needed the support of a certain number of people to maintain his political survival, which reinforced the need to rule in the interest of public welfare. In Congo, however, "Leopold was free to choose whatever institutional arrangements he wanted... Finding himself unconstrained, he chose to focus on providing private goods for a small coalition and vast opportunities for kleptocracy for himself."[25]

While institutional incentives and constraints tell us about the capacity for Leopold to do what he did in Congo, they tell us very little about the normative environment that allowed him even to think that such conduct was permissible. While transnational moral sentiment against the slave trade had been an animating force throughout the century, in the late nineteenth century, highly racialized views about the inferiority of African people were still widespread, a perspective that fueled the carve-up of Africa by the colonial powers. However, the horrific

---

[24] The relative proportion of public to private goods, in turn, depends on the size of the *selectorate*, the group of people eligible to choose political leaders, and the size of the *winning coalition*, the actual number of supporters required for a leader to get into power and to stay there. Their basic observation is that systems that have larger ratios of winning coalitions to selectorates will ultimately provide more public goods (and, from a normative standpoint, superior economic outcomes among other positive benefits) than political systems where a narrow winning coalition is required to obtain and retain political power. See chapter 4 in Bueno de Mesquita *et al.* 2003.

[25] Bueno de Mesquita *et al.* 2003, 213.

outrages in Congo would create the pressure for what Adam Hochschild called the "the first great international human rights movement of the twentieth century."[26]

It is intriguing that Bueno de Mesquita and his collaborators chose the King Leopold example to illustrate the force of their arguments. While the absence of institutional constraints may have permitted Leopold to sanction atrocities in Congo, the form and character of such brutality – such as the cutting off of hands as punishment – were a product of particular views of Africans as less than human. Indeed, the moral contestation of this practice by advocates including the Congo Reform Association and their allies in government constituted an important disciplining corrective on the foreign policy behavior of Belgium and anticipated the kinds of movements for global causes I examine in this book.

In making this connection between Bueno de Mesquita's account of King Leopold and the movement to rein in the abuses in Congo, I seek to answer a broader question: How does a framing/gatekeepers argument improve upon rationalist approaches to foreign policy? This book, though ambitious in its own right, has no pretensions of such wide-ranging generalizability as Bueno de Mesquita's magisterial effort. My focus is on liberal democracies and the circumstances under which such countries and their political leaders will support moral movement demands for the provision of public goods where the benefits largely accrue to foreigners outside the particular polity.

It is unclear if Bueno de Mesquita can explain instances of transnational altruism like those explored in this book. As the authors admit, their book does not seek to explain everything. Issues such as ideology and the choices between which kinds of public goods a polity will provide are largely left unexplored.[27] Their model presumes the existence of decisionmakers attuned to those who keep them in power. The concerns of foreigners, who have no direct say over leaders' political fortunes, are by their nature excluded. Moral motives have no place as a guiding concern of any significance for leaders or their supporters.

In previous chapters, I suggested that interest-based arguments would expect states and leaders to support moral causes when it suited them, if there were powerful incentives or at a minimum permissive material conditions. In this view, decisionmakers will support actions

[26] Hochschild 1998, 2.   [27] Bueno de Mesquita *et al.* 2003, 74.

that primarily benefit others when it is the easy thing to do or when they face overwhelming self-interested reasons to do so.

In the empirical chapters, I sought to demonstrate that states will on occasion (and within circumscribed bounds) support policies championed by moral movements when they are the hard thing to do. In such circumstances, I suggested the number and preferences of gatekeepers ultimately determine whether or not states support such costly moral action. Gatekeepers, in my approach, are actors positioned by the nature of their institutions to be able to block or at least slow down policy change. Gatekeepers are akin to what Bueno de Mesquita *et al.* call the "leadership," loosely defined as those able to decide how to gather and allocate societal resources.[28]

In Bueno de Mesquita's approach, liberal democracies have large winning coalitions that give political leaders strong incentives to provide public goods to their societies. There is very little room for agency or so-called idiosyncratic choices, either for self-enrichment, patronage, or providing transnational or global public goods to people outside that political system. Though the simplifying assumption of Bueno de Mesquita's work suggests voters care only about self-enrichment, a backdoor way to generate support for global altruism is if the voting population has strong preferences to help foreigners. However, if the public can have moral motivations, so too can leaders themselves.

While an institutional analysis of gatekeepers also plays a central role in this book, I provide a more nuanced portrait of other motivations that perform an important role in political life. Although Bueno de Mesquita and his colleagues are able to travel considerable distance with a spare assumption of survival-seeking and self-enrichment motives, I see the normative pull of prevailing moral notions and reputation informing political choices. In addition, I find more scope for agency by both gatekeepers and advocates. Given the typically low electoral salience of these issues, gatekeepers may have scope to pursue their own preferences. As I suggested in Chapter 2, gatekeeper preferences may prove to be particularly important when polities are either indifferent to the issue or when the issue has been framed to resonate with societal values but the costs of implementing the policy are high. On the advocate side, I focused on messaging, including the role of framing and the messengers themselves.

---

[28] Bueno de Mesquita *et al.* 2003, 38.

These observations lead to another question, "How often do states engage in costly moral action?" This book seeks to explain outliers and puzzles for material explanations of foreign policy outcomes among the great liberal democracies of the late twentieth and early twenty-first centuries. If these are rare occurrences, then the purchase provided by this book may be limited to the occasional instance when states are willing to absorb relatively high costs in support of moral movement aims. In exploring a diverse set of issue areas and country cases in the post-Cold War era, I have sought to demonstrate that these anomalies may be more pervasive than we might imagine. Other scholars who have written on topics such as human rights and humanitarian intervention – including Gary Bass, Darren Hawkins, Adam Hochschild, Chaim Kaufmann and Robert Pape, Oded Lowenheim, David Lumsdaine, Robert McElroy, Frank Schimmelfennig, C. William Walldorf – have demonstrated that such action by democratic powers has occurred for diverse reasons in a variety of other settings both contemporary and historic.[29] Actions to restrict the whaling trade suggest that examples extend beyond the human rights arena.[30] Additional research is needed to assess the frequency and full scope of such costly moral action. While domestic political mobilization is frequently a major contributing factor to such policy changes, moral motivations, including reputational concerns, loom large in a number of these cases. This book has suggested the set of circumstances – low costs, high value fit, supportive gatekeepers – when such attempts by advocates are most likely to succeed and the circumstances when tradeoffs between costs and values still might yield bounded support for moral commitments.

Conclusion

This book is as much about state behavior as it is about moral movements. Some readers might find the book positively state-centric: states are the main targets of political action by the movements covered here.[31] The institutional structure of decisionmaking and influence

---

[29] Bass 2008; Hawkins 2004; Hochschild 1998; Kaufmann and Pape 1999; Lowenheim 2003; Lumsdaine 1993; McElroy 1992; Schimmelfennig 2001; Walldorf 2008.

[30] DeSombre 1995, 2006; M. J. Peterson 1992.

[31] For good reason, movements that targeted private firms on corporate social responsibility (in extractive industries, textiles, and forests) were deliberately

within states shapes the potential for advocacy success perhaps more than the campaigns. The book is also about a certain set of states, the G-7 advanced industrialized countries, seven of the richest liberal democracies. As I have suggested, the role of the United States across these cases looms large.

The ways in which moral concerns affect decisionmaking over foreign policy in those states is a complex and important subject. As I noted, King Leopold's ability to act with impunity in Congo in the late nineteenth and early twentieth centuries was partially a product of prevailing moral attitudes of the day. These attitudes change over time and, as we have seen, create new pressures for action. While moral movements have a role in shaping broader international sentiment, this book has mostly focused on the internal resonance of transnational appeals within advanced democracies rather than the external legitimacy of their actions on the world stage. Where international attitudes have mattered, this has often been through the internalized logic of reputation. When the public and decisionmakers in a country believe that what others think about them is important, such beliefs have ultimately shaped state behavior in a number of circumstances.

In light of the difficult US experience in Iraq in the early 2000s, both scholars and policymakers have come to regard legitimacy – whether countries are perceived by others as engaging in morally appropriate or desirable action – as an important influence on policy success. In a sense, the normative or, in Joseph Nye's formulation, the soft power resources of a state are inextricably bound up with the national interest.[32] Many questions remain about whose perception of legitimacy matters. Nonetheless, disregarding the opinions of others, as the George W. Bush administration was accused of, is thought to have consequences, making it more costly for a country to achieve its ends because of lost cooperative opportunities, higher transaction costs of doing business, and/or a more difficult and hostile operating environment in which to get things done, including but not limited to the battlefield. As the United States discovered, being the world's dominant military power did not make it omnipotent.

excluded from this book. While movement tactics and strategies that focus on firms resemble those that target state behavior, the relative vulnerability of for-profit firms to reputational pressure from damage to their corporate brands makes them worthy of extended study in their own right.

[32] Nye 1990; 2003; 2004.

Antagonizing its friends may have increased its own costs of system maintenance.[33]

This observation complicates the distinction between interest- and values-based motivations for action. If "doing the right thing" enhances one's interests, then it becomes difficult to disentangle the underlying rationale for action. That said, distinguishing between short-run costs and beliefs about a state's long-term interests is an easy, albeit tentative way to differentiate the two.

While the United States may have discovered that limited regard for the opinions of others, even close allies, was ultimately costly, it was powerful enough to brush these concerns aside, even at the risks of policy failure. What does this say about the power of social movements, let alone other countries, to rein in the actions of powerful states through normative pressure? The US experience again suggests that the mechanism may largely be internal to the country. Some decisionmakers and states care about their international reputation, how they are perceived on the world stage. They are often guided by aspirations for global leadership and longstanding ideas about what strategies serve the national interests. While the costs they are willing to bear are not unlimited, they may be, in certain circumstances, significant enough to qualify as cases of costly moral action. These actions, while potentially materially self-interested in the long run, require investments and risks in the short run that are not obviously self-serving. While the cases in this book demonstrate that the real world rarely provides perfect instances of entirely selfless behavior, we nonetheless have observed states engaging in costly actions for reputational gain. I have ascribed such actions to a mix of ideational and material motives. What is also notable is that the values behind the issues themselves were often not enough on their own to motivate state action. For moral movements, that finding alone ought to be a humbling realization about the limits of their influence under the best of circumstances and inspire some creative agency about how to marshal their resources, however limited.

Why then do some campaigns by principled advocacy groups succeed in some places and fail in others? That question animated this book. Through an exploration of four issue areas across seven

---

[33] Kagan 2004a, 2004b. Ikenberry has written extensively on the perils of such a go-it-alone strategy (Ikenberry 2001–2002, 2004a, 2004b). For classic discussions of legitimacy, see Claude 1996.

countries, I demonstrated the importance of moral motivations, prestige, and ideas of national greatness and how these intersected with domestic institutions and the preferences of policy gatekeepers. In the process, I suggest that explanations based purely on self-interested behavior by states or politicians can get us only so far. By identifying a number of cases where states engaged in costly moral action, I show that a spare argument based on the costs of supporting movement aims is a good beginning but an inadequate basis for explaining state behavior in all instances. I emphasize the importance of framing: Where advocates' rhetoric about their cause matched the ideals and values of the countries they were targeting, campaigners were more likely to be successful. However, gatekeepers who had authority to sign off on a particular policy determined whether a country ultimately supported movement aims. As I discussed in Chapter 3 on debt relief and Jubilee 2000, where those gatekeepers were personally committed to an issue, movement success was more likely. I layer this basic argument with additional refinements, bringing in a more complex discussion of reputation in Chapter 4 on climate change, emphasizing the role of messengers in Chapter 5 on HIV/AIDS, and identifying the subjective perception of costs and the role of rhetorical entrapment and shaming in Chapter 6 on the International Criminal Court.

I opened the book with a story of Bono bringing Senator Jesse Helms of North Carolina to tears. Bono's foray into policy was so successful that by 2009 every advocacy group and international organization had adopted its own celebrity spokesperson or goodwill ambassador to drive media and public attention to their favorite issues (basketball player Yao Ming for the United Nations Environment Programme, actress Angelina Jolie for the UN Refugee Agency, Coldplay frontman Chris Martin for the Make Trade Fair campaign, and so on). While the line between celebrity and politics was crossed long ago, when Ronald Reagan transitioned from making movies to becoming governor of California and later president of the United States, the intersection of celebrity and activism became pervasive by the end of the twenty-first century's first decade, leading Daniel Drezner to write only partially tongue-in-cheek that "Foreign Policy Goes Glam." Despite the potential humor in earnest musicians and actors opining about global causes, Drezner suggests that their actions had serious consequences:

The power of soft news has given star entertainers additional leverage to advance their causes. Their ability to raise issues to the top of the global agenda is growing. This does not mean that celebrities can solve the problems that bedevil the world. And not all celebrity activists are equal in their effectiveness. Nevertheless, politically-engaged stars cannot be dismissed as merely an amusing curiosity in foreign policy.[34]

For both rich philanthropists and celebrities (sometimes one and the same), the early twenty-first century provides perhaps unparalleled power for individuals like them to shape the priorities of others, including states. Through their wealth and ability to draw media attention, the super-rich and the super-famous have altered the landscape for principled advocacy. With the global economy teetering and a new American president in Barack Obama potentially heralding a new direction in US foreign policy, it remains to be seen which of these portents will be the most important and how these and other dynamics will interact as new challenges, injustices, and moral outrages emerge on a planet that seems smaller and more tightly bound together by the day.

[34] Drezner 2007. See also Busby 2008c.

Bibliography

Acharya, Amitav. 2004. How Ideas Spread: Whose Norms Matter? Norm Localization and Institutional Change in Asian Regionalism. *International Organization* 58 (1): 239–275.

ACLU (American Civil Liberties Union). 2003. Freedom Under Fire: Dissent in Post-9/11 America. Available from www.aclu.org/safefree/general/17259pub20030508.html.

Alberts, Sheldon. 2009. Fighting AIDS in Africa: A Rare Bush Success Story, Canwest News, January 1. Available from www.canada.com/topics/news/world/story.html?id=1132130.

Allen, Mike, and Paul Blustein. 2003. Unlikely Allies Influenced Bush to Shift Course on AIDS Relief. *Washington Post*, January 30.

Amnesty International. 1998. International Criminal Court: Final Statement at the Diplomatic Conference Delivered by Pierre Sané, July 16. Available from www.iccnow.org/documents/AI_16July1998_en.pdf.

Amnesty International USA. 2007. Form 990: Return of Organization Exempt from Income Tax. Available from www.amnestyusa.org/pdf/2007990.pdf.

Andresen, Steinar, and Shardul Agrawala. 2002. Leaders, Pushers and Laggards in the Making of the Climate Regime. *Global Environmental Change* 12 (1): 41–51.

ANES (American National Election Study). 2005. Cumulative American National Election Study 1948–2004. Available from sda.berkeley.edu.

Angus Reid Global Monitor. 2007. Human Rights Trump Free Trade for Canadians, July 20. Available from www.angus-reid.com/polls/view/human_rights_trump_free_trade_for_canadians/.

Anheier, Helmut, Marlies Glasius, and Mary Kaldor, eds. 2004. *Global Civil Society 2004/5*. London: Sage. Available from www.lse.ac.uk/Depts/global/yearbook04chapters.htm.

Arieff, Alexis, Rhoda Margesson, and Marjorie Ann Browne. 2008. International Criminal Court Cases in Africa: Status and Policy Issues. Congressional Research Service, September 12. Available from http://assets.opencrs.com/rpts/RL34665_20080912.pdf.

Armingeon, Klaus, Philipp Leimgruber, Michelle Beyeler, and Sarah Menegale. 2005. Comparative Political Data Set 1960–2003. Institute of Political Science, University of Berne. Available from www.ipw. unibe.ch/content/team/klaus_armingeon/comparative_political_data_sets/index_ger.html.

Arslanalp, Serkan, and Peter Blair Henry. 2006. Policy Watch: Debt Relief. *Journal of Economic Perspectives* 20 (1): 207–220.

Associated Press. 2001. Japan Begins Preparations to Ratify Kyoto Protocol Next Year, November 12.

———. 2004. US Backs Down on War-Crimes Exemption, June 22.

Attaran, Amir, and Jeffrey Sachs. 2001. Defining and Refining International Donor Support for Combating the AIDS Pandemic. *Lancet* 357 (9249): 57–61.

Axelrod, Robert. 1990. *The Evolution of Cooperation*. New York: Basic Books.

Babington, Charles. 1999. G-7 Summit Offers Poor Nations Plan for Substantial Debt Relief. *Washington Post*, June 18.

Barnes, Fred. 2005. Pro Bono: The President and the Singer Make Common Cause on Africa. *Weekly Standard* 10 (39): 8–9.

Barnett, Tony, and Alan Whiteside. 2002. *AIDS in the Twenty-First Century: Disease and Globalization*. Basingstoke, UK, and New York: Palgrave Macmillan.

Barrett, Scott. 1999. Montreal v. Kyoto: International Cooperation and the Global Environment. In *Global Public Goods: International Cooperation in the 21st Century*, edited by I. Kaul, I. Grunberg, and M. A. Stern. New York: Oxford University Press, 192–219.

Bartley, Tim. 2007. Institutional Emergence in an Era of Globalization: The Rise of Transnational Private Regulation of Labor and Environmental Conditions. *American Journal of Sociology* 113 (2): 297–351.

Bass, Gary Jonathan. 2000. *Stay the Hand of Vengeance: The Politics of War Crimes Tribunals*. Princeton, N.J.: Princeton University Press.

———. 2008. *Freedom's Battle: The Origins of Humanitarian Intervention*. New York: Alfred A. Knopf.

Bassiouni, M. Cherif. 1998. *The Statute of the International Criminal Court: A Documentary History*. Ardsley, N.Y.: Transnational Publishers.

Baumgartner, Frank R., and Bryan D. Jones. 1993. *Agendas and Instability in American Politics*. Chicago: University of Chicago Press.

BBC. 2000. UK Pushes for War Crimes Court, August 25. Available from news.bbc.co.uk/1/hi/uk_politics/895384.stm.

———. 2002a. Canadian Parliament Backs Kyoto Protocol, December 11. Available from news.bbc.co.uk/1/hi/world/americas/2564723.stm.

2002b. Japan Ratifies Kyoto Pact, June 4. Available from news.bbc. co.uk/1/hi/world/asia-pacific/2024265.stm.

2007a. EU Plans "Industrial Revolution," January 10. Available from news.bbc.co.uk/1/hi/sci/tech/6247199.stm.

2007b. UK Soldier Jailed over Iraq Abuse. April 30. Available from news.bbc.co.uk/2/hi/uk_news/6609237.stm.

Beattie, Alan. 2000. Magic Bullet May Be Flash in the Pan. *Financial Times*, September 22.

Behrman, Greg. 2004. *The Invisible People: How the US Has Slept Through the Global AIDS Pandemic, the Greatest Humanitarian Catastrophe of Our Time*. New York: Free Press.

Benedick, Richard E. 1997. The UN Approach to Climate Change: Where Has It Gone Wrong? Resources for the Future, December. Available from www.weathervane.rff.org/pop/pop4/benedick.html.

Berger, Thomas U. 1996. Norms, Identity, and National Security in Germany and Japan. In *The Culture of National Security*, edited by P. J. Katzenstein. New York: Columbia University Press, 317–356.

1998. *Cultures of Antimilitarism: National Security in Germany and Japan*. Baltimore, Md.: Johns Hopkins University Press.

Berman, Frank. 2002. The International Criminal Court: Is It a Threat? Paper read at Chatham House, London, November 5.

Betsill, Michele M. 2000. Greens in the Greenhouse: Environmental NGO's, International Norms and the Politics of Global Climate Change. Ph.D. thesis, University of Colorado–Boulder.

Birdsall, Nancy, and John Williamson. 2002. *Delivering on Debt Relief*. Washington, D.C.: Center for Global Development.

Blackstock, Colin, and Richard Norton-Taylor. 2005. Britons Face Iraq War Crime Trials. *Guardian*, July 20. Available from www.guardian. co.uk/uk/2005/jul/20/military.iraq.

Bloomberg. 2008. Follow the $7.4 Trillion: Breakdown of the US Government's Rescue Efforts, November. Available from www.bloomberg. com/apps/data?pid=avimage&iid=i0YrUuvkygWs.

Blyth, Mark. 2003. Structures Do Not Come with an Instruction Sheet: Interests, Ideas, and Progress in Political Science. *Perspectives on Politics* 3 (1): 695–706.

Bob, Clifford. 2000. Beyond Transparency: Visibility and Fit in the Internationalization of Internal Conflict. In *Power and Conflict in the Age of Transparency*, edited by B. I. Finel and K. M. Lord. New York: Palgrave/St. Martin's Press, 287–314.

2002. Merchants of Morality. *Foreign Policy* 129 (March/April): 36–45.

2005. *The Marketing of Rebellion: Insurgents, Media, and International Activism*. New York: Cambridge University Press.

Bodansky, Daniel. 2001. Bonn Voyage: Kyoto's Uncertain Revival. *National Interest* (Fall): 45–55.

Bolton, John. 1998. What's Wrong with the International Criminal Court. *National Interest*. Available from www.aei.org/publications/pubID. 9791,filter.all/pub_detail.asp.

Bono, and Michka Assayas. 2005. *Bono: In Conversation with Michka Assayas*. New York: Riverhead Books.

Boockmann, Bernard. 2006. Partisan Politics and Treaty Ratification: The Acceptance of International Labour Organisation Conventions by Industrialised Democracies, 1960–1996. *European Journal of Political Research* 45 (1): 153–180.

Booth, Cherie. 2004. The Impact of the International Criminal Court in Strengthening Worldwide Respect for Human Rights. Speech at Graduate Institute of International Studies, Geneva (HEI), July 1. Available from hei.unige.ch/comm/files/CahierHEI10.pdf.

Bravin, Jess. 2006. US Warms to Hague Tribunal. *Wall Street Journal*, June 14.

Brem, Stefan, and Kendall Stiles, eds. 2008. *Cooperating Without America: Theories and Case Studies of Non-Hegemonic Regimes*. London: Routledge.

Brooks, Stephen, and William Wohlforth. 2008. *World out of Balance: International Relations and the Challenge of American Primacy*. Princeton, N.J.: Princeton University Press.

Brown, Bartram S. 2000. The Statute of the ICC: Past, Present, and Future. In *The United States and the International Criminal Court: National Security and International Law*, edited by S. Sewall and C. Kaysen. Lanham, Md.: Rowman & Littlefield, 61–84.

2002. Unilateralism, Multilateralism, and the International Criminal Court. In *Multilateralism and US Foreign Policy: Ambivalent Engagement*, edited by S. Patrick and S. Forman. Boulder, Colo.: Lynne Rienner, 323–344.

Bueckert, Dennis. 2002. Kyoto Vote Declared a Matter of Confidence. *Niagara Falls Review*, December 9.

Bueno de Mesquita, Bruce, Alastair Smith, Randolph M. Siverson, and James D. Morrow. 2003. *The Logic of Political Survival*. Cambridge, Mass.: MIT Press.

Burkhalter, Holly. 2004. The Politics of AIDS: Engaging Conservative Activists. *Foreign Affairs* 83, 1 (January–February): 8–14.

Busby, Joshua. 2003. Climate Change Blues: Why the US and Europe Just Can't Get Along. *Current History* 102, 662 (March): 113–118.

2004a. New Troubles for the West: Debt Relief, Climate Change, and Comparative Foreign Policy in the Post-Cold War Era. Ph.D. thesis, Government Department, Georgetown University, Washington, D.C.

2004b. Last Stop Baghdad: Origins of the Transatlantic Trainwreck. *Global Dialogue* 5 (3–4): 49–62.

2005. Good States: Prestige and Reputational Concerns of Major Powers Under Unipolarity. Paper read at American Political Science Association meeting, September, Washington D.C.

2006a. Climate Change and Collective Action: Troubles in the Transition to a Post-Oil Economy. *Saint Antony's International Review* 1 (2): 35–55.

2006b. Memo on Reputation. Paper read at Workshop on Rationality and Reputation, Woodrow Wilson School for Public and International Affairs, Princeton University, Princeton, N.J.

2007a. "Bono Made Jesse Helms Cry": Debt Relief, Jubilee 2000, and Moral Action in International Politics. *International Studies Quarterly* 51 (2): 247–275.

2007b. Climate Change and National Security: An Agenda for Action. Council on Foreign Relations. Available from www.cfr.org/publication/14862.

2008a. The Hardest Problem in the World: Leadership in the Climate Regime. In Brem and Stiles 2008, 73–104.

2008b. Who Cares About the Weather? Climate Change and US National Security. *Security Studies* 17 (3): 468–504.

2008c. Is There a Constituency for Global Poverty? Jubilee 2000 and the Future of Development Advocacy. In *Global Development 2.0: Can Philanthropists, the Public, and the Poor Make Poverty History?* edited by L. Brainard and D. Chollet. Washington, D.C.: Brookings Institution Press, 85–100.

2008d. Male Circumcision, HIV Prevention, and Support for Health Systems in Africa. CSIS Africa Policy Forum. Available from http://csis.org/blog/male-circumcision-hiv-prevention-and-support-health-systems-africa.

2008e. Overcoming Political Barriers to Reform in Energy Policy. In *A Strategy for American Power*, edited by Sharon Burke and Christine Parthemore. Washington, D.C.: Center for a New American Security, 37–66. Available from www.cnas.org/node/119.

Busby, Joshua, and Jonathan Monten. 2008a. With Us or Against Us? Public Opinion and Republican Elite Attitudes on US Foreign Policy After the Cold War. Unpublished paper, University of Texas at Austin.

2008b. Without Heirs? Assessing the Decline of Establishment Internationalism in US Foreign Policy. *Perspectives on Politics* 6 (3): 451–472.

Busby, Josh, and Alexander Ochs. 2004. Mars, Venus down to Earth: Understanding the Transatlantic Climate Divide. In *Beyond Kyoto: Meeting the Long-Term Challenge of Global Climate Change*, edited by D. Michel. Washington, D.C.: Center for Transatlantic Relations, Johns Hopkins University, 35–76.

Bush, George W. 2000. *Comprehensive National Energy Policy*. Saginaw, Mich., September 29. Available from www.bcse.org/climateact2.htm.

Cardenas, Sonia. 2004. Norm Collision: Explaining the Effects of International Human Rights Pressure on State Behavior. *International Studies Review* 6 (2): 213–232.

Carpenter, R. Charli. 2005. "Women, Children and Other Vulnerable Groups": Gender, Strategic Frames, and the Protection of Civilians as a Transnational Issue. *International Studies Quarterly* 49 (2): 295–394.

2007a. Setting the Advocacy Agenda: Theorizing Issue Emergence and Nonemergence in Transnational Advocacy Networks. *International Studies Quarterly* 51 (1): 99–120.

2007b. Studying Issue (Non)-Adoption in Transnational Advocacy Networks. *International Organization* 61 (3): 643–667.

Carr, Mathew, and Radoslav Tomek. 2009. Japan Denies Buying "Hot Air" to Meet Kyoto Target. Bloomberg News, July 23. Available from www.bloomberg.com/apps/news?pid=20601101&sid=auYplIVXDnYY.

Cass, Loren. 2002. The Dilemmas of International Climate Commitments and Energy Reform in Germany, the UK, and the US. Paper read at International Studies Association meeting, March 24–27, New Orleans.

Castellano, Marc. 1999. Japan to Expand Debt-Relief Program for Poorest Nations. *Japan Economic Institute Report* 17. Available from jei.org/Archive/JEIR99/9917w4.html.

2000. G-7 Poor-Country Debt-Relief Initiative Faces Difficulties. *Japan Economic Institute Report*, July 14. Available from www.jei.org/Restricted/JEIR00/0027w4.html.

CBC. 2002. Canada's Kyoto Documents Delivered to UN. CBC News, December 17. Available from www.cbc.ca/world/story/2002/12/17/kyoto_delivered021216.html.

Center for Global Development. 2005. Aid. Available from www.cgdev.org/section/initiatives/_active/cdi/_components/aid/.

Chamberlain, Gethin. 2007. Court "Can Envisage" Blair Prosecution. *Daily Telegraph*, March 17. Available from www.telegraph.co.uk/news/uknews/1545876/Court-'can-envisage'-Blair-prosecution.html.

Checkel, Jeffrey T. 1997. International Norms and Domestic Politics: Bridging the Rationalist–Constructivist Divide. *European Journal of International Relations* 3 (4): 473–495.

1999. Norms, Institutions, and National Identity in Contemporary Europe. *International Studies Quarterly* 43 (1): 84–114.

2001. Why Comply? Social Learning and European Identity Change. *International Organization* 55 (3): 553–588.

Chote, Robert. 1999. Japan and US Resist UK Moves on Debt Relief. *Financial Times*, June 7.

Christensen, Thomas, and Jack Snyder. 1990. Chain Gangs and Passed Bucks: Predicting Alliance Patterns in Multipolarity. *International Security* 44 (2): 137–168.

Cialdini, Robert B. 1984. *Influence: How and Why People Agree to Things.* New York: Morrow.

Claude, Inis. 1996. Collective Legitimation as a Function of the United Nations. *International Organization* 20 (Summer): 367–379.

Clinton, Hillary. 2009. Questions for the Record. Available from www.foreignpolicy.com/files/KerryClintonQFRs.pdf.

Clinton, William Jefferson. 1997. President Clinton Announces the United States Climate Policy. Speech at National Geographic Society, Washington, D.C.

1999. Remarks by the President to Conference on US–Africa Partnership for the 21st Century. The White House, Office of the Press Secretary, March 16. Available from www.state.gov/www/regions/africa/990316_clinton.html.

CNN. 2007. Climate Change Prompts Cabinet Change in Canada, January 4. Available from www.climateark.org/shared/reader/welcome.aspx?linkID=65962.

Coalition for the ICC (International Criminal Court). 2005. Country Positions on Bilateral Immunity Agreements, August. Available from www.iccnow.org/?mod=bia.

Undated. History of the ICC. Available from www.iccnow.org/?mod=icchistory.

Cohen, Samy. 2005. *The Resilience of the State: Democracy and the Challenges of Globalisation.* London: C. Hurst & Co.

Collins, Carole. 1999. "Break the Chains of Debt!" International Jubilee 2000 Campaign Demands Deeper Debt Relief. *Africa Recovery* 13 (2–3): 16. Available from www.un.org/ecosocdev/geninfo/afrec/vol13no2/sept99.htm.

Cook, Robin. 1997. Human Rights into a New Century, May 12. Available from www.guardian.co.uk/ethical/article/0,2763,192031,00.html.

Cooley, Alexander, and James Ron. 2002. The NGO Scramble: Organizational Insecurity and the Political Economy of Transnational Action. *International Security* 27 (1): 5–39.

Cortell, Andrew, and James W. Davis. 2000. Understanding the Domestic Impact of International Norms: A Research Agenda. *International Studies Review* 2 (1): 65–87.

———. 2005. When Norms Clash: International Norms, Domestic Practices, and Japan's Internalisation of the GATT/WTO. *Review of International Studies* (31): 3–25.

Crane, Barbara B. 1984. Policy Coordination by Major Western Powers in Bargaining with the Third World: Debt Relief and the Common Fund. *International Organization* 38 (3): 399–428.

Crook, Clive. 1991. Sisters in the Woods. *The Economist*, October 12.

Cushman, John H. 1997. Top Aides Urge Clinton to Ease Global Warming Emission Goal. *New York Times*, October 10.

Daily, Matt. 2001. Kyoto Treaty Becomes a Numbers Game Without the US. Reuters, July 1. Available from www.planetark.org/dailynewsstory. cfm?newsid=11534.

David Suzuki Foundation. 2002. Keeping Canada in Kyoto. June. Available from www.davidsuzuki.org/files/ClimateBrief.pdf.

De Souza, Mike. 2006. Japan's Proposal Could Weaken Kyoto Pact. Canwest News, November 4. Available from www.canada.com/ vancouversun/news/story.html?id=b4727f65-f4d7–4dac-a2d2– 67b933674fe4.

DEFRA (United Kingdom, Department for Environment, Food, and Rural Affairs). 2003. Carbon Dioxide Emissions by End User: 1970–2001 United Kingdom, September 16. Available from www.decc.gov.uk/ en/content/cms/statistics/climate_change/co2_end_user/co2_end_user. aspx.

Deitelhoff, Nicole. 2008. Isolated Hegemon: The Creation of the International Criminal Court. In Brem and Stiles 2008, 147–172.

Dempsey, Judy. 2002a. Britain Reveals Plans for Compromise on ICC. *Financial Times*, September 3.

———. 2002b. EU Ministers Back Off over Criminal Court. *Financial Times*, October 1.

Dent, Martin, and Bill Peters. 1999. *The Crisis of Poverty and Debt in the Third World*. Aldershot, UK: Ashgate.

Depledge, Joanna. 1999. Coming of Age at Buenos Aires: The Climate Change Regime After Kyoto. *Environment* 41 (7): 15–19.

DeSombre, Elizabeth. 1995. Baptists and Bootleggers for the Environment: The Origins of United States Unilateral Sanctions. *Journal of Environment and Development* 4 (1): 53–75.

2006. *Global Environmental Institutions*. London: Routledge.

Dessai, Suraje. 2001.The Climate Regime from The Hague to Marrakech: Saving or Sinking the Kyoto Protocol? Tyndall Centre for Climate Change Research, December. Available from tyndall.uea.ac.uk/sites/default/files/wp12.pdf.

Dietrich, John. 2007. The Politics of PEPFAR: The President's Emergency Plan for AIDS Relief. *Ethics and International Affairs* 21 (3): 277–292.

Dingwerth, Klaus. 2008. North–South Parity in Global Governance: The Affirmative Procedures of the Forest Stewardship Council. *Global Governance* 14: 53–71.

Dominion Institute. 2003. The 2003 Annual Dominion Institute Canada Day Poll: The Report Cards Are In, July 1. Available from www.ipsos-na.com/news/pressrelease.cfm?id=1858.

Dominus, Susan. 2000. Questions for Bono; Relief Pitcher. *New York Times*, October 8.

Domke, David. 2000. Elite Messages: The Role of Race as a Source Cue. Unpublished paper, University of Washington, May 19–20. Available from depts.washington.edu/ccce/events/domke.htm.

Donnelly, Elizabeth A. Undated. Proclaiming the Jubilee: The Debt and Structural Adjustment Network. UN Vision Project on Global Public Policy Network. Available from www.globalpublicpolicy.net/fileadmin/gppi/Donnelly_Jubilee.pdf.

Donnelly, John. 2001. Prevention Urged in AIDS Fight: Natsios Says Fund Should Spend Less on HIV Treatment. *Boston Globe*, June 7.

Downie, David Leonard. 1995. Road Map or False Trail? Evaluating the "Precedence" of the Ozone Regime as a Model and Strategy for Global Climate Change. *International Environmental Affairs* 7 (4): 321–345.

Downs, Anthony. 1972. Up and Down with Ecology: The "Issue Attention" Cycle. *The Public Interest* 28 (Summer): 38–50.

Downs, George, and Michael A. Jones. 2002. Reputation, Compliance, and International Law. *Journal of Legal Studies* 31: S95–S114.

Downs, George W., David M. Rocke, and Peter N. Barsoom. 1996. Is the Good News About Compliance Good News About Cooperation? *International Organization* 50 (3): 379–406.

Drezner, Daniel. 2007. Foreign Policy Goes Glam. *The National Interest*, November 1. Available from www.nationalinterest.org/Article.aspx?id=16012.

Drozdiak, William. 2000. Global Warming Talks Collapse. *Washington Post*, November 26.

Dugger, Celia. 2008. Bono Still Hasn't Found the African Aid He's Looking For. *International Herald Tribune*, May 15. Available from www.iht.com/articles/2007/05/15/africa/15bono.php?page=1.

Dunlap, David W. 1995. Different Faces of AIDS Are Conjured up by Politicians. *New York Times*, July 8.

Eagly, Alice Hendrickson, and Shelly Chaiken. 1993. *The Psychology of Attitudes*. Fort Worth, Tex.: Harcourt Brace Jovanovich.

Easterly, William. 2001. Think Again: Debt Relief. *Foreign Policy* November/December: 20–26.

Eftekhari, Shiva. 2001. International Criminal Justice: Rwanda and French Human Rights Activism. *Human Rights Quarterly* 23: 1032–1061.

EKOS Research Associates. 2002. Public Attitudes Toward the Kyoto Protocol, June 10. Available from www.ekos.com/admin/articles/10June02KyotoProt.pdf.

Elbe, Stefan. 2006. Should HIV/AIDS Be Securitized? The Ethical Dilemmas of Linking HIV/AIDS and Security. *International Studies Quarterly* 50 (1): 119–144.

Elsea, Jennifer. 2002. International Criminal Court: Overview and Selected Legal Issues. Congressional Research Service. Available from www.au.af.mil/au/awc/awcgate/crs/rl31437.pdf.

Elster, Jon. 2000. Rational Choice History: A Case of Excessive Ambition. *American Political Science Review* 94 (3): 685–695.

Entman, Robert M. 1993. Framing: Toward Clarification of a Fractured Paradigm. *Journal of Communication* 43 (4): 51–58.

Environics Research Group. 2004. Canadian Attitudes Toward Development Assistance. Available from www.oecd.org/dataoecd/46/9/39436670.pdf.

Environmental and Energy Study Institute. 2007. Climate Change Fact Sheet, May 4. Available from www.eesi.org/050407_Climate_Polling_factsheet.

Epstein, Helen. 2005. God and the Fight Against AIDS. *New York Review of Books* 52 (7): 47–50. Available from www.nybooks.com/articles/17963.

Eurobarometer. 1996. Standard Eurobarometer 45. European Commission. Available from ec.europa.eu/public_opinion/archives/eb/eb45/eb45_en.htm.

    1997. Standard Eurobarometer 46. European Commission. Available from ec.europa.eu/public_opinion/archives/eb/eb46/eb46_en.htm.

    1999. Europeans and Development Aid. European Commission. Available from ec.europa.eu/public_opinion/archives/ebs/ebs_126_en.pdf.

    2000. Report Number 53, October. European Commission. Available from ec.europa.eu/public_opinion/archives/eb/eb53/eb53_en.htm.

    2001. Report Number 54, April. European Commission. Available from ec.europa.eu/public_opinion/archives/eb/eb54/eb54_en.htm.

2005. Attitudes Towards Development Aid. European Commission. Available from ec.europa.eu/public_opinion/archives/ebs/ebs_222_ en.pdf.

2008. Recent Standard Eurobarometer. Available from ec.europa.eu/ public_opinion/standard_en.htm.

European Environment Agency. 2006. Greenhouse Gas Emissions Trends and Projects in Europe 2006. Available from reports.eea.europa.eu/eea_ report_2006_9/en/eea_report_9_2006.pdf.

Farrell, Joseph, and Matthew Rabin. 1996. Cheap Talk. *Journal of Economic Perspectives* 10 (3): 103–118.

Farrell, Theo. 2001. Transnational Norms and Military Development: Constructing Ireland's Professional Army. *European Journal of International Relations* 7 (1): 63–102.

Fearon, James. 1994. Domestic Political Audiences and the Escalation of International Disputes. *American Political Science Review* 88 (3): 577–592.

1997. Signaling Foreign Policy Interests. *Journal of Conflict Resolution* 41 (1): 68–90.

Fearon, James, and Alexander Wendt. 2003. Rationalism v. Constructivism: A Skeptical View. In *Handbook of International Relations*, edited by W. Carlsnaes, T. Risse-Kappen, and B. A. Simmons. London and Thousand Oaks, Calif.: SAGE, 52–72.

Fehl, Caroline. 2004. Explaining the International Criminal Court: A "Practice Test" for Rationalist and Constructivist Approaches. *European Journal of International Relations* 10 (3): 357–394.

Fekete, Jason. 2006. Harper Hints at Ditching Kyoto Accord. *Calgary Herald*, January 8. Available from www.canada.com/calgaryherald/news/story.html?id=b0480bad-6377–441e-94d6–757316019aea.

Ferguson, H. L. 1989. The Changing Atmosphere: Implications for Global Security. In *Challenge of Global Warming*, edited by D. E. Abrahamson. Washington, D.C.: Island Press, 44–62.

FIDH (Fédération Internationale des Ligues des Droits de l'Homme). 2007. Financial Statements. Available from www.fidh.org/spip.php? rubrique725.

Finnemore, Martha. 1996. *National Interests in International Society*. Ithaca, N.Y.: Cornell University Press.

Finnemore, Martha, and Kathryn Sikkink. 1999. Norm Dynamics and Political Change. In *Exploration and Contestation in the Study of World Politics*, edited by P. Katzenstein, R. Keohane, and S. Krasner. Cambridge, Mass.: MIT Press, 247–278.

Fletcher, Susan. 2001. RL30692: Global Climate Change: The Kyoto Protocol. Congressional Research Service. Available from ncseonline. org/NLE/CRs/abstract.cfm?NLEid=214.

Florini, Ann. 2000. *The Third Force: The Rise of Transnational Civil Society.* Washington, D.C.: Carnegie Endowment for International Peace.

Fukuda, Yasuo. 2008. Opening Remarks by HE Mr. Yasuo Fukuda, Prime Minister of Japan on the Occasion of "From Okinawa to Toyako: Dealing with Communicable Diseases as Global Human Security Threats." Japanese Ministry of Foreign Affairs, May 23. Available from www. mofa.go.jp/policy/health_c/remark0805.html.

Ganley, Elaine. 1995. Chirac Acknowledges French Role in World War II Deportations. Associated Press, July 16.

GAO (United States, Government Accountability Office) 2006. Spending Requirement Presents Challenges for Allocating Prevention Funding Under the President's Emergency Plan for AIDS Relief. Available from www.gao.gov/new.items/d06395.pdf.

——— 2007. Global Fund to Fight AIDS, TB and Malaria Has Improved Its Documentation of Funding Decisions but Needs Standardized Oversight Expectations and Assessments. Available from www.gao. gov/highlights/d07627high.pdf.

GAO (United States, Government Accounting Office). 2000. Debt Relief Initiative for Poor Countries Faces Challenges. GAO/NSIAD-00–161. Available from www.gao.gov/new.items/ns00161.pdf.

Garrett, Laurie. 2005. *HIV and National Security: Where Are the Links?* New York: Council on Foreign Relations.

Gellman, Barton. 2000. DEATH WATCH: The Global Response to AIDS in Africa; World Shunned Signs of the Coming Plague. *Washington Post,* July 5.

George, Alexander L., and Andrew Bennett. 2005. *Case Studies and Theory Development in the Social Sciences.* Cambridge, Mass.: MIT Press.

German Marshall Fund. 2006a. GMF Transatlantic Trade and Poverty Reduction Survey 2006: Topline Data October 2006. Available from www.gmfus.org/doc/TP2006_Toplines_v5_FINAL.pdf.

——— 2006b. Transatlantic Trends 2006. Available from www. transatlantictrends.org/trends/index_archive.cfm?year=2006.

——— 2007. GMF Transatlantic Trade and Poverty Reduction Survey 2007: Topline Data October 2007. Available from www.gmfus.org/ economics/tpsurvey/Trade_survey_2007_Topline_Data.pdf.

Glasius, Marlies. 2003. How Activists Shaped the Court. Crimes of War Project, December. Available from www.crimesofwar.org/icc_ magazine/icc-glasius.html#top.

Global AIDS Alliance. 2001. In Congress Today GAA Calls for Massive Fight to Stop AIDS, June 7. Available from www.globalaidsalliance. org/newsroom/press_releases/press060701/.

Global Fund. 2005. Pledges and Contributions. Available from www. theglobalfund.org/en/pledges/.

———. 2007. Pledges and Contributions, August 1. Available from www. theglobalfund.org/en/pledges/.

Globescan (formerly Environics International). 2002. Independent Poll Shows Drop in Kyoto Support but Little Trust in Proponents of Alternatives, November 22. Available from www.globescan.com/news_ archives/EIL_Kyoto_PR-Fin_Nov_22.pdf.

Goldberg, Jeffrey. 2006. The Believer: Michael Gerson, George W. Bush's Loyal Speechwriter. *New Yorker*, February 13.

Goldsmith, Jack, and Eric Posner. 2003–2004. International Agreements: A Rational Choice Approach. *Virginia Journal of International Law* 44: 113–143.

———. 2005. *The Limits of International Law.* Oxford, UK: Oxford University Press.

Goldstein, Judith, and Robert O. Keohane. 1993. *Ideas and Foreign Policy: Beliefs, Institutions, and Political Change.* Ithaca, N.Y.: Cornell University Press.

Goold, Benjamin. 2002. Ratifying the Rome Statute: Japan and the International Criminal Court. *Asia-Pacific News*, September. Available from www.hurights.or.jp/asia-pacific/no_29/05japanandicc.htm.

Gordon, Phillip H., and Jeremy Shapiro. 2004. *Allies at War: America, Europe, and the Crisis over Iraq.* New York: McGraw-Hill.

Gore, Albert. 2006. *An Inconvenient Truth: The Planetary Emergency of Global Warming and What We Can Do About It.* Emmaus, Pa.: Rodale Press.

Gorelick, Daniel. 2008. Law of the Sea Convention Enjoys Broad US Support. America.gov, November 2008. Available from www.america. gov/st/env-english/2008/November/20081120164958adkcilerog0. 3376581.html.

Gormley, William T. 1986. Regulatory Issue Networks in a Federal System. *Polity* 18 (Summer): 595–626.

Graham, Franklin. 2002a. Address at Prescription for Hope conference, Washington D.C.

———. 2002b. *The Name.* Nashville, Tenn.: Thomas Nelson Publishers.

Greenhill, Kelly. 2007. Extortive Engineered Migration: Asymmetric Weapon of the Weak. *Conflict, Security and Development* 2 (3): 105–116.

Greenhill, Kelly M., and Joshua W. Busby. 2009. Ain't That a Shame? Hypocrisy, Punishment, and Weak Actor Influence in International Politics. Unpublished paper, Tufts University/Harvard University and the University of Texas at Austin.

Greenpeace International. 1995. Greenpeace Climbers Still on Smokestack: Industrialised Nations Are Climate Killers, March 28. Available from archive.greenpeace.org/climate/berlin1995/index.html#report2.

Grubb, Michael, with Christiaan Vrolijk and Duncan Brack. 1999. *The Kyoto Protocol: A Guide and Assessment*. London: Royal Institute of International Affairs.

Grundmann, Reiner. 2002. Transnational Policy Networks and the Role of Advocacy Scientists: From Ozone Layer Protection to Climate Change. Paper read at 2001 Berlin Conference on the Human Dimensions of Global Environmental Change, Potsdam, Germany. Available from jobfunctions.bnet.com/abstract.aspx?docid=162618.

Grunwald, Michael. 1999. GOP's Bachus Makes Debt Relief His Mission. *Washington Post*, October 9.

Guardian, The. 1962. Britain's Role in World. December 6.

1999. Apocalyptic in America. September 20.

Gugele, Bernd, Kati Huttunen, and Manfred Ritter. 2003. Annual European Community Greenhouse Gas Inventory 1990–2001 and Inventory Report 2003. European Environment Agency. Available from reports.eea.eu.int/technical_report_2003_95/en/tech_95.pdf.

Guzman, Andrew T. 2002. A Compliance-Based Theory of International Law. *California Law Review* 90: 1823–1887.

2005. The Design of International Agreements. *European Journal of International Law* 16 (4): 579–612.

Haas, Peter M. 1992. Introduction: Epistemic Communities and International Policy Coordination. *International Organization* 46 (1): 1–35.

Habermas, Jürgen. 1996. *Between Facts and Norms*. Translated by W. Rehg. Cambridge, Mass.: MIT Press.

Hafner-Burton, Emily. 2008. Sticks and Stones: Naming and Shaming the Human Rights Enforcement Problem. *International Organization* 62 (4): 689–716.

Hafner-Burton, Emily, and Kiyoteru Tsutsui. 2005. Human Rights in a Globalizing World: The Paradox of Empty Promises. *American Journal of Sociology* 110 (5): 1373–1411.

Haigh, Nigel. 1996. Climate Change Policies and Politics in the European Community. In *Politics of Climate Change: A European Perspective*, edited by T. O'Riordan and J. Jager. London: Routledge, 155–185.

Hall, Peter A. 1989. *The Political Power of Economic Ideas: Keynesianism Across Nations.* Princeton, N.J.: Princeton University Press.

Harris Interactive. 2008. Should World Leaders Skip the Olympics? May 21. Available from www.harrisinteractive.com/harris_poll/index. asp?PID=909.

Harrison, Kathryn. 2007. The Road Not Taken: Climate Change Policy in Canada and the United States. *Global Environmental Politics* 7 (4): 92–117.

Harrison, Kathryn, and Lisa Sundstrom. 2007. The Comparative Politics of Climate Change. *Global Environmental Politics* 7 (4): 1–17.

Hathaway, Oona. 2002. Do Human Rights Treaties Make a Difference? *Yale Law Journal* 111 (8): 1935–2042.

Hawkins, Darren. 2004. Explaining Costly International Institutions: Persuasion and Enforceable Human Rights Norms. *International Studies Quarterly* 48 (4): 779–804.

Health GAP Coalition. 2001. Bush Aids Plan: PR Spectacle Instead of Desperately Needed Money for Aids in Africa, May 1. Available from www.healthgap.org/press_releases/01/051001_HGAP_PR_GWB_FUND.html.

Heavens, Andrew. 2009. China Urges Deferral of Bashir War Crimes Case. Reuters, January 7. Available from www.reuters.com/article/latestCrisis/idUSL7563091.

Hebert, H. Josef. 1997. Clinton Eyes Global Warming Plan. AP Online, October 9.

Hellerstein, Rebecca. 2004. Do Pharmaceutical Companies Price Discriminate Across Rich and Poor Countries? Federal Reserve Bank of New York. Available from www.ny.frb.org/research/economists/hellerstein/JDE2.pdf.

Henisz, Witold. 2000. The Institutional Environment for Economic Growth. *Economics and Politics* 12 (1): 1–31.

Henisz, Witold, and Bennet A. Zelner. 2006. Interest Groups, Veto Points, and Electricity Infrastructure Deployment. *International Organization* 60 (4): 263–286.

Hennessey, Peter. 2001. *The Prime Minister.* London: Penguin Books.

Herskovitz, Jon. Undated. Case Study: Japan's Banking Crisis. Unpublished paper, Initiative for Policy Dialogue, Columbia University.

Hertel, Shareen. 2006. *Unexpected Power: Conflict and Change Among Transnational Activists.* Ithaca, N.Y.: Cornell University Press.

Hertzke, Allen D. 2004. *Freeing God's Children: The Unlikely Alliance for Global Human Rights.* Lanham, Md.: Rowman & Littlefield.

Higashizawa, Yasushi. 2007. Experiences in Japan for the Coming Accession to the Rome Statute. Paper read at the Symposium on the International Criminal Court, February 3–4, Beijing, China. Available from www.icclr.law.ubc.ca/sitemap/icc/japanexperience.pdf.

Hochschild, Adam. 1998. *King Leopold's Ghost: A Story of Greed, Terror, and Heroism in Colonial Africa.* Boston: Houghton Mifflin.

Hoge, Warren. 2005. UN Will Refer Darfur Crimes to Court in Hague. *New York Times,* April 2.

Holsti, K. J. 1987. Toward a Theory of Foreign Policy: Making the Case for Role Analysis. In Walker 1987, 5–43.

Hoover, Dennis. 2001. What Would Moses Do? Debt Relief in the Jubilee Year. *Religion in the News.* Available from www.trincoll.edu/depts/csrpl/RINVol4No1/jubilee_2000.htm.

Horiuchi, Ambassador Shinsuke. 1999. Ceilings on Debt Relief Are Not "God-Given." *Africa Recovery* 13 (2–3): 33.

Huber, Evelyne, Charles Ragin, John D. Stephens, David Brady, and Jason Beckfield. 2004. Comparative Welfare States Data Set. Northwestern University, University of North Carolina, Duke University, and Indiana University. Available from www.lisproject.org/publications/welfaredata/welfareaccess.htm.

Huber, Evelyne, and John D. Stephens. 2001. *Development and Crisis of the Welfare State: Parties and Policies in Global Markets.* Chicago: University of Chicago Press.

Human Rights Watch. 2007. Financial Statements Year Ended June 30, 2007. Available from www.hrw.org/sites/default/files/related_material/finStmt2007.pdf.

ICC (International Criminal Court). 2002. Rome Statute of the International Criminal Court. Available from www2.icc-cpi.int/Menus/ICC/Legal+Texts+and+Tools/Official+Journal/Rome+Statute.htm.

———. 2004. Reports of the Committee on Budget and Finance, March. Available from www.icc-cpi.int/iccdocs/asp_docs/library/asp/ICC-ASP-3–18-Addl-Addendum_English.pdf.

———. 2008a. Frequently Asked Questions. Available from www2.icc-cpi.int/Menus/ICC/About+the+Court/Frequently+asked+Questions/.

———. 2008b. Stay of Proceedings in the Lubanga Case Is Lifted: Trial Provisionally Scheduled for 26 January 2009, November 18. Available from www.icc-cpi.int.

———. 2009. State Parties to the Rome Statute, July 19. Available from www2.icc-cpi.int/Menus/ASP/states+parties/.

———. Undated. Situations and Cases. Available from www2.icc-cpi.int/Menus/ICC/Situations+and+Cases/.

ICC (International Criminal Court), Office of the Prosecutor. 2006. Iraq Response. International Criminal Court, February 9. Available from www.icc-cpi.int.

ICTJ (International Center for Transitional Justice). 2007. When the War Ends: A Population-Based Survey on Attitudes About Peace, Justice, and Social Reconstruction in Northern Uganda. Reliefweb, December 18. Available from www.reliefweb.int/rw/rwb.nsf/db900SID/EMAE-79ZSZP?OpenDocument.

2008. Living with Fear: A Population-Based Survey on Attitudes About Peace, Justice and Social Reconstruction in Eastern Democratic Republic of Congo. Reliefweb, August 26. Available from www.reliefweb.int/rw/rwb.nsf/db900SID/ASAZ-7HVBFR?OpenDocument.

Ikenberry, G. John. 2001–2002. American Grand Strategy in the Age of Terror. *Survival* 43 (4): 19–34.

2003. Is American Multilateralism in Decline? *Perspectives on Politics*. September: 533–550.

2004a. The End of the Neo-Conservative Moment. *Survival* 46: 7–22.

2004b. The Illusions of Empire: Defining the New American Order. *Foreign Affairs* 83 (2) (Mar.–Apr.): 144–154.

2005. Creating America's World: The Sources of Postwar Liberal Internationalism. Paper read at The Future of American Internationalism, October 7–8, Austin, Texas.

ed. 2002. *America Unrivaled: The Future of the Balance of Power*. Ithaca, N.Y.: Cornell University Press.

Ikenberry, G. John, and Charles Kupchan. 1990. Socialization and Hegemonic Power. *International Organization* 44 (3): 283–315.

IMF (International Monetary Fund). 1998. The Initiative for Heavily Indebted Poor Countries Review and Outlook. Available from www.imf.org/external/np/hipc/review/hipcrev.pdf.

2005. World Economic Outlook, September. Available from www.imf.org/external/pubs/ft/weo/2005/02/data/index.htm.

2007. Heavily Indebted Poor Countries (HIPC) Initiative and Multilateral Debt Relief Initiative (MDRI): Status of Implementation, August 28. Available from www.imf.org/external/np/pp/2007/eng/08 2807.pdf.

2008. World Economic Outlook, October. Available from www.imf.org/external/pubs/ft/weo/2008/02/index.htm.

Inglehart, Ronald. 2005. European and World Values Surveys Integrated Data File, 1999–2002, Release I. Inter-University Consortium for Political and Social Research. Available from www.worldvaluessurvey.org/.

International Institute for Strategic Studies. 1998. *The Military Balance 1998–1999*. London: International Institute for Strategic Studies.

1999. *The Military Balance 1999–2000*. London: International Institute for Strategic Studies.

2000. *The Military Balance 2000–2001*. London: International Institute for Strategic Studies.

IPCC (Intergovernmental Panel on Climate Change). 2001. Climate Change 2001. Working Group III: Mitigation. Available from www.ipcc. ch/ipccreports/tar/vol4/english/192.htm.

IPS (Inter Press Service). 1998. *Terraviva – The Conference Daily Newspaper – UN Conference for the Establishment of an International Criminal Court*, July 18. Available from www.ips.org/icc/.

Islam, Shafiqul, ed. 1991. *Yen for Development: Japanese Foreign Aid and the Politics of Burden-Sharing*. New York: Council on Foreign Relations Press.

Jacobsen, John Kurt. 1995. Much Ado About Ideas: The Cognitive Factor in Economic Policy. *World Politics* 47 (2): 283–310.

JANIC (Japanese NGO Center for International Cooperation). 2001–2004. *Background of the Growth of Japanese NGOs*. Available from www. janic.org/en/en-index.html.

Japan, Cabinet Office. 2002. *Opinion Survey on Foreign Affairs*. Public Relations Office, Cabinet Office, December 24. Available from www. jinjapan.org/stat/stats/22OPN43.html.

2004. Public Opinion Survey on Diplomacy by the Cabinet Office of Japan (abridged). Available from www.mansfieldfdn.org/polls/2005/poll-05–6.htm.

2005. Public Opinion Survey on Diplomacy by the Cabinet Office of Japan (abridged). Available from www.mansfieldfdn.org/polls/2005/poll-05–12.htm.

2006. Public Opinion Survey on Diplomacy by the Cabinet Office of Japan (abridged). Available from www.mansfieldfdn.org/polls/2006/poll-06–17.htm.

Japan, House of Representatives. Undated. Guide to the House. Available from www.shugiin.go.jp/index.nsf/html/index_e_guide.htm.

Japan, Ministry of Foreign Affairs. 1999. Japan's ODA Annual Report 1999: Section 3 Efforts to Help Heavily Indebted Poor Countries, December 2. Available from www.mofa.go.jp/policy/oda/summary/1999/ov2_1_06.html.

Japan Center for International Exchange. 2005. Japan's Nonprofit Sector Fights AIDS. *Civil Society Monitor*, October. Available from www. jcie.or.jp/civilnet/monitor/11.pdf.

2007a. Breaking New Ground for NGO Advocacy in Japan. *Civil Society Monitor*, August. Available from www.jcie.org/researchpdfs/CSM/CSM_No12.pdf.

2007b. Challenges in Global Health and Japan's Contributions: Research and Dialogue Project, November 6. Available from www.jcie.or.jp/thinknet/takemi_project/.

Japan Forum on International Relations. 1998. *Japan's ODA in the 21st Century*. Tokyo: Japan Forum on International Relations.

Japan Times. 2002a. Lower House Approves Ratification of Kyoto Pact, May 22. Available from search.japantimes.co.jp/cgi-bin/np20020522a1.html.

2002b. Toothless Global-Warming Bill, May 1. Available from search.japantimes.co.jp/cgi-bin/ed20020501a1.html.

Joachim, Jutta. 2003. Framing Issues and Seizing Opportunities: The UN, NGO's and Women's Rights. *International Studies Quarterly* 47 (2): 247–274.

Jones, Bryan D. 1994. *Reconceiving Decision-Making in Democratic Politics*. Chicago: University of Chicago Press.

2001. *Politics and the Architecture of Choice: Bounded Rationality and Governance*. Chicago: University of Chicago Press.

Jospin, M. Lionel. 1998. Prime Minister's Visit to the US. Embassy of France in the United States, June 19. Available from info-france-usa.org/news/statmnts/jospin/npc-us.htm.

JPOLL (Roper Center J-Poll Japanese Public Opinion Database). 1998. Yomiuri Shimbun National Poll. Yomiuri Shimbun, July 23. Available from www.ropercenter.uconn.edu/jpoll/JPOLL.html.

Undated. The Japanese Public Opinion Database. Available from www.ropercenter.uconn.edu/jpoll/JPOLL.html.

Jubilee 2000. 2000a. An Emerging Scandal. Available from www.jubileeresearch.org/jubilee2000/reports/scandal.html.

2000b. G7 All Promise 100% Cancellation – But Debt Relief Is Still a Long Way off. Available from www.jubilee 2000uk.org/jubilee2000/news/cancel100400.html.

Undated-a. Milestones in the Campaign. Available from www.jubileeresearch.org/jubilee 2000/about.html#milestones.

Undated-b. Too Little. Too Late. Available from www.jubileeresearch.org/jubilee 2000/politic.html.

Jubilee+. 2001. Malawi's Precedent Setting Debt Relief Is Not Enough, May 1. Available from www.jubileeplus.org/worldnews/africa/malawi_debt_relief.htm.

Undated. What We Achieved: First Steps On Debt Cancellation. Available from www.jubileeplus.org/analysis/reports/world_never_same_again/what.htm.

Justus, John R., and Susan R. Fletcher. 2001. IB89005: Global Climate Change. CRS Issue Brief for Congress, April 11. Available from

www.ncseonline.org/NLE/CRSreports/Climate/clim-2.cfm?&CFID=
12157640&CFTOKEN=35944970.

Kagan, Robert. 2002. Power and Weakness. *Policy Review* 113: 3–28.

2003. *Of Paradise and Power*. New York: Alfred A. Knopf.

2004a. A Tougher War for the US Is One of Legitimacy. *New York Times*, January 24.

2004b. America's Crisis of Legitimacy. *Foreign Affairs* 83 (2): 65–87.

Kahn, Joseph. 2000. Leaders in Congress Agree to Debt Relief for Poor Nations. *New York Times*, October 18.

Kahneman, Daniel. 2003. Maps of Bounded Rationality: Psychology for Behavioral Economics. *American Economic Review* 93 (5): 1449–1475.

Kaiser Family Foundation. 2005a. Survey of G7 Nations on HIV Spending in Developing Countries, July. Available from www.kff.org/hivaids/upload/Survey-of-G7-Nations-on-HIV-Spending-in-Developing-Countries-Chartpack.pdf.

2005b. The Global HIV/AIDS Epidemic, November. Available from www.kff.org/hivaids/upload/ 3030–06.pdf.

2006a. 2006 Kaiser Family Foundation Survey of Americans on HIV/AIDS. Available from www.kff.org/kaiserpolls/upload/Chartpack-2006-Survey-of-Americans-on-HIV-AIDS.pdf.

2006b. OGAC's Abstinence, Faithfulness Requirements for PEP-FAR Confusing, Undercutting Other HIV-Prevention Efforts, GAO Report Says, April 5. Available from www.kaisernetwork.org/Daily_reports/rep_index.cfm&DR_ID=36429.

2008. Slideshow: Donor Funding for Global Health, 2001–2006, July 28. Available from facts.kff.org/results.aspx/view=slides&detail=22.

Kallenbach, Michael. 2001a. Soldiers Risk Accusations of Committing War Crimes. *Daily Telegraph*, April 11.

2001b. Tory Fears for Troops Fail to Persuade Lords. *Daily Telegraph*, March 9.

Kameyama, Yasuko. 2001. Japan: Struggling to Achieve 6%. *German Foreign Policy in Dialogue* 2 (6): 19–22.

2003. Climate Change as Japanese Foreign Policy: From Reactive to Proactive. In *Global Warming and East Asia*, edited by P. G. Harris. London: Routledge, 135–151.

Kane, Tim. 2004. Global US Troop Deployment, 1950–2003. Heritage Foundation, October 27. Available from www.heritage.org/Research/NationalSecurity/cd a04–11.cfm.

Kapstein, Ethan, and Josh Busby. 2009. Making Markets for Merit Goods: The Political Economy of Antiretrovirals. Washington, D.C.: Center for Global Development. Available from www.cgdev.

org/content/publications/detail/142 2655/. Also in *Global Policy* 1 (1): 75–90.

Kassalow, Jordan. 2001. Why Health Is Important to US Foreign Policy. Council on Foreign Relations and Milbank Memorial Fund, May. Available from www.milbank.org/reports/Foreignpolicy.html.

Kates, Jennifer. 2005. Financing the Response to HIV/AIDS in Low- and Middle-Income Countries: Funding for HIV/AIDS from the G7 and the European Commission. Washington, D.C.: Kaiser Family Foundation. Available from www.kff.org/hivaids/global.cfm.

——— 2006. International Assistance for HIV/AIDS in the Developing World: Taking Stock of the G8, Other Donor Governments and the European Commission. Washington, D.C.: Kaiser Family Foundation. Available from www.kff.org/hivaids/7344.cfm.

Kates, Jennifer, José-Antonio Izazola, and Eric Lief. 2007. Financing the Response to AIDS in Low- and Middle-Income Countries: International Assistance from the G8, European Commission and Other Donor Governments, 2006. Washington, D.C.: Kaiser Family Foundation. Available from www.kff.org/hivaids/upload/7347_03.pdf.

——— 2008. Financing the Response to AIDS in Low- and Middle-Income Countries: International Assistance from the G8, European Commission and Other Donor Governments, 2007. Washington, D.C.: Kaiser Family Foundation. Available from www.kff.org/hivaids/upload/7347_04–2.pdf.

Kates, Jennifer, and Todd Summers. 2004. US Government Funding for Global HIV/AIDS Through FY2005. Washington, D.C.: Kaiser Family Foundation. Available from www.kff.org/hivaids/global.cfm.

Kato, Kozo. 2002. *The Web of Power: Japanese and German Development Cooperation Policy*. Lanham, Md.: Lexington Books.

Katsouris, Christina. 1998. Pressure Grows for Faster Debt Reduction. *Africa Recovery* 12 (1): 1. Available from www.un.org/ecosocdev/geninfo/afrec/subjindx/121debt.htm.

Katzenstein, Peter J., ed. 1996. *The Culture of National Security: Norms and Identity in World Politics*. New York: Columbia University Press.

Kaufmann, Chaim D., and Robert A. Pape. 1999. Explaining Costly International Moral Action: Britain's Sixty-Year Campaign Against the Atlantic Slave Trade. *International Organization* 53 (4): 631–668.

Kaul, Hans-Peter. 1998. Special Note: The Struggle for the International Criminal Court. *European Journal of Crime, Criminal Law and Criminal Justice* 6 (4): 364–376.

——— 1999. Breakthrough in Rome: The Statute of the International Criminal Court. *Law and State* 59/60: 114–130.

Kawashima, Yasuko. 2001. Japan and Climate Change: Responses and Explanations. *Energy and Environment* 12 (2/3): 167–179.

Kawashima, Yasuko, and Sayaka Akino. 2001. Climate Change and Security: Regional Conflict as a New Dimension of the Climate Change. *Global Environmental Research* 5 (1): 33–43.

Keck, Margaret E., and Kathryn Sikkink. 1998. *Activists Beyond Borders: Advocacy in International Politics.* Ithaca, N.Y.: Cornell University Press.

Keefer, Philip, and David Stasavage. 2003. The Limits of Delegation: Veto Players, Central Bank Independence and the Credibility of Monetary Policy. *American Political Science Review* 97 (3): 407–423.

Keele University. Undated. Election Manifestos. Available from www. politicsresources.net/area/uk/man.htm.

Kelley, Judith. 2007. Who Keeps International Commitments and Why? The International Criminal Court and Bilateral Non-Surrender Agreements. *American Political Science Review* 101 (3): 573–589.

Keohane, Robert O. 1982. The Demand for International Regimes. *International Organization* 36 (2): 332–355.

1986. Reciprocity in International Relations. *International Organization* 40 (1): 1–28.

2002. Rational Choice Theory and International Law: Insights and Limitations. *Journal of Legal Studies* 31: S307–S319.

2005. Ironies of Sovereignty: The European Union and the United States. In *American Foreign Policy: Theoretical Essays*, edited by G. J. Ikenberry. New York: Pearson/Longman, 290–309.

Keohane, Robert, and Helen Milner, eds. 1996. *Internationalization and Domestic Politics.* Cambridge, UK: Cambridge University Press.

Kerr, Richard A. 2000. Too Little, Too Late, at the Climate Talks. *Science* 290 (5497): 1663.

Kessler, Glenn. 2003. Blair's Wife Faults Bush's Opposition to International Court. *Washington Post*, November 18.

Khong, Yuen Foong. 1992. *Analogies at War: Korea, Munich, Dien Bien Phu, and the Vietnam Decisions of 1965.* Princeton, N.J.: Princeton University Press.

2005. Seduction by Analogy in Vietnam: The Malaya and Korea Analogies. In *American Foreign Policy: Theoretical Essays*, edited by G. J. Ikenberry. New York: Pearson/Longman, 501–510.

King, Gary, Robert Keohane, and Sidney Verba. 1994. *Designing Social Inquiry.* Princeton, N.J.: Princeton University Press.

Kingdon, John. 1995. *Agendas, Alternatives, and Public Policies*, 2nd ed. New York: Addison-Wesley Longman.

Kluger, Jeffrey. 2001. A Climate of Despair. *Time*, April 1. Available from www.time.com/time/magazine/article/0,9171,104596,00.html.

Koelbl, Susanne, and Alexander Szandar. 2008. US Demands More German Troops at Taliban Front, February 1. Available from www.spiegel.de/international/world/0,1518,532476,00.html.

Koizumi, Junichiro. 2005. Address by Prime Minister Junichiro Koizumi at the Commemorative Symposium on the Fifth Anniversary of the Kyusyu–Okinawa Summit "East Asian Regional Response to HIV/AIDS, Tuberculosis and Malaria," June 30. Available from www.mofa.go.jp/policy/health_c/gfatm/address0506.html.

Kolb, Felix. 2007. *Protest and Opportunities: The Political Outcomes of Social Movements*. Chicago: University of Chicago Press.

Kowert, Paul, and Jeffrey Legro. 1996. Norms, Identity, and Their Limits: A Theoretical Reprise. In Katzenstein 1996, 451–497.

Kralev, Nicholas. 2000. Political Punch in a Package of Charm. *Financial Times*, February 26.

Krause, Joachim. 2004. Multilateralism: Behind European Views. *Washington Quarterly* **27** (3): 43–59.

Krebs, Ronald, and Patrick Jackson. 2007. Twisting Tongues and Twisting Arms: The Power of Political Rhetoric. *European Journal of International Relations* **13** (1): 35–66.

Krotz, Ulrich. 2001. National Role Conceptions and Foreign Policies: France and Germany Compared. Unpublished paper, Harvard University. Available from www.ces.fas.harvard.edu/publications/docs/pdfs/Krotz.pdf.

Krugman, Paul. 1988. Financing Versus Forgiving a Debt Overhang. *Journal of Development Economics* **29** (3): 253–268.

Kupchan, Charles. 2002. *The End of the American Era*. New York: Alfred A. Knopf.

Kupchan, Charles, and Peter Trubowitz. 2007. Dead Center: The Demise of Liberal Internationalism in America. *International Security* **32** (2): 7–44.

Kyodo News International. 2001a. 64% of Those Familiar with Kyoto Pact Want Japan to Lead, July 16. Available from findarticles.com/p/articles/mi_m0XPQ/is_2001_July_16/ai_77058105/pg_1.

——— 2001b. Pronk Criticizes Japan for Wavering on Climate Treaty, July 10. Available from findarticles.com/p/articles/mi_m0XPQ/is_/ai_77058116.

Labour Party (UK). 1997. New Labour Because Britain Deserves Better. Available from www.politicsresources.net/area/uk/man/lab97.htm.

Lake, David A., and Robert Powell. 1999. *Strategic Choice and International Relations*. Princeton, N.J.: Princeton University Press.

Lancaster, Carol. 1999. *Aid to Africa: So Much to Do, So Little Done.* Chicago: University of Chicago Press.

Larson, Deborah Welch. 1997. *Anatomy of Mistrust: US–Soviet Relations During the Cold War.* Ithaca, N.Y.: Cornell University Press.

Larson, Deborah Welch, and Alexei Shevchenko. 2005. Status and Power in a Unilateral World. Paper read at American Political Science Association meeting, September 1–4, Washington, D.C.

Lebow, Richard Ned. 1985. Generational Learning and Conflict Management. *International Journal* 40: 555–85.

———. 2005. Fear, Interest, and Honor: A Theory of International Relations. Paper read at American Political Science Association meeting, September 1–4, Washington, D.C.

Lederer, Edith. 2002. Both Sides Bruised After US Deal over War Crimes Court. Associated Press, July 14. Available from www.globalpolicy. org/security/peacekpg/us/2002/0714sol.htm.

Lee, Henry, Vicki Arroyo Cochran, and Manik Roy. 2001. US Domestic Climate Change Policy. *Climate Policy* 1: 381–395.

Lee, Roy S., ed. 1999. *The International Criminal Court: Making of the Rome Statute.* The Hague: Kluwer Law International.

Lefkowitz, Jay. 2009. AIDS and the President: An Inside Account. *Commentary*, January: 24–29. Available from www.commentarymagazine.com/ viewarticle.cfm/aids-and-the-president–an-inside-account-14057.

Leggett, Jeremy, ed. 1999. *The Carbon War.* New York: Routledge.

Legro, Jeffrey W. 1997. Which Norms Matter? Revisiting the "Failure" of Internationalism. *International Organization* 51 (1): 31–63.

———. 2005a. Making the Coalition that Made US Liberal Internationalism. Paper read at The Future of American Internationalism, October 7–8, Austin, Texas.

———. 2005b. *Rethinking the World: Great Power Strategies and International Order.* Ithaca, N.Y.: Cornell University Press.

Lepgold, Joseph. 2001. Reassessing the Roots of American Ambivalence Toward Multilateralism. Paper read at annual meeting of the American Political Science Association, August–September, San Francisco, California.

Levi, Margaret. 1997. A Model, a Method, and a Map: Rational Choice in Comparative and Historical Analysis. In *Comparative Politics: Rationality, Culture and Structure*, edited by Mark Lichbach and Alan Zuckerman. Cambridge, UK: Cambridge University Press, 19–41.

Levy, Marc A. 1993. European Acid Rain: The Power of Tote-Board Diplomacy. In *Institutions for the Earth: Sources of Effective International Environmental Protection*, edited by P. M. Haas, R. O. Keohane, and M. A. Levy. Cambridge, Mass.: MIT Press, 75–132.

Lewis, Neil A. 2002. US to Renounce Its Role in Pact for World Tribunal. *New York Times*, May 5.

Lincoln, Edward W. 1993. *Japan's New Global Role*. Washington, D.C.: Brookings Institution Press.

Lipson, Charles. 1981. The International Organization of Third World Debt. *International Organization* 35 (4): 603–631.

Litfin, Karen. 1995. Framing Science: Precautionary Discourse and the Ozone Treaties. *Millennium* 24 (2): 251–277.

Lomborg, Bjorn, ed. 2004. *Global Crises, Global Solutions*. Cambridge, UK: Cambridge University Press.

Lowenheim, Oded. 2003. "Do Ourselves Credit and Render a Lasting Service to Mankind": British Moral Prestige, Humanitarian Intervention, and the Barbary Pirates. *International Studies Quarterly* 47 (1): 23–48.

Lumsdaine, David Halloran. 1993. *Moral Vision in International Politics: The Foreign Aid Regime, 1949–1989*. Princeton, N.J.: Princeton University Press.

Lynch, Colum. 2002. EU Ratifies Global Warming Treaty. *Washington Post*, June 1.

MacAskill, Ewen. 1998. Short's Debt Lifeline for Africa's Poorest. *Guardian*, October 1.

MacAskill, Ewen, David Pallister, and Richard Norton-Taylor. 1998. Write Off Debt, Say Agencies. *Guardian*, May 12.

Mallaby, Sebastian. 2000. Why So Stingy on Foreign Aid? *Washington Post*, June 27.

———. 2004. *World's Banker: A Story of Failed States, Financial Crises, and the Wealth and Poverty of Nations*. London: Penguin Books.

Mannheim, Karl. 1952. *Essays on the Sociology of Knowledge*. London: Routledge & Paul.

Mansfield, Edward D., Helen Milner, and John Pevehouse. 2005. Vetoing Cooperation: The Impact of Veto Players on International Trade Agreements. Paper read at American Political Science Association meeting, February, Washington, D.C.

Mansfield Asian Opinion Poll Database. 2007. Yomiuri Shimbun May 2007 Opinion Polls. Available from mansfieldfdn.org/polls/2007/poll-07–24.htm.

———. 2008. List of Polls. Available from mansfieldfdn.org/polls/polls_listing.htm.

March, James G., and Johan P. Olsen. 1998. The Institutional Dynamics of International Political Orders. *International Organization* 52 (4): 943–969.

Markey, Daniel. 2000. The Prestige Motive in International Relations. Ph.D. thesis, Department of Politics, Princeton University, Princeton, N.J.

Martens, Christiane N., and Paul V. Rafferty. 2002. COP 6: An Unusual Blend Of Failure and Success. *UN Observer*, November 2. Available from www.unobserver.com/printen.php?id=22.

Masaki, Hisane. 2001. Japan Ready to Seek Ratification of Kyoto Protocol. *Japan Times*, October 12. Available from www.japantimes.co. jp/cgi-bin/getarticle.pl5?nn2001 1012a4.htm.

———. 2006. JBIC Also Bankrolls Kyoto Projects. OhmyNews, December 22. Available from english.ohmynews.com/articleview/article_view. asp?no=336209&rel_no=1.

Mathews, Jessica. 1997. Power Shift. *Foreign Affairs* 76 (1): 50–66.

Mayhew, David R. 1974. *Congress: The Electoral Connection*. New Haven, Conn.: Yale University Press.

Mazetti, Mark. 2006. US Cuts in Africa Aid Said to Hurt War on Terror. *New York Times*, July 23.

McAdam, Doug, John D. McCarthy, and Mayer Zald. 1996. *Comparative Perspectives on Social Movements*. Cambridge, UK: Cambridge University Press.

McDonnell, Ida, Henri-Bernard Solignac Lecomte, and Liam Wegimont. 2003a. Public Opinion and the Fight Against Poverty. OECD Development Centre Studies. Available from www.oecd.org/document/ 31/0,2340,en_2649_33731_2498143_1_1_1_1,00.html.

———. 2003b. Public Opinion Research, Global Education and Development Co-operation Reform: In Search of a Virtuous Circle. OECD Development Centre, March. Available from www.oecd.org/dataoecd/39/ 8/1840009.pdf.

McElroy, Robert W. 1992. *Morality and American Foreign Policy: The Role of Ethics in International Affairs*. Princeton, N.J.: Princeton University Press.

McManus, Mike. 1999. Jubilee 2000: Debt Relief for the Poor. *Birmingham News*, October 17.

Mead, Walter Russell. 2001. Back to the Future. *Newsweek*, December 3.

Midford, Paul. 2002. The Logic of Reassurance and Japan's Grand Strategy. *Security Studies* 11 (3): 1–43.

Milner, Helen. 1997. *Interests, Institutions, and Information: Domestic Politics and International Relations*. Princeton, N.J.: Princeton University Press.

Moravcsik, Andrew. 1997. Taking Preferences Seriously: A Liberal Theory of International Politics. *International Organization* 51 (4): 513–554.

———. 2005. The Paradox of US Human Rights Policy. In *American Exceptionalism and Human Rights*, edited by M. Ignatieff. Princeton, N.J.: Princeton University Press, 147–197.

Mori, Yoshiro. 2001. Statement by Former Prime Minister Yoshiro Mori, Head of Delegation of Japan, at the United Nations Special Session on HIV/AIDS. Japan, Ministry of Foreign Affairs, June 25. Available from www.mofa.go.jp/policy/pop_aids/session0106/state.html.

Morrisette, Peter M. 1991. The Montreal Protocol: Lessons for Formulating Policies for Global Warming. *Policy Studies Journal* 19 (2): 152–161.

Morrissey, Wayne A. 1998. Global Climate Change: A Concise History of Negotiations and Chronology of Major Activities Preceding the 1992 UN Framework Convention. Congressional Research Service. Available from ncseonline.org/nle/crsreports/climate/clim-6.cfm.

  2000. RL30522: Global Climate Change: A Survey of Scientific Research and Policy Reports. Congressional Research Service. Available from ncseonline.org/Nle/Crsreports/climate/clim-24.cfm.

Morrow, James D. 1994. *Game Theory for Political Scientists*. Princeton, N.J.: Princeton University Press.

  1999. The Strategic Setting of Choices: Signaling, Commitment, and Negotiation in International Politics. In Lake and Powell 1999, 77–114.

Müller, Benito. 2000. The Hague Climate Conference: Impressions of the North American Press Coverage, December. Available from www.oxfordclimatepolicy.org/publications/hague.pdf.

Murray, Shoon Kathleen. 1996. *Anchors Against Change: American Opinion Leaders' Beliefs After the Cold War*. Ann Arbor: University of Michigan Press.

Naimon, Jon, and Debra S. Knopman. 1999. Reframing the Climate Change Debate. Progressive Policy Institute, November 1. Available from www.ppionline.org/ppi_ci.cfm?knlgAreaID=116&subsecID=149&contentID=1348.

Nankani, Gobind, and Timothy Geithner. 2003. Enhanced HIPC Initiative: Creditor Participation Issues. International Monetary Fund, April 8. Available from www.imf.org/external/np/hipc/2003/creditor/040803.pdf.

Nanto, Dick K. 2004. 9/11 Terrorism: Global Economic Costs. Congressional Research Service, October 5. Available from digital.library.unt.edu/govdocs/crs/permalink/meta-crs-7725:1.

Nau, Henry R. 2002. *At Home Abroad: Identity and Power in American Foreign Policy*. Ithaca, N.Y.: Cornell University Press.

No Peace Without Justice. Undated. NPWJ's Judicial Assistance Program (JAP). Available from www.npwj.org/No+Peace+Without+Justice/International+Criminal+Justice/ICJP+Priorities/Judicial+Assistance+Program.

Noguchi, Motoo. 2006. Criminal Justice in Asia and Japan and the International Criminal Court. *International Criminal Law Review* 6: 585–604.

Nolte, Georg. 2003. The United States and the International Criminal Court. In *Unilateralism and US Foreign Policy: International Perspectives*, edited by D. Malone and Y. F. Khong. Boulder, Colo.: Lynne Rienner, 71–93.

Nye, Joseph. 1990. Soft Power. *Foreign Policy* 80: 153–171.

——— 2003. *The Paradox of American Power: Why the World's Only Superpower Can't Go It Alone*. Oxford, UK: Oxford University Press.

——— 2004. *Soft Power: The Means to Success in World Politics*. New York: Public Affairs.

Oberthür, Sebastian, and Hermann E. Ott. 1999. *The Kyoto Protocol: International Climate Policy for the 21st Century*. Berlin: Springer.

Observer, The. 2005. Interview: Admiral Sir Michael Boyce, May 1. Available from observer.guardian.co.uk/politics/story/0,6903, 1474607,00.html.

OECD (Organisation for Economic Co-operation and Development). 2006. International Development Statistics Online. Available from www. oecd.org/dataoecd/50/17/5037721.htm.

——— 2007. Statistics. Available from stats.oecd.org/wbos/default.aspx.

Ohta, Hiroshi. 1995. Japan's Politics and Diplomacy of Climate Change. Ph.D. thesis, Columbia University, New York.

Olson, Mancur. 1965. *The Logic of Collective Action: Public Goods and the Theory of Groups*. Cambridge, Mass.: Harvard University Press.

O'Neill, Barry. 1999. *Honor, Symbols, and War*. Ann Arbor: University of Michigan Press.

Orr, Robert M. 1990. *The Emergence of Japan's Foreign Aid Power*. New York: Columbia University Press.

Ott, Hermann E. 1998. The Kyoto Protocol: Unfinished Business. *Environment* July–August: 16–20, 41–45.

Oxfam. 1998. Making Debt Relief Work: A Test of Political Will. Oxfam International Position Paper. Available from www.id21. org/id21ext/9brn1.html.

——— 2002. False Hope or New Start? June. Available from www.oxfam. org/en/policy/bp0206.

——— 2007. The World Is Still Waiting, May. Available from www.oxfam. de/download/the_world_is_still_waiting.pdf.

Padgett, John, and Christopher Ansell. 1993. Robust Action and the Rise of the Medici, 1400–1434. *American Journal of Sociology* 98 (6): 1259–1319.

Parker, Andrew. 2001. Cook Reassures MPs over War Crimes Court Prosecutions of British Soldiers. *Financial Times*, April 4.

Parker, Larry, and John Blodget. 1998. Global Climate Change: Reducing Greenhouse Gases – How Much from What Baseline?

Congressional Research Service. Available from ncseonline.org/ NLE/crsreports/climate/clim-13.cfm.

Parsons, Craig. 2003. *A Certain Idea of Europe*. Ithaca, N.Y.: Cornell University Press.

Passell, Peter. 1997. Wanted: A Global Warming Policy that Stands a Chance. *New York Times*, October 2.

Pattberg, Philipp. 2005. What Role for Private Rule-Making in Global Environmental Governance? Analysing the Forest Stewardship Council (FSC). *International Environmental Agreements* 5 (2): 175–189.

Patterson, Amy. 2006. *The Politics of AIDS in Africa*. Boulder, Colo.: Lynne Rienner.

Payne, Rodger. 2001. Persuasion, Frames and Norm Construction. *European Journal of International Relations* 7 (1): 37–61.

PBS (Public Broadcasting Service). 2000. National Security Threat. NewsHour with Jim Lehrer Transcript, May 2. Available from www.pbs. org/newshour/bb/health/jan-june00/aids_threat_ 5–2.html.

——— 2006. Interview with Franklin Graham. Frontline, May 30. Available from www.pbs.org/wgbh/pages/frontline/aids/interviews/graham.html.

Pempel, T. J. 1978. Japanese Foreign Economic Policy: The Domestic Bases for International Behavior. In *Between Power and Plenty*, edited by P. J. Katzenstein. Madison: University of Wisconsin Press, 139–190.

Peterson, Jonathan. 2001. The Rock Star, the Pope, and the World's Poor. *Los Angeles Times*, January 7.

Peterson, M. J. 1992. Whalers, Cetologists, Environmentalists, and the International Management of Whaling. *International Organization* 46 (1): 147–186.

Peterson, Susan. 2002/2003. Epidemic Disease and National Security. *Security Studies* 12 (2): 43–81.

Peterson, Susan, and Stephen Shellman. 2006. AIDS and Violent Conflict: Indirect Effects of Disease on National Security. Unpublished paper, College of William and Mary. Available from www.wm. edu/irtheoryandpractice/security/papers/AIDS.pdf.

Petty, Richard E., and John T. Cacioppo. 1981. *Attitudes and Persuasion: Classic and Contemporary Approaches*. Dubuque, Iowa: W. C. Brown.

——— 1986. *Communication and Persuasion: Central and Peripheral Routes to Attitude Change*. New York: Springer-Verlag.

Pew Center on Global Climate Change. 2001a. Conference of the Parties 6 (COP 6) Bis, Bonn, Germany, July. Available from www.pewclimate. org/what_s_being_done/in_the_world/cop_6_germany/index.cfm.

——— 2001b. Conference of the Parties 7 (COP 7) Climate Talks in Marrakech, Morocco, November. Available from www.pewclimate.org/what_s_ being_done/in_the_world/cop_7_morocco/.

Pew Research Center. 2006. Conflicting Views in a Divided World. Available from pewglobal.org/reports/pdf/DividedWorld2006.pdf.

Pew Research Center for the People & the Press. 2002. What the World Thinks in 2002. Available from people-press.org/report/165/what-the-world-thinks-in-2002.

———. 2007. Pew Global Attitudes Project: Spring 2007 Survey. Available from pewglobal.org/reports/pdf/256topline.pdf.

Pianin, Eric. 2001a. 160 Nations Agree to Warming Pact: US Was on Sidelines in Morocco Talks. *Washington Post*, November 10.

———. 2001b. EPA Chief Lobbied on Warming Before Bush's Emissions Switch: Memo Details Whitman's Plea for Presidential Commitment. *Washington Post*, March 27.

———. 2001c. US Aims to Pull Out of Warming Treaty. *Washington Post*, March 28.

———. 2001d. Warming Pact a Win for European Leaders. *Washington Post*, November 11.

Pianin, Eric, and Amy Goldstein. 2001. Bush Drops a Call For Emissions Cuts. *Washington Post*, March 14.

PIPA (Program on International Policy Attitudes, University of Maryland). 2001. Americans on Foreign Aid and World Hunger: A Study of US Public Attitudes. Available from www.pipa.org/OnlineReports/ForeignAid/ForeignAid_Feb01/ForeignAid_Feb01_srcdata.pdf.

———. 2006. 30-Country Poll Finds Worldwide Consensus that Climate Change Is a Serious Problem. Available from www.worldpublicopinion.org/pipa/articles/btenvironmentra/187.php?lb=bte&pnt=187&nid=&id.

Pisik, Betsy. 1998. Global Court Is No Done Deal. *Washington Times*, June 15.

Pittman, Mark, and Bob Ivry. 2008. US Pledges Top $7.7 Trillion to Ease Frozen Credit. Bloomberg, November 24. Available from www.bloomberg.com/apps/news?pid=20601109&sid=an3k2rZMNgDw&.

Pomerance, Rafe. 1989. The Dangers from Climate Warming: A Public Awakening. In *Challenge of Global Warming*, edited by D. E. Abrahamson. Washington, D.C.: Island Press, 259–269.

Price, Richard. 1998. Reversing the Gun Sights: Transnational Civil Society Targets Land Mines. *International Organization* 52 (3): 613–644.

———. 2003. Transnational Civil Society and Advocacy in World Politics. *World Politics* 55: 579–606.

Purvis, Nigel. 2004. Europe and Japan Misread Kerry on Kyoto. *International Herald Tribune*, April 5. Available from www.brookings.edu/opinions/2004/0405energy_purvis.aspx.

Putnam, Robert. 1988. Diplomacy and Domestic Politics: The Logic of Two-Level Games. *International Organization* 42 (3): 427–460.

Bibliography

Randle, Michael. 2004. *Jubilee 2000: The Challenge of Coalition Cam[ing*. Coventry, UK: Centre for the Study of Forgiveness and Rec[ation.

Raustiala, Kal. 2005. Form and Substance in International Agreements. *American Journal of International Law* 99 (3): 581–614.

Reich, Michael R, Keizo Takemi, Marc J. Roberts, and William C. Hsiao. 2008. Global Action on Health Systems: A Proposal for the Toyako G8 Summit. *Lancet* 371 (9615): 865–869.

Reiner, David M. 2001. Climate Impasse: How the Hague Negotiations Failed. *Environment* 43 (2): 36–43.

Reuters. 2008a. Japan to Buy Excess Czech Emissions Allowance, September 23. Available from www.planetark.org/dailynewsstory. cfm/newsid/50332/story.htm.

2008b. Wall St. Crisis Might Mean Less Foreign Aid: Biden, October 2. Available from www.reuters.com/article/politicsNews/ idUSTRE4920SZ20081003.

Riddell, Peter. 2003. *Hug Them Close: Blair, Clinton, Bush and the Special Relationship*. London: Politico's.

Rieffel, Lex. 2003. *Restructuring Sovereign Debt: The Case for Ad Hoc Machinery*. Washington, D.C.: Brookings Institution Press.

Rifkin, Jeremy. 1988. The Greenhouse Doomsday Scenario. *Washington Post*, July 31.

Riker, William H. 1986. *The Art of Political Manipulation*. New Haven, Conn.: Yale University Press.

Risse, Thomas. 2000. Let's Argue: Communicative Action in World Politics. *International Organization* 54 (1): 1–39.

Risse, Thomas, Stephen C. Ropp, and Kathryn Sikkink, eds. 1999. *The Power of Human Rights: International Norms and Domestic Change*. Cambridge, UK: Cambridge University Press.

Risse-Kappen, Thomas. 1991. Public Opinion, Domestic Structure and Foreign Policy in Liberal Democracies. *World Politics* 43 (4): 479–512.

1995a. *Bringing Transnational Relations Back In: Non-State Actors, Domestic Structures, and International Institutions*. Cambridge, UK: Cambridge University Press.

1995b. Ideas Do Not Float Freely. In *International Relations Theory and the End of the Cold War*, edited by R. N. Lebow and T. Risse-Kappen. New York: Columbia University Press, 187–222.

Ritholtz, Barry. 2008. Big Bailouts, Bigger Bucks. The Big Picture, November 25. Available from www.ritholtz.com/blog/2008/11/ big-bailouts-bigger-bucks/.

Rogowski, Ronald. 1989. *Commerce and Coalitions: How Trade Affects Domestic Political Alignments*. Princeton, N.J.: Princeton University Press.

Roodman, David. 2008. History Says Financial Crisis Will Suppress Aid. Center for Global Development, October 13. Available from blogs.cgdev.org/globaldevelopment/2008/10/history_says_financial_crisis.php.

Roskin, Michael. 1974. From Pearl Harbor to Vietnam: Shifting Generational Paradigms and Foreign Policy. *Political Science Quarterly* 89: 563–588.

Rubin, James P. 1998. US Department of State Office of the Spokesman Press Statement, April 2. Available from secretary.state.gov/www/briefings/statements/1998/ps980402.html.

Rutherford, Kenneth R. 2000. The Evolving Arms Control Agenda: Implications of the Role of NGOs in Banning Antipersonnel Landmines. *World Politics* 53 (1): 74–114.

Sampson, Martin W., and Stephen G. Walker. 1987. Cultural Norms and National Roles: A Comparison of Japan and France. In Walker 1987, 105–122.

Sandholtz, Wayne. 2005. Europe, the United States, and the International Criminal Court. Paper read at Transatlantic Relations Workshop Program, November 11–12, Princeton University, Princeton, N.J.

Sandler, Todd. 2004. *Global Collective Action*. Cambridge, UK: Cambridge University Press.

Sarewitz, Daniel, and Roger Pielke. 2000. Breaking the Global-Warming Gridlock. *Atlantic Monthly*, July. Available from www.theatlantic.com/issues/2000/07/sarewitz.htm.

Sato, Shigeru, and Michio Nakayama. 2008. Japan to Buy Emission Credits from Czech Republic. Bloomberg News, September 23. Available from www.bloomberg.com/apps/news?pid=20601081&sid=a7s4z4qAsHz E&refer=australia.

Sault Star (Sault Saint Marie, Ont.). 2002. Chretien Officially Inks Kyoto: Takes Shot at Opponents of Plan, December 17.

Schimmelfennig, Frank. 2001. The Community Trap: Liberal Norms, Rhetorical Action, and the Eastern Enlargement of the European Union. *International Organization* 51 (1): 47–80.

——— 2003. *The EU, NATO, and the Integration of Europe: Rules and Rhetoric*. Cambridge, UK: Cambridge University Press.

Schneider, Stephen. 1997. *Laboratory Earth*. New York: Basic Books.

Schoppa, Leonard J. 1993. Two-Level Games and Bargaining Outcomes: Why Gaiatsu Succeeds in Japan in Some Cases But Not Others. *International Organization* 47 (3): 353–386.

Schreurs, Miranda A. 2002. *Environmental Politics in Japan, Germany, and the United States*. Cambridge, UK: Cambridge University Press.

Schuerch, William E. 1999. House International Relations Committee, Subcommittee on Africa Testimony by Treasury Deputy Assistant Secretary for International Development, Debt and Environmental Policy, April 13. Available from www.treas.gov/press/releases/rr3079.htm.

Schultz, Kenneth. 1998. Domestic Opposition and Signaling in International Crises. *American Political Science Review* 92 (4): 829–844.

Schuman, Howard, and Cheryl Reiger. 1992. Historical Analogies, Generational Effects and Attitudes Towards War. *American Sociological Review* 57 (3): 315–326.

Sebenius, James K. 1994. Towards a Winning Climate Coalition. In *Negotiating Climate Change: The Inside Story of the Rio Convention*, edited by I. M. Mintzer and J. A. Leonard. Cambridge, UK: Cambridge University Press, 277–320.

Sell, Susan K., and Aseem Prakash. 2004. Using Ideas Strategically: The Contest Between Business and NGO Networks in Intellectual Property Rights. *International Studies Quarterly* 48 (1): 143–175.

Serieux, John, and Yiagadeesen Samy, eds. 2003. *Debt Relief for the Poorest Countries*. New Brunswick, N.J.: Transaction Publishers.

Sheler, Jeffery L. 2002. Prescription for Hope. *US News and World Report*, February 12. Available from www.usnews.com/usnews/news/articles/aidshelp020212.htm.

Shiffman, Jeremy. 2006. HIV/AIDS and the Rest of the Global Health Agenda. *Bulletin of the World Health Organization* 84 (12): 923.

Shiffman, Jeremy, and Stephanie Smith. 2007. Generation of Political Priority for Global Health Initiatives: A Framework and Case Study of Maternal Mortality. *Lancet* 370 (9595): 1370–1379.

Shogren, Jason, and Michael Toman. 2000. Climate Change Policy. Resources for the Future, May.

Simmons, Beth A. 1998. Compliance with International Agreements. *Annual Review of Political Science* 1 (1): 75–93.

———. 2000. International Law and State Behavior: Commitment and Compliance in International Monetary Affairs. *American Political Science Review* 94 (4): 819–835.

Simmons, Beth A., and Zachary Elkins. 2004. The Globalization of Liberalization: Policy Diffusion in the International Political Economy. *American Political Science Review* 98 (1): 171–189.

Simmons, Beth A., and Daniel J. Hopkins. 2005. The Constraining Power of International Treaties: Theory and Methods. *American Political Science Review* 99 (4): 623–631.

Simon, Herbert. 1956. Rational Choice and the Structure of the Environment. *Psychological Review* 63: 253–283.

——— 1959. Theories of Decision-Making in Economic and Behavorial Science. *American Economic Review* 49 (3): 253–283.

——— 1979. Rational Decision Making in Business Organizations. *American Economic Review* 69 (4): 493–513.

——— 1982. *Models of Bounded Rationality.* Cambridge, Mass.: MIT Press.

Singer, P. W. 2002. AIDS and International Security. *Survival* 44 (1): 145–158.

Skidmore, David. 2005. Understanding the Unilateralist Turn in US Foreign Policy. *Foreign Policy Analysis* 1 (2): 207–228.

Snow, David A., and Robert D. Benford. 1988. Ideology, Frame Resonance, and Participant Mobilization. In *From Structure to Action: Comparing Social Movement Research Across Cultures*, edited by B. Klandermans, H. Kriesi, and S. G. Tarrow. Greenwich, Conn.: JAI Press, 197–218.

Snow, David A., E. Burke Rochford, Jr., Steven K. Worden, and Robert D. Benford. 1986. Frame Alignment Processes, Micromobilization, and Movement Participation. *American Sociological Review* 51 (4): 464–481.

Snyder, Jack. 1991. *Myths of Empire: Domestic Politics and International Ambition.* Ithaca, N.Y.: Cornell University Press.

Snyder, Jack, and Leslie Vinjamuri. 2003. Trials and Errors: Principle and Pragmatism in Strategies of International Justice. *International Security* 28 (3): 5–44.

Söderberg, Marie. 2002. The Japanese Citizens Increasing Participation in Civil Society: Implications for Foreign Aid. Stockholm: European Institute of Japanese Studies. Available from swopec.hhs.se/eijswp/papers/eijswp0159.pdf.

Staggenborg, Suzanne. 2008. *Social Movements.* Oxford, UK: Oxford University Press.

Stephen, Chris. 2003. ICC Launch Bolsters Human Rights Cause. Institute for War and Peace Reporting, February 28. Available from www.globalpolicy.org/intljustice/icc/2003/0228rights.htm.

Stolberg, Sheryl Gay. 2003. The White House Gets Religion on AIDS in Africa. *New York Times*, February 2.

Struett, Michael. 2008. *The Politics of Constructing the International Criminal Court.* Basingstoke, UK: Palgrave Macmillan.

Struett, Michael J., and Steven A. Weldon. 2006. Explaining State Decisions to Ratify the International Criminal Court Treaty. Paper read at the American Political Science Association annual conference, August 31, Philadelphia.

Sugiyama, Taishi. 2003. Climate Policy in Japan. Centre for European Policy Studies, May 20. Available from www.ceps.be/content/what-2nd-commitment-period-kyoto-protocol-some-initial-views-japan.

Summers, Lawrence H. 2000. Moving Forward with Millennial Debt Relief. Reception to Celebrate HIPC House Banking Committee Room, US Congress, Washington, D.C., February 1. Available from www.treas.gov/press/releases/ls363.htm.

Sundstrom, Lisa McIntosh. 2005. Foreign Assistance, International Norms, and NGO Development: Lessons from the Russian Campaign. *International Organization* 59: 419–449.

Takemi, Keizo. 2008a. *Japan's Role in Global Health and Human Security.* Japan Center for International Exchange, January 15. Available from www.jcie.or.jp/thinknet/takemi_project/cgh-jc01.pdf.

Tamamoto, Masaru. 1993. The Japan that Wants to Be Liked: Society and International Participation. In *Japan's Emerging Global Role*, edited by D. Unger and P. Blackburn. Boulder, Colo.: Lynne Rienner, 37–54.

1999. The Uncertainty of the Self: Japan at Century's End. *World Policy Journal* 2 (Summer): 119–128.

Tarrow, Sidney G. 2005. *The New Transnational Activism.* New York: Cambridge University Press.

Thompson, Clive. 2009. Can Game Theory Predict When Iran Will Get the Bomb? *New York Times*, August 12.

Thurner, Paul W., and Michael Stoiber. 2001. Comparing Ratification Processes Within EU Member States: The Identification of Real Veto Players. Unpublished paper, University of Mannheim. Available from www.unizar.es/euroconstitucion/library/working%20papers/Amsterdam/Thurner.pdf.

Tiberghien, Yves, and Miranda A. Schreurs. 2007. High Noon in Japan: Embedded Symbolism and Post-2001 Kyoto Protocol Politics. *Global Environmental Politics* 7 (4): 70–91.

Tilly, Charles. 2004. *Social Movements, 1768–2004.* Boulder, Colo., and London: Paradigm Publishers.

Toman, Michael, and Marina Cazorla. 1998. The Clean Development Mechanism: A Primer. Resources for the Future, September. Available from www.weathervane.rff.org/features/feature048.html.

Tomz, Michael. 1998. Do Creditors Ignore History? Reputation in International Capital Markets. Paper read at Latin American Studies Association meeting, September 24–26, at Chicago.

2007a. Domestic Audience Costs in International Relations: An Experimental Approach. *International Organization* 61 (4): 821–840.

2007b. *Reputation and International Cooperation: Sovereign Debt Across Three Centuries.* Princeton, N.J.: Princeton University Press.

Toulin, Alan. 2002. New Democrats, Bloc Help Grits Pass Kyoto: "Incredibly Stupid." *National Post*, December 11.

Traub, James. 2005. The Statesman. *New York Times Magazine*, September 18.

Trueheart, Charles. 1997. France Splits with Court over Bosnia; General Won't Testify in War Crimes Case. *Washington Post*, December 16.

Tsebelis, George. 1995. Decision Making in Political Systems: Veto Players in Presidentialism, Parliamentarism, Multicameralism and Multipartyism. *British Journal of Political Science* 25 (1): 289–325.

———. 2002. *Veto Players: How Political Institutions Work*. New York: Russell Sage Foundation.

Tyrangiel, Josh. 2005. The Constant Charmer. *Time*, December 17.

UNAIDS (Joint United Nations Programme on HIV/AIDS). 2005a. AIDS in Africa: Three Scenarios to 2025, January. Available from www.unaids.org/unaids_resources/images/AIDSScenarios/AIDS-scenarios-2025_report_en.pdf.

———. 2005b. Resource Needs for an Expanded Response to AIDS in Low- and Middle-Income Countries, August. Available from data.unaids.org/pub/Report/2005/jc1239_resource_needs_en.pdf.

———. 2008. Global Facts and Figures. Available from data.unaids.org/pub/GlobalReport/2008/20080715_fs_global_en.pdf.

———. 2009. More than Four Million HIV-Positive People Now Receiving Life-Saving Treatment, September 30. Available from www.unaids.org/en/KnowledgeCentre/Resources/FeatureStories/archive/2009/20090930_access_treatment_4millions.asp.

UNDP (United Nations Development Programme). 2004. Human Development Report. Available from hdr.undp.org/en/statistics/.

UNFCCC (United Nations Framework on Climate Change). Undated. Kyoto Protocol. Available from unfccc.int/kyoto_protocol/items/2830.php.

United Kingdom, Department for Environment, Food, and Rural Affairs, see DEFRA.

United Kingdom, Foreign and Commonwealth Office. 2000. Government to Introduce International Criminal Court Bill, June 12. Available from www.fco.gov.uk/servlet/Front?pagename=OpenMarket/Xcelerate/ShowPage&c=Page&cid=1007029391638&a=KArticle&aid=1013618408101.

———. 2001. The Ponsonby Rule, January.

United Kingdom, Mission to the United Nations. 1995. Statement by the Representative of the United Kingdom in the 6th Committee of the UN General Assembly on the Establishment of an International Criminal Court (New York, USA), November 2. Available from www.iccnow.org/documents/UK1PrepCmt2Nov95.pdf.

1997. Statement by the Representative of United Kingdom of Great Britain and Northern Ireland to the UN, before the 6th Committee of the 52nd UN General Assembly, Regarding the Establishment of an International Criminal Court (New York, USA), October 23. Available from www.iccnow.org/documents/UK6thComm23Oct97.pdf.

United Kingdom, Parliament. Undated. Factsheet P14-Treaties. Available from www.parliament.uk/parliamentary_publications_and_archives/factsheets/p14.cfm.

United Kingdom, Prime Minister's Official Spokesman. 2002. Briefing: 11 am Monday 1 July 2002. 10 Downing Street. Available from www.number10.gov.uk/Page2446.

2005. Press Briefing: 1100 BST Wednesday 20 July 2005. 10 Downing Street, July 20. Available from www.number10.gov.uk/Page7961.

United Nations Association of the United States of America. 2003. Comparison of the Clinton and Bush Administration Positions on the International Criminal Court, October. Available from www.unausa.org/site/pp.asp?c=fvKRI8MPJpF&b=345925.

United Nations Treaty Collection. 2009. 10. Rome Statute of the International Criminal Court, July 7. Available from treaties.un.org/Pages/ViewDetails.aspx/src=UNTSONLINE&tabid=1&mtdsg_no=XVIII-10&chapter=18&lang=en.

United States, Department of State. 2006. Action Today, Hope for Tomorrow: The President's Emergency Plan for AIDS Relief, Second Annual Report to Congress, February 8. Available from www.state.gov/documents/organization/60598.pdf.

United States, Department of State, Office of the US Global Aids Coordinator. 2009. PEPFAR: Latest Results, September 30. Available from www.pepfar.gov/about/c19785.htm.

United States, Government Accountability Office, *see* GAO.

United States, Government Accounting Office, *see* GAO.

United States, White House, Office of the Press Secretary. 1997. Press Conference Transcript, December 11. Available from clinton2.nara.gov/Initiatives/Climate/19971212–6024.html.

Van Evera, Stephen. 1997. *Guide to Methods for Students of Political Science*. Ithaca, N.Y.: Cornell University Press.

Védrine, Hubert. 1997. Address Before the United Nations, September 24. Available from www.un.int/france/documents_anglais/970924_ag_france_pleniere.htm.

Védrine, Hubert, and Dominique Moïsi. 2001. *France in an Age of Globalization*. Washington, D.C.: Brookings Institution Press.

Victor, David G. 2001. *The Collapse of the Kyoto Protocol*. Princeton, N.J.: Princeton University Press.

Victor, David G., and Lesley A. Coben. 2005. A Herd Mentality in the Design of International Environmental Agreements? *Global Environmental Politics* 5 (1): 24–57.

von Stein, Jana. 2005a. Do Treaties Constrain or Screen? Selection Bias and Treaty Compliance. *American Political Science Review* 99 (4): 611–622.

——— 2005b. Saving the Environment? Ratification and Compliance in the International Climate Change Regime. Paper read at American Political Science Association, September 1–4, Washington, D.C.

Vreeland, James. 2004. Institutional Determinants of IMF Agreements. Unpublished paper, Yale University. Available from escholarship.org/uc/item/69d9b6kq.

Wagner, John. 2000. In Helms, Bono Finds the Ally He's Looking for. *Raleigh News and Observer*, September 21.

Walker, Stephen G. 1987. *Role Theory and Foreign Policy Analysis*. Durham, N.C.: Duke University Press.

Walldorf, C. William, Jr. 2008. *Just Politics: Human Rights and the Foreign Policy of Great Powers*. Ithaca, N.Y.: Cornell University Press.

Walt, Stephen M. 2005. *Taming American Power: The Global Response to US Primacy*. New York: Norton.

Wang, Hongying. 2001. *National Image Building: A Case Study of China*. Paper read at International Studies Association, July, Hong Kong.

——— 2004. National Image Building and Chinese Foreign Policy. *China: An International Journal* 1 (1): 46–72.

Wapner, Paul. 1995. Politics Beyond the State: Environmental Activism and World Civic Politics. *World Politics* 47 (3): 311–340.

Washington Post, The. 2001. The Warming Debate. March 9.

Wax, Emily. 2008. Wall Street Greed? Not in This Neighborhood. *Washington Post*, October 11. Available from www.washingtonpost.com/wp-dyn/content/article/2008/10/10/AR200810100 2937.html.

Wedgwood, Ruth. 1998. Fiddling in Rome: American and the International Criminal Court. *Foreign Affairs* 77 (6): 20–24.

Weiner, Jonathan. 1997. Designing Markets for International Greenhouse Gas Control. Resources for the Future, October. Available from www.rff.org/RFF/Documents/RFF-CCIB-06.pdf.

Weingart, Peter, Anita Engels, and Petra Pansegrau. 2000. Risks of Communication: Discourses on Climate Change in Science, Politics, and the Mass Media. *Public Understanding of Science* 9 (3): 261–283.

Wheeler, Nicholas J., and Tim Dunne. 2004. Moral Britannia? Evaluating the Ethical Dimension in Labour's Foreign Policy. Foreign Policy Centre. Available from fpc.org.uk/fsblob/233.pdf.

WHO (World Health Organization). 2008. Towards Universal Access: Scaling up Priority HIV/AIDS Interventions in the Health Sector, June 2. Available from www.who.int/hiv/pub/2008progressreport/en/.

Wilson, James Q. 1980. *American Government: Institutions and Policies.* Lexington, Mass.: D. C. Heath.

Wippman, David. 2004. *The International Criminal Court,* edited by C. Reus-Smit. Cambridge, UK: Cambridge University Press.

Wirth, Tim. 1996. Statement by HE the Honourable Mr Timothy Wirth, Under-Secretary of State for Global Affairs of the United States of America, at the High-Level Segment of the Second Session of the Conference of the Parties to the United Nations Framework Convention on Climate Change. Paper read at Second Conference of the Parties Framework Convention on Climate Change, July 17, Geneva, Switzerland.

Woolley, John, and Gerhard Peters. 2006. The American Presidency Project. University of California (hosted), Gerhard Peters (database). Available from www.presidency.ucsb.edu/sou.php.

World Bank. 1999a. HIPC Debt Tables. Available from www.worldbank.org/hipc/about/debt-table/debt-table.html.

———. 1999b. Outcome of the 1999 Review. Available from www.worldbank.org/hipc/hipc-review/outcome_1999_review/outcome_1999_review.html.

———. 2001. The HIPC Initiative: Background and Progress Through December 2001. Available from www.worldbank.org/hipc/progress-to-date/May99v3/may99v3.htm.

———. 2006. HIPC Initiative: Status of Implementation, March 21. Available from siteresources.worldbank.org/INTDEBTDEPT/ProgressReports/20894658/032106.pdf.

———. Undated-a. Debt Issues. Available from web.worldbank.org/WEBSITE/EXTERNAL/TOPICS/EXTDEBTDEPT/0,,menuPK:64166739~pagePK:64166681~piPK:64166725~theSitePK:469043,00.html.

———. Undated-b. HIPC Map. Available from www.worldbank.org/hipc/about/map/map.html.

World Bank Development Committee. 2005. Note on the G8 Debt Relief Proposal. World Bank/IMF, September 21. Available from siteresources.worldbank.org/IDA/Resources/G8DebtPaperSept05.pdf.

Worldpublicopinion.org. 2006. World Citizens Reject Torture, BBC Global Poll Reveals. Program on International Policy Attitudes, University of Maryland, October 18. Available from www.worldpublicopinion.org/pipa/articles/btjusticehuman_rightsra/261.php?lb=bthr&pnt=261&nid=&id=.

2008. World Public Opinion and the Universal Declaration of Human Rights. Program on Public Policy Attitudes, University of Maryland, December. Available from www.worldpublicopinion.org/pipa/pdf/dec08/WPO_UDHR_Dec08_rpt.pdf.

WRI (World Resources Institute). 2004. CAIT: Climate Analysis Indicators Tool. Available from cait.wri.org/.

2006. CAIT: Climate Analysis Indicators Tool Version 4.0. Available from cait.wri.org/.

Wylie, Lana. 2006. We Care What They Think: Prestige and Canadian Foreign Policy. Paper read at the 2006 annual meeting of the Canadian Political Science Association, June 3, Toronto. Available from www.cpsa-acsp.ca/papers-2006/Wylie.pdf.

Yasutomo, Dennis T. 1995. *The New Multilateralism in Japan's Foreign Policy.* New York: St. Martin's Press.

Yee, Albert S. 1996. The Causal Effects of Ideas on Policies. *International Organization* 50 (1): 69–108.

Yoshida, Reiji, and Junko Takahashi. 2003. Lower House Dissolved. *Japan Times,* October 11. Available from search.japantimes.co.jp/cgi-bin/nn20031011a1.html.

Zald, Mayer. 1996. Culture, Ideology and Strategic Framing. In McAdam, McCarthy, and Zald 1996, 261–274.

Interviews

This book is based on hundreds of interviews, many of them conducted in person in Berlin, Bonn, Boston, Brussels, The Hague, London, Milan, New York, Paris, Seattle, Tokyo, Vienna, Washington, D.C., and other cities. Only a subset of them is ultimately cited in the text.

Barrett, Marlene. 2003. Personal communication. London, August 13.

Benn, Christoph. 2003. Personal communication, December 10.

Callahan, Sonny. 2005. Personal communication, January 27.

De Brichambaut, Marc Perrin. 2007. Personal communication. Vienna, May 18.

De Charette, Hervé. 2007. Personal communication. Paris, May 23.

Drummond, Jamie. 2001. Personal communication. Washington, D.C., January.

French Foreign Ministry official. 2007. Personal communication. Paris, May 22.

Fukawa, Yoko. 2005. Personal communication. Tokyo, March 8.

Garrett, Laurie. 2006. Personal communication. New York, November 10.

Gartner, David. 2006. Personal communication, November 19.

Gerson, Michael. 2006. Personal communication. Washington, D.C., November 14.

Hart, Thomas M. 2001. Personal communication. Washington, D.C., January.

——— 2006. Personal communication. Washington, D.C., November 13.

Hatch, Scott. 2005. Personal communication. Washington, D.C., April 6.

Isaacs, Ken. 2007. Personal communication, January 11.

Japanese industry official. 2004. Personal communication, March 29.

Japanese MOFA (Ministry of Foreign Affairs) official-a. 2004. Personal communication, July 22.

Japanese MOFA (Ministry of Foreign Affairs) official-b. 2008. Personal communication. Tokyo, May 27.

Jenns, Nicola. 2006. Personal communication, June 5.

Konukiewitz, Manfred. 2008. Personal communication, June 16.

Lagon, Mark. 2005. Personal communication. Washington, D.C., June 15.

Lovett, Adrian. 2003. Personal communication. Oxford, UK, August 15.

Maas, Joerg. 2008. Personal communication, June 17.

McCormick, Jamie. 2005. Personal communication, February 10.

Morgan, Jennifer. 2003. Personal communication. Berlin, May 21.

Munson, Lester. 2005. Personal communication, May 27.

Nakao, Takehiko. 2004a. Personal communication. Tokyo, March.

——— 2004b. Personal communication, August 22.

Nakao, Yutaka. 2004. Personal communication, April 5.

Northover, Henry. 2003. Personal communication. London, August 22.

Okazawa, Kazu. 2004a. Personal communication. Washington, D.C., February 12.

——— 2004b. Personal communication. Washington, D.C.

Purvis, Nigel. 2003. Personal communication. Washington, D.C., October 2.

Reifsnyder, Dan. 2004. Personal communication. Washington, D.C., February 13.

Roll, Katja. 2003. Personal communication, December 15.

——— 2007. Personal communication, October 24.

Sandalow, David. 2003. Personal communication. Washington, D.C., October 10.

Scheffer, David. 2007. Personal communication, April 30.

Shimizu, Yasuhiro. 2004. Personal communication, Tokyo, April 27.

Sulzer, Jeanne. 2007. Personal communication. Paris, May 23.

Summers, Larry. 2004. Personal communication. Boston, December 9.

Takemi, Keizo. 2008. Personal communication, June 4.

Védrine, Hubert. 2007. Personal communication, Paris. Paris, May 21.

Yamada, Yoichiro. 2005. Personal communication, March 14.

——— 2007. Personal communication, October.

Index

50 Years Is Enough US Network for
Global Economic Justice 89

Abu Ghraib 220
Acharya, Amitav 50, 55
Acheson, Dean 240
ACT UP 154, 169–170, 172, 180,
191, 205
ActionAid 263
advocacy movements
aspirational goals 36–37
broadening of scope 3–4
conditions favorable to 268,
270–272
countermovements 7, 41, 46
defined 35–36
donor priorities 262–264
failure to emerge 256, 261
funding 8, 36
history 2–3, 4, 5
incidental role 67
influence 63–68; distinguished from
success 55, 64–65
leverage on states 44
motivations 36
points of focus 8–9
political mobilization levels 45–46
strategic approaches 35, 39–42
studies 5–7, 10–11, 50, 268
Afghanistan 221
2001 invasion 5
Africa Faith and Justice Network 89
African Development Bank 76
agenda, global, prioritization of issues
261
agents/structures, interactions between
7
AIDS see HIV/AIDS
AIDS Treatment Action Campaign
154

Aisawa, Ichiro 199
Akao, Nobutoshi 143
Aktionsbündnis gegen AIDS 192, 205
Amnesty International 215, 226,
235–236, 249
Annan, Kofi 152, 155, 161
Arbour, Louise 249–250
Argentina 112
Aristide, Jean-Bertrand 139
Armey, Dick, Representative 90
ARV (anti-retroviral therapy)
154–155, 188
costs 160–161, 162, 186, 190
funding 155
Asia Pacific Partnership on Clean
Development and Climate (APP)
115
Asociación pro Derechos Humanos
215
Attaran, Amir 154
Australia 149

Bachus, Spencer, Congressman 12, 88,
90, 91
Bangladesh 99
Barnett, Tony 153
Barrett, Scott 127
al-Bashir, Omar Hassan 221
Bass, Gary J. 4, 59, 268
Bassiouni, Cherif 229
Belden, Nancy 208
Benn, Christoph 191–192, 195
Bennett, Andrew 49, 87
Berman, Frank 211
Berscheid, Ellen 167
Betsill, Michele M. 55
Bible, citation of 71, 185
Biden, Joe, Senator 257
Birmingham G-8 summit (1998),
protests at 1, 74, 85

Black Death 153
Blair, Cherie (née Booth) 238, 242, 244
Blair, Tony 191, 237–238, 240–242, 244
Bob, Clifford 262
Bodansky, Dan 130
Bolten, Joshua 185–186
Bolton, John 224, 239
Bonino, Emma 249, 250
Bonn Agreement 113
Bono (Paul Hewson) 1–2, 70, 81, 89–90, 154, 164, 169, 176, 183, 185, 187, 188, 193, 198, 271
Boockmann, Bernard 132
"boomerang model" 6, 236
Booth, Cherie *see* Blair, Cherie
Boyce, Sir Michael, Admiral 245
Brady Plan 72
Bread for the World 89, 262
Brookings Institution 262
Brown, Gordon 242
Bueno de Mesquita, Bruce 264–265, 267
Buffett, Warren 263
Burundi 227
Bush, George H. W. 108
Bush, George W. 10, 14, 15, 169, 224, 244, 260, 269–270
 climate change policies 105, 113, 115, 129
 HIV/AIDS policies 151, 172, 177, 178–180, 181–182, 184–187, 190, 191
 policy toward ICC 212, 218, 227, 237
Byrd–Hagel Resolution 112
Byrne, Donn 167

Cacioppo, John T. 167–168
CAFOD (Catholic Agency for Overseas Development) 100
Callahan, Sonny, Congressman 88, 92–93
Cameroon 76
CAN (Climate Action Network) 107–108, 127–128
Canada
 and climate change 12–13, 34, 105–106, 107, 115–116, 117,

149; emission levels 123–124; failure to meet commitments 260
 cultural importance of religion 83
 and debt relief 77–78, 80, 84
 global profile 146–147
 and HIV/AIDS 152, 156–158, 160, 173
 internal politics 116, 135, 145–146, 149
 NGOs 146
 overseas troop deployments 223–224
 political structure 132–133
 public opinion 173, 209, 233
 ratification of Kyoto Protocol 113, 119–120, 131, 145, 148, 255; costs 124; motivations 138–140, 145–147; public opinion 119, 147
 role of reputation 145–147
 support for ICC 142, 223–224
 treaty ratification procedure 132–135
carbon sinks 113, 115
CARE (Cooperative for Assistance and Relief Everywhere) 89, 263
Carpenter, Charli 50, 264
Castellano, Marc 100
celebrity/ies, role in success of movements 167, 193–194, 271–272
Center for Global Development 159, 263
Central African Republic 220
Chad 221
Chaiken, Shelly 167, 168
Chancellor of the Exchequer, role in UK politics 62–63
Chandy, Tom 255
cheap moral action 57, 65, 67
 on climate change 125
 on debt relief 84, 87
 on foreign assistance 174
 vs. costly 58, 234–235
Checkel, Jeffrey T. 8, 37, 55
Chicago Council on Foreign Relations 173
China
 and climate change 112, 150, 260

China (*cont.*)
  female footbinding,
    nineteenth-century protests
    against 4
  non-ratification of Rome Statute
    219
Chirac, Jacques 15, 191, 238,
  239–240, 247–249, 250, 252–253
Chrétien, Jean 133, 135, 145,
  146–147
Cialdini, Robert 167
CICC (Coalition for the International
  Criminal Court) 215
Clarke, Kenneth 73
clean development mechanism 112
climate change 5–6, 9–10, 12, 13, 38,
  64
  activist rhetoric 120, 125–126
  binding reductions timetable,
    adoption of 110, 127–128,
    129–130
  common but differentiated
    responsibilities, principle of 109
  framing of issues 65–66, 120–131;
    in environmental crisis terms
    120–121, 125–128, 131,
    147–148; flaws 130–131
  history of initiatives 106–108, 116,
    127
  public opinion 119–123
  research 107
  "safety valve" policy 129–130
  see also emissions trading; Kyoto
    Protocol
Clinton, Bill 1, 12, 15, 41, 139,
  259–260
  climate change policies 104,
    109–110, 112, 129, 130
  debt relief policies 74–75, 87, 88,
    89
  HIV/AIDS policies 178, 187
  stance on ICC 216, 218, 227, 239
Clinton, Hillary 222
Cold War 214
Cologne G-8 summit (1999) 1, 74–75,
  76, 191
  protest activity 1, 74–75, 85 (*see
    also* G-8)
Colombia 221
colonial past, impact on AIDS policies
  160

Columban Justice and Peace Office 89
complementarity principle *see under*
  ICC
"complex social learning" 52
compliance 8–9
  monitoring 138–139
  non-penalization of failure 115
  "pull" 117, 149
  vs. commitments 13, 80
concordance *see* cultural match
Congo, Democratic Republic of the
  220, 229
Congo (Belgian), nineteenth-century
  abuses 4, 265–266, 269
constructivism 36–37, 42, 53
Consumer Project on Technology 154
consumers, targeting of 3
Cook, Robin 241–242, 243
Cooley, Alexander 3
Copenhagen
  climate negotiations (2009) 148
  Consensus (2004) 261
corporate social responsibility
  268–269
corporations, targeting of 3
Cortell, Andrew 55
cost–benefit ratio (of state
  actions/policy) 43–45, 55
  changes in 67–68
costly moral action 57–59
  on climate change 125
  conditions favorable to 270–271
  on debt relief 85
  on foreign assistance 174
  frequency 268
  on HIV/AIDS 165
  on ICC participation 234–235, 245
cost(s) 142
  intersection with values, mapping of
    56–63, 120–121, 170, 174–177,
    234–238
  as motivating factor 12–13, 33–34,
    43, 44, 68–69
  subjective quality 34, 58–59
  see also cost–benefit ratio
Côte d'Ivoire 221
"credit culture" 12, 97
crisis in global economy (2008) 16,
  255, 256–258
  rescue attempts 258
  undermining of foreign aid 257

cultural match
  importance in framing of issues
    51, 55–56, 65–66, 166–167,
    271
  and climate change 131
  and debt relief (in US) 93
  and HIV/AIDS 170–173, 181
  see also salience

DAC (Development Assistance
  Committee) 156, 158
Darfur 6, 220–221, 235, 244–245
DATA (Debt, AIDS, Trade, Africa)
  89, 151, 154, 172, 182, 188–189,
  205, 262
David Suzuki Foundation 146
Davis, James W. 55
Davis, K. E. 167
De Brichambaut, Marc Perrin 247,
  249, 250, 252
De Charette, Hervé 247, 248–249
de Vries, Gijs 251
Debt Action Coalition (1991–1993)
  89
Debt Crisis Network (1985–1990)
  89
debt crisis (1980s) 95
debt relief 9–10, 12, 58, 68–69,
  258
  calls for 1–3, 70–103 (*see also*
    Jubilee 2000)
  conditionality levels 79–80
  costs/benefits 78–82
  history 72, 78, 89, 94–96
  interest-based arguments 88–93
  moral basis 37
  national levels, compared with GDP
    82–83
  slow pace, criticisms of 75–76,
    80
Deitelhoff, Nicole 228–230, 233
Dent, Martin 71
Deutsche AIDS-Hilfe 191–192
developing countries
  emissions reduction exceptions
    112
  HIV/AIDS in 14
  social movements 6
  support for human rights treaties
    230
  see also debt relief; HIPC

DeWine, Mike, Senator 184
Dietrich, John 187
Doctors Without Borders 154
domestic structure, analyses based on
  59, 61, 79
Domke, David 167
Downs, George 138
Drezner, Daniel 271–272
Drummond, Jamie 74, 85, 154
Dunne, Tim 242
Durban conference (2000) 154

Eagly, Alice 168
economic conditions, as motivating
  factor 44
economy, global *see* crisis in global
  economy
Efran, M. G. 167
Eftekhari, Shiva 250–251
Elkins, Zachary 43
Elster, Jon 46
emissions trading 112, 113, 114–115
  see also under European Union
energy crisis (1970s) 95
Entman, Robert M. 55
environmental crisis frame *see* climate
  change: framing of issues
Environmental Defense Fund
  127–128, 129–130
Epstein, Helen 189
Eritrea 76
"ethical foreign policy" *see* Labour
  Party (UK)
Eurobarometer 208
European Law Students Association
  215
European Union 142
  Emissions Trading System (EU ETS)
    114, 119
  Environment Council 109–115
  and Kyoto Protocol 144–145
external threats, as motivating factor
  43

Farmer, Paul 190
Fearon, James 128
Fédération Internationale des Ligues
  des Droits de l'Homme (FIDH)
  215, 226, 227, 249
Fehl, Caroline 221, 228
Finnemore, Martha 39, 50, 140

foreign assistance, public attitudes to
    172–174, 175, 191, 207, 208–209
  see also debt relief; HIV/AIDS
foreign policy, studies 264–268
  see also specific policy areas
framing 15–16, 49–50, 63–64, 82–86,
    120–147, 267
  appeal to causal beliefs 53–54,
    88–91
  appeal to principled beliefs 53–54
    (*see also* religious values, appeal
    to)
  coercion/conversion effects 52, 60,
    100–101
  counterframing 54–55
  factors in success 55–63
  impact on policy arguments 50–51
  multiple positions 53–54, 60,
    90–93, 170–172
  nature of appeal to decisionmakers
    52–53
  recasting of issues 65–66, 85
  see also climate change; cultural
    match; environmental crisis frame;
    HIV/AIDS
France
  cultural importance of religion 83
  and debt relief 34, 77–78, 80;
    percentage of GDP 83; share of
    costs 84–85
  and HIV/AIDS 156–158, 160
  and the ICC 14–15, 16, 40–41, 58,
    212–213, 227–228, 234–253;
    attempts to limit powers
    216–218; fears for service
    personnel 246–247; impact of
    change of government 246–247,
    248–249, 252–253; initial
    hostility 246–247; pressure of
    European partners 249–251;
    public opinion 249; ratification
    251–252, 255; reasons for stance
    225–226, 233; rhetorical
    entrapment 239–240; role in
    Rome negotiations 249–251, 252;
    seeking of concessions 251
  NGOs 163, 227, 236
  overseas troop deployments
    223–224
  role in ICTY 247–248

Friends of the Earth 104, 108
Friends of the Global Fight (US)
    205
Friends of the Global Fund Japan
    (FGFJ) 198–199, 206
Frist, Bill, Senator 184
Fukawa, Yoko 101–102
Fukuda, Yasuo 199
Fukuyama, Francis 5

G-7 group 4, 9–10
  debt relief policies 76–78, 82–83
  pressure on members to conform
    100
  public opinion, national variations
    173–175
  rankings on human rights index
    231
G-8 group 4, 49
  hosting of meetings 140, 193, 201
    (*see also* Japan)
  summits *see* Birmingham; Cologne;
    Heiligendamm; Okinawa
game theory 8, 37, 117, 128, 142
Garrett, Laurie 153, 187
Gartner, David 187–188
gatekeepers 34, 55, 60, 67–68, 82,
    234, 255–256, 267
  changes of personnel 237–238
  and climate change 131–138
  and debt relief 76; complication of
    issues 85–86, 87
  defined 267
  importance of support 56, 59–63,
    166–167, 176–177, 267, 271
  as institutional impediment 66
  in Japanese politics 197
Gates, Bill/Gates Foundation 157,
    198, 262–263
Gellman, Barton 153
Geneva Conventions 213
George, Alexander 49, 87
Georgia 221
Germany
  and climate change 117; emission
    reductions/targets 110, 114;
    ratification of Kyoto 133–134
  cultural importance of religion 83
  and debt relief 77–78, 80, 85
  economic situation 142, 160

and HIV/AIDS 14, 152, 156–158, 176–178, 190–195, 200–201; domestic campaigns 172, 191–192; public opinion 190–192, 208
internal politics 128, 178
NGOs 46
overseas troop deployments 223–224
Gerson, Michael 185–188, 190
Gladstone, W. E. 241
Global Aids Alliance 151, 154, 181, 187–188, 206
Global Fund to Fight AIDS, Tuberculosis, and Malaria 152, 154, 156, 161, 172, 195–196, 204
contribution levels 156, 158, 170
global warming *see* climate change
Goldman, Rachel 167
Gore, Al 65–66, 110, 126, 154
governments, movements' targeting of 3, 35
see also specific countries/issues
Graham, Billy 14, 152, 168, 169, 182
Graham, Franklin 14, 152, 168, 169, 176, 182–183, 185, 200
The Name 182–183
Gramm, Phil, Senator 88, 92
Green parties 119, 128
Greenhill, Kelly M. 139
greenhouse effect/gases, defined 106, 110
see also climate change
Greenpeace 108, 125, 127–128
Greenstock, Jeremy 243
Grohemeyer, Herbert 194

Habermas, Jürgen 40, 55
Hafner-Burton, Emily 230
The Hague, 2000 protests 104
Haiti 76, 139
Hall, Christopher 235
Hall, Peter A. 55
Hansen, James 107
Harper, Stephen 116
Harrison, Kathryn 133, 146–147
Hart, Tom 90, 91, 154, 182, 186–187, 188

Hastert, Dennis, Representative 90
Hatch, Orrin, Senator 89
Hatch, Scott 91, 92
Hathaway, Oona 230
Hawkins, Darren 50, 268
Health GAP 154, 172, 181, 206
Heiligendamm G-8 summit (2007) 193–194
Helms, Jesse, Senator
stance on debt relief 1–2, 12, 70, 87, 88, 91–92, 271
stance on HIV/AIDS 168, 169, 176, 180, 181, 182, 183–184
stance on ICC 216, 232–233
Henisz, Witold 61
Hertzke, Allan 91, 103
HIPC (Highly Indebted Poor Country) initiative 37, 71, 79, 81–82
costs 80
eligibility 73
HIPC I 72–74
HIPC II 74, 75
scale of debt 72, 76
HIV/AIDS 5–6, 9–10, 14, 34, 58, 64
advertising campaigns 193–194
bilateral contributions 156, 158
history/death tolls 151, 153
international initiatives 151–152, 153–159
moral stigma attached to 180, 182
NGOs/lobby groups 162–163, 188–189, 198, 199, 205–206
(potential) opposition to initiatives 163, 164
prevention programs 155
public opinion 172–175, 191, 192
reasons for (variations in) state policies 48, 151–152, 159–177, 195; economic factors 160–165
(re)framing of issues 53–54, 65, 170–172, 176, 180–183, 190
as security issue 172
share of global health budget 263, 264
threat to developed nations 160
treatment programs *see* ARV
see also Global Fund to Fight AIDS, Tuberculosis, and Malaria; PEPFAR
Hochschild, Adam 265–266, 268

hostility 57
  on debt relief 85
  on foreign assistance/AIDS funding
    175, 196–197
  moves away from 66, 93, 181, 200
Huber, Evelyne 61
human chains, forming of 1, 2, 70,
  74
human rights
  AIDS funding linked to 172
  organizations 214–215, 226, 249;
    national support, linked with ICC
    participation 232; role in
    establishment of ICC 226,
    235–237
  public opinion 233–234
  turn toward, in international law
    231
Human Rights Watch 215, 226

ICC (International Criminal Court)
    9–10, 40–41, 58, 142
  accommodation of major powers'
    interests 211–212, 217
  administration 210
  Asian representation 225
  complementarity principle 217
  costs 222, 224
  degree of independence of major
    powers 228–229
  differing national attitudes toward
    14–15, 16, 34, 68, 212–213,
    221–252; changes of government,
    impact of 237–238; diversity of
    motivations 229–231;
    framing/gatekeeper-based
    explanations 227–238, 252–253;
    interest-based explanations
    221–227; variations in rhetoric
    237
  enshrined in UK Labour manifesto
    241
  framing of issues, in public interest
    terms 233–237, 252, 255
  historical background 213–221,
    228–229
  investigative activities 220–221
  jurisdiction 210–211, 216–217
  lack of public awareness 227, 229
  (ostensible) benefit to all states 221

  restriction of prosecutor's role 217
  risks of prosecution 210–212,
    222–226
  support base 216
  see also Rome Statute
ICJ (International Court of Justice)
    211, 222
ICTR (International Criminal Tribunal
    for Rwanda) 214
ICTY (International Criminal Tribunal
    for the former Yugoslavia) 214
  French (non-)participation
    247–248, 249–250
ideational arguments see values
IFIs (international financial
    institutions), role in debt relief
    program 80–81
Ikenberry, G. John 55, 270
Imai, Takashi 136, 137
IMF (International Monetary Fund) 2,
    72–73, 76
Inconvenient Truth, An (2006) 126
India 112, 150, 219
indifference 57, 65
  on HIV/AIDS 174–175, 176–177
Indonesia 121
institutionalism 117–118
InterAction (relief organization) 89,
    262
interest(s)
  as basis of arguments/behavior
    33–34, 41–49, 68, 78–82,
    116–120, 159–166, 221–227
  contrasted with framing/gatekeeper
    scenario 82–83, 266–267
  individual 45–46, 79, 81–82,
    162–164, 187–188, 221,
    226–227
  limitations of theory based on
    46–49, 91, 119–120, 164–166,
    225–227, 255, 266–267
  state 43–45, 78–81, 159–162,
    186–187, 221–226
  studies 264–265, 267
International Commission of Jurists
    215
international context, impact on state
    behavior 44, 100–101
International Law Commission 214
international relations theory 33

IPCC (Intergovernmental Panel on
Climate Change) 107, 108,
123–124
Iraq, 2003 invasion 5, 242
(alleged) impact on US AIDS policy
160, 186–187, 190
(alleged) war crimes/human rights
abuses 210–211, 212, 220,
245–246
impact on United States'
international image 269–270
Isaacs, Ken 183, 184, 189
Israel, creation of 4–5
Italy
and climate change 123
cultural importance of religion 83
and debt relief 77–78, 80, 84
and HIV/AIDS 156–158, 160
overseas troop deployments 223

Jackson, Patrick 50–51, 52
Jacobsen, John Kurt 55
Japan
civil society/NGOs 46, 101–102,
137, 198, 199; limited
numbers/impact 46, 162–163
and climate change 12–13,
105–106, 115–116, 117; emission
levels 123–124; emissions trading
119; failure to meet commitments
260
concern for international profile
103, 143, 145, 197
and debt relief 12, 34, 57, 66,
77–78, 80, 86–88, 93–99, 103,
255; opposition to project 96–97;
percentage of GDP 83; policy
switch 97–100; pressure to
conform 97; reasons for change
100–103; share of costs 84–85
dependence on US for security 225
economic situation 44, 95–96, 142,
160, 200, 257
foreign assistance programs 93–94,
96
grant aid 98–100; reasons for
continuing 98–99; reasons for
discontinuing 99–100
and HIV/AIDS 14, 152, 156–158,
173, 176–178, 190, 195–201;

commitments to Global Fund
196, 199; governmental structure
197
hosting of summits, impact on
decisions 140, 143–144, 178,
195–196, 199
and the ICC 235; change of position
225
internal politics 137
(lack of) Christian tradition 83, 93,
102
overseas troop deployments
223–224
public opinion 173–174, 190, 196,
208–209
ratification of Kyoto Protocol 113,
119, 131, 136–138, 255; costs
124, 148, 149; implementation
programs 115, 119, 149;
motivations 138–139, 143–145;
public opinion 122, 145
role of reputation 91, 103, 143–145
treaty ratification procedure 134
Japan Bank of International
Cooperation (JBIC) 94, 97–98,
99–100
Japan Steel 136
Joachim, Jutta 50
John Paul II, Pope 70, 74, 93
Jones, Bryan D. 53, 126
Jones, E. E. 167
Jones, Michael 138
Jospin, Lionel 237–238, 239, 248,
250
Jubilee 2000 1–2, 12, 63, 70–71, 74,
79, 85, 154
framing of issues 66; in religious
terms 55–56, 83–85, 88–89,
91–92
genesis 71
influence in Japan 101–102
Jubilee+ 75–76
Jubilee 2000/USA 89–92
political pressure 81, 88, 92–93
success 37–38
JUSSCANNZ (ad hoc group on
climate change) 109

Kaiser Family Foundation 190
Kameyama, Yasuko 143

Kasich, John, Congressman 88, 89–91, 92
Kates, Jennifer 158, 204
Kaufmann, Chaim 51, 57–58, 245, 268–270
Kazakhstan 112
Keck, Margaret, and Kathryn Sikkink, *Activists Beyond Borders* 5, 6, 64, 262–263
Keefer, Philip 62
Keidanren (Japanese business association) 136–137
Kelley, Judith 225, 230
Kenya 4, 221
Keohane, Robert 47, 103
Kingdon, John 55, 126
Kinkel, Klaus 251
Koizumi, Junichiro 136, 144, 196, 198
Kolb, Felix 5–7
Konukiewitz, Manfred 194–195
Krause, Joachim 194
Krebs, Ronald 50–51, 52
Kristof, Nicholas 263
Krupp, Fred 129–130
Kyoto Protocol 12–13, 34, 38, 41, 104, 110, 116
   achievement of targets 123–124, 125
   costs of implementation 118–119, 120–124, 125, 139, 147–148
   explanation of national variations: framing/gatekeeper-based 125–147; interest-based 116–120
   flexibility mechanisms 112
   joint implementation 112
   proposed delay 144
   ratification 104–106, 113–114, 131–138 (*see also* Canada; Japan; United States)
   role of non-state actors 128–131, 144–145, 146, 147–148
Kyrgyz Republic 76

Labour Party (UK) 252
   "ethical foreign policy" 241–242, 243
   mission on return to power 241–242
   rebranding 242–243

Lagon, Mark 91–92
Lancaster, Carol 101
Larson, Deborah Welch 142
Law of the Sea Treaty 132
Lawyers Committee for Human Rights 215
Leach, Jim, Congressman 87, 88, 90–91
leaders, motivations of 139–140, 141–142
   see also interest(s): individual
Legro, Jeffrey W. 55, 140
Leopold II of Belgium 265–266, 269
Leviticus, Book of *see* Bible
Levy, Marc 139–140
liberalism 33
Lincoln, Edward W. 95, 102
Lomborg, Bjorn 261
Love, James 154
Lovett, Adrian 90
Lowenheim, Oded 140, 268
Loy, Frank 105
Lubanga, Thomas 220
Lumsdaine, David 268

Maas, Joerg 193, 194, 195
MacDonald, Ramsay 243
Mallaby, Sebastian 85
Mandela, Nelson 187
Marshall Fund 207, 208
Martin, Paul 135
Maryknoll Office for Global Concerns 89
maternal mortality 264
McAdam, Doug 43–44
McCarthy, John D. 43–44
McCormick, Jamie 87, 91
McElroy, Robert 268
Mead, Walter Russell 241
Merkel, Angela 178, 193–195
messaging 63–65, 267
messengers 14, 34, 63–64, 152, 166–177, 200, 267, 271
   balance vs. content of messages 66–67
   elite ("grasstops") 168
   factors in effectiveness 167, 169–170, 183, 185, 199
   new, emergence of 181–182

race 167
relationship with gatekeepers
168–169, 184
Mexico 72, 220
military action (by movements for
change) 39
Millennium Challenge Account (MCA)
185
moral arguments, power of 49, 255
and AIDS assistance 181, 189–190
and foreign aid 173
see also values
moral credibility, search for 140–142,
165
as individual motivation 141–142
moral hazard, arguments based on 63,
70, 73, 80–81, 86, 96–97
Moravcsik, Andrew 33, 128, 131
Moreno-Ocampo, Luis 210–212
Morgan, Jennifer 144–145
Mori, Yoshiro 195–196, 198–199
Morrow, James 128
Moynier, Gustave 213
Multilateral Debt Relief Initiative
(MDRI) 76
Munson, Les 184
Museveni, Yoweri 229

Nakao, Takehiko 97, 99, 100, 102
Nakao, Yutaka 143
National Rifle Association 41, 188
national role conceptions 140, 142
NATO (North Atlantic Treaty
Organization) 100, 219, 220
Natsios, Andrew 154–155
Nau, Henry 141
neo-classical realism 33
neo-liberalism 33
neo-realism 33
Nepal 76
NGOs (non-governmental
organizations) 46, 101–102, 163
environmental 107, 108, 128–131,
137, 144–145, 146; differences
between 127–128
human rights 214–215, 228–229,
233–236
nature of influence 188–189
Nicaragua 211
No Peace Without Justice 215, 227

Noguchi, Motoo 225
norms
opposing (domestic vs. international)
63
role in theoretical systems 36–37
Northover, Henry 100, 102
Nuremberg trials 213–214
Nye, Joseph 269

Obama, Barack 10, 148, 256, 257,
259, 272
Ohta, Hiroshi 134
Okazawa, Kazuyoshi 136
Okinawa G-8 summit (2000) 97–98,
100, 102, 195–196, 198–199
Okuda, Hiroshi 136–137
Oppenheimer, Michael 125
Orr, Robert M. 95
Ottoman Empire 4
"oughtness" 36–37
Oxfam 89, 90, 194, 262

Pace, William 215
Pacific Asia Resource Center (PARC)
101
Pape, Robert 51, 57–58, 245, 268
Paris Club 72
Parliamentarians for Global Action,
Rights and Democracy 215
Patterson, E.W.J. 167
Payne, Rodger 40, 55
PEPFAR (President's Emergency Plan
for AIDS Relief) 151–152,
154–155, 172, 178–180, 186–190
Petty, Richard 167–168
Pew Research Center 121, 190
Pielke, Roger 130
Pitts, Joseph, Representative 189
pluralism 33, 118–119
see also interest(s): individual
political culture *see* cultural match
political psychology 67
political science, study methods
48–49
Ponsonby, Arthur/Ponsonby Rule 243
Popular Revolutionary Army 262
Poverty Reduction Strategy Papers
(PRSPs) 75
Prakash, Aseem 3, 54
preference change 53

Prescription for Hope (conference)
  182–183
prestige 165
  defined 139
  see also reputation
Price, Richard 6, 55
principled advocacy 3–5, 35–36
process-tracing 48–49, 165–166
Prodi, Romano 164
Pronk, Jan 144
protest activity see locations, e.g.
  Seattle, and methods, e.g. human
  chains
public health, global, prioritization of
  issues 263, 264
  see also HIV/AIDS
public interest frame see under ICC
public opinion see individual
  countries/issues
punishment, fear of 138–139
Purvis, Nigel 129
Putin, Vladimir 114
Putnam, Robert 37

QELROs (Quantified Emission
  Limitation or Reduction
  Objectives) 108–109

Radelet, Steve 255
rape, wartime 264
rational choice theory 33, 45
rationalism 47, 53, 116–120,
  138–139, 221
  see also interest(s), as basis of
  arguments/behavior
Raustiala, Kal 260, 271
Reagan, Ronald 271
Red Army Faction 39
Reifsnyder, Dan 127
Reiner, David M. 127
religious values, appeal to 55–56
  and debt relief 83–85, 88–89,
  91–92
  and HIV/AIDS 176, 177, 181–186
  lack of impact in Japan 102
reputation, as motivating factor 34,
  103, 118, 138–148, 213, 269,
  270, 271
  and being a "good international
  citizen" 12–13, 143, 149, 194

and national role conceptions
  140–142
resonance see cultural match
resource mobilization theory 5–7, 43,
  79
Results (relief organization) 263
rhetorical entrapment 34, 138–139,
  201, 213, 237
  and ICC participation 239–240, 271

NGOs' strategic use of 235–237
relationship with shaming see
  shaming
Rice, Condoleezza 185–186
Richard, Alain 249–250
Rifkin, Jeremy 125
Risse(-Kappen), Thomas 40, 55
Robertson, Pat 70, 91, 92
Rokeach, Milton 167
Roll, Katja 192–193, 195
Romania 220
Rome Statute (establishing the ICC,
  2002) 210, 212, 213, 221
  preliminary negotiations 215, 233,
  247
  state signature/ratification 218–219,
  239
Ron, James 3
Rubin, Robert 90
Rudd, Kevin 149
Rumsfeld, Donald 239
Russia
  famine (1920s) 4
  gas emissions 114
  non-ratification of Rome Statute
  219
  ratification of Kyoto Protocol 114
Russonello, John 208
Rwanda 247
  see also ICTR

Sachs, Jeffrey 70, 154
salience
  defined 52–53
  low levels of 50, 119–120, 227,
  267, 271
  particular 242
Samaritan's Purse 14, 168, 182–183,
  188, 189
Samy, Yiagadeesen 81

Sandalow, David 129
Sandholtz, Wayne 225, 231–232
Sandler, Todd 138
Santorum, Rick, Senator 184
Sarewitz, Daniel 130
Scandinavia, 1991 financial crisis 257
Schavan, Annette 195
Scheffer, David 232, 251–252
Schimmelfennig, Frank 50, 268
Schmidt, Ulla 195
Schoppa, Leonard 101
Schreurs, Miranda 139, 144, 145
Schroeder, Gerhard 74, 80, 191, 195
Schwarzenegger, Arnold 89
Seattle, 1999 protests 2, 32, 85, 102
secession movements 262
Sell, Susan K. 3, 54
separating equilibria 47–48
September 11 attacks 5, 16, 126, 172,
    218, 256
  impact on global economy 256–257
  impact on national policies 51, 52,
    255–256
Serieux, John 81
shaming 15–16, 52, 92–93
  and rhetorical entrapment 138–139,
    213, 235–237, 271
shared lifeworld *see* cultural match
Shiffman, Jeremy 263–264
Shimizu, Yasuhiro 137, 143–144
Sikkink, Kathryn 39, 50
  (and Margaret Keck), *Activists
    Beyond Borders* 5, 6, 64,
    262–263
Simmons, Beth A. 43
"Singapore compromise" 217
slave trade 57–58
Smith, Chris, Representative 189
Smith, Stephanie 264
Snow, David A. 50, 55
social psychology 167–168
Soros, George 263
South Africa, initiatives on AIDS 154
"spiral model" 6, 236
Staggenborg, Suzanne 5–7
states
  acceptance (of advocacy), defined
    36–38
  acting against own (apparent)
    interests 33–34, 47–48, 70, 165,

225–226, 255, 267, 270 (*see also*
    costly moral action)
  reasons for behavior 9, 11, 33,
    40–63, 268–270
  see also cost(s); interest(s); values;
    individual states/issues
Stewart, Kate 208
Stoiber, Michael 133
Struett, Michael 224, 229
success (of movements)
  definitions 8, 36–38
  reasons for 6–8, 33
Sudan *see* Darfur
Suedfeld, Peter 167
Suez Crisis (1956) 240
Sulzer, Jeanne 227
Summers, Larry 81, 83, 88, 89,
    90–91, 92
Sundstrom, Lisa McIntosh 50

Takemi, Keizo 199
Tarrow, Sidney 50
Thurner, Paul W. 133
Tiberghien, Yves 139, 144, 145
TICAD IV (Fourth Tokyo
    International Conference on
    African Development) 199
Tilly, Charles 5, 35
Tobias, Randall 188
Tomz, Michael 142
Toronto goals (greenhouse gas
    emissions) 107, 125, 127
Toronto terms (debt relief) 72
Toyota 136–137
transnational advocacy, rise of 2–5, 32
  see also advocacy movements;
    principled advocacy; *specific
    organizations/areas of concern*
treaties
  calls for support 8–9
  compliance-pull 117, 149
  ratification 13, 259–260; benefits
    117–120; motives 230; national
    procedures 131–134
  see also specific instruments, e.g.
    Kyoto Protocol
Trinidad and Tobago 214
troops, overseas deployment 68,
    222–226
"true persuasion" 40

Truman, Harry S. 169
Tsebelis, George 61
Tsukada, Tamaki 96
Tsutsui, Kiyoteri 230

Uganda 74, 75, 78
  dealings with ICC 220, 229
United Kingdom 4, 57–58
  and climate change 117; emission
    reductions/targets 110, 114
  and debt relief 78, 84; leading role
    76, 77–78, 80
  domestic structure 61, 62–63,
    132–133, 243
  and HIV/AIDS 48, 152, 156–159,
    160
  and the ICC 14–15, 16, 34, 58,
    212–213, 227–228, 234–240,
    241, 252–253, 255; brokering of
    compromises 217, 220, 244–245,
    246; downplaying of costs 245;
    reasons for stance 225–226, 233;
    risk of prosecution of service
    personnel 210–211, 212,
    245–246; role in Rome
    negotiations 243, 245
  internal politics 241–243 (*see also*
    Labour Party)
  overseas troop deployments
    223–224
  pressure groups/NGOs 46, 162–163
  relationship with United States
    240–241, 244, 245
  treaty ratification procedure 132
United Nations
  Framework Convention on Climate
    Change 108–109, 110, 117–118,
    134
  Genocide Convention 214
  role in establishment of ICC 214
  role in initiatives on AIDS 152, 154,
    155–156, 172
United Nations Foundation 262
United States 4, 9–10, 272
  appearance before ICJ 211
  civic creed 141
  and climate change 117; clashes
    with European powers 104–105,
    109; Congress/Senate proceedings
    107, 112, 113; emission levels
123–124; multilateral initiatives
    115; non-ratification of Kyoto
    Protocol 38, 104–106, 116, 148,
    149–150; proposed reductions
    105, 110, 113; public opinion
    122–123
  Constitution/gun law 41
  damage to international reputation
    269–270
  and debt relief 12, 58, 66, 72, 80,
    82, 84, 86–93, 255; contribution
    to HIPC 75, 77–78, 88; cutbacks
    94; political pressures 81;
    Republican support 90–93
  domestic structure 39, 62–63,
    131–132
  Energy Information Agency 112
  foreign assistance ranking 159
  gatekeepers, number/importance 60,
    62, 88, 131–132, 232–233,
    238–239, 259–260
  global hegemony 142, 256, 259
  and HIV/AIDS 14, 34, 48, 58, 65,
    66, 152, 175–176, 178–190, 200,
    202, 255, 257; allocation of funds
    155, 187, 189–190; amendments
    to plan 189; contributions to
    Global Fund 156–158, 159;
    motivations 160; Office of the
    Global AIDS Coordinator 189;
    public pressure 188; puzzling
    nature of policies 165–166, 176,
    177; scale of commitment 151,
    258; switch in policy 180–190
  and the ICC 14–15, 212–213,
    234–237, 238–239, 252; attempts
    to limit powers 216, 218;
    ideological objections 224–225,
    232; moves to undermine
    219–220, 224, 230; reactions to
    229–230; reasons for
    non-participation 224–225,
    231–233; vote against Rome
    Statute 218–219
  impact on other states' behavior
    260
  internal politics 104–105, 256, 259
  NGOs 46, 163, 226
  obstructionism 260
  Office of Global Change 127–128

overseas troop deployments
223–224
public opinion 173–174, 181, 208
relationship with Canada 146–147
religious elements: cultural/political
importance 55; disapproval of
AIDS assistance 180, 182; role in
debt relief 83, 91–92; support for
AIDS assistance 181–186
response to 9/11 2, 257
response to 2008 crisis 256–258
treaty ratification: abstention from
232, 260 (*see also treaties/specific
subheadings*); procedure
131–132, 134, 259–260

values, as basis of arguments/behavior
41–42, 83–85
overlap with self-interested motives
270
(perceived) limitations 47
public vs. elite impact 45
see also cost(s)
Védrine, Hubert 41, 227, 248, 249,
250
veto players theory 56, 59, 60–62, 63
datasets 61–63
see also gatekeepers
violence, movements' resort to 39

Walldorf, C. William 268
Walster, Elaine 167
war crimes
allegations before ICC 210–211,
212

domestic trials 212
ICC opt-out 217–218, 225–226,
251
studies 264
Weldon, Steve 224
whaling 268
Wheeler, Nicholas J. 242
White, Ryan 180
Whitman, Christine Todd 113
Wieczorek-Zeul, Heidemarie 178,
192, 194–195
Wolfensohn, James 73, 74
women, role in AIDS policies
195
World Bank 2, 72–73, 76, 81–82
World Federalist Movement 215
World Trade Center, attacks on *see*
September 11 attacks
World Values Survey 55–56, 83, 121,
181
World War II, aftermath 213–214,
225
World Wide Fund for Nature 108
WTO (World Trade Organization) 2,
39, 114
Wylie, Lana 224

Yamada, Yoichiro 196, 199
Yamamoto, Tadashi 198
Yasutomo, Dennis 95
Yugoslavia (former) *see* ICTY

Zald, Mayer 43–44, 50
Zapatistas 39, 262
Zeitz, Paul 181

Cambridge Studies in International Relations

103 Beate Jahn
(ed.) *Classical theory in international relations*
102 Andrew Linklater and Hidemi Suganami
The English School of international relations
A contemporary reassessment
101 Colin Wight
Agents, structures, and international relations
Politics as ontology
100 Michael C. Williams
The realist tradition and the limits of international relations
99 Ivan Arreguín-Toft
How the weak win wars
A theory of asymmetric conflict
98 Michael Barnett and Raymond Duvall
Power in global governance
97 Yale H. Ferguson and Richard W. Mansbach
Remapping global politics
History's revenge and future shock
96 Christian Reus-Smit
The politics of international law
95 Barry Buzan
From international to world society?
English School theory and the social structure of globalisation
94 K. J. Holsti
Taming the sovereigns
Institutional change in international politics
93 Bruce Cronin
Institutions for the common good
International protection regimes in international security
92 Paul Keal
European conquest and the rights of indigenous peoples
The moral backwardness of international society
91 Barry Buzan and Ole Wæver
Regions and powers
The structure of international security

90   A. Claire Cutler
     Private power and global authority
     Transnational merchant law in the global political economy
89   Patrick M. Morgan
     Deterrence now
88   Susan Sell
     Private power, public law
     The globalization of intellectual property rights
87   Nina Tannenwald
     The nuclear taboo
     The United States and the non-use of nuclear
     weapons since 1945
86   Linda Weiss
     States in the global economy
     Bringing domestic institutions back in
85   Rodney Bruce Hall and Thomas J. Biersteker
     (eds.) *The emergence of private authority in global governance*
84   Heather Rae
     State identities and the homogenisation of peoples
83   Maja Zehfuss
     Constructivism in international relations
     The politics of reality
82   Paul K. Ruth and Todd Allee
     The democratic peace and territorial conflict in the twentieth century
81   Neta C. Crawford
     Argument and change in world politics
     Ethics, decolonization, and humanitarian intervention
80   Douglas Lemke
     Regions of war and peace
79   Richard Shapcott
     Justice, community, and dialogue in international relations
78   Phil Steinberg
     The social construction of the ocean
77   Christine Sylvester
     Feminist international relations
     An unfinished journey
76   Kenneth A. Schultz
     Democracy and coercive diplomacy
75   David Houghton
     US foreign policy and the Iran hostage crisis
74   Cecilia Albin
     Justice and fairness in international negotiation
73   Martin Shaw
     Theory of the global state
     Globality as an unfinished revolution
72   Frank C. Zagare and D. Marc Kilgour
     Perfect deterrence

71 Robert O'Brien, Anne Marie Goetz, Jan Aart Scholte, and Marc Williams
   Contesting global governance
   Multilateral economic institutions and global social movements
70 Roland Bleiker
   Popular dissent, human agency, and global politics
69 Bill McSweeney
   Security, identity, and interests
   A sociology of international relations
68 Molly Cochran
   Normative theory in international relations
   A pragmatic approach
67 Alexander Wendt
   Social theory of international politics
66 Thomas Risse, Stephen C. Ropp, and Kathryn Sikkink
   (eds.) *The power of human rights*
   International norms and domestic change
65 Daniel W. Drezner
   The sanctions paradox
   Economic statecraft and international relations
64 Viva Ona Bartkus
   The dynamic of secession
63 John A. Vasquez
   The power of power politics
   From classical realism to neotraditionalism
62 Emanuel Adler and Michael Barnett
   (eds.) *Security communities*
61 Charles Jones
   E. H. Carr and international relations
   A duty to lie
60 Jeffrey W. Knopf
   Domestic society and international cooperation
   The impact of protest on US arms control policy
59 Nicholas Greenwood Onuf
   The republican legacy in international thought
58 Daniel S. Geller and J. David Singer
   Nations at war
   A scientific study of international conflict
57 Randall D. Germain
   The international organization of credit
   States and global finance in the world economy
56 N. Piers Ludlow
   Dealing with Britain
   The Six and the first UK application to the EEC
55 Andreas Hasenclever, Peter Mayer, and Volker Rittberger
   Theories of international regimes

54 Miranda A. Schreurs and Elizabeth C. Economy
   (eds.) *The internationalization of environmental
   protection*
53 James N. Rosenau
   Along the domestic–foreign frontier
   Exploring governance in a turbulent world
52 John M. Hobson
   The wealth of states
   A comparative sociology of international economic
   and political change
51 Kalevi J. Holsti
   The state, war, and the state of war
50 Christopher Clapham
   Africa and the international system
   The politics of state survival
49 Susan Strange
   The retreat of the state
   The diffusion of power in the world economy
48 William I. Robinson
   Promoting polyarchy
   Globalization, US intervention, and hegemony
47 Roger Spegele
   Political realism in international theory
46 Thomas J. Biersteker and Cynthia Weber
   (eds.) *State sovereignty as social construct*
45 Mervyn Frost
   Ethics in international relations
   A constitutive theory
44 Mark W. Zacher with Brent A. Sutton
   Governing global networks
   International regimes for transportation and communications
43 Mark Neufeld
   The restructuring of international relations theory
42 Thomas Risse-Kappen
   (ed.) *Bringing transnational relations back in*
   Non-state actors, domestic structures, and international institutions
41 Hayward R. Alker
   Rediscoveries and reformulations
   Humanistic methodologies for international studies
40 Robert W. Cox with Timothy J. Sinclair
   Approaches to world order
39 Jens Bartelson
   A genealogy of sovereignty
38 Mark Rupert
   Producing hegemony
   The politics of mass production and American global power

37 Cynthia Weber
Simulating sovereignty
Intervention, the state, and symbolic exchange
36 Gary Goertz
Contexts of international politics
35 James L. Richardson
Crisis diplomacy
The Great Powers since the mid-nineteenth century
34 Bradley S. Klein
Strategic studies and world order
The global politics of deterrence
33 T. V. Paul
Asymmetric conflicts: war initiation by weaker powers
32 Christine Sylvester
Feminist theory and international relations in a postmodern era
31 Peter J. Schraeder
US foreign policy toward Africa
Incrementalism, crisis, and change
30 Graham Spinardi
*From Polaris to Trident: the development of US Fleet Ballistic
Missile technology*
29 David A. Welch
Justice and the genesis of war
28 Russell J. Leng
Interstate crisis behavior, 1816–1980: realism versus reciprocity
27 John A. Vasquez
The war puzzle
26 Stephen Gill
(ed.) *Gramsci, historical materialism, and international relations*
25 Mike Bowker and Robin Brown
(eds.) *From Cold War to collapse: theory and world politics in the 1980s*
24 R. B. J. Walker
Inside/ outside: international relations as political theory
23 Edward Reiss
The strategic defense initiative
22 Keith Krause
Arms and the state: patterns of military production and trade
21 Roger Buckley
US–Japan alliance diplomacy 1945–1990
20 James N. Rosenau and Ernst-Otto Czempiel
(eds.) *Governance without government: order and change
in world politics*
19 Michael Nicholson
Rationality and the analysis of international conflict
18 John Stopford and Susan Strange
Rival states, rival firms
Competition for world market shares

17 Terry Nardin and David R. Mapel
   (eds.) *Traditions of international ethics*
16 Charles F. Doran
   Systems in crisis
   New imperatives of high politics at century's end
15 Deon Geldenhuys
   Isolated states: a comparative analysis
14 Kalevi J. Holsti
   Peace and war: armed conflicts and international order 1648–1989
13 Saki Dockrill
   Britain's policy for West German rearmament 1950–1955
12 Robert H. Jackson
   Quasi-states: sovereignty, international relations, and the third world
11 James Barber and John Barratt
   South Africa's foreign policy
   The search for status and security 1945–1988
10 James Mayall
   Nationalism and international society
 9 William Bloom
   Personal identity, national identity, and international relations
 8 Zeev Maoz
   National choices and international processes
 7 Ian Clark
   The hierarchy of states
   Reform and resistance in the international order
 6 Hidemi Suganami
   The domestic analogy and world order proposals
 5 Stephen Gill
   American hegemony and the Trilateral Commission
 4 Michael C. Pugh
   The ANZUS crisis, nuclear visiting, and deterrence
 3 Michael Nicholson
   Formal theories in international relations
 2 Friedrich V. Kratochwil
   Rules, norms, and decisions
   On the conditions of practical and legal reasoning in international relations
   and domestic affairs
 1 Myles L. C. Robertson
   Soviet policy towards Japan
   An analysis of trends in the 1970s and 1980s